D1622708

'Membering

813.54 Clark

Clarke, A.
'Membering.

PRICE: $23.99 (an/m)

PETERBOROUGH PUBLIC LIBRARY   NOV   2015

AUSTIN CLARKE

'Membering

DUNDURN
TORONTO

Copyright © Austin Clarke 2015

All rights reserved. No part of this publication may be reproduced, stored in a retrieval system, or transmitted in any form or by any means, electronic, mechanical, photocopying, recording, or otherwise (except for brief passages for purpose of review) without the prior permission of Dundurn Press. Permission to photocopy should be requested from Access Copyright.

Editor: Shannon Whibbs
Design: Courtney Horner
Cover design: Sarah Beaudin
Cover image: © Mohan Junja
Printer: Friesens

Library and Archives Canada Cataloguing in Publication

Clarke, Austin, 1934-, author
    'Membering / Austin Clarke.

Issued in print and electronic formats.
ISBN 978-1-4597-3034-2 (paperback).--ISBN 978-1-4597-3035-9 (pdf).--
ISBN 978-1-4597-3036-6 (epub)

    1. Clarke, Austin, 1934-. 2. Clarke, Austin, 1934- --Childhood and
youth. 3. Authors, Canadian (English)--20th century--Biography.
4. Authors, Barbadian--20th century--Biography. 5. Barbados--Social life
and customs. I. Title.

PS8505.L38Z49 2015   C813'.54   C2015-904684-X
                                              C2015-904685-8

1   2   3   4   5   19   18   17   16   15

 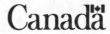 

We acknowledge the support of the **Canada Council for the Arts** and the **Ontario Arts Council** for our publishing program. We also acknowledge the financial support of the **Government of Canada** through the **Canada Book Fund** and **Livres Canada Books**, and the **Government of Ontario** through the **Ontario Book Publishing Tax Credit** and the **Ontario Media Development Corporation**.

Care has been taken to trace the ownership of copyright material used in this book. The author and the publisher welcome any information enabling them to rectify any references or credits in subsequent editions.
— *J. Kirk Howard, President*

The publisher is not responsible for websites or their content unless they are owned by the publisher.

Printed and bound in Canada.

VISIT US AT
Dundurn.com | @dundurnpress | Facebook.com/dundurnpress | Pinterest.com/dundurnpress

Dundurn
3 Church Street, Suite 500
Toronto, Ontario, Canada
M5E 1M2

For tee,
Haddie

and for Howard Matthews
the First Floor Club
Betty Clarke
The Honourable Roy McMurtry

"You 'member?"
"I 'member."
"I 'member, too!"
"What you 'member?"
"I 'member everything you want me to remember!"
"You really 'member everything, in-true?"

— From a conversation seventy years ago, on a humid afternoon, in a school, in Barbados, the St. Matthias Elementary School for Boys

A time has come and gone.
Some memories are
captured in a song.
Some stories told,
an artist's hand,
something to find
among the sand,
something to hold,
remembering,
another world.
Another world.

— ABBEY LINCOLN, "ANOTHER WORLD"
(FROM THE ALBUM *WHOLLY EARTH*, NEW YORK CITY, 1998)

Contents

CHAPTER ONE

The Little Black Englishmen

I am sitting in my study on a Friday afternoon in 2004, forty-nine years after I came limping through a hurricane whose name I cannot remember, although it is the name of a woman, and I always remember the names of women, but this is 1955, on the twenty-ninth day in September, fifty years later, almost to the day, in this same weather that used to be called, and could be called "Indian Summer," a term which to me, a novelist, is filled with romantic notions and presumptions, but which the pervading decency of political correctness, like the fury of the hurricane … I 'member the name we called it by now! Janet! Janet, Janet, Janet! Hurricane Janet. I have known many Janets. And all of them were harmless, beautiful women … but here I am, in this study that looks across a road well travelled in the rushing mornings to work, and hardly travelled with such anxiety and intent during the hours that come before the rush to work, walked on, and peed on, by the homeless, and the prostitutes and the pimps, and the men and women going home to apartments in the sky, surrounding and overlooking Moss Park park, as I like to call it. Moss Park park is where life stretches out itself on its back, prostrate in filthy, hopeless, bouts of heroism and stardom, for these men who lie on the benches and the dying grass, are heroes to themselves and to one another, in a pecking order that is full of right-eous daring, and righteous chances of stupidity like crossing the road in front of speeding cars that put the brakes — at the last minute — on with a squeak. The image of a smashed head on the shining bonnet of a Mercedes-Benz is not on the menu for tonight's dinner in Cabbagetown; or the delay caused by the dying words of the homeless man about his residence in a filthy halfway house behind the bastions of Victorian and Georgian townhouses that hide this degradation from the fleeing man in the German-made automobile.

Such homelessness — as politicians like to call this layer of detestation — greets me every day on the green grass cleaned by the morning and the dew, like a set of teeth passed over by a smear of toothpaste; or by warm water seasoned in salt; or by bare fingers that had dug during the night in the five minutes ticking off on a Rolex watch, or counted off in seconds by the friction of a French-leathered hectic moment behind the fences of the townhouses, deep into the panties of the woman who stands like a sentry at the corner of two streets, punctual and reliable as a security guard, and whose colour or cleanliness he wisely cannot see in the dark, leaf-shaking night hidden by the trees that have no tongue in the chastising speechless mouth of satisfaction.

And I wonder why these men with their picked-out women, all standing in the darkness of street corners shaded by trees and the darkness of their own intentions should choose such a little, such a small, short hiatus from their lives of homelessness — or lovelessness?

I have been homeless once. In a most dramatic manner, with a knock on the door, in the rough, brutal manner of the bailiff; but this is nothing to boast about. I saw my homelessness in the colour of black and white: racism, at its most brutal and unfeeling and uncompromising display. But I saw it also in the insistence that I would overcome this temporary reversal of fortune. I saw it, too, as a revisiting of the importance or the fatalism associated with Fridays. Fridays in my early life in Barbados, were days of terror, when I had to face homework at Harrison College that was almost the equal of one term's work at Combermere School for Boys, the previous "second grade" I attended. Harrison College was a "first grade" government school. At Harrison's, which is what we called our school, a normal Friday afternoon's homework for me as a boy in the Lower Sixth Form of Modern Studies (I was specializing in Latin and English grammar and English literature, with subsidiary subjects of

Roman history and religious knowledge), meant "learning" two chapters of the Acts of the Apostles; two chapters in Roman history; one hundred lines of Virgil's *Aeneid* Book II, two chapters in Caesar's *Gallic Wars*; two chapters of Livy Book XXI; and as our Latin master (Joe Clarke, no relation of mine!), who had no idea of the lives we lived away from Harrison College, always suggested, "Well, you can open your book and look at a few chapters of Tacitus's *Histories*, after you have pushed your Sunday dinner plates aside."

"One act of *Macbeth* by Shakespeare; a few stanzas of T.S. Eliot's 'The Hollow Men'; and one act in Eliot's *Murder in the Cathedral*; one hundred lines of 'Hyperion' by John Keats; and a few pages of A.C. Bradley's prefaces to *Shakespearean Tragedies*, with particular attention to *Macbeth*," said the English Literature master, an American from Harvard University (a university which none of us had heard of before his arrival at Harrison's in loose-fitting linen and cotton suits, brown moccasins with a penny fitted into the instep of each shoe, outfits which we held bets on that he would not repeat in the same week, or month, or term … and he did not!). And anything we wanted to "learn" would improve our chances of winning the prestigious Barbados Scholarship. I was entered for the scholarship; but it was known by the "bright boys" and by my own honesty that I did not have a chance against three other boys in my form, unless two of them suddenly dropped down dead. Fridays at Harrison College were mind-numbing days; days of terror; days that ensured that the entire weekend would be unhappy.

At Combermere, which we called "Cawmere," Fridays were days of relaxation, of play, of exercising the power and privilege of being a prefect, or a house captain, or even as Head Boy. Of preparing the body and not the mind for the rigours of the weekend: cricket, "social hops," the cinema, dropping-round by boys and visiting girlfriends, and eating black pudding and souse, sugar cakes, coconut bread, "cou-cou and harslick"; and "cakes" and puddings made, sometimes, by the girls who had listened to their mothers' memorization of old recipes, delivered like dictation; and going to the beach to loll in the warm, salty, enervating waves, and wash your face with sea water that burned your eyes, that made the hair round your forehead red and tough, and that you drank as a kind of purgative to "clean-out the bowels"; while men took it home in bottles, or else drank it from their palms as they would drink "a drop o' hot sauce," and afterwards cry out "Hem! Uh-hem!," exclaiming at its marvellous recuperative qualities. Going to church, as a little Anglican to the English Church of England; or to the Methodist church; or to the Church of the Nazarene, or to the Pilgrim Holiness, either to worship — a term never used in Barbados — or to sing in the choir, and as a gesture more to illustrate social class and status, than to demonstrate any contention of being religious, attending church "in your Sunday best" was the only interruption of the two-and-a-half-day holiday, beginning on Friday afternoon, and ending on Sunday after Evensong and Service. But during the weekend when I was at Cawmere, the spine of a textbook was never broken as we tromped through the weekend in our noisy glee; and if the Bible was in fact looked into, it was in order to follow the reading of the two lessons by the vicar. It was certainly not considered the same as reading Scripture, our first class on Monday mornings at Cawmere: "The Axe of the Postles." Bright and early at nine-fifteen — after prayers — in the class of Mr. L.L. Webster, who never looked into a book himself while he heard the lesson of Scripture. At the beginning of his class, he asked, "What is the lesson today, boys?"

"Axe of the Postles," the monitor, Armstrong, A.E., reminded him.

"Uh-huh!" he told the monitor and the class of thirty other boys.

And when the monitor, A.E. Armstrong, told him a second time, "Axe of the Postles, sir!" all Mr. Webster would do was close his eyes, pass his hand over the few remaining strands of hair on his balding grey head, and, with his eyes still closed, as if calling up memory and strength to paint the picture of the verses about Ananias and Sapphira more clearly in his retentive mind, he would hear us in the lesson, orally, having us complete the words in a verse he had picked, at random, out from his expansive mind.

"Uh-huh!" he would keep saying. "Uh-huh!"

Mr. Webster was the brother of the owner of Wildey Plantation, of vast fields of sugar cane, and which produced raw sugar and crack liquor, another name for molasses, and which is the model, only in its physical dimension, though not in racial and moral disposition, of the plantation in my novel *The Polished Hoe*.

Fridays became for me, at Cawmere, signposts of the long journey I did not know I was about to begin, but which I found myself on, a journey going backwards, always on a Friday while I lived in the Island; and now in this country of greater size and lesser self-assurance, similar in some ways to the indecisiveness of colonial power, and the people who lived under that power, going backwards to a Friday; a Friday in September that marked the change in my life which cannot be altered now; and in some cases, be redeemed. But in this journey backwards, I am discovering more about myself and the heritage that brought me, through ancestry, to this part of the bigger world, the First World. I have never been concerned with the history of my hijacking from some place in Africa, to the West Indies; and I have never really contemplated that I was a slave, even through that ancestry, and association with slaves, in history books, and in fact; even though former slaves and slavery are painted in the picture of my origin. We were brought up to imagine that the page had not been stained by this "passage." But it did not mean that I could not see, as I did, traces of this terrible experience in the body and physical and mental disposition of my grandmother, Miriam. I do not know whether she regarded, and could remember when her mother was a slave. Or if she herself was a slave. But there was something about her complete satisfaction with her life, her acceptance of it, whatever it was — mostly a terrible, spare, and bare existence — that alarmed me into thinking that I had been hoodwinked in those Sunday School classes by parables and Christian tracts; seduced into feeling that I would inherit the earth because of my injection with Christian principles.

Friday, September the twenty-ninth, in 1955, was a dramatic day in my life. I arrived at the airport in Toronto, bound, as a student, for the University of Toronto. Since then, my search in life and in literature has been to find the meaning of myself, my personality, my reason for entering the relationships I have formed, with friends and enemies and lovers; my abandonment of women who could have been amongst women chosen as wives, recognizing the old-fashioned, and chauvinistic implication of putting this sentiment in this archaic language; my reasons for remaining in this country when it was possible to go to England and enter the London School of Economics to which I had been admitted in 1952, to enter the Middle Temple, and satisfy the craving for big, autocratic and even dictatorial power in a small island; and become prime minister, or an autocrat, like other West Indian prime ministers; to ruminate upon disastrous decisions I have made in private life, in literary life, in love; quite simply I wanted to know what would become of me, with the decisions I have made. And this search, though not of the kind that I see in historical inquiry, I am reminded of it, in the retelling of that very history, narrated from the mouths of the women who have lived through it.

And when these Barbadian Fridays had got the better of me, and had fashioned my outlook on things more than homework, I was now forced to face Friday afternoons at Trinity College in the University of Toronto.

Friday afternoons, much later on: in marriage; and later still in separation; and in broken love affairs ...

And then, there is Good Friday! Eleven o'clock Matins at the Anglican Cathedral church on the northeast corner of King and Church Streets, where Good Friday comes back to me in full, sweeping emotions that began in another Anglican church, a smaller church built by the English and by slaves, in St. Matthias Church; and then, with the change in status, and the change in my voice, I am in the choir stalls of the St. Michael Cathedral Church in Bridgetown, where I "cooed" like a dove during solos, or carrying the descants; and like a bird singing psalms measured and announced in Roman numerals, which I had just begun to learn at Cawmere, in Second Form, in L2D; and sometimes could not find the psalm in time before the singing ended. And when this happened, I would watch the mouths of the more certain boys, who had mastered Roman numerals like little mathematicians; and in time I developed a mastery of lip-reading, following not only the words of psalms, hymns ancient and motets, and all that liturgical music in the high-ceilinged chancels in two churches, but I also learned to read lips in other situations, of passion, of defending myself in crises, of reading minds through the movements of women's lips, when it was important for me to know what she was thinking before she spoke the truth that set me free.

Practising to delude the choirmaster that I knew the words, that I could read the intractable Roman numerals fast enough to open the red-leather psalter in time to sing the first notes, and fooled myself that

I was deluding him, until his eyes grew larger in the mirrors placed above the rows of organ keys which he had taken from the right and the left side of a motor car.

I do not know, and cannot remember if the hurricane that was the harbinger of my departure from Barbados, that delayed me through its fury, was the voice of fate that cast me up on these shores of Lake Ontario on the twenty-ninth of September 1955, and whether Janet had something in mind for me. But I do remember trees stripped of their leaves and boughs, just like the sugar cane is stripped of its green blade-like leaves by the glistening fierceness of the cane cutter's cutlass; and how the land seemed bare, uninhabited, barely discovered by men who claimed to be English; and suddenly to be in serene and peaceful Toronto, even at the ungodly hour of two in the morning, when my plane, a Trans-Canada Air Line that roared in its uncomfortable flight from the British Bahamas, on that raining September morning in 1955, a land I did not know, and a land I never went back to, a land that was segregated. I had never come up against this method of distinguishing black skin from white skin in Barbados. Not that Barbados was Elysium. Barbados was always Little England. But the rawness of segregation in the Bahamas, and the acceptance of it by those who were made to suffer under its apartheid, was crippling. All of a sudden I was frightened, scared to continue my journey, fearing more segregation at the destination.

Many years after this first confrontation with racism, I would write narrative about a train ride from Miami at a time much earlier than 1955; and that journey is told by Mary-Mathilda, the main character in my novel *The Polished Hoe*, who is travelling with the plantation manager, her lover, Mr. Bellfeels, with whom she has a son, Wilberforce. They are going to Buffalo to buy second-hand machinery for the sugar factory. Mary-Mathilda describes her discovery of segregation with the same alarm as I would experience many years later in 1955, at the seating arrangement on the train going from the South to the North, from Miami to Buffalo. To her, it was "not normal." She called this seating arrangement, "serrigated." I chose the term "serrigated" instead of the traditional spelling, because I wanted to invent a word that expressed the rawness of racism, like a wound made on the most delicate part of the body, a woman's belly, with a knife with a serrated blade.

And in all this time, travelling by now hundreds and hundreds o' miles, Mr. Bellfeels is seated in a different section of the train, invisible to me, and separated from me. Mr. Bellfeels is sitting in one section, a reserved compartment of the train, a sleeper. And in a next section they called third class, sitting up, my back hurting me, all through this journey north.

And when I finally notice that something wasn't sitting too good with me, that something wasn't normal, I could only shake my head.

I was serrigated from Mr. Bellfeels.

I was travelling through serrigated country!

And, as usual, in these matters of racism, involving the white man and the black woman, the white man never goes, publicly, to the defence of the woman he foops in the privacy of his physical and material power.

The episode in the British Bahamas on that sunny, humid September morning almost dampened my spirit about continuing to Canada to go to university, to study economics and political science. It was, nevertheless, a stain; a spot, similar to the dot of shit that a pigeon drops on your freshly laundered white shirt. You remove it with a Kleenex, or you shake it off, or in disgust, you flick it off with your finger.

The stain disappears later the same morning, either under the sink or because it is by nature not an enduring assault of nature. I would encounter and experience many more blemishes to my clothes, now, in the fifty years I have been on this journey, which I am deliberately narrating backwards.

This backwards journey in the narrating of this 'membering, this remembrance, is a lesson I learned from Geoffrey Chaucer's *Canterbury Tales*, and which considers how language, in this case, English, the only language I know, is at present of profound interest, when used in a non-traditional manner. I have used this language in *The Polished Hoe*, and I call it many things, but the most precise definition I have given it is contained in a booklet published by the Giller Prize Foundation, celebrating the tenth anniversary of this literary prize. In that review of the literary problems I faced in the writing of *The Polished Hoe* in 2002, my main concern was to find a language, or to more strictly use the language I already knew, in such a way that it became, in my manipulation of it, a "new" language. And to explain the result of this experiment, I said that I intended to "creolize Oxford English."

What I meant by that was that I wanted to show, through the narrative of the novel's heroine, Mary-Mathilda, her deliberate claim of ownership of the English language, ironically and coincidentally, the language of her own colonization. But I feel that English has been used so unrelentingly to describe Mary-Mathilda, in ways that were more derogatory than complimenting, that as the object of that narrative she has at least an equal right in deciding what kind of descriptive language ought to be used to describe her life. She has a claim to that language. And with no feeling of inferiority that seems to have been in the minds of French-speaking, French-colonized African poets who invented the literary term "Negritude." But Negritude was nothing more than the "creolization" of French, which in turn was approved by the French Academy. It seems as if they were asking the French Academy for permission to use the language of their colonization, whereas, like Mary-Mathilda, they should have claimed ownership of the French language, and should have used the language as a weapon, as the justification of their anger against such a system of colonialism.

Writing about Mary-Mathilda has released from within me a literary and cultural anger against Europe, so much so that I am disposed to taking a second look at the Europeanization of my thoughts, percolated like coffee through the mechanism of English Colonialism. It is not only Mary-Mathilda who rejects European supremacy — so-called! — as it manifests itself in culture, in diplomacy and in art, but as the creator of the portrayal of her character. But getting back to Chaucer, and the advice he gives in constructing narrative — narrative in fiction and narrative in autobiography, although *'Membering* is not autobiography. It is not intended to be. Nor is it biography. It is memoir.

I am controlling, through choice and selection, the things about myself that would become public knowledge the moment you have taken this book from the shelf or from the table in a bookstore.

It is a Friday morning on Shuter Street, in 2004, and there is mist and white long-beaked birds whose names I never learned to remember, and pigeons struggling with the white unknown birds for bits of bread thrown on the grass by a man who drives a limousine. This man parks the automobile illegally, thinking that a traffic cop would not bother him as he is performing this human act of kindness to birds who cannot use words and tell him thanks for his startling generosity. And to show his appreciation, the limousine driver drops the two large white plastic bags on the ground, in the gutter, and they blow up and down the gutter, and add to the garbage that the homeless men contribute to, dropping paper cups, pizza shells eaten down to the rim and crust, condoms whose lifespan is as short as their pleasure in the dark back alley behind the townhouses built in the years and architecture of former graciousness — Georgian and Victorian ages — when this dalliance with sex was certainly not tolerated; was not the done thing. But the man driving the limousine does not look back, and the white plastic bags that contained the late breakfast that the pigeons and the white birds that live in lakes, picked over in a multicultural accommodation with the white-feathered cranes ... sea gulls!... (remembering their names) ... men with grocery carts but with no intention and hope of going and coming from Loblaws or Dominion or the No Frills grocery stores; men with bundles hoping for someone, limousine driver or traffic cop, to bring some slices of hardened white bread and throw them to relieve their homelessness and hunger ... this happens every morning, not only on Fridays.

On other Fridays, in the strangulating humidity that drains all energy and intellectual alertness from the body, and which seems purposeful as if it is inflicted upon us boys at Combermere School, in the slow-paced afternoons, we came into adolescence disguised thinly as man-hood; and we faced the first frightening demands and the meaning of this tricky growing up circumscribed by strict discipline. Combermere School trained us to enter the teaching profession at elementary level; and as middle-ranked civil servants; sanitary inspectors, and we took this declaration of manhood, as it was imposed upon us, not in our stride as more egoistical young men would declare our daily escape from mother and father, household, and coterie of friends, not to mention our Latin master, our French master and the master who was a captain in the Cadet Corps — to say nothing of the Scout Troop leader, the 3rd Barbados Scouts … but we accepted this singling out by Latin master, Cadet Captain, Scout Troop leader, as the privilege that rightfully was ours, being "Cawmere boys" who "could smell our pee, and see it foaming while we peed," becoming men in the process, men who would in short time be leaders in the Island. We were being trained to be leaders. Either as test cricketers, as barristers-at-law, doctors, politicians, reverends in the Anglican Church, secondary school teachers just like our own Latin and French masters … or, we might become senior sanitary inspectors looking into closet pits and stagnant water collected in pools around chattel house, after the rains, looking for "larvees," carrying out these tests with a white enamel ladle with a long handle, making it look like a soup spoon for Gulliver, or Robinson Crusoe, or for the one-eyed giant.

We picked our models from amongst our masters. The term "mentor" had not entered our puny vocabulary, and even if it had, we would not, being of a different culture and myth from Americans who invented this term, we would not have understood what it really meant, when it was used in the context of North American foreign culture. "Mentor" was a clumsy word, that had no meaning to us. We chose "example" instead. My mother never tired of telling me, "Boy! Take a' example from Mr. Smith. And grow up to be a teacher like him. You hear me?" At other times, when she had just left the surgery of her doctor, Dr. Massiah, who would in turn become my doctor, searching my body for mumps, appendicitis, problems with groins, colds and coughs that lingered too long for his liking, and testing to see if I had "pulled" muscles from too much running, my mother would change her mind and shake her finger in my face, and say, "Boy, take the example from Dr. Massiah. And you grow up to be a doctor like him. You hear me?"

But on those Friday afternoons, ambition did not spread its wings to embrace the study of medicine. We all wanted to be masters like our teachers. Their life appeared to be so enjoyable. All they had to do was learn the lessons set, by heart, and sit and hear boys repeat them by rote. And they had almost three months' vacation a year!

We boys listened to their voices coming from the Masters' Room. Noisy and sometimes boisterous, these men, now lordly in the Masters' Room, had come through the same alleys and backyards as us Fifth Formers; and had climbed that same ladder of ambition, had become the "examples" that mothers swore by; and these same men who had first introduced us through experiment and "example," to try our hands at "running the school," while they gloried in their absence playing dominoes or bridge on Friday lazy afternoons, who had put us in charge of discipline, laid down in laws of no talking, "keeping silence," making certain that the level of noise and vulgarities and mild delinquency, the slamming of the lids of our desks. The desks were arranged individually, "one desk per boy: one boy per desk," from one to thirty-one, in three rows. We called the desks "desses." These desks bore the slight, one-line histories of our ancestry: the names of fathers and uncles, older brothers, distant cousins and claimed cousins, when he was an important man like a barrister-at-law, or a cricketer; and we gouged these histories into the wood that was sometimes too tough to receive the gouge of letter, or initial cut into it, by razor blade, pen knife, or piece of broken bottle. With this love of the annals, we wanted to herald forever, to bear the dignity forever, and to show forever the proof of this patrimony, to all the generations to come.

We indulged in games, shouting in imitation of the voices and antics and eccentricities of our masters. We were the new leaders: boys being turned into men. We knew that each of us would be in the vanguard to lead the Island, a Crown Colony into independence, would be the constitutional lawyer to trade intricacies with the colonizing English up in Westminster, would be the permanent secretary to guide the files in the right direction to keep their secrets confidential, would be the headmaster to guide the coming generation following our "example." Or, with that choice and cockiness of ambition, could, if we wanted to, become the most notorious murderer, thief, criminal, gambler throwing dice under a tamarind tree, in any neighbourhood; or be a seaman, or stoking furnaces in a boiler room on a merchant ship, roaring like the fires of hell, but making "good money" from it; or, going to America and Panama; and becoming a stowaway when faced with the majesty and promise of the Statue of Liberty.

Our possibilities began at the top of the scaffold of ambitiousness. And these possibilities swarmed over each step in the ladder of social and moral decorum in the Island.

The Island is the Island of Barbados. A Crown Colony. "Bimshire." Little England.

The irony in the last two names, "Bimshire" and "Little England," stamped us, for life, and made us act like black Englishmen: in our upbringing, in our attitude towards one another, and toward other West Indians. And other West Indians smiled with amusement and with a tinge of taunt, to our face, called us "little black Englishmen"; and behind our back, "black bastards suffering with a' inferiority complex." But we had the education. And the literacy measured in the numbers, 99.9 percent. Never mind the education was placed in a syllabus patterned, patented and exported from the English public school system. Latin and Greek, and ancient history and mathematics and religious knowledge and English literature, with no regard for American literature … ("What is that?") … and less regard for the Spanish language, whose tongue surrounded us just like the Caribbean Sea, and the Atlantic Ocean; and none at all for French. The Battle of Trafalgar was memorized; and we fought that battle over and over, each morning as we passed the magnificent statue in green bronze of Lord Horatio Nelson, making him look as if his face was breaking out in some West Indian disease. Yes, the French language was not for us. Our tongues were too heavy from drink and with glory. It seemed as if Lord Nelson's words, "England expects every man to do his duty," were his avowal to us not to learn the French language. We were English. British. Britannia ruled the waves. This was our virtue. And it became, through our indoctrination, our ideological and moral liability. We were loved and disliked in equal proportion of intensity, by other West Indians, because of these two "virtues."

Especially were we despised by Jamaicans and Trinidadians.

Combermere School for Boys, beloved by us, was in 1948 situated in the crowded business section on Roebuck Street, in Bridgetown, the capital, where small- and medium-sized merchants sold bags of sugar, flour, salt fish and rum in various strengths to sting the throat, where there were handcarts and donkey carts and mule carts; and there were people, women with bags and bundles on their heads padded with cloths that looked like turbans worn by Muslims and Indians, neither of which groups lived in Barbados in significant number in those days. Muslims and Indians, whom we lumped together as one race, came in droves in the sixties, piled one on top the other, animals and people, just like a city in India; and in the midst of this river of people, moving like water manouevring through the obstacles of stones in its path, along Roebuck Street, and Baxters Road, bustling with other fortune-making, fortune-telling, men and women swept over the land from Saint Lucia, from Saint Vincent, and Martinique and Montserrat.

We changed "Saint" when referring to Saint Lucia and Saint Vincent, to "Sin," to suggest suspicion of their "different ways" and our reservation about "small-island people." But we especially fell in love with these beautiful, sweet-talking women who wore gold bangles and rings on almost every finger, and whose "patois" lulled us into indolent, slow-walking "mannish-boys" always looking to see the seam of the panties that marked their bodies, to catch the lucky glance of their breasts when they laughed, looking-back boys "smelling our pee." So, we watched these "foreigner" women selling things and selling themselves, and the middle-class matrons who lived in the spacious, airy but dark apartments above the small-merchant stores, were more plentiful than the flies that buzzed over the uncovered cakes and coco- nut bread, rock cakes and coconut turnovers, in the cases that showed off these confectioneries, made from glass and wood, delicate as white coffins for children. But the flies got into the glass-cased cases, and travelled slowly over the barrel with chunks of pigs' tails in them, and over the tastiest salted mackerel that could decorate a bowl of corn meal cou-cou, slobbered in steamed fresh okra, snapping in their green freshness. Corn meal cou-cou, eaten in the humid afternoons, with a mackerel sauce and with enough small tomatoes in the sauce … in this environment, in this place, in that Island of Barbados, we boys in the Fifth Form, 5-A, to be distinguished from 5-B (boys older and not so bright); from 5-C (boys who were not taught Latin, but had to settle for Spanish, regarded as a commercial language); and from 5-D (boys who were not expected to pass the Senior Cambridge School Certificate Examination, set in England, the Mother Country). We the 5-A boys, would one day run the affairs of the Island, as we ran the working of the entire school, on the Friday afternoons when the Masters were engrossed in their games of dominoes, and chess, and poker, and bridge, in the cool Masters' Room freshened by the cross breeze — wind coming over the playing field, wind coming from the fish heads and mango peels in the gutters.

"5-A boys, man! The A-form boys, man! I am not talking about 5-B! Or 5-C ... and don't mention 5-D, where they only learn Spanish! Spanish? Where in Barbados are you going to use Spanish when you finish school, when you matriculate? If, at all, you do matriculate? Are you thinking of going to Venezuela? Or, Brazil? ... Or ... Panama?"

"Canada!"

So, with this attitude of superiority, cultivated through the curriculum itself, we the 5-A boys, patterned like Siamese twins with the English public school system, changed our way of talking, of walking, of dressing, custom vouchsafed over generations, in neighbourhood and in ancestry, from birth and practised until the grave; adopted a new posture of sauntering and not walking, in the thickness of the afternoon humidity that clutched us around one o'clock, by the throat, as we endured this new education, like English boys in this imported English school called "Cawmere" by us. But in spite of our new status, we remained tied to the cries of the congested Roebuck Street and Baxters Road, close enough to the rawness and the stagnant gutters which flowed like tributaries of rivers filled with molten lead. Along Roebuck Street and Baxters Road we were exposed to the shouts of warring of bargains and demands for settling debts, and pleas to enter into more debt; we were close enough that we could hear the details and the venom in the arguments, some of them using the logic we had just been taught about at Cawmere, but did not ourselves employ in our littler arguments. We could hear the victory of a man, a debtor most likely, as he exulted in his escape from the clutches of the money lender; or the police; and sometimes, in the gloominess of skies turning mauve with the threat of rain, while our teachers, lingered in the Masters' Room, and were still playing rummy, and whist, and bridge, or were slamming dominoes, we in the classrooms liberated from their supervision, remained unattended, and in our freedom, instead of slamming the seeds of dominoes — it was forbidden to play games in classrooms — we slammed the lids of our wooden desks, instead; in a loud, destructive peal that was like thunder. And we did not even wonder at the stupidity of these clamouring desks.

In the clap of a lid of a desk, similar in sharpness and noise, to the clap of thunder that announces rain or storm or hurricane, equal almost to the clap of victory in the slamming of the last domino seed that announces a "six-love," we shouted in our illegal freedom and smug licence, as we noisily ate our "roly-poly" candies, left over from our lunch; or tried to hide and eat the leavings of a "bread-and-fish," because we did not wish to share it with our best friend. A bread-and-fish, certainly with hot pepper sauce and perhaps a fresh leaf of lettuce, and cod fish cakes fried to a golden crispiness, in a freshly baked loaf, called a "salt bread," this "bread-and-fish" is a more substantial and sophisticated lunch for a boy than a fish sandwich sold in Toronto.

So, as we ate our "bread-and-fish" in the classroom, knowing it was prohibited; and as we slammed the lids of our "desses," we ignored what was happening around us. We were privileged boys. We knew and we felt that we were assured a place of importance in status, in job and in calling, in the society that was being built around us. And the builders of this society were Barbadians like ourselves, many of whom were black like us.

The Island was becoming de-colonized. And even though we were too young, and too uninterested in this political ideology of independence — even though the fervour of freedom was surrounding us like the sea, lapping at our consciousness, from the shores of Trinidad, from Jamaica, right down in the south, into British Guyana, and as far away as the African countries colonized by the English, Mau Mau and Zulu, countries whose names we could not even pronounce — still we knew, through instinct, through the new behaviour expressing independence, and through the self-assurance of the sound of the domino seeds being pounded in the Masters' Room, by young Barbadian men not much older than ourselves, we knew in our blood, and through instinct, that something very important was happening.

It seemed to us as if the Caribbean Sea had changed into the Atlantic Ocean, washing us with the skeletons and bones and myths of its importance as a conveyor of men and women in bondage, but being cleansed by the currents and lashing of that ocean, against our bodies to make us alert to the changes happening round us. We were once more living upon the waves of an ocean. The Atlantic Ocean.

But in a real sense, and being able to point a finger at our own self-discovery, in an individual manner of defining ourselves, in apposition to the white Englishman, one by one, we still did not know — even those of us who were prefects, and house captains and definitely, as the Head Boy — we did not really understand, at that time, why we were being singled out by our masters, and given this new authority to "take their classes," to "run things" while they continued their arguments with dominoes and white rum mixed in with the diminutive bottles of Coca-Cola, imported from America, or diluted in lemonade sweetened with white sugar, and made from limes growing in their backyards, close to the outdoor WC, and the prolific tree that dropped green and ripe pawpaws, good for purging the bowels and making us regular; and of course deliciously diluted in fresh coconut water. Not many of us had running water in our homes, bursting through lead pipes, fizzing just like the refreshing Coca-Cola. In England, our Mother Country, many years after these humid afternoons at Cawmere School for Boys, these same WCs, or outdoor toilets, were prevalent in London, adding surprise, and irony, to our wholesale imitation of English customs.

On those Friday afternoons, acknowledged to be periods when no significant work was expected to be done, and the concentration of energy was pointed to cricket practice in the nets, or training for athletics, or just talking on the edge of the playing field, watching boys pretending to be Frank Worrell, or Jesse Owens; not many amongst us could really make the connection between taking a class for a master, keeping his pupils disciplined, and the greater significance of that assignment, that a boy was acting for a master: that it was what is called nowadays "training for leadership."

I wonder if the 14th of February 1955, is a Friday. It won't take me much to look it up, but my hesitation, even in this small point of inflated significance, was born by the fact that at Cawmere we were not taught history. In more than one respect, Cawmere was a "secondary" government school. But the date is important. It is the day a Mr. C.D. Solin, assistant dean in the Faculty of Arts & Science, of McGill University, wrote me the letter of my acceptance, addressed to Mr. Austin A.C. Clarke, Flagstaff Road, Clapham, St. Michael 22, Barbados (there is a typographical error made by Mr. Solin's secretary — she had typed "Bargaros," and her eraser did not conceal her error!) — B.W.I.

> Dear Sir,
> I am glad to inform you that your application for admission to the first year of the course leading to the degree of Bachelor of Arts has been accepted for the 1955–56 Session.

There is a space, larger than the normal space between words, that separates *first* and *year*; and between *of* and *Arts* and *Arts* and *has*, as if either Mr. Solin, or his secretary were in two minds about my admission. The letter goes on to enumerate certain regulations:

> All students entering this Faculty for the first time are required to attend a meeting in the Sir Arthur Currie Gymnasium on Wednesday, September 21st, at 9 a.m.

Incidentally, I never did get to the Sir Arthur Currie Gymnasium, for on that very day, and for days before and after, my small Island was in the clutches of a hurricane, named Janet. And I never did go to McGill. When I eventually arrived in Canada, on the twenty-ninth of September 1955, I came to Toronto, instead. This now becomes ironic, and speculative: I would be bilingual today; and probably a separatist, had I entered McGill in 1955. Certainly, in the nationalistic political theology of the 1960s in Montreal, I would be a "black white nigger of Canada," if you can pardon the tautology. Mr. C.D. Solin, thought it prudent to warn me, that:

> This letter is your *Official Acceptance*. It must be presented at registration as your authority to register. It does not, however, constitute an acceptance to any other Faculty of the University either now or at some later date.
> Yours very truly.

In other words, I cannot ask, at this late stage, to be admitted. I cannot journey to Montreal and take an intensive course in French, I cannot qualify as a "black white nigger of Canada."

But I am still concerned by what had gone through the secretary's mind, when she came to write the name of my Island, Barbados. Why did she type *Bargaros*, and did not succeed in concealing her error, even though the eraser and the heavier striking of the two convicting letters, *g* and *r* were, unsuccessfully, pounded out into erasure, by striking those two keys to do the job which the rubber could not?

In Calgary, in May 2002, forty-seven years later, a similar confusion was made in the pronunciation of the name of my Island, Barbados. The woman introducing me to an auditorium filled with third-year students of English, said, with characteristic Canadian confidence, "Mr. Clarke is a Barbarian … and he had a Barbarian education at the best schools in Barbados."

This slip of the tongue did not much offend me, as there were no sniggers, making it seem that this woman introducing me, a chairman of the Department of English, at the college I was visiting, did not realize her slip. But I have had enough time after the first slip in spelling, to see that there was … could be … an element of the psychological, something hidden beneath the slip, something exposing the attitude of the chairman, as with the secretary, that was more unmentionable than the separatists of Quebec seeking emotional and cultural brotherhood with their myth of my person, by presuming a symbiosis, and calling themselves "white niggers," and by extension, calling me a "black white nigger." At least, it is less deadening than the greetings of "Look the nigger!" Or "Spook!" that I received on the subway, on the streetcar, on the streets of Toronto, during that first year in 1955. What would the Quebec Canadian have called me, then?

But before there was an opportunity by Canadians living either in Montreal or Toronto, to give me my new identity, defined in racial terms: "nigger," "monkey," "Spook," "Did you know they have tails? Look good behind them, when they walk" … I had first to leave Barbados, as a student, or as an immigrant. But Canada was, like us, only a colony; and you didn't leave your own colonized life, with its un-understood meanings, and seek refuge in another colony. It was the Mother Country that called all of us. We would show the Mother Country, to use the words of Frantz Fanon, a Martinique intellectual who wrote of race and phobias in his groundbreaking book, *Black Skin, White Masks*, published in 1967. And I would have to do better in the Mother Country, better even than those bred and born in the United Kingdom. So, we practised this encounter with the Mother Country, even before we had sat our school-leaving examination, which was set, characteristically, and colonially, in England, and graded by professors, presumably at Cambridge. The examination was the Senior Cambridge University School Certificate. We gave ourselves passes in this examination and we took the next step and gave ourselves admission to universities in the United Kingdom — to the best universities. I chose Cambridge University, using its Latin name, *Cantabria*. This sounded more impressive than Oxford, or *Oxonensis*. I became, in the stroke of a pen, A.A.C. Clarke, BA (Cantab), MA (Cantab), MPhil (Cantab), PhD (Cantab), DPhil (Cantab); and in case I was missing something, I conferred upon myself, LLD (Oxon). No other boy in my class could therefore match my academic degrees.

And so I left Cawmere well-endowed with these academic degrees that I had conferred upon myself. I also left as Sergeant-Major, the highest rank a schoolboy could reach in those days. And according to *The Combermerian*, the school's magazine, for the year 1948, under the heading "Athletics," for my house, Set C, is this comment:

> The Set has some fairly promising athletes; nevertheless it achieves the last place at every inter-house … In the senior division we saw Hal Brewster, "Tom" Clarke of Class II and I respectively, outrunning their colleagues. Brewster is an athlete of great promise and is capable of being the 1950 Victor Ludorum [champion of the games] … Clarke who was Victor Ludorum for the 2nd year, was a Class I champion at the last inter-school Meet, with the Husbands brothers of Harrison College. We are anticipating good results from Brewster and Clarke at the coming Inter-School Meeting.

I was looking at *The Comberemian* magazine recently, and had to wonder why as a school boy there, from 1944 until 1949, I never noticed the association of this secondary government school, founded in 1819, with the topography of the Island, that is to say, with sugar cane and all the things associated with the culture of sugar cane: hard, back-breaking labour in the fields in the hottest of suns; with the sun and the rain; with sweat, and sex; and with slavery.

The motto of my school is *Religione, Humanitate, Industria*. Three concepts consistent with a colonized society. The school crest itself is oval in shape, and inside a double-lined oval, is the name COMBERMERE SCHOOL. BARBADOS. And inside that oval, are two pieces of sugar cane with the blades, or leaves attached, in the middle of which is a book opened at the middle, and below which are, on the left an opened bottle of ink, the kind in which people like Charles Dickens, Samuel Pepys, Goldsmith, and prime ministers would dip their quill pens; and at the right, is a quill pen itself. But it is the irony in the motto, juxtaposed with the reminder, and the precept that would have been driven into the head of the slave, just as the whip had been driven into his back, to make a point to him, to remind him of his place, and of the "commandments" of *Religione, Humanitate, Industria*. But Combermere was established for the education of poor whites, whose parents could not afford the more expensive and upper class institutions of Harrison College and Queens College. Those lower-class white boys would have got the same lesson about their status in the society of the Island, as a black boy in 1944.

I am mentioned again in the 1948 issue of *The Combermerian*, under the heading, "The 1948 Inter-School Athletic Meeting":

> A.A.C. Clarke of Combermere won the 880 yards event in a style that gained him much applause. E.R. Cumberbatch of College seemed to have the race in hand in the first stages, but Clarke coolly kept himself in hand and set a tremendous pace near the end.

Incidentally, I ran that 880 in 1948, in two minutes, twelve and a half seconds.

In 1955, when I compared my times in the Island with the records posted in the Athletic Department of the university of Toronto, I was surprised to see that almost all the times I had done in Barbados as a high school athletic were better than the university's. And I wonder why I did not get involved in athletics at the university?

One afternoon I wandered into a basement room at Varsity Stadium. And I remember the feeling of confidence. And I remember the feeling of being out of place, being in the wrong place, as if there was some unwritten directive that I should have known, smelled, intuitively understood. In 1955, there were not, to my recollection, any black students on the university's athletic team — perhaps not even on the college team, not to mention the varsity team. A few of us kicked about the football, for our colleges. A smaller few played soccer for the university. If my memory serves me correctly, the university record in 1955, for the 100 yards, was eleven seconds. I had done it in ten seconds flat in 1949.

In the same issue of *The Combermerian*, is another reference to my athletic ability, and, as I read it now, I wonder what happened so soon after my schoolboy successes in track that I neglected athletics when I came to Canada in 1955? Was it that I expected to have been "approached" by a coach and asked to compete? Was it that I did not know the protocol required to be admitted to the varsity track team? Was the university's Athletic Department racist?

The School Athletic Meeting. A.A.C. Clarke — Victor Ludorum.

The conclusion of the annual Athletic Sports Meeting of Combermere School, found A.A.C. Clarke Victor Ludorum for the second year in succession.

Clarke won three events, came second in one, and third in another to pile up nineteen points, the highest of the meeting. He was winner of the flat races 220 yards, 440 and 880. He turned out for Division I of which he also emerged champion.

My times for those three races all run on the same afternoon: 24 and 3.5 seconds in the 220; 58 and 4.5 seconds in the 440; and 2 minutes, 12 and 2.5 seconds, in the 880.

At Speech Day that year, the headmaster, an Englishman — noted for his proficiency in French, as well for his proficiency in conducting "public floggings" — in his Report to the Board, under the heading, "Corporate Activities, section 28," said:

> In the Inter-School Athletic Meet held last Easter we came into Second Place, after Harrison College, and one of our boys — A.A.C. Clarke — tied with two Collegians for the honour of Victor Ludorum. I would remind you that the Second-Grade schools [of which Combermere was one], are severely handicapped by virtue of the age-clause operating which turns our boys out at 18 plus, whilst the First Grade Schools, [Harrison College and The Lodge School], may go on for a further two years. We are therefore compelled to compete in all branches of Sports and Athletics under a possible age-handicap of two years, with all that is involved in terms of greater physical development and stamina.

My headmaster's concern for the disadvantages of age and physical development as I competed against Harrison and The Lodge School boys, though admirable, was never a real indisposition. And what was ironical in his statement of good faith, was the fact that the very next term, I was "going over the fence" to Harrison College, into their Sixth Form, in a first-grade school, and would compete against them and also against Combermere — for I was labelled, not a Harrisonian, but "a transfer from Combermere School!" — an appellation and an identity similar to the "dog tags" worn by U.S. Armed Forces, men and women, round their neck! — and this appellation followed me through the two years I attended Harrison College. The distinction was understood, was etched in the mind, indelible as a wound that caused a mark on the black skin, like a birth mark.

"One of our boys," the headmaster's term, a term with a somewhat double entendre that might cause resentment and reservation, became "a transfer from Combermere," a term implying greater invisibility, implying encroachment and non-belonging. It was as if the headmaster of Harrison College was saying that I had, physically and morally, "climbed under the wire," which separated Combermere School from Harrison College, and thereby had committed an act of trespassing.

CHAPTER TWO

The Court Martial

I can still see the small pebbles in the playing field, like rubies or diamonds, although I had never seen a ruby or a diamond, not even in a magazine of Technicolor conspicuousness; and I can see the small black pellets from the sheep as they roam the desert of a playing field, similar to deserts I had learned about in geography class — deserts in Africa; deserts in Australia; deserts of ice in the Alaskan wilds of Canada; sheep trying "to get blood outta stone," as my mother would characterize their determination and resolution, to graze, which caused me to remember the only lines I remembered in class, of Proverbs quoted in my Wordsworth school book:

> Go to the ant, thou sluggard,
> Consider her ways and be wise.

And I am now at the end of the wire, the boundary that separates the tough neighbourhood of Carrington's Village, which is not a village, for there is no grass, no paved road, no running water, no trees except the few pawpaw trees, which, with their closeness to the outdoor WC, seem to be planted there deliberately to suck up the nourishment from the feces; this boundary is a wire. We place our well-polished brown shoes on the bottom strand and widen the space that already exists, and make it larger, large enough for our bodies to crawl through, without touching the desert of the playing field, littered now with broken pieces of bottle, with the droppings of the sheep that grazed the green with the efficiency of a gentleman's straight razor, with the "diamonds" and "rubies" or stones spread throughout the brown, unwatered grass, and, after a quick wash of the face from the public stand pipe, I walk along Hall's Road, incongruous with the general appearance of these poor men and women, crawling on their bottoms because their legs have disappeared from amputation, the crippling result of sickness, too much sugar in the blood, deformity at birth; and the women dressed in their see-through cotton frocks that look more like nightgowns than dresses to be worn in the daytime, and I come to the quieter, more village-like section where Halls Road meets Constitution ... Constitution is up from Queen's Park, known as the Park. Spartan Cricket Club, whose members are middle-class and brown-skinned, play cricket and football on this playing field. Queen's College, still predominantly white and upper-class, and "light-skinned," is situated here. It is a bastion, a fort, a boundary, an example of excellence in the brains of women. And to complete the triangle of power, Harrison College, where the guarantee to your success rests confidently in its classrooms, especially in the Classical Sixth; and should you be bright enough, or white enough, or rich enough, or lucky enough — if you had possessed none of the qualities or "qualifications" for entrance — if you were lucky enough to have an aunt, or an uncle in America, who could send you five Yankee dollars, in a money order, once a month, you too could squeeze through the iron gates of Harrison College, on which the motto *In Deo Fides* is emblazoned. "Wukking for the Yankee dollar!" my mother said, as if she was characterizing whores. But whores have always been with us. The Waterfront is painted with them: young, brown, luscious, lipsticked in red, smeared in that danger-ous colour round their mouths, which are always just, barely, seductively open, to let out a breath, to let out a kiss, and have it travel its imaginary short journey from those lips to your groins. And with those thoughts of ambition whirling in your head, you come to the last monument against whose walls, in whose desks, on whose playing fields, and in whose hall, your name — if you are a woman — may be scrawled. St. Michael's Girls School. A secondary government school for girls.

There is a rocky lane beside St. Michael, and the mile trees growing out of the rock, warn you that you are entering Belleville, a garden, a village, a small town, a small fort, a small beautiful "neighbourhood," where people like me work, but do not live. We water the lawns, we water the gardens, we clear the gutters of the fish heads, and the guts, and the little pieces of paper which you never see in my neighbourhood, or in Carrington's Village, that float like foam on the tops of waves at Gravesend Beach, near Needham's Lighthouse. The Lighthouse-man, meaning the man in charge, has a daughter. She is very beautiful. She is very bright. She goes to The Foundation Girls' School. Another secondary government school for girls. If you behave yourself, and be decent, you will be invited by Joan, and shown the anatomy of the lighthouse, similar to walking through the guts of a large fish, through the ribs along the spine, going through a channel, vertical, like a worm, like the worm you are — for you have wriggled the visit out of Joan, by deceiving her that you and she will be practising and rehearsing the lines you and she are to know by heart before Monday's rehearsal, to be performed in the musical play, *Tea for Two*, produced by Madame Ifill, a hairdresser who learned her trade in America, in Brooklyn, who became a millionaire.

I am walking the two and a half miles to get home, to Flagstaff Road. My bicycle, a ladies' wheel, black and a Raleigh, needs a new rear tire. Travelling this same journey, this same distance last week, I rode over a nail. The nail remained in the tire. The tube of patching paste is like a wound that has dried before it has healed. The paste is now part of the tube. And the Yankee dollar bills have not arrived yet. My mother wonders whether the civil servants in the post office down in Town — we live on a hill; we live in a neighbourhood that is above the topography of the post office; we live "above them, boy," — my mother wonders with the confidence of a conviction whether they have opened her letter from her sister in the Canal Zone, in Ancon Post Office, in Panama ... whether the postal workers in that post office across the red-white-and-blue air-mailed seas, so many miles of unknowledgeable distance, in a foreign country, has already tampered with the seal on the envelope, put their hands into her letter, and taken out her U.S. money order? So, today the sweat of effort, and the sweat of my brow, an exhausting condition praised only by people who are poor, instilled into the behaviour of slaves, and ignored by boys who come to school in chauffeur-driven cars, or in school buses, or who are picked up by their civil servant parents, or who have a green, three-speed-ticking Raleigh bicycle, the sweat pours down both sides of my face.

How many days, especially on Sunday afternoons, when homework became inexplicable and intractable, did I wallow in ignorance and consider myself ignorant because the Latin prose exercise was too difficult? I am a sluggard. Only in an English book was this word used. In the better lexicon that the neighbourhood of Flagstaff Village used, I was simply, "a blasted lazy boy, boy!" Who said that? My mother, or the boy with whom I had "reading races"?

The daily journey from school, whether on the ladies' wheel, or by foot, end at the Corner. We called it simply The Corner. Because it is a corner. Where Flagstaff Road meets the Front Road. The Front Road, like The Corner, has no formal government-chosen name. The Corner is where the public water standpipe is cut out of the tough rock of The Corner; where the grocery shop stands in its rotting board and shingle pride and where the shop owner, Miss Edwards — no one has ever called her by her Christian name; no one knows if she has a Christian name — sits behind the counter that hides her from sight, reading the *Barbados Advocate* daily newspaper, over and over again, until she has memorized it, as she had memorized Proverbs 6:6 at St. Michael's Girls School, and would relate it to me, the same two lines as punishment.

> Go to the ant, thou sluggard,
> Consider her ways and be wise.

Customs, and manners, and the number s of hymns sung in Sunday School, and at Matins; at weddings and Services-of-Song, and naturally at funerals; the jokes you tell a boy; the words you tell a girl; the food you eat, none of this changes, just as Miss Edwards sits behind her counter, reading the *Barbados Advocate* — except on Sundays, when the shop is closed for respect of "the Lord's Day, boy!" From generation to generation, we repeat the same rhetoric, the same lies, the same promises, when they are not kept, as they are not usually kept. So, Miss Edwards is comfortable and wise, and rich, and malicious, and knows the social, sexual, moral, monetary, and bedroom history of every woman and every man in this neighbourhood, so long as he breathes, so long as she breathes. Miss Edwards extends credit to every last household in this neighbourhood. She knows that when "Mistress Jones's husband went overseas, picking cotton in the South, the man had hardly left the Harbour, before the sweet-man came through the back door whilst the the children were sleeping … and this went on for years and years, and it only stop the night following the afternoon when the postman knock on her door, when she get the letter that he coming back on the thirteenth. It was a December …"

The shop is more important than the Church. And the shop is superior to the school in meaning and realism.

It was a Friday. We were in the country. In the eighteen years of my life, living in this Island shaped like a pear, the longest part of which is twenty-one miles, I had never visited this part of the Island, the country district of plantations and sugar canes and large fields that grew green grass. "For the cows and the sheeps," somebody said. I was in Sin-Joseph. It was a cadet camp. Harrison College, The Lodge School, and Combermere School. I was Sergeant-Major, in the Cawmere Cadet Corps, the highest rank a Combermere boy could achieve. It was a Friday night, the night before camp was to be broken. My best friend, Gillie, also a sergeant-major, of the Lodge School Cadets, had found his taste whetted for a woman who lived in the nearby village of Shop Hill, and he needed to make one last visit before he went home to his own parish, St. John. Gillie needed support. Gillie needed a cover. Gillie needed a go-between. Gillie needed a "backup." I was his "backup" on this Friday night, when the moon had forgotten to come out and shine, when the rain was threatening, but did not fall, when my arch enemies, the Harrison College cadets were on patrol (I was going there the following term, a matter of weeks from this Friday night; and I had beaten their best athlete, Edward Cumberbatch, in the 880; and I was the highest ranking cadet at Combermere; so as all their officers, second lieutenants, were leaving school, I would automatically become the highest-ranking cadet at Harrison College! And Victor Ludorum. And school captain. And everything else). This Friday night was an important and dramatic Friday night. Fraught with possibilities; poised upon the fascinating heel of accomplishment and distinction: Sixth Former in modern studies, winning the Barbados Scholarship, becoming a second lieutenant, and for the third time, Victor Ludorum, topped off by Head Boy.

Gillie insisted upon wearing his topee. Perched on his head, as he would wear it on parade. On the right side. Just at the correct angle and cock, to show off the part in his hair, gouged out not by the fine-tooth comb, but by the steady hand of his uncle, using a razor blade. And after two weeks in manufactured "darkness of warfare, in trenches, in fox holes, in training as close as possible to war," the batteries in Gillie's torchlight were like the eyes of a scolded dog in the same manufactured darkness of warfare. Down we went, into the hillside of St. Joseph, the sea on one side of us, the "enemy" — Harrison College cadets on watch! — on the other side, and we crawled on our bellies, although there was no need to, and we imagined enemy soldiers coming against us, and we trusted our safety to silence, and the moonless night, down, down, into the roiling bowels of the enemy, reciting to ourselves, silent and respectively, "The Charge of the Light Brigade" and "England expects every man to do his duty!"

Gillie was in the Upper Classical Sixth Form at The Lodge School, and therefore knew the names of many other battles fought in Greece and in Rome, and throughout the Roman Empire, in the prose of Tacitus, of Livy, of Caesar, and the plays of Euripides; and he knew the sting in the flesh from a thrust of a spear, and the reverberating *zzzzzing*s in the eardrums from a blow from a sword to that part of the head covered by an iron helmet. He was silent in his reconstructing of classical battles.

We faced the Rubicon. It was the home of the girl he loved. It was the tent of his Helen. Perhaps, she was his Cleopatra. She would remain inside the house, standing at the window, pretending to be admiring the darkness of the night, while it was the dark thoughts of love — not all classical and platonic — that consumed her body. And Gillie's body. We two soldiers, AWOL, like true officers in the army of Rome, legionnaires, would not betray the young girl's honour, or her deceit. Her mother thought she was already in bed, after having digested her own homework:

thirty lines of Virgil's *Aeneid*, Book One. If the moon was shining. If it was a moonlight night. If the silver of the moon had matched the silver of the waves of the sea, breathing peacefully nearby. If Gillie's batteries had been stronger. If the Harrison College cadets were not our "enemies" that Friday night. If I could have convinced Gillie to pull the straps of his topee down, and buckle them under his chin, as we always did, to make it look like a pilot's helmet.

If ... if ... if ...

"If," as my mother used to say, "if shit had wings, it would fly ..."

Gillie lost his topee. In the sand on the hill, in the darkness of the night, the light-green, woollen topee did not ever become conspicuous against the background of the crystal sea, now almost as black as the night. But tomorrow, and tomorrow, as that procrastinating prince of Denmark used to say: Tomorrow we break camp. Gillie needed his topee to appear at the parade. Rise and shine. Bright and early. Spit and polish. "Hip-hip! Hip-hip! Eyeeeees, right! Roy-yalll, Sah-lute, preeeee-zent arms! Hih-pipp-poray!"

We found the topee. The bulb of Gillie's searchlight, eighteen inches long, and its colour of fake silver, was now a weapon, and no longer a light. The sea had gone to bed. The beach grape trees were dozing, as they dozed even during the day, in their gnarled, twisted bodies; no dog was barking; there was no wind, and we could not imagine fishing boats returning to the side of the jetty in the silent, thick, smelling night ... for the Harrison College "enemies" were on guard, at every possible loose wire that a cadet breaking camp would think to slide under, like a worm slithering on its belly, through a hole half its size ... Gillie was breathing hard beside me. I can see his eyes. I could see his spectacles. I could see his spectacles. See his disappointment. The girl did not tell him what he wanted to hear. His question was, "When I going see you again? After camp break tomorrow? Tomorrow is Saturday. Saturday in Town?" The window closed with a sound as loud as a sigh. But she was decent enough, well brought up enough, to leave her perfume as a kiss. Goodbye. A promise. Not good night. But not a promise clothed in a word, either.

"When, nuh?" Gillie asked, too loud, for I could hear his words fifty yards off, in the dark night, standing like a watchman or a guard.

"I don't know," she told him, in a voice that said she knew, but did not want to tell him; in a voice that said that someone, mother, father, big brother, little brother would come any moment now, and catch her, and catch her at the window, talking to a man dressed like a soldier ...

And we trudged up the hill, disappointed and unrequited, in the shifting sand, in total darkness now, as the bulb refused to answer the switches Gillie's thumb was putting it through, and we imagined that we were at Sebastopol, in the Dardanelles; in Bataan, in Japan; and that we were surrounded, in a jungle, by Japanese soldiers identical to the black jungle by the silence of their bodies, until the knife was at your throat ...

"Who goes there?" The voice was young. But the intention and tone were serious and adult. A real soldier!

Silence. We were, after all, in a jungle in Japan, in the Eastern Theatre of War. Silence.

"Advance to be recognize?" In the heat of acting, in the enthusiasm of being a "real" soldier, syntax and grammar were sacrificed.

I saw him. I saw his eyes. They were full of fear. I recognized his spectacles. Horn-rimmed. I recognized his "fizziogomy," as my mother would say. He was my neighbour. A Third-Former. A private. Arresting a sergeant-major. In 1951. On a dark night, on a hill where the sand was shifting, where the camp was in darkness, where the ranking cadets, second lieutenants from Harrison College, were in their tents, drinking gin and bottled lime juice, when they "got Tom Clarke, boys! We catch-he-brekking out o' camp!"... in almost total darkness, in the informal night, with Gillie wearing his topee at the correct angle now, showing his razor-blade part in the left side of his hair, proper in the correct "spit and polish" of the conscientious "mock-soldiers" as envious boys who were not admitted to the Cadets, called us ...

Gillie was stripped from sergeant-major to private that morning when only the wood dove welcomed us, democratically, casting his praise for the morning alike to commanding officers, as to the two breakers of the code. In that soft cooing, as comforting as the soprano soloist in the choir of St. Matthias Anglican Church, and in that identical punishment, the stripping away of status given by our masters, a bond was sealed. In all this time, from 1949 until 2004, when, on one of my trips back to the Island, I last saw Gillie, attending the book launching of *The Polished*

Hoe, we never talked about that bleak morning in Walkers. We never have sought the meaning for our closeness, never questioned whether it would, or could, simmer into formality. We have never thought that our court martial could have had a fundamental effect upon our lives.

~

It is a Friday afternoon, in July 2004, and I am in the library of the University of the West Indies, (UWI), on the Cave Hill campus, in Barbados, signing copies of *The Polished Hoe*. A man comes up to me. I know him. I was at Harrison College with him. I remember more from his rank in the Cadet Corps. He was a second lieutenant in 1951. He was at the cadet camp in Walkers, on that August Friday night. He remembers the night fifty-three years ago. And he gives me details that only a man who knows the history of an event, its fomenting, its plotted beginning, and the detailed putting into effect of this plot, and I know I am in the presence of one of my predetermined "enemies" who must have prayed for that Friday night, for the fates to be on their side — who had laid the plot like a small boy lays a trap, a "down-fall" to snare a small animal like a wood dove, and had had the luck fall upon their spiderwebbed jealousy similar to Iago's enmity against Othello, a web that was spun on that Friday night in 1951, to entrap and kill two sergeants-major — with one stone.

"And I have carried this all these years, fifty is it?… Fifty-four!…" he says, standing beside me, as I sign the piles of *The Polished Hoe*, which was a bestseller in Barbados and the West Indies. "But how are you, man? Congratulations on the book … but I never really had the opportunity to tell you about that night at Walkers, at the cadet camp. I have been impressed that you carried no enmity for any of us, Harsun College boys, who were quite aware you were 'coming over the wire,' the next term, in six' form. I never really understood why you didn't write anything about this … I admire you for it, man …"

This man introduces himself to me as Cecil Clarke.

~

In *The Harrisonian* magazine, edited by us Sixth Formers, is my name, A.A.C. Clarke of the Modern VI, under which is a short story, "Off the Beam." The publication date of the magazine is January 1951. Robert Weaver must have somehow seen this story before I came to Canada in 1955. I reproduce the story here, and as I read it over sixty years later, I wonder what had got into my head to write such a work of art?

Omnibused, I arrive.

Water Street was pregnant with inquisitive-coyish looks. Rustic dwellers. Sunday-crowd elastic-stretched along young rum-fields.

An almond tree-guarded house — my destination!

Musical "tap-tap" upon the door; excited interior feet beat a country-dance.

Smiling-spectacled-beauty answered the call. Atmosphere aromatized by provocative perfumes.

"Come in."

Greetings exchanged.

Aunt. Sister. Brother-in-law. Friends. All there — seated on cloud-cushioned-chairs. Wild chatter.

Sudden patter-patter of rain on window-panes. Inquiries, semi-embarrassing: the girl ... her name ... 'tis true!

Truth concealed. Hostess bloody-raged.

Conscience-prickled-confessions.

Hostess indignant-painted. Situation over-tense. Transitory chillness pervading body and soul. Bewitched ... bothered ... bewildered ...

Colleague-rescued by saviour. Gratuitous-understanding-looks exchanged.

Reconscioned! Saved!

Expositioned:

Former-suited — addresses nullified and void. Shocking revelations. First-named-spidered-pest knocked off the beam ... hated, despised.

Semi-relieved-heart-beats 'gainst jawboned-compressed-mouth.

Exclamation, open-mouthed!
Stimulated-grimness. A lapse.
Interim-icecream-entertained. Fervid heart turned chilly
... death-cold.
Ticking-mantlepieced-contraption declaring "eight,"
farewell-kissed; lark-happily omnibused home.

Now that I have read this over, after sixty-four years of its "creation,"
using "creation" in its greatest clemency of critical evaluation, I think
I am reminded that my ambition was to have been an English-trained
barrister-at-law. This realization is most consoling when I see that in
this one-paged short story, I have broken all the "rules" I have made for
my students in creative writing classes, at the University of Toronto, at
Yale, Brandeis, Smith, Williams, Duke, and the Universities of Indiana
at Bloomington, and of Texas at Austin. And I'm glad that they never
saw this early example of their instructor's writing.

It must have been something in my mind, in my makeup, in my experiences at this young age, that always made me see humour in situations
of great horribleness. And this is the way I looked at it, lived in it,
and became the main character, the tragic hero ... Macbeth. We were
studying *Macbeth* for our Senior Cambridge School Leaving Certificate.
The three "characters" were mixed into one: witness, observer, and
victim. Years before, or it could have been only weeks before, I had
seen the movie, *The Life of Emile Zola*, starring Paul Muni, concerning
a senior ranking officer in the French Army who was court-martialed
for his political views. And even though my misadventure did not have
that tragic significance, and could not have harmed the court of either
Combermere School or Harrison College, no one was concerned if
I had proved to have been disloyal to King George the Sixth, but the
dramatic ripping off of Dreyfus's gold-braided epaulettes of "scram-
bled-egg," attesting to his former importance, and then the deliberately
slow but dramatic and vicious ripping of the medals off his chest; and
then, when it was over, there was a silence in the cinema, in that parade

square somewhere in Paris, and here in Barbados at Walkers, bright and early, at nine o'clock, it seems that I faced my new nakedness, the three khaki stripes above which was the Imperial Crown, making me a sergeant-major; I was reduced in rank, in confidence, in status, in shame, and in the calculated vengeance of my "enemies" at Harrison College, even before I entered this school, to a naked boy.

A.A.C. Clarke, Private, Company 3, Combermere School Cadets.

Through my mind, on that morning in the bookstore of the University of the West Indies, at Cave Hill in Barbados, induced by the comment of the former Harrison College second lieutenant, I was remembering a history that bound me to customs and to the drama of seriousness, which I could not really understand, in my circumstances that were so different from the disposition of my masters; and I used the word in both senses: those who were appointed to teach me, and those who appointed themselves, through wealth, status, colour, or meanness, to teach me. In the first case, teach me Latin and English literature. In the second case, manners. "Manners maketh man." It was driven into me from my five-year-old days on the backless, hard, wooden benches at St. Matthias Elementary School for Boys.

Master and the headmaster were taking life more seriously than me. To me it was a case of not leaving my best friend in a lurch, or insisting upon that kind of allegiance; of daring the command culture of the "Mock Soldier" establishment. Board guns and blanks, and road marches, and singing "It's a Long Way to Tipperary," "John Brown's Body" (without knowing its racial application to me, and to the majority of these "mock soldiers," from homes in the villages and neighbourhoods, and not from Belleville and Stratchclyde, known as "esplanades" and "terraces"), and "What Do You Do with a Drunken Sailor?"

Years later, in the writing of *The Polished Hoe*, published in 2002, more than fifty years after my fall from rank, I remembered the songs we sang as "mock soldiers," and the hymns my mother sang following my fall, and military court martial. What I thought was a comedy, a pageant, inferior in its significance to a Shakespearean comedy, that it was a long vacation holiday, when we would play impromptu and invented games of cricket — "marble cricket" — to suit our world, in place of first-class cricket for organized teams; what I had thought was a pageant, and could therefore not touch me when with any serious scolding or detentions, was actually harsh reality. When we became more studious, entering the Sixth Form, when I entered the Modern Studies Sixth, to study Latin, Roman history, English literature and language, and religious knowledge (as a pass subject), preparing for a real life, overseas; to the Mother Country; or immigrating to America, Canada completely out of the picture, because Canada was, like us, a colony, and did not play cricket, and was lock-jawed in cold more bone-chilling months, than the life of a summer; and who had gained our wrath by receiving premium rum made from our sugar cane reaped amidst violence with the sun, cow-skin, rape and sweating labour, for boxes of thin, bony, "white-skin" salt fish, called cod, from the Grand Banks. No wonder then that my mother increased the intensity of voice and punctuation, when she sang "Nearer My God to Thee."

I resigned from the cadet corps and concentrated my extra-curricular activities to athletics, dabbling on Friday nights in writing poetry at the home of a senior civil servant, Mr. Hope, along with Magistrate H.A. Vaughan, from a hill in the neighbourhood of Britton's Hill. I spent time listening to their more mature and professional poetry which sounded more like the poems we studied in Sixth Form, the poems of Tennyson, Wordsworth, Keats, Milton, Chaucer, than they sounded like any home-grown versifying or poetastering, since in those days, the early fifties, the BBC's "Caribbean Voices" radio programme, which slammed against our ears, every Sunday, to wake us up into the unbelievable recognition that we had something important to say in our short stories, in our poems, in our literary journeys about ourselves. And that what we heard, edited, and judged and sent back to us, in better estate than Canadian salt fish, by the English, still was able to give us that less shitty end of the stick of colonialism.

With this new origin of our Island's creative talent, and its winning the approval of the BBC, we, individually, and in "writing clubs," became more brave, more creative, more licentious with the English language; and from those Sunday evenings in the fifties, we abrogated the English language and used it as our own, and enriched it in the process, with the help of Samuel Selvon, Earl Lovelace, V.S. Naipaul, Dionne Brand, Derek Walcott, Archie Markham, Caryl Phillips, Jan Carew, Wilson Harris, Edgar Mittelholzer, Martin Carter, Mark McWatt, Fred D'Augiar, Tessa McWatt, George Lamming, Kamau Brathwaite, Lionel Hutchinson, and many others who came later.

~~~

> Nearer, my God to Thee,
> Nearer, to Thee.

In times of stress, in times of sadness, no credit extended at the shop by Miss Edwards; the delay in the arrival of the U.S. postal money order making my mother have "bad headaches," that begin in America, and are coming all the way from Miss Eloise Clarke, Ancon Post Office, Canal Zone, Panama, Central America; the accidental burning of the white rice she is cooking, to be served with steamed flying fish, all these "calamities" were best illustrated by her soprano voice, in an off-tune improvisation of "Nearer My God to Thee."

Gillie went on to take a degree in classics. I never found out whether he too resigned from the cadet corps of the Lodge School; or whether he remained, and stared them in the face, and re-climbed the ranks, and reached second lieutenant.

I had to face the headmaster of Harrison College, and face captain George Hunte, almost every day, the latter of whom, in his twin capacities — commanding officer of the cadet corps, and games master, even though the latter was still an informal arrangement. About the first, I resigned; about the second, I was determined to use athletics as an avenging weapon, to be Victor Ludorum, for the two years I would be "the Transfer." I remained in all this time, "the Transfer." Was even identified as such in my school-leaving testimonial:

> A.A.C. Clarke entered Harrison College as a transfer from
> Combermere School. He is at present taking the Oxford &
> Cambridge Higher School Certificate, at Scholarship Level.

He is an outstanding athlete, and shows a flair for literary writing. Signed, J.C. Hammond, M.A. (Cantab), Headmaster.

On your school-leaving testimonial, a document without which your prospect of getting a job; a document which like a police record is negatively as important in your not getting a job; a document in which your headmaster does not mention, not necessarily in blazing comment, a word of your deportment, your promptness, your tidiness, your extra-curricular activities, your manners, your academic record in detail, and whether you were a prefect, Set Captain, or Head Boy, and your punctuality — without this document saying all these things, you are lost; washed up on the beach like a high-smelling carcass of a fish that the sea and larger fish have nibbled at. You are dead, you are lost: court-martialed, stripped of any possibility. You are better off to leave the Island, and "emigrade to Amurca," England, "if yuh can't do any better." Or even Venezuela. "You could-even learn to speak the brabba-rabba of the Spanish language." The size of the Island, and its predilection for gossip and general knowledge would make it impossible for you to hide this wound to your spirit.

CHAPTER THREE

Toranno!... Toranno!... Toranno!

Mr. W.R. Martin, the registrar of Canadian citizenship, in the Department of the Secretary of State, wrote me this letter on October 30, 1968. It is written under File 30533-68; and it is addressed to me, at 46 Asquith Avenue, Toronto 5, Ontario. (In 1968, 46 Asquith Avenue was opposite to the First Floor Jazz Club, run by Howard Matthews; and at which Archie Alleyne, Wray Downes, Dougie Richardson, P.J. Perry, Gerry X — who died recently — Nobbie Watanobe, and the Thompson brothers, one on tenor saxaphone, the other on string bass — which we still called " the mother-fiddle" — and at the corner of Park Road and Asquith Avenue, cutting each other at right angles, was the Oscar Peterson School for Jazz, where Ed Thigpen and Ray Brown were instructors.):

> Dear Mr. Clarke;
> I am very sorry to say that the Minister has found it necessary to reject your application for citizenship.
>
> The information on which the decision was based is confidential and it would not be in the public interest to reveal it.
>
> Section 14 of the Citizenship Act provides that you may again apply after a period of two years from the date of

rejection, October 29, 1968.
Yours truly,
W.R. Martin
Registrar of Canadian Citizenship.

In the same way as I had refused to see the seriousness with which certain persons viewed behaviour, even when I myself was the subject of that behaviour being discussed, I do not often take the censure that was bound to follow, seriously enough, believing that as I have said, I was protected by some Fate, by the Three Weird Sisters, by God, perhaps, to overcome what my mother was certain was "lack o' decentness on their behalfs." So, the glancing blow of racism on the part of the headmaster of Harrison College — or was it his succumbing to the culture of class that surrounded him, a stranger to the Island's code of behaviour? — in his attempt to bury my ambition and my possibilities, in my own Island, whose culture, myths, and modus operandi mystified the smallness of his stature, physically and morally (he was four feet ten inches short), could not have touched me in the Island. It turned out that his testimonial, with all its innuendo and glancing irony and sarcasm, was futile in achieving the result it was intended to have, by its curtness of language. I was the champion schoolboy athlete for seven consecutive years. And as we know in Canada, and in America, and in the United Kingdom, "star-boys" in sports have a way of squeezing through and walking around certain encumbrances put in their way, when they deserve to be curbed by those reservations, like the bars placed in the path of the hurdler, who is to clear them, or be confounded by them, as we all saw at the Olympics in Athens, when the Canadian champion hurdler Perdita Felicien misjudged the height of the first hurdle, something she had not done before. Misjudging, caused, perhaps, through overconfidence, or her belief that adversity will not strike her.

A hurdle was placed in my path. And as a champion athlete, a schoolboy notwithstanding, I had been acquainted personally with adversity. So, it must have been this determination to win, which is utilized so economically by the champion athlete, which caused me — in my reaction to the court martial and to the testimonial — to disregard their intended disastrous meaning. Friendship and loyalty to

Gillie, and to my neighbour, who was guarding the gate, even though on that night at Walkers, he was, as the cadet on guard duty, a declared "enemy" (he was a Harrison College boy, wasn't he?), that placed me in that predicament. And then, in 1968, living in another landscape, to face this tricky hurdle to Canadian citizenship, based, as Mr. Martin's letter stated, upon "information" that is "confidential," and "not in the public interest to reveal …"

What does Mr. Martin mean by the "public"? And what is the meaning of "information"? Does Mr. Martin's information mean "facts"? The information-gathering agencies that I know of are CSIS, MI5, the CIA, and the FBI. And everyone knows by now, from the publication of these "confidential" pieces of "information," that much of this "information" cannot be accused of accuracy; but is prejudiced. I have never been so curious that I needed for my peace of mind, to inquire and investigate each statement, each act in which I am involved. I can keep gifts at Christmas and birthdays wrapped for months after they have been given, without feeling the tug of wonder enough to want to know their contents. This is not a lack of regard for the felicitation behind the giving of the gift. It is probably based in history, a history of not expecting too much, goodness, reward, assistance, gifts, that I have developed this cynical attitude to things and to matter, persons, and friends, from whom I do not expect unquestioning loyalty, that Mr. Martin's letter, written at a time when I was going to Yale University as a visiting lecturer, in the midst of the civil rights movement in America, at a time when it was important to me, as a man, as a black man, and a beginning writer (by 1968, I had published only *The Survivors of the Crossing, Storm of Fortune, Amongst Thistles and Thorns,* and *The Meeting Point*). And I was in a hurry. The terrible times of segregation, police violence against black people, the snarling of dogs trained to snarl, and the thunderous, limb-breaking force of water hoses used more suitably by the fire brigades of America's Southern states, than by firemen bent upon cutting off the limbs of non-violent protestors for freedom; most of these hoses levelled against the spread of women's buttocks, against their breasts, tore their panties off in full view of jeering policemen and sheriffs and marshals, these terrible times in America, and to some extent modified in their application and moderated, in Canada, too, the times caught my intellectual interest — my cultural and social interests were axiomatically already engaged — and it became imperative that I go to Yale, and to America, and see first-hand the torment which "the brothers and the sisters" were being put through, and to see, by breathing in that American animosity, "what's happening, baby?"

Maclean's magazine had published a subjective piece I had written about my experience of racial discrimination in Toronto — and in Canada. My piece dealt with personal experience between 1955 and 1968. *Maclean's* magazine, imitating the brusqueness of headlines that we were all reading in the American papers, headlines that warned of a black-white race war, or the second American Civil War, headlines screaming about large-scale lynchings, in other words, of Armageddon ... Malcolm X was coming into prominence as a "firebrand" and a "racist extremist" ... inducing James Baldwin to give the title of his book of essays *The Fire Next Time*, which every thinking man and woman, black and white, expected to descend upon the land, at any moment, *Maclean's* magazine took the occasion of the publication of my piece about Toronto's and Canada's version of segregation, to use the headline, "Canada's Angriest Black Man." I had earned a label. My position and my presence in Toronto were therefore categorized and dipped in the ink of unworthiness to be a citizen. "Canada's Angriest Black Man."

The "angry blacks" of America and of this world, were the Black Panthers, the Black Muslims, the Black Nationalists, who were all, in the eyes of the press, meaning the white press, the *Globe and Mail*, the *Toronto Telegram*, the *Toronto Star*, the *Financial Post*, all black racists. They did not care to admit to their monotheistic racism, by failing to explain that everyone who was black in those days was not a member of the Black Panthers, or the Black Muslims — even though the reality of their lives might very well induce them to taking out membership! But, by the 1960s, we all knew — both black and white — that "all blacks look alike." Angry and black, both at once? And the euphemism "Canada's angriest black man" did not faze any thinking person. The hidden meaning was simply "Canada's most anti-white black man." But the sadness was that I was given no opportunity, in the minds of the readers of *Maclean's* magazine, to say why I was an angry black man — not to mention "the angriest" in all of Canada!

The truculence in the photograph of the face of "Canada's angriest black man" and the scowl on his face that the photograph focused on, is similar to the visage of a newspaper photograph of "the last man black man to be hanged in Canada," Mr. Arthur Lucas! The photograph of me was published after the gallows snapped Mr. Lucas's neck in 1962 … pop!

With this obstacle of image placed in my path, I knew I had to leave Canada. I had intended to leave Canada for good, earlier. After Yale, I would go to England, where Notting Hill and Brixton, England's metaphors for race riots, segregation, and lynchings was extant, but with a polite British Oxonian and Cantabrian stiff upper lip, that spoke a most "civilized racism, if you see what I mean, old chap!"

I had to leave.

But I had never considered leaving Canada for America, even though my education at Harrison College was paid for by the "ill-gotten gains" my mother said. America had given me, after having given my aunt, Eloise; permission to live in America as an immigrant was not in my stars, even though at that time, and in the present time, my mother, my stepfather, five brothers, and a sister were living in Brooklyn, in suburban New Jersey, in the Bronx, and other cities in America. It would be England, completing the unfinished journey that would have begun with my going up to Oxford, as I had been promised a place in 1953 and 1954, at New College, if I had the fees for tuition, or knew how to acquire the fees — not counting in the cost of the passage, in the steerage, third-class in a reverse journey across the Atlantic Ocean.

By the beginning of 1968, I had begun to hear horror stories about the neglect the British were now showing some of the West Indian writers living in London. Among these writers are Andrew Salkey, Samuel Selvon, Jan Carew, Wallace Collins, Archie Markham, and others. The only West Indian who during this time of racial baiting and violence in London's Notting Hill Gate and in Brixton, giving the riots their name, was V.S. Naipaul. But we, those of us who had not achieved any recognition equalling his British and international acclaim, concluded, through a touch of jealousy, and justified convincing criticism, that Naipaul had sold out the black race, and his own Indian castes, in order to get into bed with the white Englishman, the same man who, earlier in the 1950s, had judged the standard of our literary production, just as he had administered our social and agricultural production, during the height of African colonization. The invisible Englishman, accustomed to his word being sanctioned as law, went beyond his limitations of the apprehension of the cultural and racial character of the West Indies, and presumed to be the arbiter of value and appropriateness — and the definition of West Indian — and judged the literary worth of our novels and poems and travel writings by the standard laid down by Naipaul. The rule of colonialism, over tribes and races, protectorates and colonies, and islands and dots of islands in the Indian Ocean, and in other seas, achieved its paramountcy. The presumption of superiority was applied to our writing. You were a successful writer if your books were published by a "reputable" London house. I would not dismiss our criticism of Naipaul as purely jealousy, for there is, in criticism, an element of the subjective that gives the critical judgment its balance, and a certain acerbity that is another name for bite.

But to get back to Mr. Martin's characterization of me, in the sentence, "The information on which the decision was based is confidential and it would not be in the public interest to reveal it." This is an ominous statement. And when this sentiment is out against the title of my article in *Maclean's* magazine, "Canada's Angriest Black Man," it becomes, in the terminology of the athlete, an obstacle similar in meaning, to the two hurdles that faced Perdita Felicien.

Harry J. Boyle is a burly, cheerful, self-contented, and very intelligent man. He is a creative man. He is a fair, Christian-minded, honest man. I came to this conclusion before I found out that in addition to being the best executive producer in radio, at the CBC, in its historic, beautiful building on Jarvis Street, he is a published author. I was somewhat puzzled by his egoism in naming — or agreeing with his editor's suggestion — one of his novels, *The Great Canadian Novel*. What after all was the great Canadian novel? When Harry J. Boyle abrogated to himself this questionable honour, Margaret Atwood, Graeme Gibson, Margaret Laurence, Marian Engel, Farley Mowat, David Lewis Stein, Hugh Garner, Robert Mirvish, and Morley

Callaghan, were at that stage in their careers, all writing the "great Canadian Novel" … although they did not, with smaller egos, say so. It is true, if not indelicate to say so, that their "great Canadian novels" might have outstripped Harry Boyle's. But the honesty of his achievement lies in the honesty of his endeavour, and in its treatment of all those ambitious, quarrelsome, cocksure, creatively talented young men and women (Howard Engel, Dita Vadron, Elizabeth Barry, Alex Frame, Max "Rawhide" Ferguson, Allan McFee, Barbara Frum, Robert MacNeil, Phyllis Webb, and the two very skilled radio technicians who dedicated their brilliance to the CBC, in the producing of shows, such as Glenn Gould's piano recitals, and *Ideas*, and the Project Series. I feel that Harry J. Boyle was to the radio documentary, which he took to its highest limits of excellence and relevant subject matter, every Sunday night, what Robert Weaver was to Canadian literature. They were both pioneers, with a profound confidence in struggling freelance broadcasters and writers. Their generosity of spirit helped to launch many careers in broadcasting, and in writing: Alex Frame and Alice Munro, to name just two.

In 1963, I had this conversation with Harry J. Boyle, in his office, cluttered with audio tapes awaiting to be used in tape recorders, Nagras and other models, and audio tapes for the machine on which recorded interviews are edited. Harry is smoking a hooked Peterson of Dublin pipe. I think of Irish goblins, I think of Father Christmas, I think of James Joyce. I think of myself imitating Harry J. No man, artist or layman ever looked so impressive as Harry J. Boyle with his Peterson of Dublin pipe, with its band of silver, certified to be silver by the things, letters and figures, and numbers etched and stamped into it. It looked like a very elegant wedding ring. The beautiful, European woman, an immigrant from Hungary, his secretary, is outside in greater chaos of tapes and scripts and yellow-paged transcripts of interviews, proposals of programmes for the Project Series, and a few young idling men who want to be taken seriously as freelance broadcasters.

Howard Engel is across the hall, trying against time, to reduce a verbose interview to two minutes, the greatest space he has to spare.

"Well," Harry J. Boyle says. "What can I do for you?"

"I want to be a freelance broadcaster, sir."

I had just been fired from the CBC stagehand crew, for "lateness"; arriving too late with my hammer to pound nails part-way into the wooden "flats." My mind had not been on learning to be a stagehand, although the money was good.

"Ever done any broadcasting?"

"No, sir."

"How do you know you can be a broadcaster?"

"I just feel so."

"Who would you like to interview?"

"James Baldwin."

"James Baldwin? We already have about twenty hours of tape on Baldwin, and ..."

"I can do a better job."

"Why do you think you can do a better job?"

"Because I am black, and I am a writer."

Great, thick, whitish-grey clouds came billowing out from the silver-bound Peterson of Dublin pipe. Harry J. sucked on the impressive pipe with its sparkling silver ring, for a few more minutes, in silence.

"Tell you what!" The pipe was still billowing white-grey clouds. I could hear his breathing; and I could hear the puff each time he exploded the very aromatic smoke into the ceiling of his cluttered office ... Condor? Erinmore Flake? Amphora, in a brown plastic pouch, mixed into the two Irish flavours? Even if this was not his home-made blend, I wanted it to be so. "Tell you what! You go down to New York you're on your own. You interview Baldwin. I'll even let you do the interview in our New York studios on Sixth Avenue. Our woman there, Dorothy McCallum, will assist you. By the way, have you ever used a tape recorder?"

"No, sir."

"She'll give you a few lessons."

"Thank you, sir."

"You go and interview Baldwin, send it back to us through Miss MacCallum, we'll listen to it, and if it is any good, we'll pay you ... your travel, plane fare to and from New York, per diem, hotel, and the regular fee for a Project documentary."

"Who do I report to in New York, to learn how to use the tape recorder?"

"Miss McCallum."

The pipe was smouldering.

"Ever used a Nagra tape recorder?"

"Never used a Nagra, sir."

This conversation has returned to me, inhabiting my head, in its detail, an exact recapturing of the words we exchanged that morning. And I feel that if the roles were reversed, and I was interviewing a young black man, and he had told me that he could do a better job than those already done by established CBC freelance broadcasters, without having studied those interviews, and if he had insisted that he could do better interviews, principally because he is black, I would, I think, have thought of throwing him out of my office.

But Harry J. Boyle could not have said that to me, not because of race, but because he was a gentleman willing to give a chance to a young black man, with "no Canadian experience," but ambitious and confident enough though unskilled in the profession he sought to enter.

I had never even seen a Nagra tape recorder. But my more pressing problem was transportation to New York "by whatever means possible!" How was I going to get to New York? I had no place to stay. I had no money. Not even enough to buy a one-way bus ticket on Greyhound. I had no money for food. And what if I could not get the loan of the Nagra tape recorder, which I soon learned was used for the audio in Hollywood movies because it was such a brilliant tape recorder. I was buried in my own boastfulness. But I was determined to interview James Baldwin.

Baldwin's novel *Another Country* had just been published. I had read it in Toronto. When I read it the second time, in New York, part in Harlem and part in a hotel downtown, I had a stronger feeling of its pulsing power of violence barely restrained. I identified with Rufus, the main character, who committed suicide by jumping off a building in downtown New York. That manufactured violence coursing through *Another Country* I transposed into my first novel, *The Survivors of the Crossing*. Where there was no natural violence, not the same violent confrontations: lynchings, brutal beatings of Negroes (the term used at the time), where there was none of this occurring in my Island, I invented it, and showed a tension to exist between the two races, and made them live, in what Frantz Fanon calls, "a psycho-existential complex." Where, in my contemporary landscape in the Island there was no violence, no action, no brutality, I invented riots and strikes and beatings. Baldwin therefore was my spiritual brother. *Notes of a Native Son* would warn me, however, that Baldwin's treatment of Richard Wright, and his comments on the latter's novel *Native Son*, that Baldwin was mean-spirited and vengeful, and had mastered a facility with patricide.

It is 1963. Out of the blue, a Trinidadian friend of mine, who was at university with me, was going to New York, by car, for the weekend. His Canadian girlfriend owned the car, and would be doing most of driving; and he would share the driving with her. This was a very important detail, more important than any superficial meaning given to it. She would make sure she was driving when we stopped to face the U.S. immigration officer.

"Toranno!... Toranno!... Toranno!"

The words were repeated until they came close to the proper colloquial pronunciation of a woman born in Toronto. The reason? At the Niagara Falls border, the American immigration officer will ask this question, first:

"Where were you born?"

This is an absurd question now that I think of it. You are black. A Negro. A nigger in the way most American immigration officers look at you. What chance then is there that you were born in Canada? In America, more likely!

And you had better have learned the proper pronunciation of Toronto.

"To-ranno!" you will tell the immigration officer.

But we are still on the 401 West, still on Canadian soil, and this soil is important to you, because in your short time in Canada, you have heard all aspects of the symbolic meaning in the term "Underground Railroad." In Canada, slaves from just across the same border you are about to cross, illegally … because you have no visa to enter the United States … slaves found freedom by merely landing on Canadian soil. But in your short time in Canada, in *Toront-to*, you do not, because of your experience, associate Canada — in a personal realistic sense — with the same freedom the runaway slaves found.

So, you practise the pronunciation with the Canadian woman, as she is driving the car, and who is acting as your tutor. My friend is arrogant. He is a Trinidadian. He is convinced he knows the correct pronunciation. And he is characteristically, and culturally, self-assured. He knows all about everything: Biology, in which he gets only A's. And immigration matters: he is here, illegally.

"What the ass is this, eh? Eh-eh!"

"You have to learn to say it correctly," she tells him.

"What the ass is this, eh? Eh-eh!"

I practise the word, to myself, repeating it, with her guidance, over and over, and I think I am getting it right and can pronounce it with ease, like a real Canadian.

"Toranno!... Toranno!... Toranno!"

I become so good at it, that I say it with an added nuance that only "real Canadians" can imitate. "Tranno!... Tranno!... Trannah!"

We are at the border. He has by now convinced his Canadian girlfriend to let him drive. He is stubborn. He is a Trinidadian man. He is macho. He is a graduate of the University of Toronto in Biology, first class honours. His student visa is expired. She is a first-year student, in a general B.A. degree course. He is a know-it-all. His Canadian girlfriend does not argue. She remains quiet. She has right on her side. I become nervous; for my career in broadcasting is on the tip of his tongue, should he mispronounce "Toronto" and cause us to be sent back across the border, into the cold, dark blackness that is a Canadian night in November. But I am practising my pronunciation, just in case the immigration officer should ask me first, "Where do you live, sir?," since we do not have the visa necessary to enter the United States.

"Trahnnnh! Tranno! Trannah!"

We are silent in the car. And we extinguish our cigarettes, as if this act will save us. The radio, WLIB, a Buffalo station popular among black people in Canada, that plays good jazz and better rhythm-and-blues, is turned down. We do not want to appear uncultured, shady, illegal students skipping across the border, to live in the luxury of American wealth and full employment, and generous unemployment benefits.

"Turn the radio to CBC. The classical programme."

I do not know who has said this.

"Why?"

I do not know who has said this.

"Sounds better."

And suddenly Beethoven's Symphony No. 6, "Pastoral," comes through the speakers, like a tin, or a large grater, being scratched by a nail.

We can see the border. It is dark and foreboding, meaning the cement structure, and the stalls, and the Stars and Stripes; and the music coming through the tinny speakers does not help our mood, and before we know it, the three of us shaking inside the darkened car, and, beside us, bending down, to see who sits in the darkness inside the car, and making a sign with his hands that the window should be rolled down, is an American, an immigration officer, shivering in the Canadian cold to which he has been exposed during his eight-hour shift. And when the Trinidadian has succeeded in his fumbling to lower the window — it is a manual window — we hear the foreboding question ...

"Where were you born, sir?"

Silence is no measurement of time, or of fear, or of success. Beethoven is no longer soothing to the nerves, no longer the symbol of our sophistication. Beethoven is now like the night: cruel, and silent and no longer effective for the case of nerves. We sit in the silence. We know the American is losing his patience. It is cold outside where he is standing with his hand on the cold side of the car. The loss of voice becomes the fear in our bodies that the Trinidadian, the man at the wheel, has now forgotten his coaching in the pronunciation of a simple word, like "Tranno." But he regains his voice.

"Toe-ron-toe!"

Under different circumstances, the two of us would have applauded his repossession of voice. We would have cheered that he had not lost his vocal chords completely. But in the unbelievable coldness, in the unbelievable Trinidadian pronunciation of the word — "Toe-ron-toe!" — following the miles and miles on the 401 West, and now into this winding road, no larger than an alley; after all these hours driving in a rickety car with faulty steering, and faulty speaker system, and faulty windows, and having to return to Toe-ron-toe ...

"Where, sir, do you live?"

And we prayed that he would ignore the immigration officer, and refuse to answer, and not put us deeper into the jeopardy of his egotistical attitude with the pronunciation of strange words, especially cities.

"Toe-ron-toe!"

I cannot remember if the immigration officer said, "Turn round, sir." I cannot remember if his words were, "You are refused entry," and we therefore knew that we had to turn round and retrace our steps. I cannot remember if the immigration officer said anything, at all.

But I do remember that since we were in the hands of the Trinidadian, and since the Trinidadian had sunk the carload of us, by uttering one word — "Toe-ron-toe" — all of us probably would be better off had we made the wrong turn and had fallen into the roaring Falls just outside our window; and by his recalcitrance and bad pronunciation of a simple word, the name of a town — in which we had been living for eight years! — we were, metaphorically, over the Falls.

"Erie!" he said, in a voice pronouncing cheerfulness that was not understandable. "Let we try the Border at Erie!" he said again, unnecessarily. "And why you don't drive, girl? You are a better driver. And you know how to say 'Toe-ron-toe' the right way!" he said, pronouncing it the wrong way, again.

In silence, but in a silence of a different thickness, the car was pulled over to the side, and he got out, and she got out, and when they passed each other, she placed her lips on his lips, and passed her left hand on his back, as if she was massaging him there; and then she fastened her seat belt, and he settled himself in the seat beside her; and in this silence of declaration and surrender, we rambled, and made the wrong turns, and corrected those mistakes in the same silence, and then we saw the name, in lights, Fort Erie.

"Where were you born, ma'am?" the immigration officer asked. She had the window rolled down before the American official had reached the car. There was a smile on the American's face. He looked past her to the back seat, and saw what he saw, and I did not know what it was that he saw; and with his eyes, he asked me the same question he had asked her, and she, in whose hands we were now languishing, she answered for me, and she answered for him, her boyfriend. She answered for the three of us.

"Trannah!"

"Have a good weekend."

"Incidentally," she said, "what is the best way to get to New York?"

"Take the 95 South, then the 96, then the 93, then back to the 95 South, ma'am, and after that, plain sailing," he said, calling out highways, as if he were calling out numbers at a bingo game.

"Thanks very much, sir!"

"Drive carefully, y'all. And y'all have a good weekend, now ..."

"You're welcome!" she said.

In our boisterous self-congratulations, with the window closed, we rocked in the rocking car, and Beethoven was switched off, and the Buffalo radio station WLIB, was turned on and turned up; and, through the tinny speakers straining under the volume, came the voice of James Brown telling us to shout and shimmy.

"Let we stop at the first bar, and celebrate."

But we did not find one from amongst the maze of streets and roads and lanes which all seemed to be one-way streets, going in the direction away from our thirst for a sip of celebration. And like this, buried in the silence that came back and inhabited the car, in our regained confidence, we headed in this interminable, black, cold Friday night, to New York City.

That inability of my Trinidadian friend, a man knowledgeable in the polite brand of racism, was repeated and crystallized two times each year when we visited the immigration office on Bedford Road, a spit's throw from Dupont Street, an address that gained fame, or notoriety, when it was associated with the 1994 Just Desserts murder. But in those days, in the mid-fifties, it was a desolate, nondescript place, like a huge suburban parking lot with no cars, but with buildings more suitable for soldiers to learn how to use rifles and bayonets, than for frightened, insecure, discriminated-against students from the West Indies, to put their future in the hands of an immigration officer, whom we learned had more power than the regulations — if there is such a manual of rules in a manager's desk — outlined, or suggested. As foreign students attending university, we were not permitted to have even part-time employment.

But everyone — including the immigration officer holding our file in his hands — knew that you had to have a job, to help pay your fees, to pay your rent, and to buy food; and the occasional bottle of rum, not even Mount Gay Rum, from your own country; or a bottle of Coca-Cola, and pray that the West Indian nurse you were dating, or that you knew, would remember to procure for you, an equally large bottle of rubbing alcohol: I learned this tactic from a student from Jamaica. He was in first year medicine. You mixed the rubbing alcohol with the Coca-Cola, in proportion to suit your tolerance for alcohol, and that increased the liquor supply to assist in the limping of your party into success.

But each time we presented ourselves to the biannual interview, to reassure the authorities that we had not failed our year, that we had not wandered into delinquency, that we were still law-abiding, and that we had not taken part-time employment, we arrived at the nondescript offices, beaten, paranoid, visibly shaking, and really frightened by our imagination that at the end of the curt, aggressive interview with the smiling immigration officer — reminding me of my mother's repeated warning, "Boy, every skin-teeth is not a laugh, you hear?" — we soon realized that there were traps, buried devices that could explode when you stepped on them and pelt you back in the explosion, deported to the Island from whence you came; land mines laid to trap you into confessions, pulled into candour by the smiles of the man sitting before you, to confess that, "Yes, when you come to think of it, I did take a little job, part-time, mind you, washing dishes at the restaurant on that Harbord and St. George"; and yes, that you had broken the immigration law of Canada.

And I must say, for emphasis, that in those days of the fifties, West Indians were the most law-abiding immigrant group in this city, if not in the entire province of Ontario. Perhaps in the whole country.

In those days, it was an irrevocable act of great shame if you got a parking ticket. But the suspicion was that you had broken the law; had accepted illegal part-time employment, serious blots spewed against your clean West Indian character. Or that you would marry a Canadian woman, and side-step the regulations about becoming a landed immigrant; your first steps in the long training-to-walk journey toward the altar, and the first steps to becoming a Canadian citizen.

"I see you have passed your term exams."

"Yes, sir."

"And of course, you know the rules about not working."

"I know the rules. I have never worked, sir."

"Well, if you have never worked, how you pay your fees?"

"I am on study leave. Teachers' leave to study, with pay."

"You are not to work. Remember. But I don't see how you can study at the university, without a scholarship, or something ... I don't know about study-leave ... and still pay fees in Canadian money!"

"My leave with pay covers that."

"Did you say full pay, or half pay?"

"Half pay."

He stamps the extension into my passport, does not smile, and gives it back to me.

"See you the end of the term!"

I wait on the stairs for the Trinidadian who did not learn how to say "Trannah" like a Torontonian, to compare what his experience with his examining officer was. You never went to this immigration office by yourself; you never went into a strange restaurant by yourself; you never went to a jazz club on Yonge Street by yourself; you never went to a white barber by yourself. You always went with a friend. In case. You might need the evidence of a witness ... he had to witness, and to report your deportation to your parents — and whether fate would underline the date of his deportation, should he have been found guilty of working part-time at Gooderham & Worts Distilleries, and in the post office at Front Street East across from the new Hockey Hall of Fame, in the rushes to deliver mail, at Christmas and at Easter; and in the previous summer, on the Canadian National Railway, as a porter. Sel was a very serious student. He was the last person to leave the Wallace Library, and the first to arrive after dinner; and it seemed that when he finished his shift at Gooderham & Worts Distilleries, at nine o'clock in the night, he went straight to the Wallace Library.

"Jesus Christ, boy! Guess!"

"Deportation?"

"Permission to work! He tell me, how the ass I going pay for graduate school, if I don't work? This is a democratic country, he tell me. Get a job, he tell me. And then he stamp my passport. 'Immigrant recu,' in your ass, boy! Eh-eh! How your interview went?"

"I can't work."

"The information" on which the decision to deny me Canadian citizenship was based (not that "decision" in the letter W.R. Martin wrote to me in October 1968, twelve years later) that information could not have been "confidential," and it could not "… would not be in the public interest to reveal it."

Years later, just before that trip to America to interview James Baldwin in 1963, as if that journey, almost aborted through the mispronunciation of an insignificant city in the eyes of the Americans (for they insisted upon having visas from us in order to visit the United States for a weekend), as their aggressive interviews of us at the border suggested, they suspected we had no intention to return to Canada. America has always been a lure. But who in his right mind would have wanted to immigrate to America in the 1960s, during the virulent times of the riots and other civil rights demonstrations? And during the protests and the draft-dodging days of the Vietnam War? So, Mr. Martin's letter of rejection in October 1968, to my application for Canadian citizenship, was not surprising. It would be a disappointment if I was not able, because of the denial of Canadian citizenship, to take up the appointment at Yale University. As the almost tragic rejection of entry at the border at Niagara Falls, about five years before Mr. Martin had to write his letter, bears an ironic relationship to the tragicomic evening in 1963, when my fortune was almost fractured by one Trinidadian's un-ethnic pronunciation of the word *Toronto*.

CHAPTER FOUR

1960s Toronto

In Toronto at this time, in the firmament of the civil rights movement in America, and which spread throughout the world, there was an easier, and closer relationship between black people and Jews. This relationship has its historical roots in the days of the Depression; and apart from the predilection of the two groups toward a socialist and Marxist philosophy, this closeness was fostered significantly through the profession of writing. Jews, such as Saul Bellow, encouraged black American writers through the various creative writing programmes paid for by the American government during the Depression. The bond was formed, and it became stronger, with the publication of such black American novels as *Native Son* by Richard Wright, and *Invisible Man* by Ralph Ellison. In the vanguard of this African-American–Jewish literary brotherhood, was the leading literary critic, Irving Howe. This alliance suffered, from time to time, by the exigencies of the nature of the civil rights movement, juxtaposed by the rise of Black Cultural Nationalism. And it found its weakest links toward the old brotherhood, with the popularity of Malcolm X.

In the sixties in Toronto, I formed a friendship with Rabbi Feinberg of the Beth Tzedec Temple on Bathurst Street. Rabbi Feinberg, side by side with me, led the demonstration from his temple, I think, right down Avenue Road to Queen's Park, where we both spoke against the "assassination" of the civil rights leader, Medgar Evers. It was one of many demonstrations Rabbi Feinberg and I would lead, including lying on the cold concrete sidewalk in front of the U.S. Consulate General on University Avenue, when the "sit-in" — as the "sleep-ins" — was all the popular rage, and the expression of peaceful protest. Historically, the important aspect of these demonstration, which would take place almost every weekend, for these were hectic days when we felt that the moral obligation of Jews and Negroes (to use the contemporary term), we had, for the very sake of our lives, or our physical safety, to form this coalition, this partnership, and encourage this symbiosis. What had begun in America much earlier, during the Second World War, and that was concentrated on writing and the arts, now found its resurrection in Toronto, in social issues regarding racism, segregation, and violence against minorities.

Out of the blue, years earlier, coming out of the West of the country, like a thunderbolt, or rather, a Chinook, were the candid, explosive, and embarrassing articles and columns written by Pierre Berton, who single-handedly threw this embarrassing light upon the Canadian version of a respectable, silent disposition of racism, regarding the renting of cottages in the Lake Muskoka District, "cottage area" to Jews; and the refusal of membership in the Granite Club (I am sure in other clubs, too) to Jews. The Jews built and opened their own club, the Jewish Club. From Pierre Berton's justified exposure of the racism in renting cottages, which was sometimes hidden, and always embedded in the silence of a gentleman's agreement, I was informed that there were quotas on Jews entering certain professions, such as law, medicine, and dentistry. But this could well have been before I came to Canada to attend university; and we were embarrassed to assert, even if with a pinch of dishonesty, that this condemnation should have come from a Canadian, much earlier. For I am living, with Rabbi Feinberg, in the sixties, in the atmosphere of great physical fear, of the expectation that a policeman might shoot me — bang-bang, you're dead, dead — of being refused the renting of a basement room, or an apartment in a public building, that I would find myself standing noticeably longer than other customers at a counter in Eaton's store, at the corner of Yonge and College Streets, that I might be thrown out, sometimes physically, from a restaurant, or a nightclub, as Oscar Peterson was, and face the embarrassment of being told by a barber that he does not cut niggers' hair. This is my Toronto. When I joined the happy band of artists, or "artists-to-be," mainly painters and sculptors, some of whom were still attending the Ontario College of Art, in those days a magnificent, desirable place to study; and a handful of actors; and an even smaller handful of writers, men and women, playing they're serious writers, musicians who are always there, whether following the social footsteps of the artists, which was the name we called painters — nobody called me "a black man playing I am a serious writer!" — by the name of "artist," for those days were days of love, and "love-ins," of nights of "paint-ins," days when we welcomed the dramatic huge influx of German immigrants, whom I did not know, or could not at that time have known, why they were all Jews; and these women — we ignored the men! — were all blond and beautiful, and spoke English with a sensual sweet destruction of the language, sometimes ignoring the fundamental laws of syntax. But who cared? They knew their jazz. And we who accompanied them to the First Floor Club on Asquith Avenue, where I lived opposite; or to the Towne Tavern, just east of Yonge Street on Queen, in a toned-down lighting atmosphere, seductively soft, because we were listening in these sweet times, "when we were free and young and we used to wear silks," to cool jazz. "Dear Old Stockholm," "Round About Midnight," where the music was more American and international; or to the Colonial Tavern on Yonge just up from College and Yonge; and this riff-raff of souls, wearing blue jeans, professionally daubed with the oils and charcoal and crayons of their specialization, aiming to be the new Picassos, or another member of the Group of Seven … abstract art and cool jazz … we the riff-raff in the most pleasant sense of that term, were dressed in thick home-made sweaters, deliberately torn in places to appear casual, and "artistic"; and Clark desert boots, or black leather boots, and scarves like the one given to Dylan Thomas when he was a child in Wales, "that could be tug-o'-warred down to the galoshes." We wore galoshes made of black rubber, with badly installed zippers that tore off your flesh so easily and so often as they tore off your trousers legs. But in winter, which I have always felt to be the season of social occasion, and dressing up, and parties, in winter, if you were cool, and an artist — and which artist is not cool? — you wore a discarded, second-hand, war-surplussed duffel coat, preferably one from the British Royal Navy, in light brown, almost tan, coarse cloth like a horse blanket, and with pieces of stick, or bone, like large animal fingernails, or small horns from a small animal, for buttons, that you took from the flimsy wire hangers in the section of men's used clothing of the Goodwill Store on Jarvis Street, at Richmond, near the St. Lawrence Market, where after three o'clock on Saturday afternoons, most everything was sold at half price; near the St. James' Cathedral Church. The Crippled Civilians was the name in those days of the Goodwill Store. And you kept your hood off, to fall on your shoulders, to expose the home-made knitted sweater that a lover or a wife had given you the previous Christmas. And this merry group met every single night, in varying number, in the Pilot Tavern. The moving aeroplane from the First, or Second World War, whose lights symbolized the flights from disaster, or victory, and the pilot himself with his air-man's cap, "showed us the way to get home," as we used to sing, in our mild drunkenness, back in the Island; but here at the corner of Bloor and Yonge, not so drunk, because we were artists, and therefore were broke, penniless most of the time … one beer could be nursed from nine until closing time at eleven, sharp! "Come, drink up! Drink up! Last call!" Or, if you had sold a painting, or had been given a commission such as Graham Coughtry, or his brother Arthur, the photographer, got with regularity; or, had been promised an exhibition at the Isaacs Gallery just up the street, almost opposite Asquith, across from the Toronto Reference Library; or if you had sold a poem or a short story, to Robert Weaver, for *CBC Anthology*; or a story idea to Harry J. Boyle, for *Project '68* … or, if your girlfriend has lent you five dollars from her small wage on a Friday afternoon, you splurged on a whiskey and soda; or you stayed longer at the black-topped square table and drank three beers instead of one, without nursing them. These artists sat at the back, just one step up from the hoi-polloi of respectably employed stores clerks, bookshop assistants; and men who worked in the CIBC bank at the corner beside the Pilot, who refused a loan to you because you were an artist, reminding you that you were a "risk" because you were unem-ployed, meaning that they were one and the same thing. The artists sat mainly on the south wall of this section. The chairs on the north wall were occupied by the riff-raff artists, meaning men and women "playing they were serious writers," by the actors; and the remaining riff-raff sat in the centre row of chairs, at tables. The seating on the south wall and the north wall were high-backed, long, upholstered chairs. Each wall was taken up by one chair; and the chair followed the shape of the room, and curved on both walls to face the cash register, or face the rest of the patrons. You did not dare enter the Pilot, walk past the row of leather-bound chairs stood at the bar, walk past the black-topped, square tables opposite, arranged in booths in which you could have a private conversation of seduction, pass all these customers, mainly the respectably employed, and walk past the owner at the cash register, holding his fat hands deep into the coins and dollar bills, playing with them, like a child at the seaside, playing in the sand, like a big, congenial, happy father, an uncle, a teddy bear of a man. From Greece. Bill. Only Bill. Because we never asked his surname; and probably if he had told us, we couldn't pronounce it. The Danforth was not so Greek in those days. So, you would not walk all that distance from the entrance on Yonge Street, and presume, because this was a public restaurant and bar, to be able to sit where you chose. Certainly not in the company of the artists. The artists ruled the waves of beer, draft and bottled, and the economical sips of the rare glass of Scotch, or Canadian Club, or dark rum from down East, Nova Scotia, since many bars in Toronto, in these days, had not yet discovered Barbados Mount Gay Rum, or Jamaican Appleton's. There were drops of Cuban Bacardi, and that terrible rum from Puerto Rico.

But what did we talk about? Books, and plays, and roles in plays for the stage or on CBC television; and advances for a story not yet written, for the *Tamarack Review*; or the coming exhibition at the Isaacs, or the Dorothy Cameron, who took a chance with the paintings of Robert Markle, and had the Toronto Vice Squad close down the exhibition, to the rage of protests raging in the *Toronto Telegram* and the *Toronto Star*. And we talked about the best movie being shown at the Towne Cinema, down the street on Yonge, or at the few art cinemas dotting the city. And if it was Christmas, if Christmas was in the air, about parties: six artists to a case of beer, and two bottles of Chianti wine, and when we had drunk off all, we stuck a red candle into its mouth, as if to keep it silent and bear witness to our lasciviousness; six girlfriends and wives to match the number of artists; and a "mickey" of Canadian Club because it is Christmas; and Dylan Thomas in vinyl form, played on a blond Seabreeze record player, with a record arm changer that plunked down on the thirty-three-and-a-half with such a noise that you thought the record had cracked. You got the Seabreeze from Bay Bloor Radio, with a down payment of ten dollars, and a promise to pay, regularly, five dollars a month, from Sol, because Sol was an artist himself: more than a mean-spirited businessman. He wrote poetry. And if he liked you, he read it to you, while you stood thinking of your financial health and whether or not your monetary arrangement would be accepted. "Drop in anytime! Pass by. Even if you don't have the installment …"

One Christmas was so much like another, in those years around the sea-town corner now and out of all sound except the distant speaking of the voices I sometimes hear a moment before sleep, that I can never remember whether it snowed for six days and six nights when I was twelve or whether it snowed for twelve days and twelve nights when I was six.

We would sit on the floor, in an artist's studio, most parties had the floor as the best furniture, for not always was a bargain to be had at the Goodwill Store; but we sat, and leaned our backs against the wall, and listened to Dylan Thomas, and tried to imitate his voice and pitch and his swagger and his capacity for whiskey, and believed that we had his genius. Just as the six men, all painters, imagined that they had John Coltrane's genius and Miles Davis's genius and Philly Joe Jones's genius, when they formed the Artists' Jazz Bann, and played in many diverse tempos and keys, playing the new mad jazz of Ornette Coleman, who played deliberately off key, while they could not help the dissonant notes escaping from their horns and strings and skins and ivories, performing at Openings on Fridays, and in mixed-media concerts on Sunday afternoons, at the Isaacs Gallery; and in private homes, such as Bill and Betty Kilbourn's mansion, in Rosedale. At one of these mixed media concerts,

Bill Kilbourn read from Dante's *Inferno*, and I, from Leroi Jones's *The System of Dante's Hell*; somebody joined the two ends of a piece of tape with Elastoplast, and we heard the same phrases for the three hours of the concert. I cannot remember whether it was a speech from Professor Kilbourn's biography of the firebrand, Mackenzie King, or a chosen few chords from "A Love Supreme" by John Coltrane. So, the six merrie men of the Artists' Jazz Band, all true and talented — with the paint brush, not necessarily with the drummer's brushes for playing waltzes — and creating more noise in their artistic crescendos, which we all stomached, liked, and applauded as if we were listening to John Coltrane, Elvin Jones, McCoy Tyner, Jimmy Garrison, and Miles Davis; and were not listening to Graham Coughtry, Gordon Rayner, Sadao "Nobbie" Watanabe, Robert Markle, and sidekicks, Harvey Cohen, an architect student at the university; and Dennis Burton, famous for his Garter Belt series.

These were halcyon days for Dennis Burton. He had just got a commission from Dr. Morton Shulman to paint a portrait of his beautiful wife, Mrs. Shulman. Dennis, who had recently befriended me, had invited me to his studio — whenever a painter invites an artist who is not a painter to his studio, this was an honour — in a second-floor apartment in Yorkville, at the corner of Yonge and Yorkville Avenue, across the parking lot from Pickering Farms — a place which sold the best meat, the best fruits, the best everything, before stores started coming on strong, as specialty shops, selling special "produce": a place where more Mercedes-Benzes, Volvos, and BMWs were parked in the lot east of the Yorkville Public Library and the Yorkville Fire Station, more than at the Granite Club.... Dennis decided to paint the portrait, in a triptych. Things were good for Dennis. And to paraphrase Dylan Thomas, everything was good, everything was easy. Dennis was parading in an individual fashion parade, the moment May arrived each year, in a houndstooth, custom-made suit, probably from Lou Myles, or the House of Mann, both on Yonge Street. But it could have been bought from the advance he got on his commission to paint the beautiful Mrs. Shulman.

The German women, with their love of beer and cool jazz, to be followed by the Hungarians fleeing another kind of holocaust, but the majority of whom were convincing you that they were counts and czars and emperors and countesses, back home in Hungary, and who made the best beef stew to be served in Toronto, and called it by a European name, goulash; and then had the audacity to gouge their culinary and cultural identity into the thick wall of Toronto business and private landscape, by opening a restaurant on Bloor Street just west of Spadina Road, and call it The Goulash. We dined there. With a new appetite and a new taste of our taste buds that had been deadened for years by the roast beef cooked to a burn, and overcooked Brussels sprouts, overcooked carrots, and mashed potatoes flooded by brown gravy. And there was no hot sauce! We revelled in this new immigrant cuisine, in the same way as we devoured the blintzes, latkes, boiled braising beef of the Jewish restaurant on College near Spadina. The Bagel. Oh, these days of protests and posture. These days of immigrants who could not speak the same English, but together we dragged Toronto into the twentieth century on its belly, too filled, for too long with the fodder cooked by Anglo-Saxon culinary blandness. Free form in painting, free expression in dress, especially by the Germans and the Hungarians — the Italians, with their characteristic and cultural clannishness, and love of family, kept to themselves, in a cultural self-imposed segregation, and had not yet shared their risotto, their sliced ham (prosciutto), and their corn meal cou-cou, which they called *polenta*, a more sophisticated term than ours, but tasting not so good! — free expression, too, in opinion, and ideas and themes in their writing; free expression in love, and, I am told, in love-making.

In those days, in the Pilot Tavern, surrounded by all this talent, I tried my hand at writing stories, which I would send to Robert Weaver, to be broadcast either on one of his literary radio programmes at the CBC, or in the literary magazine of which he was editor, the *Tamarack Review*. One story I wrote in this new form, not new form, but perhaps more correct to be described as formless, was "When He Was Young and Free and He Used to Wear Silks," from the book of the same name. Weaver did not buy it.

It was "inspired" not by women from Germany or Hungary who drank their beers at the Pilot Tavern with us, but by Enid, the sister of the actor Michael Sarrazin — was he a teetotaller? — a woman who wore hats and who loved hats, and who loved beer, and who loved artists, and who loved Hendy, or Henderson, a sculptor who had come up from the United States, and who was not in love with me. Meaning the hat-wearing woman. But I was in love with her — from this distance. I never spoke a word to her, in all the years I drank my ration of beer, sometimes in cash; sometimes on Bill's credit. But once, on a cold afternoon, in early December, I met her walking up Bloor Street, in the direction of Holt Renfrew, where she said she was heading to buy a hat; and I told her I had been "inspired" by her to write the story. "And why didn't you tell me?"

"That I had been inspired by you?"

"All those years?"

"You mean that I've been inspired by you?"

"No, stupid! That you were in love with me! My marriage was on the rocks all the time you were seeing me wearing my hats, and sitting in the Pilot, drinking beer. Was I drinking beer in those days?"

She knew me well enough now, to be personal.

"Did you go to see *They Shoot Horses, Don't They?* You should have told me …"

The night her movie-making brother got his first contract to be an actor in *They Shoot Horses, Don't They?*, he entered the Pilot and sat with the painters, and held to his principle of drinklessness.

"You should have told me," she said.

And I said:

> In the lavishness of the soft lights, indications of detouring life that took out of his mind the concentration of things left to do still, as a man, before he could be an artist, lights that put into his mind instead a certain crawling intention which the fingers of his brain stretched towards one always single table embraced by a man and his wife who looked like his woman, her loyalty bending over the number of beers he poured against the side of her bottle he had forgotten to count, in those struggling days when the atmosphere was soft and silk and just as treacherous, in those days in the Pilot Tavern the spring and the summer and the fall were mixed into one chattering ambition of wanting to have meaning, a better object of meaning and of craving, better meaning than

a beer bought on the credit of friendships and love by the
tense young oppressed men and women who said they were
oppressed and tense because they were artists and not because
they were incapable, or burdened by the harsh sociology of
no talent, segregated around smooth black tables from the
rest of the walking men, and walking women outside the light
of our pilot of the Snows; and had not opened or shut their
minds to the meaning of their other lives; legs of artless girls
touching this man's in a hide and seek under the colour blind
tables burdened by conversation and aspirations and promises
of cheques and hopes and bedding and beer and bottles; in
those days when he first saw her, and the only conversation
she could invent was "haii!" because she was put on a pedestal
by husbandry, and would beg his pardon without disclosing
her eyes of red shots and blots and blood-shot liquor; the
success of his mind and the woman's mind in his legs burnt
like the parts of the chicken he ate, he was free and young
and he was wearing the silks of indecision and near-failure.

This opening to a short story, written in 1970, while I was teaching at
Yale University, is the longest opening sentence I am guilty of having written. I always use my openings to compare them with three openings, Dylan
Thomas's in "A Child's Christmas in Wales"; Ian McEwan's in *Amsterdam*;
and Caryl Phillips's in *Crossing the River*, which I quote here, respectively:

One Christmas was so much like another, in those days
around the sea-town corner now and out of all sound except
the distant speaking of the voices I sometimes hear a moment
before sleep, that I can never remember whether it snowed
for six days and six nights when I was twelve or whether it
snowed for twelve days and twelve nights when I was six.

Two former lovers of Molly Lane stood waiting outside the
crematorium chapel with their backs to the February chill.

A desperate foolishness. The crops failed. I sold my children.

I remember.

You walk in this quadrangle: from Asquith Avenue, straight across the road, and pass beside the First Floor Jazz Club, and, if it is daytime, the place will be closed, the downstairs where the music is played and sandwiches sold, smoked ham or smoked beef on rye bread; but upstairs, if you look carefully, through one of the large windows, you will see Mandel Sprachman, the architect, standing at his drafting board; and you have just enough time to look to the right, east to Yonge Street, with your eyes passing the sign board of a French restaurant, La Maison Doré, beside which is a Model T Ford, put there, unmoving and immovable, with no gas in it, and no engine, slaughtered, it seems, and plucked like one of the chickens the chef of the restaurant, who stands outside smoking and blowing his clouds into the cracked leather upholstery of the Model T, and thinking of transforming the chicken on his mind, into the gutless cleaned-out automobile. But you are not going toward Yonge Street. Not yet. You are passing through the "back," an informal parking lot, heading to Bloor Street, where there used to be a street lamp, almost directly outside of Grand & Toy, who were located beside the subway entrance. I have just passed the coach house in which there is a theatre where Dora Mavor Moore has been teaching generations of men and women how to remember lines and postures, and *Macbeth* and *Hamlet*. "To be, or not to be. That is the question." I wanted to be a professional actor, once. And I used to hang out with Norman Ettlinger on Prince Arthur Avenue, Number 27, as I boarded there, in the attic, or crow's nest, if you please. I have never seen Dora Mavor Moore in person, only in the newspapers, or heard her on CBC. Norman Ettlinger is the person who told me I should take acting seriously, and play Othello; and I took him seriously, and applied for a place in the Actors' Studio in New York, and was accepted, and chickened out, because I had cold feet: the first three months of my acting career, "playing I am an actor," and getting principal parts, to play the role of a black butler, all of a sudden, parts vanished. And I spent three months without a call. Acting, and wanting to be an actor, was too precarious. I would see Barry Morse, Norman Campbell, Bruno Gerussi, an older actor, Christopher Plummer, who was the spitting image, even in voice, of Alec Guinness, but was not; and other actors such as Gordon Pinsent; and other actors who appeared in General Motors ninety-minute dramas, in plays in The Unforeseen Series; and at Stratford; and I saw them all in Norman Ettlinger's kitchen, sitting round the round breakfast table, with the English marmalade bottles, and warm milk, and teapot with the tea cozy on, and half-used China teacups and saucers. Norman encouraged me to go to Stratford to see how it is really done, but I balked at the idea. I have never visited Stratford to see a play. In the sixty years I have lived here. I have never visited the Royal Ontario Museum. Nor the Science Centre — except to listen to jazz and hear Ted O'Reilly introduce Toronto musicians on Monday nights when there is jazz there.

But I am wandering from my quadrangle of habitation. I am going to Grand & Toy to buy the cheapest typing paper on which to write my novel: it is *The Meeting Point* I am working on, on a Noiseless Remington Rand. I am too poor to purchase, even on installment, an IBM Selectric. The Bay store is obviously not built yet, on the lot through which I am passing. I enter Grand & Toy, and the manager, a slim, tall man with his head shaven bald, looking as if he is undergoing treatment for cancer, but is not; he is just a man of class and style, ahead of his time, with a clean-shaven head and well-pressed trousers. He attends to me, all the time. In time, he is most considerate when one or two of my cheques, written in the best Christian uprighteousness, bounced. And in time, when time had cured that little indiscretion, he gave me a card with which to charge typewriter paper, carbon paper, typewriter ribbon — with the card I could still afford only the cotton ribbon, not the silk — and Liquid Paper, which looked like a vial that contains lady's lipstick, and which reminded me of milk turning bad.

The door to Grand & Toy is a double door, with two vertical halves. With a horizontal bar made of aluminium, just above waist height, in each half of the door.

Habit tells me that the right hand half is open. It is always open when you push it. This afternoon I am in a hurry. My two daughters, Janice and Loretta, aged three and one, are in my care. My wife, Betty, a head nurse at the Toronto General Hospital, is on the day shift. I "mind" the children during the day, and I scratch out a few hours' writing during that time, but am relieved from my duty during the night, beginning at four or five o'clock in the afternoon, when nurses on the day shift usually get off work. Before I slip out to get the typing paper, I ask my friend, next door, Gordon Peters, to listen for the children, in case of emergency …

It is not much more than one hundred yards from 46 Asquith to the door of Grand & Toy, and the children are in their playpens. And Gordon Peters is next door, listening through the paper-thin wall that joins my townhouse to his. I put the playpens on the floor, to prevent the children from wanting to climb out. Infants like to climb. Climb in and climb out of playpens. This afternoon I am in a good mood. My work is going well. And I am broke. But I have the card that the bald-headed gentleman has entrusted me with. I want only typing paper. And Liquid Paper. And I know that the bars are there on the door I am about to enter, on the right side, and the door is unlocked. And I walk to the right-hand side, and am about to place my hand on the metal bar, and I do not feel a bar, and continue walking, into the store; and I stand for a foolish moment, looking at the bald-headed manager, and then I realize that something is wrong. The right hand half of the door was not unlocked. I had walked through a glass door. And my hand is bleeding. And the manager's pate is shining more than usual. And he utters a strange admission. "You are the second person today to walk through this door."

My writer's mind is working fast. Lawsuit. Sue. Get as much money out of Grand & Toy, that I can purchase a brand-new IBM Selectric, red in colour, and with silk ribbon, and a built-in erasure. And be able to drink pure Scotch at the Pilot Tavern, and follow Dennis Burton and buy my suits at Lou Myles. And go to Ibiza, as all successful Toronto artists do, on the money they get from the Canada Council. Blood is coming from my left hand. And somebody says that dreadful word. "Concussion." And I feel faint, and I am having a concussion. It is my first concussion. I do not know if I am playing the role of a man having a concussion, correctly. I should have gone to the Actors' Studio. And before I know it, for I am having something — if not a concussion, something. "Take him to St. Mike's, and see if he has a concussion." And they do that. And I am attended to, immediately on arrival. And I think it is serious, that the concussion will kill me. And my left hand is stitched up, most unprofessionally, so that to this day there is a scar. The nun did not pull the skin back enough to cover the raw, bloodied wound. And my grey worsted trousers bought at the Crippled Civilians are torn, ironically, along the crease. In those days, I never wore a pair of trousers without first ironing them. The tear is about three inches. I cannot remember how I get to the Emergency of St. Michael's Hospital. I cannot remember who takes me there. And I do not remember who drives me home. Perhaps the man with the shaven head. But I know that I do not return home with the typing paper and the Liquid Paper.

The children are both at the window, low enough for them to see me approaching up the short walk. In cases like this, you are not sure you want to see the damage done. Either to the house, or to themselves.

I open the door. I open the inside door. Peals of laughter and giggles as only small children can behave, greet me in the short hallway. They are both naked. Have unclipped the large safety pins on their diapers. Have climbed out of their playpens. And, as you would expect, need a bath.

~~~

"Lawsuit in their ass!" my Trinidadian friend screams in delight. He likes the law. He is not a lawyer. Not even a law student. He is a graduate in biology. But he dresses like a lawyer, in dark blue, pin-striped double-breasted suits with a tie of blue and white stripes, the colours of the University of Toronto; and a spotless white shirt with starch in the collar and the cuffs.

But he practises law. "I will defend you, free. Lawsuit in their ass, pappee!" And he pats his briefcase. It is a very expensive-looking leather briefcase.

~~~

If I had taken my constitutional with my two daughters, in the English perambulator, I would not have stopped at Grand & Toy, but would have walked between the two buildings, in the long lane going south still, and come out on a small street, Hayden, famous for two things: The Nut House. You get the best peanut brittle there. And if you turn east a little bit, a drinking establishment — frequented by the painter Kenneth Seager, who eats hamburger lathered in Heinz tomato ketchup, and chips every day; and who paints with thick colours the chapel attached to the Anglican Church of St. Paul's on Bloor Street, near Jarvis — comes into view. In this drinking establishment, you can eat delicious hard-boiled eggs, cured in vinegar with onion. Small glass shakers containing salt are still placed on the plastic-covered tables. As you entered, you face two signs. MEN. LADIES & ESCORTS. Decency, propriety, and Christian-mindedness do not look kindly on women who sit in the same saloon as men, drinking hard liquor. Ladies and Escorts. But if you are wise, or tricky, you get your cashews, red-skin peanuts already shelled, and peanut brittle, before you go for your draught beer.

From here you go back to the west to Yonge Street and turn left, and walk as far as the bank at the corner of Charles and Yonge — now, like everything else, turned into a coffee shop! — to go to Coles Bookstore, to buy a book cheaper here than you can get it at Britnell's bookstore, north of Bloor, north of the Pilot Tavern. You may go as far as the cinema, cross the street, past Charles Street, pass another cinema on the west side, come to Frank Stollery's men's store, overpriced even in the sixties; wait for the light to change; and change your mind and go into the tuck shop that is west of Stollery's, that sells Erinmore Flake and Condor tobaccos, imported from London along with the *Times*, and other English magazines; and then you cross the street, and your eye sees the pilot in the Pilot's sign of blinking lights, giving you half of the bodies of the patrons and waiters sitting at the long counter, cut in half; and you imagine that Gladstone must have been sitting at the same bar in the Pilot Tavern, dreaming over his beer, and watching the profiles and silhouettes, the left sides of beautiful women walking north on Yonge Street, in front of the picture window of the Pilot Tavern. And I make a mental note that the next time I enter the Pilot Tavern, I shall not sit with the riff-raff of artists, but at the bar, with the respectably employed, bank tellers, store clerks, managers of stationeries, even men who sell suits and ties and shirt and "monkey suits" and Aquascutum, and watch the walking women pass, and put them in a short story.

Anticipating "disciplinary measures" in response to my lateness at work as a stagehand, I must have contacted Robert Weaver, in my fear of being "measured" disciplinarily: and I must have shown him a poem or two before I had done sufficient revision, and could not help myself from showing them to him in such a raw form. I wanted to be a poet then. But Robert Weaver's letter of rejection was so savage that it clogged the last remaining poetical veins in my body. Bob did not extend the same helping hand as Norman Ettlinger. But he was kinder in other ways.

I have just passed Cumberland Street — the nut-selling woman has her store near here, before she made so much money, and had to move to a larger place, on Hayden Street — and Harry. Oh, Harry. Of Harry's Records and Books. The records Harry sold, mainly classics and blues, were special. He introduced me to Paul Robeson, singing "Ol' Man River." And he introduced me to Robeson's politics, and to Robeson's acting roles, especially his historic role as Othello. And his travels in Russia, and his persecution by the United States, his own country, by their withholding his passport. If you were to go to the bank on a Friday afternoon, do not stop at Harry's Records and Books, do not even glance in his direction. Look instead to your left, and admire the books in the showcase at the Albert Britnell Book Shop. Mr. Britnell never put one of my books in his showcase, in all the time I lived on Asquith Avenue, passing his store, and looking in, but not venturing in, at least four times a day. He held this embargo on the two books I had written at this time, *The Survivors of the Crossing* and *Amongst Thistles and Thorns*, until just before he died. He apparently did not see eye to eye with the moderate praise that William French, books editor at the *Globe and Mail*, had given to my first two novels. It was only when William French, in giving greater praise to *The Meeting Point*, my third novel, was Mr. Britnell stirred from his lack of notice. But he had not been the only bookseller to embargo my books from their showcases. It happened again, years later, with my cookbook, *Pig Tails 'n' Breadfruit*, being absent from the showcase of a bookseller, who specialized in cookbooks. *Pig Tails 'n' Breadfruit* was shortlisted for the award of the Best Cookbook, in New York.

But Harry's conversations, and his informal seminars, as he stood amongst the boxes made with three-ply wood, sawed and built with his own hands, in which the records were kept; and the shelves filled with books which he said he had brought back from New York in his car, having bought them at book sales; and he called the names of the giant bookselling firms, and I forgot their names immediately; and then he asked me if I wanted to go with him one of these days, to New York. Harry and his young, beautiful, intelligent wife, Verna. She must have been a German immigrant, too. She liked dogs. She walked with a dog that reached her to her waist. The hair of the dog, whose pedigree I would not know, since I hate dogs, was the same reddish-brown texture as hers. Now that I remember the colour of her hair, I think she must have been Irish. Verna liked Harry. And she liked dogs, as I have said. But I think she liked music better. Perhaps, it was she who taught Harry so much about classical music and classical blues. He introduced me to Rimsky-Korsakov, and Borodin. And he told me that Beethoven was black. And so was the Russian poet Alexander Pushkin. "Two black giants!" Harry called them. Harry told me that one of the best modern composers of classical music was the African, Fela Sowande. "Never heard of *Freedom Now Suite*? Sell it to you. Give you a good price." I could hear Verna playing her cello in the office at the back of the store. I would watch her playing her instrument, with her dog, the size of her animal-sized instrument, tight between her legs, and imagine the sensation that the echo ... tremulo? ... vibrato? ... from the bow, was taking a toll on her legs. Verna's legs were more beautiful than her hair. Verna and Harry. Harry liked William Faulkner. And Eugene O'Neill. And John Steinbeck. And Richard Wright. "Did you know he is a communist? Chased him out of the United States. Fled to France. The State Department did. Made him go and live in Paris." *Native Son*. And, *Crime and Punishment*. *Crime and Punishment* drove me into a deep depression when I read it in two days. Dylan Thomas's "A Child's Christmas in Wales," even out of season, was my only balm. Dostoevsky and *Russian Easter Overture* were my diet. "Did you know that Billy Eckstein is a better singer than Frank Sinatra?" I had listened to Billy Eckstein back in Barbados; and I entered a singing competition at the Globe Cinema, near my school; and sang ... some people who were witnesses on that historical Friday night, might say otherwise ... "Blue Moon"; and I got to the end of the second line; and then, all words and phrases and lyrics left my mind. I was more concerned with the slur Billy Eckstein always gave to the last word in each verse, than on remembering the lyrics. When the booing ended, and the missiles — large home-grown parched peanuts — smashed on to the stage; I was already walking through the pit, to bury my shame in a large glass of Mount Gay Rum and Coca-Cola ...

We shall leave Harry. And Verna, with the animal of a cello between her legs, and stop listening to her notes flying out from its well-polished torso, just like her hair blows in the Yonge Street wind, in winter and in summer, when she takes the large business chequebook, and its larger cousin, the book in which entries are made, to the Canadian Imperial Bank of Commerce, immediately south of the Pilot Tavern.

Let us leave Harry's Records and Books, and pass to the Isaacs Gallery, through whose large picture windows you can see large paintings by Coughtry, and Raynor, and Markle. Dorothy Cameron could not take the hassle from the Vice Squad of the police; and she closed her gallery, whether immediately as a consequence, or because galleries weren't making money. And leave the Isaacs Gallery; and leave the stairs that lead to an apartment on the third floor, where Jimmy plays the best rock and roll music, and some jazz, and some blues, and where he cooks you a three-course meal, specializing in fishes, where you have to call the name of a well-known person, an artist obviously, before you could get past the eye-opening, eye-balling, eye-peeping-hole door.

At the corner of Yonge and Yorkville, up to the second floor, lives Dennis Burton, busy now, painting in three copies, the face of, and some of the body of, Mrs. Morty Shulman. I have looked upon her beauty and upon Dennis's genius with faces and bodies and garter belts that decorate women's bodies. "She comes here, to sit." Well, naturally. Where else would she come? Where else does she want to come? To get her portrait triplicated in oils? I wish I were a painter. I start to envy all painters I know, who drink with me in the Pilot Tavern. They live a better life than a writer. A poor painter is better than a poor writer. He has, at least, the luxury and the torment of, the luxury and the wealth of observation of a beautiful woman, painting her face, and her body, her breasts, if he is lucky, and her full nakedness if he can prove that he is lucky. But they tell me, painters I mean, that when you see a woman naked, and you rub your paint brushes over her delicious parts nothing happens in your jeans. It is like stone.

"Tell that to the Marines!"

Stand at the side door leading to Dennis's studio, and you can see Pickering Farms, and the parked Mercedes-Benzes, Volvos, Cadillacs, and the BMWs; and you wish you were not a starving writer. But as you turn your back upon the T-bone steaks, the racks of lamb, the joints of pork roasts, and turn and walk on the west side of the street, you stop at the tuck shop and you buy a stick of chewing gum, wait for the traffic to become a trickle, and you enter the street on which you live. Asquith. In the short distance, on the south side, is the Bell Company, where beautiful black women and beautiful white women, the long-distance operators, come out, at all hours of the night, and get into taxis, to be driven to their doors; going home. Or, in the cars of men waiting like hawks, or piranhas, whose back seats are like moveable bedrooms. The Maison Doré is busy. You can smell onion soup. You can smell the onion soup every day. I have never eaten at the Maison Doré. I would have to complete and sell to Weaver a piece of an acceptable first draft of *The Meeting Point* to afford a cup of coffee there. There is no bride, none from the Bell Company, who has made a reservation to be married, and have her photograph taken by the photographer of the firm that is advertised in the small black Model T, which is forlorn at this time in the early afternoon back seat. I do not know what *doré* means in French.

Everything on this street is quiet. I can look over the roofs of the few houses along this street, and along Park Road, and see the top of Crown Life Insurance, from whom I rent Number 46. And I am glad that they cannot see me. The rent is due. A strange feature about this house: it has two floors only, for a townhouse in the middle of the city of Toronto. It has no garden, no front walk, and it has no backyard, only a space for three cars to park, which we rented out to Mr. Moriyama, the architect who would, in time, design the Toronto Reference Library, which now sits at the top of Asquith Avenue and Yonge Street. I always wondered, whether when he was trying to get his small car in the small space behind Number 46, he was thinking of the economy of space, and how space affects size and so on; and whether the ruminations of iron and steel and concrete were going through his mind? And I wondered whether his assistants, or partners, who also parked in the small space, were thinking of similar things? Or, only of the delicious-smelling onion soup of the Maison Doré, two doors to the west? The rent was due …

… and I have been remembering that in these days, I really wanted to be a poet. But Robert Weaver, in the firmness of his honesty, thought that my submission was so poor that it belied improvement through editing, even over years. He must have been sure of his prejudice, for he was publishing Al Purdy, Margaret Atwood, Earle Birney, the Montreal Group, including Irving Layton and Phyllis Webb and Leonard Cohen … Alice Munro's short stories; and I venture to face the wrath of some, to say that Robert Weaver made Alice Munro!… Dean French of University College, Richard Outram, and Leonard Cohen, whom I consider to be the best poet in the country — before he considered himself a crooner and not a writer of sonnets. Of course, there were others whom Weaver published either in his CBC literary programmes, or in the *Tamarack Review*. There was this professor in the Department of English of the university, who wrote poems, who won the Governor General's Literary Award one year. Fiction and poetry were, I think I am correct in saying this, in the same category. His winning the prize obliterated the chances of *The Meeting Point*, because it was said, by those who knew, that he was dying of cancer, "and therefore we feel he would not live long …"; and so on and so forth. I have the distinct opinion and I harbour my conviction, after all these years, that race colours the rules and regulations that govern the decisions of literary matters: prizes, promotion of your book, reviews, and acceptance. But in addition to this gentleman, Weaver published many more young poets in the 1960s, including Gwendolyn MacEwen and Miriam Waddington, a book of whose poems I bought this year, at the weekly book sale held in a small room, on the first floor of the Toronto Reference Library. And, browsing through this thin volume of poems, I remembered that when poetry was ripped untimely from my ambition, I fell upon writing plays in verse, as my saviour from complete extinction. *Murder in the Cathedral* was my favourite book when I was in the Sixth Form, back in Barbados; and when I tried to drown my disappointment at Weaver's rejection, which said in gist — though not in jest — something like "You do not show that you have a grasp of poetic idiom, and I see no future in these poems, which I am returning to you."

I do not know if he thought that I had a future in fiction. But I had told him, many times in the past twenty years, that he is responsible for Canada not having a great poet born in the West Indies, and that he should take the blame for this. Weaver took a deeper puff on his straight pipe, unfolded the yellow plastic tobacco pouch, forgot to take tobacco out to put into his pipe, re-folded the yellow plastic pouch, thick and bulky as if he were carrying a .38 revolver in the side pocket of his grey worsted sports jacket; and then he blew the smoke, into my face, not disrespectfully; and all the time, implying, and then suggesting, "Put that in your pipe, and smoke it, Clarke!"

And, standing in that small book store on the first floor of the library, the name of the playwright on whom I would base my plays, so far unwritten, appeared on the spine of a small book, not so small as Miriam Waddington's, and I remembered the name of the playwright I wanted to be like, from when I first saw it on the spine of another book, in the Britnell bookstore, in a second edition, published in 1950. Christopher Fry. (There is an obituary in the *Globe and Mail* today, the 8th of July 2005, announcing that he died on the 30th of June 2005, at age ninety-seven; and a note that "in 1939 he wrote a play called *The Tower* that was seen by Mr. Eliot, with whom his name was thereafter indissolubly linked. 'I suppose, he had some influence on me,' Mr. Fry once said, 'but, to me, the names of Eliot and Fry always suggested a pair of famous photographers who were around at the time.'" Today is the first time I have seen his photograph, and the first time I knew of the literary relationship the two of them shared.) For two dollars, I bought the copy of *The Lady's Not for Burning: A Comedy*. I wrote the first act of my play in verse, imitating the style and enough of the dramatic technique of my two "literary ancestors" to use Ralph Ellison's term, that my small talent could apprehend at the time. T.S. Eliot and Christopher Fry were beyond me. Weaver had assured me of this: not only in poetry, but also plays in verse. So, I consoled myself when I noticed that Christopher Fry's name had the same cadence, and the same number of syllables as mine. And at this stage in the birth of my swaddling career as a playwright in verse, I clung, proving a literary ancestry that had nothing to do with literature, but to the significance of the similar cadences and the multisyllabic spelling of our two names; and I wrote my name, on the first pages of drafts of plays in verse, and just in cases, on a few poems, not as Austin Clarke. Or, Austin C. Clarke (which Heinemann, my British publishers, insisted I should use in deference to the more established career of a real poet, Austin Clarke of Dublin, Ireland). I became A.A. Chesterfield-Clarke. Written with the hyphen. The hyphen did not improve my poetry. And one day in disgust, tempered with a small bout of depression, I dug into my past, back to Barbados, in old papers that gave off a smell of neglect and of old age; and decided to try my hand at writing "common fiction," as a friend of mine who writes "in the poetical consciousness," told me to do.

∼∩

Beside the Grand & Toy store on Bloor Street, east of Yonge and before Church Street, an arrow's shot from my house on Asquith Avenue, there used to be a Loblaws supermarket store. A report was published in the *Toronto Star* about a man named Garfield Weston. Mr. Weston, I knew, owned a bakery somewhere in the west end, perhaps on Dupont Street where it becomes Davenport Road; and as we discussed the statement Mr. Weston was alleged to have made in South Africa, I was told that he owned Loblaws, too. Mr. Weston was a very wealthy man. He was also a man who had vast investments in South Africa. South Africa in the fifties was a country that boasted of its racial segregation and its demonization of black people. We in the Canadian Anti-Apartheid Committee were boycotting South African goods and South African athletes in international sports competition, like cricket and the Olympics. Not many nations supported all the boycotts.

In these times, we inspected the labels on wine bottles to see if the wine was made in South Africa. And also the labels and the advertising print on oranges. And then we felt our hearts skip a beat when we discovered that the oranges that before the boycott might have been imported from South Africa, had disappeared from the shelves of supermarkets, and had reappeared as oranges from Israel. It was the identical orange now packaged as a "product" of Israel. Our intelligence wondered if an arrangement to switch the labels had been made between Israel and South Africa. Until we realized the dissimulation, we had been eating South African oranges with Israeli stickers on their fleshy, beautiful skins.

But to get back to Mr. Weston: in one of his meetings, as a board member of an important enterprise in South Africa, he made a statement that was felt to have demonized not only black people in Canada, and in South Africa, but throughout the world. The statement was: "Every black piccaninny or black mammy can call on the government for solutions to every social problem." When I read the statement in its full context in the *Toronto Star*, I could not believe my eyes.

Mr. Weston used to produce in his bakery on Davenport Road, a loaf of bread called Wonder Bread. The slices were cut to precision. If you held a fresh loaf of Wonder Bread in your hand, and squeezed it, it seemed as if the size of the entire loaf could be reduced to almost the thickness of one slice of an ordinary loaf. All Toronto children, including Janice and Loretta, grew up on this bread; and many of our wives and husbands worked for Mr. Weston.

We were in a quandary about what to do in protest of this raw, stupid, new expression of the disregard for black women's dignity.

First of all, I stopped buying Wonder Bread for my children. And I spread the word amongst like-minded members of the Canadian Anti-Apartheid Committee, headed by a gracious, intelligent Canadian Negro (to use the contemporary term), Mrs. Jean Daniels, to make more firm and illustrative our disapproval of the allegiance and the support that Canadian businessmen, and the Canadian government itself, during this black time of apartheid, had been giving, through duplicity, to the Verwoerd government. The University of Toronto also had huge investments in South Africa at this time. So, Israel was not alone in its furtive financial support of South Africa. Nelson Mandela was still in prison on Robben Island and we assumed he would rot in that incarceration. Margaret Thatcher was a staunch supporter of the apartheid government of South Africa.

We decided to hold a demonstration at each of the Loblaws stores in downtown Toronto, at which we could muster picketers. But with our small membership and number of supporters, there were too many stores and we could not cover Mr. Weston's domain with picketers. In times like these, many dramatic things go through your mind: fear of police brutality; the police insisting that we were blocking the right of way of "legitimate" customers entering the store; recruiting and encouraging enough persons to make the demonstration significant, and hearing their reservations about joining, and about having their photographs taken by the newspapers, and secretly by the police on rooftops, for the number of demonstrators was the main — and the only — factor on which the newspapers evaluated that the demonstration was significant and had achieved its purpose. The newspapers were not necessarily our allies. In these days I conducted a running quarrel with Toronto's newspapers, accusing them, with justification of evidence and occurrence, of blatant racism. And not least of which was the example of their own hiring practices. There was not one black reporter on staff at the *Star*, or at the *Telegram*. There was one at the *Globe and Mail*. Newspapers counted only the number of picketers, disregarding the morality of the demonstration, before they decided that black protest against racism was worthy of coverage.

But we could do nothing to increase our membership. And when I say membership I refer to a ragtag group of very intelligent men and women: Canadian-born Negroes, African-Americans who had crossed the border in protest of the Vietnam War, Africans from South Africa itself, and Jewish people. My greatest support in all the demonstrations that Rabbi Feinberg and I organized and led, came from Jewish people. This is another aspect of the allegiance, the brotherhood that used to exist between Negroes and Jews.

Stokely Carmichael and H. Rap Brown, during the worst, black days of segregation in America, made the strategic decision to exclude Jews from participating in demonstrations organized by the Student Nonviolent Coordinating Committee (SNCC) and by the Congress of Racial Equality (CORE). But here in Toronto — and in Canada — there was a demonstrably supportive allegiance, something approaching a symbiotic reaction of Jews to the horrors of the racism that stunted Negroes. After all, in 1955, we were only ten years past the end of the Second World War. And in our midst all of a sudden, were all these Germans and Hungarians, and some of whom we got to know were Jews from Europe. Who did not, in moments of great brotherhood, and closeness, see the blue-veined penciling of the tattooed number on the flesh of a man's right arm, or in the softness of a woman's arm? When I saw the tattooed number for the first time, it was on the arm of Gershon Iskowitz, a painter of heart-wrenching social realism. He wore his number exposed in summer, exposed in defiance and dignity about that experience, and he wore short-sleeved shirts, to let the world be the witness.

And so it was, that with the decision to deploy — the usage of military terms in our demonstration is ironical and deliberate! — the puny ranks of protesters (we sometimes had one person only) to stand in front of a Loblaws store on that Saturday morning. The wind was chilly and had already heralded the arrival of winter, and we did not have numbers to shield us, through rubbing shoulders and bodies against the onslaught of the weather not much different from the political weather in South Africa. In these days, the name in our minds, on our lips, was Chief Albert Lutuli — not Nelson Mandela who was "forgotten" in prison. Nor Bishop Tutu, who was not, then, even immortalized by Miles Davis in the beautiful, mournful epic, "Tutu."

Some black women walked up to us, looked at us with disdain, with pity, but also with anger. We were embarrassing them. And I did not understand their embarrassment at first, but later knew to be the embarrassment of the victim, exposed publicly by this demonstration. It seemed as if we were reminding the public that these black people in Toronto were without rights; and people without rights do not wish the limitation to be too publicly noticed, or protested. Besides, Loblaws stores did not prevent them from shopping at any of their stores, as was the case in America — with restaurants, water fountains, barbershops, and hotels — but here was this "nigger" (Negroes called us that to our face, loudly, sometimes) "making things bad for everybody." Making things bad for everybody. This was the conclusion. This was the reaction to visible protest against racial discrimination — by letters to the editor, by speeches, by marching in a demonstration, such as the one against George Wallace, who was given permission to speak at the Maple Leaf Gardens, by a mayor who was Jewish, Mayor Philip Givens. "You West Indians're always making things bad, for everybody!" I got the impression that I could best bear the brunt, and defeat racial discrimination, personal, collective, individual or systemic, if I kept my "damn" mouth shut. That way, they argued, nobody would get hurt in Toronto, racially or physically.

Some few black women saw us picketing, sometimes no more

than two at a store, and read the words on the placards we held like crosses in a procession down the aisle, remembering South Africa, remembering Sharpeville, remembering the burning of the pass books, remembering graphically, the slaughter, the merciless, brutal slaughter of black people throughout all of South Africa ... and Rhodesia, too! And Congo! And postponed their shopping, for the day. Some smiled with us. Some said, "Right on!"

And some, whites only, spat their condemnation of us, in the glare of their looks. My mother, had she been with us on that Saturday morning, would have characterized their disapprobation, by "cutting their two eyes at we."

Our demonstrations, and our letters to the editor, and my own columns published in the *Toronto Telegram* and the *Toronto Star*, did absolutely nothing to lessen the incidents of abuse caused by racial discrimination. So, when Mayor Givens gave Governor George Wallace permission to speak at Maple Leaf Gardens, a man who at the same time, only yesterday then, had been leading the political force and the raw physical violence in support of racial segregation, in his state of Alabama, personally; and advocating it throughout America, culturally and morally, extolling "serrigation now, serrigation tomorrow, serrigation forever" — he did not need to add, "over my dead body!" We were appalled at the mayor's insensitivity.

So, on the bleak afternoon, perhaps it was also a Friday, since as I have said, Friday is the most ominous day in all my life, on that Friday, I was at the head of a phalanx of protesters, Negroes and Jews, going westward from Church Street, along the north side of the Gardens, on to Wood Street, when, out of nowhere, I see this man, bigger than a lumberjack, wearing a ten-gallon hat; looking like a Southerner, thick in the shoulders, his eyes covered in dark glasses, jaw firm as steel, and his hand, through the custom and instinct born in his home down in the Southern pines and magnolias, he was caressing his holster; this man who moved silently, like a ballet dancer, like a cobra, with physical power coming even from his eyes, this man could land a blow with his body that could land me in the gutter; or with his butt. He was now a blocker, or better still, a guard. And his moves that he must have practised, like moves over the football field, schooled in many marches and protests and demonstrations; and now to "put them down," in support of racial segregation, this Southern visitor hit me with his body. Once. Fast, and impossible to see. The cobra's strike. And I went, "cat-spraddled," into the middle of Wood Street. The man was dressed in a well-tailored suit that hid the bulk of his "piece" from the eyes of witnesses, even those walking beside me.

Governor Wallace moved freely, safely, through the thin line of protestors to enter the Gardens. And Mayor Givens was waiting, relieved and safe inside the thick walls of Maple Leaf Gardens, where bigger, more bruising, blows were delivered every "Hockey Night in Canada," by the Toronto Maple Leafs hockey team.

Governor Wallace gave his speech. I did not hear it. I did not read the *Star* or the *Telegram* or the *Globe and Mail* the next day, so I wouldn't have to see it. But I could guess that it was peppered by the words in his philosophy of inequality: "Serrigation now, serrigation tomorrow, serrigation forever"

~

And many years after Governor Wallace's visit to Toronto, I am just leaving Silver Springs, Maryland, just outside Washington, D.C., on another Friday, leaving the home of a former colleague at Yale University, coming back home to Canada. Over the radio comes a bulletin. It cuts into the jazz I am listening to.

"… and Governor George Wallace, Democratic candidate campaigning for the presidency of the United States, has been shot … he is believed killed, and …"

There was only my wife in the Mercedes-Benz with me; and not even she knew the words I uttered at the news. We looked at each other. And said nothing. We could only listen. "It is believed, police say, that the would-be assassin is driving a foreign-made car …" She had not been in the demonstration outside Maple Leaf Gardens, years before. Did I remember the words Malcolm X spoke when President John F. Kennedy was assassinated, sentiments that got him — so it is said — into trouble with his leader, the Honourable Elijah Muhammad head of the Muslims in America. Malcolm's comment on Kennedy's assasination was based on an old Negro philosophical saying: "… chickens coming home to roost."

Or, it could be clothed in the homonym, in imitation of H. Rap

Brown, that "Violence is American as apple pie!" Philosophies and rage, political retort testifying to church bombings in Birmingham; the Southern Negro Churches' flaming graves of children; the attempt to register Negroes to make them eligible to vote in elections hijacked by the kidnapping, the torture, the murders, and the burning of three bodies of civil rights workers: one black, one white, one Jewish, the exact reflection of the largest racial groups in America. The irony of it all. And the man known to have been the ringleader, tried in a court of law, as recently as June 2005, and sentenced shortly afterward, in one day, or in two days, to thirty years in prison, for each of his three victims. The man is in his eighties. It took the American "justice system," which I sometimes felt was not only blind, but lame, forty-something years to catch up with a man in a wheelchair, crippled by his personal history.

He became a lay preacher, because no established church would have him, because he needed the space of the evangelist; and he put his body and soul in the hands of Jesus, just as Captain John Newton, for years had sailed the Atlantic Ocean, bringing slaves from Africa to the New World; and who had, suddenly sought grace, and redemption. Captain John Newton became a born-again slave-catcher, and a devout church-going composer, and who gave us "Amazing Grace." It became a song whose lyrics describe the beauty and the pleading for grace, which now has its fullest aesthetic and moral voice in the mouths of black Americans, singing Amazing Grace!

"The fact that you are eighty years old, an old man, who will probably die before you have served your sentence," the sentencing judge seemed to be saying, "does not save you from having to serve thirty years for each of these murders."

Can grace and the plea for redemption find their moral justification to forget the March on Selma, Alabama, one hot weekend?

And then, there was another bulletin: "… the attempted assassination of Governor Wallace, who was giving a campaign speech in the Maryland suburb of Silver Springs … police have informed this station, that the suspect is believed to be heading north, in a foreign European car …"

What will I say to the State Trooper, when I come to the next stop, at the next toll, at the next point where money is taken from you to let you pass into another state, another country? How much will it be? One

American dollar bill? Do I throw two quarters into the tray and speed off? Or, is it five Yankee dollars? I am confused and frightened. He will see my "foreign European car." But why would an assassin choose such a conspicuous car to get away in? To flee to Canada on a modern-day Underground Railroad? Because of its engineering?

Rabbi Feinberg and I continued to lead demonstrations, and we changed the intensity of mood, of obsession, of evaluation, of all this work, all this intellectual, contentious argument about racial discrimination and segregation, and we found our temporary solace at the Jewish restaurant on College Street, just west of Bathurst. And then we would walk farther down Spadina Avenue; going south; and the Rabbi would introduce me to a friend of his who made cigars. We would blow the thick blue-white smoke from our cigars into the air to mix with the low-hanging clouds. Our cigars were from Havana — Cuban cigars. The Rabbi, who liked the thin ones, not much larger than a cigarette. And we praised God and Javeh, and Fidel Castro that we lived in Canada, and that we did not live in America, and that Canada had not banned Cuban cigars or Cuban rum.

But in spite of the soothing intoxication of strong, Cuban cigars, the chats about jazz, and snippets of autobiographical 'memberings, the nourishing food from the Bagel Restaurant on Spadina Avenue and College Street, we were just, only two men, too weak, in spite of our commitment to "racial integration," too poor in influence and resources, we were still powerless to make any real change. And we went about our other lives, the Rabbi to his congregation at Beth Tzedec Temple, and I to the beginning toil of wanting to be a writer.

CHAPTER FIVE

The CBC Stagehand

I had recently moved from a two-bedroom apartment on Vermont Street, the first street south of Dupont, and west off Bathurst. In those days, you could count the number of black residents in this area on your left hand. From Vermont, we moved to Rosedale. Rosedale! Glen Road, north of Bloor Street, east from Sherbourne. In a basement apartment.

The landlord was in his kitchen at the rear, on the first floor, when I knocked on the door; and he himself answered, and I said I had come "to see the apartment advertised in the *Star.*" And he said, "Fine!" and he guided me down the back stairs, to the basement, and when I entered the screen door, which was the entrance to the apartment, I saw the pipes running in all directions along the ceiling, and I think I saw this first time, the sweating beads on the pipes, and I could not see into the farther darkness to the front of the basement apartment, but this did not deter me, so I shouted, "I'll take it!"

Allan, as it turned out was his name, was, as it turned out, gay. The term was not yet in full currency. The term people used, in public and in private, was "queer," or it was "homo," or it was "fag," if you wanted to be crude; and it was "a philosopher," if you were out to hide things. I had never met a man who claimed he was gay — openly. But he was, more than that, a good man. A perceptive man. He knew what I meant by accepting an apartment before I had hardly inspected it. He would know the history of my rejections and of my rare welcome, looking for an apartment or a room, to rent.

"You haven't even seen the place," he said, with the cigarette dangling from the right side of his mouth.

And then he re-climbed the stairs, back to his kitchen, bending his head, at the appropriate stages in the stairs that went around two right angles. And I made a note to remember where the stairs demanded a lowered head.

Allan did not ask for the two months' rent "in advance," as was the custom, and the condition of renting in those days of 1959.

We had a garden to look at during the summer; and we placed the two English perambulators in this garden, for Janice and Loretta, my young daughters, babies, really, to "catch the air." And we had our own entrance, though it was at the rear, through bushes that declared flowers and a perfume during the summer, walking distance to Bloor near Yonge, to the same Loblaws grocery store I would picket, years later.

I had got a job as a stagehand, at the CBC, in Design Staging, on 354 Jarvis Street, across the road from what was then The Four Seasons Motor Hotel, where Robert Weaver would later hold court, guiding the fortune and literary progress of the beginning of something somebody called Canadian Literature, or CanLit; and hold in his hands the future, and the failure of all Canadian writers. I was a stagehand. This closeness to the Czar of Literature probably explains how I got to know Weaver. All I needed to qualify for this stagehand job was my declared familiarity with a hammer. A hammer. Some people, including kings and fleeing dictators have asked for a horse, and in modern times, for a "flying horse," a private jet. But all I needed was a hammer. A simple, ordinary Canadian Tire Canadian hammer, a tool, so long as it had claws. I learned afterwards, that to be a stagehand, you had to know how to use this hammer, your own hammer bought from Canadian Tire, at the corner of Yonge and Davenport, to rip apart "flats," and to rip nails out of "flats," and to pound nails into "flats," leaving about a quarter of an inch, a nail head, exposed, so that the next shift of stagehands, "the strikers," could more easily rip the nails back out.

If the crew chief liked you, he gave you lots of overtime shifts. If he didn't like you, you lived off your salary, only. I never liked many of my crew chiefs. They were racists, mostly. They had never seen a black stagehand before — except Martin Carrington, a painter at the start of his studies at an art college in Toronto, wearing jeans with blobs of paint on them, just like Markle, Coughtry, and Dennis Burton.

Martin was a "Canadian Negro." And there was another Canadian Negro, whose name slips my mind, who worked on the trucks that brought the "flats" to the television studios on Jarvis Street, to be put up, by us; and then to be pulled back down, by us; left outside the studios by him, because this is the way it was done in these days and nights of "live television." And then the "flats" would be taken back to Sumach Street, from whence they had come, to be stored in the shop there, where they were also built.

James Bacque, the author of *Other Losses*, an investigation into the mass deaths of German Prisoners at the hands of the French and Americans, after the Second World War, was a stagehand. Graham Coughtry, the distinguished painter, was in the paint shop, decorating "flats" for the scenery in plays and children's programmes. Michael Nimchuk, known around town as the best University playwright, was a stagehand. Richard Outram, the poet, was a stagehand. Outram, as we called him, became a crew chief, soon after I joined Design Staging. He was not a racist. Outram gave me a poem once, beautifully printed in tasteful font and design, "Ophelia Illumined," published by the Gauntlet Press. I have just read the first two stanzas, again; and I note that it is my Christmas present from Richard and his wife, Barbara, in 1965.

> SIR, she is couched
> Under the willows,
> Watching the water;
>
> You shall not find her
> Where she attends
> The slightest of motions:

And Don Owen, who went on to make movies and films and to make a name for himself at the National Film Board, down in Montreal, speaking broken French, at the NFB.

And then, there appeared a man named W.H. Linklater. He was supervisor of the stage crew (Studio Operations). Other men, most of whom were recent immigrants, from England, Ireland, and Scotland … perhaps also from Australia…trained by the BBC, they let you know, these gentlemen … there were no women then … boasted a superiority of experience and talent because of their origins outside of Canada. In this hierarchy, were Leonard Crainford, director of design, and A.E. Bentley, studio co-ordinator.

In these 1959 days, I was looking after Janice and Loretta during the day, spending more time bathing babies; powdering them; burping them, cleaning them, changing them, feeding them … singing to them; singing them to sleep, so I could sneak … "on tip-toes now, boy, yuh don't want to wake-up the children from sleeping …"

"Rockabye baby on the tree top

"when the wind blow, the cradle going rock …"

From Monday to Friday; from seven o'clock in the morning, until five when Betty got home from the Toronto General Hospital, head-nursing adults, and trying to make sense of the madness of my decision to be a writer. I was nurse and nursemaid during the day, and, at night, in the basement with the sweating pipes overhead, following me like fifth columnists, stalking my movements from one room to the next babysitting and baby-screaming room, hitting keys on the Noiseless Remington Rand that made the same sharp noise as my stagehand hammer striking partially exposed heads of nails on "flats" in CBC television studios; trying to write plays in verse, in imitation of Christopher Fry, and not knowing another living writer with whom I could exchange a word to help solve my literary confusion. But I was reading. *The Lady Is Not for Burning*. And listening to Miles, and Coltrane, and Bird, and Art Blakey, and Beethoven. Yeah! I was cool down in that basement, remembering to duck my head from banging it, from not getting my head cracked against the sweating pipes that lined the low ceiling, that caused me to walk with a stooped back, like an old man, like the homeless men who looked into the galvanized, shiny garbage cans, left out like bombs waiting to blow up the houses in front of which they lined the peaceful peaceable houses they were left outside to guard. The homeless men were regular, on garbage days, as policemen who strolled, every day, all day, through these Rosedale streets, silent and smiling, and touching the peaks of their caps. "Morning, sir! Have a good day, sir." And I far from home, far now from Barbados, am here. "Where you was such a blasted fool to choose, choosing Canada over England, by yourself, to live in that damn cold place, Canada as if you is a real Foolbert." My mother said that in a letter in a red-white-and-blue air mail envelope from Barbados. "And by the way, I send you a little parcel, with the thing you ask for in the parcel. I hope the bottle don't break. Or somebody in the post office up there don't pinch it. And you up, in Canada, where it so cold. Your very loving Mother. Mother."

In those days of uncertainty, I was tormented by personal demons (to use the threadbare term in a context of fear) with no one, no other writer, with whom I could share these misapprehensions of writing that hugged me like a wet, cold shirt.

Babysitting in the daytime, squeezing an hour here and an hour there, to put a word on paper the days that seemed shorter every day, to slam my frustration out on to the noisy keys of the Noiseless Remington Rand; and working as a stagehand, hammering nails into "flats" on the night shift.

CBC's Studio Nine was on Yonge Street, just up from the Summerhill Liquor Store, across the street from a fancy meat store that sold steaks for more money than I spent on furniture and corduroy trousers, at the Goodwill Store — still called The Crippled Civilians — and facing the entrances to Rosedale's intractable streets which could take you walking in never-ending circles and in mazes and roundabouts, for hours and hours. It is also near — or used to be — to the art gallery that Ted, a Hungarian immigrant, a painter, owned; and who before that was the impresario, and owner of the jazz club, The Cellar, a basement on Avenue near Davenport Road, where Canadian and American musicians played in the key of John Coltrane and Charles Lloyd and Keith Jarrett and Jack DeJohnette; and imitated Thelonious Monk and the Bird; and where I read poems that no one would publish. But who gave a damn? This was a time for poetry readings and love-ins, and paint-ins, and one night stands in the low-ceilinged Cellar Jazz Club, where Michael Nimchuk read a scene from a play in progress, and did not call it a poem. But which jazz club owner would pay a starving poet to read his poems? This was free publicity, man. The audience, sometimes no bigger than the size of the group playing Miles Davis tunes, were themselves poets!

In Studio Nine, the well-liked, well-known, well-designed musical programme, *Country Hoedown*, was produced live, with the help of cue cards; and with a crew of six stagehands, "chiefed" by an Irishman, whose name I think was Carey. We were assigned to put up the scenery. Carey, if this was his name, would rip the designer's drawing into half, and give each half to three stagehands, with a leader he had appointed on the spot. After a while, we learned how to set up *Country Hoedown* in thirty minutes. We were not taught how to do things; there was no welcome to make you feel at home, no indoctrination. You watched the man beside you hammering nails into "flats" and you hoped by God, that his hammer didn't slip, and land you in the land of seeing stars and reverberating pains. "Crew chief? Crew chief, come over here! A fellow ..."

One night, we set up *Country Hoedown* in twenty minutes.

How did we spend the time left over? I suspect that amongst the older stagehands, those who had worked together for a long time, those who were neighbours, coming over on the same ship from England, there would be secrets and confidences and cliques. I learned afterward that they went to their favourite late-night restaurant, Mars, on College Street, near Bathurst. Amazingly, the last time I journeyed in that area, Mars was still alive and kicking, and sputtering out those damn delicious hamburgers. But those of us who did not want to be driven to Mars, went home, or went elsewhere, with the understanding that we would be back in time to clock out. And nobody — not the supervisor of Stage Crew, not the director of design, and not the studio co-ordinator were seen during this hiatus. They all had their own schemes, hiding in secret places of retreat — probably in the basement of the Celebrity Club across from the CBC building, on Jarvis Street.

From my own basement apartment with the sweating pipes, to Studio Nine on Yonge Street, you would walk out to Sherbourne Street, turn right, walk along Bloor Street, turn left, and pass the Ranch House Restaurant, which sold the best chili con carne, where, years later when I used to play poker in the Oakwood-Whitmore-Park Hill neighbourhood, we would find ourselves: weary and beaten by the cards and by the interminable hours over Five Card Stud, Kings and Little Ones, Follow the Queen, and Low in the Hole, and order bowls of chili con carne to regain strength, to have enough strength to face wife or woman, or "deputy"; the strength needed to try to explain our long absence from home. So, you pass this restaurant now, and continue past the small bridge leading to Bayview Avenue and the Branksome Hall private school for girls. You have already passed the lawns of Crown Life Insurance and Manufacturers Life, mowed to such perfection that they looked unreal, like the fields where football is played, artificial; and when Christmas comes, you travel to see their Christmas lights shine and twinkle like stars, decorations that presage hope of a better year, next year. With a job. A better apartment. "Man, all the best for the New Year, man!"

And I make my landmark by the corner of Roxborough Street East. This is where I would emerge from the circuitous route, had I been fearful the children would be wakened from their long-winded winter sleep. But the writing got the better of me, in the sense that everything else, the crying of babies, the rage of the wife at the crying of the babies, the crying of the babies, which babies do especially at nights, tampering with my concentration in the small time I had in the basement from the cold and the snow, and the anger of the crew chief, not to mention the supervisors, all hanging over my head, inspecting the words I was hammering onto the store-bought typing paper from Grand & Toy, and the un-bought typing paper which friends and wife and allies smuggled out from their various jobs in their briefcases, handbags, and under their winter coats, keeping out more than the chilling wind at the corner of Bloor and Yonge … rambling in my thoughts, I completely lost sight of the time, and forgot I had to punch out; and in my rush to be punctual, and avert the stern warning written on another Remington Rand Noiseless, by Miss "odh," the typist, and from the anger and the pen of Mr. W.H. Linklater, I left the unfinished page in the typewriter, got up from the chair in the low-ceilinged basement front-house, where there was only one pipe which did not sweat, walked on tip-toed softness through the long corridor to the rear-door entrance, not even realizing how stupid this behaviour was, as I had ignored my noise disturbing the three sleeping souls in the two-bedroomed catacomb. I trounced out, wearing my faun-coloured British Navy duffel coat, green corduroy suit, dark brown Clark suede desert boots, and a scarf; and instead finding my way in the anonymous streets white-painted in snow, streets that did not lead to any destination once you had begun to trample on their crunching cover of ice, like echoes of muffled shouts from a child; and turning right instead of left; and finding too late that I am going in another direction along Sherbourne, which I know; and knowing this, I know from short memory, that this street turns left and then becomes another street, and that this new street, which I had seen, fleetingly from a bus, or from a car … never from a taxi … for what would I be doing in Rosedale? Which person, writer, which person, writer or no writer, would I be visiting in this white no-man's land, like a lake of power, glittering in parts where a star, or a lamplight from the room of an insomniac, or from the study of a man counting his treasures in one-dollar bills, I walk like a man trapping bears, or wolves, animals that eat men, and that men eat, and find none; but I am hearing the beating of my heart. And my bravery fades.

I am not fleeing before the footprints of paws that will haul me back, like a contrary wind, and fit me easily, appetizingly into the jaws of doom.

Doom rises in my breast. Doom rises in my limbs. My crew chief. The arthritis of the snow-biting wind. The wind accompanies me around turns in the uncharted streets. The trees and the telephone poles are now the same colour of white. The leaves are like decorations, and the glittering snow like flakes thrown onto the green growing tree; and the lights on houses are white. They are not like the riot of lights and carnival flashing and bursting from houses in the poorer district … red, green, white, red, blue, and yellow, glittering; and some like dead eyeballs; lifeless, and staring at you. They are not like Scarborough's multicultural explosion of passion and love. In these days, people of respectability, people like the people who live in Rosedale and in Forest Hill, and people who think themselves civilized, who get into their cars late on Christmas nights, "to help digest all this turkey"; and drive, and drive down University Avenue, going south as they went every other day, into the vaults of Bay Street, "to see the lights" on the trees and statues and monuments and on hospitals, in their brave, crude colours of green and red and yellow, on places and on things where "you'd never expect to see such wildness" in colour, where coloured immigrants dared to run lines of coloured lights in trees, bringing the trees back to life in the deepness of winter, and around houses, on roofs, in front garden beds, as if they were rebuilding the houses built in repeated monotony, in their own individual choice of architecture…. Had I marked a house during the infrequent daytime ramblings through Rosedale, I would have remembered the shape of the boughs, the way the leaves hung, related the house at the corner to the name of the street, and found some bearing. But the streets were anonymous. Not visible. Just as you feel the sudden panic, sitting in a bus, in November with its disappearing light, and its windows covered in vapour and mist and breath and the accumulation of the stain of snow. And the breathings of people in a new panic of early nighttime, their breath fogging up the windows, "fucking up your vision," you do not, all of a sudden know where you are. I sometimes wonder how explorers explored streets that had no names before they began stumbling in the white darkness of being lost.

I am passing the cemetery on the other side from the one I would take if I were walking along Yonge Street. My feet remain almost buried in the snow. My feet disappear for a few seconds, with each step in the story-telling snow of men buried in avalanches and the wilderness of snowbanks, of women found days after they first went lost, frozen stiff in an act of attempted escape, or animals stiffer than the roasted pig we ate on Christmas afternoon, back in Barbados. And I think of the Three Wise Men. Nowadays in the dawning of a new black consciousness, we are insisting that we should have, and have acknowledgement of the "fact" that at least, one o' these three men was black." Give us a black Wise Man, to let the world, which is white as this convicting snow, know there is a "wise man" who is black; and that every black man, or coloured man, or Negro man out of three wise men, is therefore, a wise man. Wise Men do not get lost. They use the stars as their compass, just like the one in the car that my Trinidadian friend helped to drive to get us lost, on our way to Niagara Falls and the American border. That compass sways and moves and turns corners and stops and goes, imitating the movements of the car; still remaining still and fixed, correct, steady, and reliable. I look up into the heavens for stars and see more than I am able to count and pin down, and declare. And then I give up. It is the courage of the timid. Throw yourself upon the mercy of the cold, believe you will freeze to death and no one would know, or care.

> ... and a Negro was yesterday found frozen to death in a path that enters the Mount Pleasant Cemetery. Police, investigating the death, said they do not know why the man was walking in the Mount Pleasant Cemetery. They have no knowledge as to any relative of the dead man who was buried there. Police informed this newspaper that because of the Christmas holidays, at this busy time in December, authorities might not know the cause of death, until after an autopsy on Boxing Day. No relatives have been discovered as at press time ...

But, in its unrevealing, life is more simple than that. Life has no miracles. No complexities. "The man get-lost. The type o' man the man was, is the type o' man who won't know how to get outta Rosedale, particular on a night with snow covering the ground and making everything more whiter than it already is! He bound to get-lost. That type o' man don't live there, don't work there, don't have friends up in there, don't know no blasted body up there, and can't, therefore, quod-a-rat, call-on 'pon nobody to extricate him from field-after-field of whiteness. He must end-up in Mount Pleasant Cemiterry."

So, when the man saw from the distance, a subway station, and could pick out a few letters in the name on the white horizontal board on a telephone pole, and could guess at the correctness of a few other letters, he realized he was at LAWRENCE AVENUE. And he knew where he was. He was lost.

He ducked down and raised the wire over his head, and he straddled the wire for a moment, and then picked himself up from the thick snow. He was now white. When he returned to his true colour, of fear and shame, he was able to run and slide and stumble down a slight incline to the street, and put up his hand, now black from slapping against his British Navy duffel coat, and the bus driver saw him, and slowed down and slid a little, making meandering river beds with the tires, and he thought again, not for more than one second, trying to unravel the mysteries of the streets of Rosedale, why didn't he take a taxi from his basement, to the CBC Studio Nine?

When he opened the door to Studio Nine on the side street, there was a man in the small office, the size of the section in a bank where a teller sits and checks your identity, asking you for your name which is written down on the cheque you have just given her; asking for your address which is written down on your ID; asking if you have an account here in this bank, although your passbook says you have; and asking you these questions two times, in order for her to trust you; or sometimes, standing before her, asking you no question that is verbal, but that is imagined, before you can get your cheque cashed, because a previous cheque of yours, "not so long ago," came back "with not sufficient funds" stamped horizontal, rising from the left corner, at an angle of forty-five degrees … and I see the supervisor sitting, and I cannot tell him that that cheque that came back "not so long ago, with not sufficient funds" stamped on it, in red, was written for a delivery of oil, in the middle of January, one winter ago, and the bath towels had to be boiled in water in the saucepans; and the Lilliputian-sized bathtubs for Janice and Loretta, had to be filled with water boiled in the large enamel saucepan that rice and peas had been cooked in, earlier; and the water bottles, and bottles filled with water had now to be filled with water from the kettle that screamed steaming-mad when the water, unlike the heat in the rented house, reached boiling point. I would rub my larger hand over the soft, innocent, shivering hands and bodies of the two babies, who did not know why all of a sudden they were cold in this deathlike January; and this was always after I had walked into the basement, and had placed my hands on the pipes, which I knew were cold, when I came down the previous five minutes, expecting as a fool expects luck to save his poverty, hoping as a poor man hopes that a miracle would happen. In the thin line of another man's footprints in the snow, that January 18th in 1958, a man I would never know, would never track down to his lair, I felt the denuding cold in my bones, and in the desperation, and in the hope that "the game is up," that you "gonna freeze your arse off, this winter, boy! That's for goddamn sure!" I was that man, a man from Detroit, who tracked another man down, driving over the speed limit from Detroit to find Walmer Road, to find the man who had run off before he had settled his account, with the drugs, in a darkened room on the east side of the second-floor staircase, telling him, "Ma-fucker! Mafucker! You's mine now, ma-fucker!" And he shot him dead. And was himself tracked down through unknown drifts and rooming houses in Toronto, and became, at his death by hanging in the Don Jail, more famous than when he was in the quick. "The last man to be hanged, and hanged back-to-back with a French-Canadian, a murderer like himself, was …"

But black Americans, like this stranger from Detroit, have always helped themselves with the notoriety that made us, less interesting people, famous. He is even a clue in a crossword puzzle. "Who is the last Negro to be hanged in Canada, for murder?"

They have never posed the question from the other side: "Who is the first Negro to be hanged in Canada, for murder?"

"Clarke?" the supervisor said.

"Clarke," I said.

"It-is-a'-hour-and-forty-five-minutes-you-late," he said, making his sentence into a one-word conviction. "Two hours almost …"

"Almost two hours?" I said.

"Yes," he said.

"Yes," I said.

"I'm gonna send you home, Clarke."

"Yes, sir."

On Mr. W.H. Linklater's memo, there is the entry: "Jan. 18 — 1 hour 45 minutes late, sent home."

I have that memo, under the subject "Lateness." The word is underlined. And written in capital letters. It is written and signed by W.H. Linklater. It is "dated at Toronto, Ontario, February 16, 1959, WHL: odh" — referring to the initials in the name of the secretary, whose name I never did know.

Since November your punctuality has been terrible as the following record will attest:

Nov. 10	punched in at 08.16	scheduled for 08:00
17	21.55	21:50
Dec. 10	08:56	08:00
18	11:02	11:00
22	08:05	08:00
25	12:55	12:50
28	08:08	08:00
Jan. 11	23:10	23:00
18	1 hour 45 minutes late, sent home	
19	punched in at 06:55	scheduled for 06:50
21	08:10	08:00
29	21:58	21:50
Feb. 1	20:55	20:50
4	10:06	10:00

This incidence of lateness is far too high and, unless I see an immediate improvement, I shall have to recommend disciplinary measures.

I had not looked carefully at this memorandum, when I received it. I must have put it into my file and ignored it. I must have misunderstood its significance. I must have deliberately wiped it from my mind. The sweating pipes that criss-cross my environment must have dropped an inch or two from their anchoring in the ceiling, and had smashed my head, temporarily damaging my brain. I had become a Foolbert. A late one.

"Disciplinary measures" had indeed been taken. I was fired. But the next morning, I was back in the studios. Without my hammer with its two claws. In my hand, I carried a script. For a "principal role." In a "live" television drama. Directed by a man named Jarrett. Barbara Chilcott and Julie Christie starred. I was an actor, all of a sudden. As a stagehand, I'd always wondered what you had to do to be an actor. Turned out, not very much. They saw me on the set as a stagehand and invited me to be an actor. The euphoria made me think I was the great Percy Rodriguez from Montreal; or Paul Robeson; or the Negro actor who went before him, the greatest of all black actors, Laurence Dunbar — in the role of Othello, the Moor of Venice, at the Shakespearean Festival at Stratford, Canada. Not, Canada! On the London stage. Why not?

CHAPTER SIX

"Jesus Christ, boy! You is a running-fool, a race horse!"

It had come to its most dramatic crossing, my life, which contained a direction, a logic which although incomprehensible to me, at the time of crisis and terror that I might not be employed again, that I might be thrown upon the pile of the newspapers' statistics about Negroes and Negro immigrants, "who come here to live on the dole" when they are not taking jobs from "decent white Canadians." I could trace my predicament back to Barbados, and examine two events which were my explanation for the action taken by Mr. Linklater on January 18, 1959.

The first is the play-play military seriousness on the parade ground at Walkers cadet camp, when I was stripped of my rank as sergeant-major, because of my loyalty to a friend, a greater loyalty than I could ever have had toward the regulations of the Cadet Corps. Loss of rank, and status, pseudo-military and social, was small punishment of my attitude and understanding of friendship and loyalty. And I carried no rancour, was not diminished, did not accept it, with all its panoply and assumed British seriousness, as a reversal. It did not, and could not mark me as a failure.

The second event took place in the cellar underneath the George Challenor Stand, at Kensington Cricket Oval in Barbados, where the annual Inter-School Sports Day, participated in by all the government secondary boys' schools, is held. The year is 1951. It is the last race of the day. The half mile, or 880 yards, race. My school, Harrison College, has to win this race, to win the cup — for the third successive time. In the race with me, from Harrison, is one other boy. Michael Simmons. Michael is in the Classical Fifth Form. He will be my pace setter. The rivals, and perennially they have been our rivals, are the boys from the Lodge School, a boarding school favoured by English expatriates, local whites, local blacks who pass for whites, Venezuelans who come to learn how to speak English, and three black boys, one of whom is my main rival. Glasgow. It is very tense in the basement. And more tense in the stands. The girls from all the government secondary schools have chosen their heroes. Queen's College girls are with Harrison College. The one "white" girls' private school, St. Winifred's, cannot compete in this athletic event because it is a school, privately-endowed ... Sin-Winifred's are with the Lodge School.

Into the basement, sweating through anxiety and the surrounding tension and the humidity, comes the same man who had signed the orders placed in the glass case, protected by lock and key and history, outside the door of the Classical Sixth Form, proclaiming that "A.A.C. Clarke has the rank of Lance-Corporal, (Acting)." It was signed by Captain George Hunte, a kind of unofficial sports master, in addition to being the commanding officer of the cadet corps. I would see him stand on the boundary line of the college's main playing field, and watch the boys sweating from their sprints, and stretches, and press-ups, without the benefit of a coach.

"Clarke, we're depending on you. You have to win this race. We can't win the cup, otherwise. You can't come second, neither, Clarke. You have to come first ..."

He did not ask me how I felt. He did not ask me if I needed a drink of water. He did not ask me if I needed a massage. Or a handkerchief soaked in ice water, to wipe the sweat from my face ...

... but I had been winning the 880, the last race of the meet, for the past three years; and everybody expected that I would win this one, a fourth time. This was also the last race I could run before leaving Harrison College. So, Captain George Hunte's words, even though not words of encouragement, but of expectation, were understandable, nevertheless; and in my own "tenseness" and nervousness before the race ... before every race ... they did not seem to be spiteful coming from a man whom I had grown to hate; really hate, so much so that I made every attempt not to be in the same space as him; and luckily for me, Captain Hunte was a junior master, and he was not qualified to teach Sixth Form English and Latin; so Captain Hunte went his merry way, teaching Latin and French in the first form.

"First" was driven into me, from the time my mother carried me about in her hands, because I was small and fragile for her shoulder, in the two neighbourhoods of Sin-Matthias and of Dayrells Road. "You gotta come first! Hear? Everything after first is last! There is only one first." And it is probably my inhaling this philosophy of egocentric determination, accepting her attitude, too, that "coming first" was a declaration that I was trained not to share my laurels with anyone. I chose athletics, not without reason. In cricket, in football, in basketball, you needed the team as much as you needed your individual excellence. In athletics — except for the relay race! — you hit the tape first. And every other runner was "last." You shared your glory with no one. You were Victor Ludorum.

"On your marks!"

The voice was a familiar one. He had started all the races I ran at Combermere, for five years, and at these Inter-School Sports meet, for three years.

I steadied myself in my "blocks."

They were not the starting blocks athletes use today. They were holes gouged into the ground by your heel. I inhaled one of the three deep breaths I would take.

"Set!" He drew the word out, making it almost three syllables long.

In all these years, with the same starter, I had got to know his rhythm. And as I had been a cadet, with a little knowledge of rifles and guns, and the meaning of first and second pressure on a trigger, I knew when to expect the sound of the starting pistol. There would be no false start in such a long race.

Count two, my mind reminded me, after the echo of "Set!" had settled in the tall casuarina trees and the coconut trees surrounding Kensington Oval; and in the hush, and the coolness of the late afternoon, I counted off the two pauses, like heartbeats. And true enough. The pistol went, *bang*! Too close to my moving out of the "blocks," to call it a false start. But it was a long race … get to the inside; get in behind the pace setter;

do not get locked in, and be no farther back than third at the end of the first 220 yards. Yes!... settle into your own rhythm and pace; try not to breathe too hard; relax, relax ... yes!... the end of the second 220, you should be moving up into second place; watch out for the spikes of your rivals, the boys from the Lodge School, "those bastards!" ... and then, suddenly, out of the pack, in a move that had never happened before in the five years I had been running and winning the 880, a boy sprinted, as we were rounding the beginning of the last turn; and before I could readjust my pace, a second Lodge School boy slipped by. Yes! In all the years, in all the sweating victories, I always made my move at the top of the last turn, just where the 220 yards dash started. And in those previous times, I would glance over my right shoulder, we ran counter-clockwise in those days, and never once over my shoulder would I glimpse a competitor, only his breath I would hear, "blowing like a horse!" and I would know ... he was exhausted; the pace was too much for him ... it was the end. No! This time, one slipped past. Then a second. And my arch-rival, Glasgow, was not seen. And when, with characteristic confidence, I looked over my right shoulder, as I had done, all those five long winning years, there was Glasgow, coming at me with a new confidence and greater wind and speed, that I knew this was the end. No one had challenged me like this before in all my years as a middle-distance runner. My athletic career was sinking. The sun was below the roofs of the houses surrounding the grounds. And when it happened on this Friday afternoon at Kensington Oval, in the presence of the girls from Queen's College, the girls from St. Michael's Girls School, the girls from Green Lynch, from the Modern High School, from the Ursuline Convent and the girls from Sin-Winifreds; and the boys from the Lodge School, Combermere School, the Boys Foundation School, the Alleyne School and the Coleridge & Parry School, and my own Harrison College fans, the stands became noisier than when filled with spectators applauding the making of test cricket centuries by Barbadian batsmen ... it all ended at that last corner, when the body is slightly leaning to accommodate turn and speed and endurance and pain; and guts. It all ended there. In the last 220 yards. I could not face the failure of coming second.

"Yuh can't come in second!" Captain George Hunte had said, unnecessarily, minutes before, in the basement of the George Challenor Stand.

"Yuh have to come first, otherwise we can't win the cup!"

I had never come second in the 880 yards, not since that first Saturday morning at Combermere, when athletes were running heats, when I joined in the last heat, the half mile, just for the fun of it, to see how long I could keep up with bigger boys, and couldn't stop running. I liked the excitement so much that I continued running and running; and came third, and never stopped running since then; but I had been prepared, unknown to myself, for this "long-long race and you are still a lil' boy! Jesus Christ, boy! You is a running-fool, a race horse!" I had practised my art of running, attempting to escape from my mother, at the slightest threat of a flogging. And she was a young woman, and vigorous and beautiful, and I am sure the men found her sexy and "looking sweet"; and if I was not careful, meaning if I wasn't "a little more faster than she," she would have crippled me with her fat rod of chastising tamarind, or with an old shoe, or a window stick, a broom handle, a slap, with her opened palm if she caught me, and then collared me.

The ancient windows and the floors of Harrison College, reliable thick floors, made of oak, because in all the books we read about steadiness, strength, long-lasting usage, sturdiness, the strongest things in the world: ships, boats, oars, the doors of fortresses, were all made of oak. There was not one oak tree in Barbados. The walls were made from the limestone cut by prisoners in the broiling hot sun, with an iron drill, almost as tall and almost as heavy as the prisoner himself. For all the time of my life in Barbados, I walked past rock quarries and saw the perspiration like righteous priceless pearls pouring down the black shining face of Mr. Mawn, standing erect in the rock quarry, with the shining iron drill, hitting the earth, metal hitting stone, like a muffled cry of shame, a cry of sorrow, cutting sense and dimension and beauty out of the ugly, white, tough rock. When you met Mr. Mawn on the road from the quarry to his house, you greeted him loudly by his name. And you moved away from his outstretched hand. You would have shaken his hand, once, years before. But the warts and corns and muscles and hard stumps started appearing in his right hand, and they crushed your own soft greeting; and caused wrist-snapping pain for hours afterwards. This kind of rock mined from a quarry in our Neighbourhood of Clapham, helped, years before Mr. Mawn was born, to build the sturdy walls of

Harrison College, in 1733. And the prison. *In Deo Fides,* Harrison College boasted. The Latin scholars of the college never were able to agree on the correct translation. One side said it meant, "Trust in God." The other side argued that the translation is, "There is trust in God." Whatever the nuance you accept, I modelled my philosophy, when I was big enough to know that such things may be called a philosophy, after the first translation: "Trust in God."

～

"Appendicitis!"

I said this to the doctor, in the appropriate tone suggesting alarm, fear, pain, and doubt of being treated successfully by him, Dr. H.G. Massiah, who also was educated at Harrison College. He was an Old Boy.

I was holding my left side.

"Appennicitis?" my mother screamed, holding her own stomach. She was realizing the danger; searching in her mind for that day when she might have fed me the wrong thing to cause the calamity of this disease "Appennicitis?"

She had taken the correct steps; had fed me the correct things. She was relieved. We were in Dr. Massiah's surgery as he consoled her. The cold fingers of his cold hands dug deep into my well-conditioned stomach, on this side and on that side — he alone amongst the three of us, knew which was the correct side to feel for the "appennicitis." And then he got it. On the right side.

I had held my left side. The side near the heart.

"This blasted boy, eh? Trying to fool two big people like we, that he got a blasted 'pendicitis, Mistress! This blasted boy let down the whole school, the whole Island, the entire College, a place built in the year 1733! He let down the college. He is a disgrace. This boy who let down the blasted college, last Friday at the Inter-school Sports, don't have no blasted 'pendicitis, Mistress!"

It was not a time for rejoicing. Not for me. I had already told the newly appointed games master, Mr. Stanton Gittens, that my health was cleared. Stanton had been chosen to accompany a team of Harrison College boys to Trinidad, to compete in cricket, football, and athletics against Queen's

Royal College, QRC, our arch enemies, in Port-of-Spain. I had blamed my appendicitis for my dramatic failure in the 880. "Appendicitis, sir," I had told Mr. Gittens, limping off the track. But now my health was cleared. My appendicitis had suddenly disappeared. Been dissolved.

But I was aware of the weight of disappointment and disapproval that followed the collapsing act that caused so much sadness. The race became legendary. Twenty years later, in 1971, the old boys of Harrison College still talked about how Glasgow beat me in the 880; and then he would talk about having just the two of us re-run the race; and some, like myself, in more critical·attitude, would use my defeat in that race to symbolize the end of my athletic career.

"And he could have gone to the Olympics!"

But it was more than the end of my athletic career. That defeat was like the repeating whirring sound of a tightly wound-up spring you hold in your hand and try to steady, and control, but the spring has its own mind, and reverberates against your will. This whirring followed me for years: after leaving Harrison College in the Sixth Form; after teaching for three years in a government secondary boys' school, The Coleridge & Parry School, in Sin-Peter, in the country; and into Canada, in 1955; and still, the wound-up spring does not unwind; and the pain did not abate its reminding, monotonous whirring of my moral weakness and obvious lack of physical fortitude; and the repetition of thinking about it, that this "weakness" could raise its head of reminder to illustrate that I might never complete any important endeavour, task, wish, prospect, or ambition. That unfinished race marked the end of a career. Forever it dogs my footsteps in whichever journey I undertake in this country. And the mechanism of doubt continues like the unending whirring of a spring.

So, the afternoon that I ventured into that basement room, in Varsity Stadium, at the corner of Devonshire Place and Bloor, and read the "best times" of the University of Toronto athletes in 1955, I suffered the pang of defeat once more, with dramatic immediacy, reliving that 880 yards race, four years before; but even in this melancholy, I was aware that I had beaten most of the times posted on the board. And why, why did

I not sign up for athletics? Was it that there was no one who welcomed me into this basement room? The basement and the feeling I had while I was there that afternoon, was similar, if not identical to that feeling of fear that came over me when Captain George Hunte told me, back in that other basement below the Pavilion in Barbados, "You have to come first, Clarke! The weight of this race is on your two shoulders!" And he said it again, that I had to come first, that I had the weight of stone, and solid beams of oak, and Harrison College itself, *in deo fides*, on my shoulder — or to be more precise, in the muscles of my legs.

Or did I not put my name down, "to run track," because I could taste the veneer of racism in that basement? In these days, in matters other than academics, business, the quarterback in a football team, in activities that demand excellence, it was felt, generally, and kept silent about, in profound immorality of gentlemen's agreements, that one could not really expect too much ... too much intelligence from a Negro, for this intelligence was the bulwark and the characteristic, "as a matter of fact," as a matter of nature, in white people only.

Perhaps, it was racism.

Perhaps, it was the repeating aftermath of that last 880, back in Barbados. For years, I could not watch athletics on television. I would relive my own defeat, and failure and fear and tenseness and nervousness. For years, I could not watch the sprints without experiencing the feeling of emptiness that inhabits the stomach, I almost said the guts ... for it is all guts ... as it had been guts at the beginning of the last 220 yards, when, in all the previous races, no one was within sight, when I glanced over my right shoulder; and to find someone on that Friday afternoon, in my final race, was misinterpreted by me, as defeat.

Years later, in a banter of reminiscence, Glasgow told me, "Man, Tom, if you had taken another stride, just one more, I would have collapsed. Not you!"

Guts. I see it all the time, in athletics especially; but in all sports; and certainly, in my life as a writer, which I had not intended to be, a life that is encircled with uncertainty, with no objective way of measuring my talent, with the pervading attitude of suspicion and the feeling that my contribution, defined as black, might bear an inherent inferiority to other social endeavours, such as being a stockbroker, or an engineer. There is no regard in this country for the dignity and the inherent contribution of the arts to the social fabric of the country. The crudity of modern-day life suggests that any viable contribution to society in which we live, is to be measured in dollars and cents.

Guts. That I know I am the best. That I have been taught by my mother to believe I am the best. And if I have transferred this belief in the sinews of my physical and mental training for the 880, then I ought to think, that running is a thinking man's game — or woman's game! — that there is no surprise if a competitor draws up beside you, when you already know the amount of energy he has lost in order to draw so close. It is your guts against his physical power. Training, and energy, and muscles and massaging of those muscles now rely upon one factor. Guts.

Imagine, over fifty years later, I see the repetition of my own defeat in the tragedy at the finals of the ladies' 100 metres hurdles, at the Athens Olympics, when the Canadian hurdler, acknowledged to be the best in the world, stumbled at the first hurdle. Stumbled. Without being pushed. Stumbled from her own mistake. Or, was it bad luck? It suggested to me more than the physical act of having struck the hurdle at the wrong point. Stumbled? A world-class hurdler? It was the culmination, I think, of the days of pressure — and fear; and questioning of herself — against the declarations in the attention the media was giving to her, even before the race was run. And my advice to her, which I gave to the nearest friend with whom I watched on the days that included her heats, her semi-finals …

… I think she is giving the media too much time; talking to them too much; dissipating her energy, both moral and physical; and being "sucked in" to believing that the race had already been run — and that she had won. The "stumble" was caused by the sudden fear that she might not be the best, the fear of coming second.

CHAPTER SEVEN

Christmas, 1960

Many years later, when the demonstrations and protests, the violence of American sheriffs and police, in urban ghettos and small towns of the South, the delusion of inter-racial peace had settled on the land, including Canada, and "we were moving on up," as the weekly sitcom later said, adding further to the disillusionment that the civil rights movement had erased the hatreds and the disparities that characterized black life and white life. And I had now put aside active participation in civil rights. It was no longer an aspect of my life, because I had found that there was a close linking of my freelance broadcasting work, interviewing all the important leaders participating in the movement, to my writing; and it was not a linking only, but an open association, approaching a conclusion that I held the same thoughts as the men and women I interviewed. I was now being introduced as "Austin Clarke, the friend of Malcolm X." I did become more acquainted with him before his death in 1965, but I would not presume to have been his friend, not at the time I left Toronto by car for New York, where I interviewed him.

So, it was years later that I found out the meaning of the second sentence in the letter from Mr. W.R. Martin, registrar of Canadian Citizenship; and not only its meaning, but the source that contributed to Mr. Martin's conclusion: "The information on which the decision was based is confidential and it would not be in the public interest to reveal it." And even though this "information" was without value to have brought about that decision, it must be remembered that during this time, the American and Canadian agencies that looked into these matters, saying there was national paranoia toward any black person, citizen or immigrant, who raised a voice against the waves of racial discrimination, against the killing of Negro demonstrators, against the burning of churches, and the lynching of black men. And of course, part of this sentiment related to the merciless and senseless beatings of blacks by the police. "Racial profiling" had its origin in these flinty days.

"The information" on which my unsuitability to be a Canadian citizen, came from a letter written by a white Canadian woman, in response to the article I had written for *Maclean's*, which the magazine published under the title, "Canada's Angriest Black Man." I suppose since the article contained no treasonable thoughts, the author of the "information" detested black men who are angry about the treatment they got from white Canadians.

But there are other "crimes" that I committed, which must have given point, in the context of the times, to the 1968 letter of "rejection." And these are, in addition to demonstrating against Garfield Weston's racist comments about South Africa, and the demonstrations and sit-ins in front of the U.S. Consulate General on University Avenue, and marching with Rabbi Feinberg regarding the assassination of Medgar Evers, who had led the Mississippi integrationist movement; marching against the welcome given to Governor Wallace by Mayor Givens. I had been involved in the following anti-Canada activities.

I stood up to a policeman for a Jamaican taxi driver. The taxi had stopped in front of the Bank of Nova Scotia, on Bloor Street, just a few doors west of Frank Stollery's menswear shop. In a "No Standing" zone. The policeman said, "Move along," even before I had got completely out of the taxi. And he continued to harass the taxi driver as I was walking toward the bank. I stopped. I went back to the frightened taxi driver and told him, "If this policeman gives you a ticket, I'll be your witness." And to the policeman, I said, "Where did you want the man to stop, to let me off? At the corner of Bloor and Yonge?"

You did not talk back to a policeman in those days. You might be taken into a dark lane, or down Rosedale Valley Road, in the greater darkness with trees and graveyards, and no street lights, and told a few simple home truths, with a policeman's fist, or billy club.

This policeman got on his walkie-talkie. And called somebody. Backup, most likely. I prepared my body and my mind for the confrontation. There were many confrontations in these days. Some ended mortally. Some ended with arrest. Some ended with broken bones. Some ended with a warning about those things. "I am going to this bank. Where should he drop me off?" He asked for my name. I gave him my name. My address. My telephone number. Just then, out of the blue, my friend, colleague, permanent guest, universally regarded as a man who could smell a party miles away, but to me, an intellectual and bibliophile, Mr. Kenneth Reid, of Dublin, Ireland, was passing. On his way to the Pilot, or to my house. He would pass by the Pilot, or my house, on Christmas Day, on Easter Day, or Good Friday. I went up to him and whispered information into his ear. My stepfather, a policeman back in Barbados, had taught me a few tips of wisdom about protecting myself against policemen who were quick on the draw with a billy club, or their fists, or a gun. He was teaching me how to save myself. I knew that the police knew who I was. Something in his body language spelled it out for me. The policeman walked away, along to Yonge Street. I walked into the bank. And withdrew twenty dollars. My spending money for that Friday, for Saturday, for Sunday, Monday, and for Tuesday ...

It is Christmas, 1960. I have just returned from Kirkland Lake, where I had been a reporter for the *Northern Daily News*. A painter I met there, Fred Schonberger, an immigrant from Holland and his wife, comes down to spend Christmas with us. Fred and I take the chance and sneak out of the busy, turkey- and pork-smelling house, to visit a friend, promising to return before the first cut was to be made into the breast of the turkey. We go to Bedford Road, the street of horrors on which the Department of Immigration is located. The wine that year is Zing. It is a lovely name. A most un-French-like name, exposing you to the oblivious when it is sipped, with ice cubes in a plastic glass, with a Christmas motif on it. And on an empty stomach, you experience the full "zing" of Zing. Well, from one zing to another, Fred and I stumble out of the apartment on Bedford Road, and wind our way to Dupont, looking for a taxi. A taxi stops. We get in. It is not a taxi. We immediately try to get out. But the doors are locked. And then they are unlocked. We get out.

The colour of the cruisers of the Metropolitan police was identical to that of the Metro taxicabs. We had been sure that when we hailed the first car coming through the driving snow toward us — at the corner of Dupont and Bedford Road — that we were hailing a Metro cab.

We stand in the road, looking stupid and appearing drunk. Our two breaths creating small clouds and mists and vapour in the policeman's face. It is cold. It is December the twenty-fifth. It is snowing. Snow in the sixties was still powdery and thick like ice cream. And it came thick. And it rose up to your knees. Sometimes. Not only in snowbanks. It is snowing like this. All of a sudden there are two more police cars. Two men in each.

One of the things my step-father had advised me about policemen was "… never, never, never-ever taunt a policemen. Particular if he is accompanied by a next policeman. One against two, boy. One against two, don't make sense!" And he added, "Particular if it is a dark night. Or if they have you in a one-way alley!"

It was the Zing. It was the cold. It is the fear that the white snowing day had produced two more policemen. They get out of the car and surround us. Two policemen can surround two big strapping men. Particularly if they have been drinking Zing.

"Tell your friend to take his hand off my uniform."

It is a policeman who says this. But I do not know to whom he is referring. Whose hand was touching his uniform? Mine? Or Fred's?

But I remember that I was pleading with the policemen. And as a West Indian, we gesticulate and touch the shoulder, touch the skin of the person we are addressing; and slap him on the back.

"Tell your friend to take his hand off my uniform."

By now, I realize I was the "friend" who has been putting his hand on the policeman's uniform.

They decide to arrest my friend. For drunkenness, "in a public place" — namely the street, Dupont, at the corner of Bedford Road. And they give me a ride to the police station. I think it was west of Bathurst Street, on a back street.

"Leave him here for a couple o' hours, till he sobers up," the station sergeant says to me. "And by the way … happy Christmas! Come back for him in an hour …"

I take a taxi. I rush back to Asquith Avenue. I whisper to my wife to hold the Christmas dinner for an hour. Fred is in a little difficulty. We'll be back soon …

And she suggests I get my friend, Michael Sylvester, a second-year law student at the university, to "defend" me, in case I need defending. I get Mike. In all his imposing, handsome height, walking like a lawyer, talking like a lawyer, acting like one, Lawyer Mike accompanies me back to the police station, to face the station sergeant. Mike stands at his tallest, full lawyer's height, and gives the station sergeant a lecture on *habeas corpus*. On torts. On common law. On the Bill of Rights. On the Canadian Constitution. And he concludes his defense of my friend by telling the station sergeant, "You's a racist. Toronto is racist. Canada is racist, and …"

"Geddouttahere!" the good-natured station sergeant says, not in a loud or in a cruel manner; but in a firm voice. "Before I put you in one o' them cells … and keep your friend till New Years!"

It is all a misunderstanding. A misunderstanding made worse by blurred vision. And the blood-freezing wind. The snow is coming down like a curtain of voile cloth at a window. The wind is blowing the snow like flakes of shaved ice into the face.

On the appointed hour, I take another Metro taxi and go back to the police station, to get my friend, and take him to my home, to Christmas dinner.

"Get-him-outta-here!" the pleasant station sergeant says. "I can't stand more of his damn singing!"

Nobody could have had a merrier Christmas! — to paraphrase Dylan Thomas.

CHAPTER EIGHT

Timmins and Kirkland Lake

December 1959, cold, unemployed, the burden of poverty, made heavier because this is the Christmas season, the holly and the ivy, drinks being bought and assembled, in hiding places from myself; one-by-one; wishing I was back home, reliving the warm blood in the sun in the West Indies; and standing up to the supervisor, who had me moving tons and tons of mail ... so it seemed ... in this gadget which I had never seen, nor driven before, in my life ... "If you don't like it, you can leave!" I think he had a fat cigar between his teeth. His teeth were slightly brown from the strong tobacco smoke. I did not consider Christmas. Six days to come. I did consider my slowly accumulating bottles of liquor, Barbados rum, one bottle of Scotch, one bottle of red wine — with LCBO gouged out in unromantic letters on its white label; none of this had entered my head when I left the main post office. I was at the bottom of Yonge Street. On the first floor; of the first building west of the O'Keefe Centre; and I was facing the long walk up Yonge, turn left at College and walk to Bay; walk farther west on College, looking at the Christmas decorations on stores in the windows of businesses, and drugstores, and the men and women going in and coming out from banks, and banking, with a smile on their faces, pass the hospitals on the left; and the police headquarters; and the university on my right; and the school whose floors and walls and inkstands and blackboards and toilets I had cleaned for weeks, one

Christmas season, and after the first two weeks in the New Year … after the Old Year's bank holiday; and thinking of the Christmas facing me, for no reason that was obvious or that was relevant, into my mind came:

> … I can never remember whether it snowed for six days and
> six night when I was twelve, or whether it snowed for twelve
> days and twelve nights when I was six … all the Christmases
> roll down …

I was admiring the stores and restaurants on College Street, just before I came to the Tuberculosis Centre, where, once a year, you coughed up sputum while a nurse held an enamel cup, or a chipped white enamel pan in the shape of a kidney, and you were asked to spit into the enamel cup, to check that you did not have TB; or that you had not contracted TB since your last visit two terms ago. My head was not registering sense or common sense, and I gave up mentioning to myself the names of the streets I was passing. I continued, just walking, and repeating in my head, what words I might use to swallow up and contain and absorb the anger of the woman waiting. My wife. And what explanation would satisfy her expectations. Even of a meagre Christmas. But a Christmas, nonetheless. She was waiting at home to greet me.

"How it went?" she asks me.

"Fine."

"You like the job?"

"… all right."

"What is it?"

"Well …"

And I told her. And her eyes got larger. And redder. And she said something.

I was not supposed to hear what she said. It was the flash of her eyes she wanted me to observe. And I found myself, like a child, telling her all the things I did not intend to tell her; and she listened with patience, listened as she would listen to her children, knowing that what they were telling her not the whole truth, but were little while lies, while their countenances protested innocence.

"You left the job you had? The only job? And Christmas coming?"

She did not have to say any more. But she did. "Christmas coming … and you left the only job you had, at the post office, and and …and … Christmas is one week away?"

She handed me my coat. And said unnecessarily, "And put your coat on properly. It's cold. What they said the temperature was going to be today?"

"Ten," I told her. "Ten."

"Put your scarf on properly. And keep out the cold. I expect you to find a job before-you-come-back-in-here …"

There is a black man standing at the corner of Bay and Queen Street, across from the Old City Hall, where there are cells, where men and prisoners, and weddings are held; on this cold afternoon, so close to Christmas, this black man standing lost; trying to make head, or tail, but making neither; seeming to have no reason for his standing up here, standing in the midst of people, all white, and staring across the intersection at the tough, solid buildings that have one planted stone slobbered in cement, one stone exactly above the other, in measured calculation; and upon the other, on this cold afternoon, when the chimes of the City Hall clock is confusing him, making him feel, because Christmas is around the corner from here, from this spot. And he has no plans for Christmas.

The chiming of the clock wakes him to his present reality. Here, where the chimes bring him back to the consciousness of time, and to the consciousness of the hour …he has been standing now for fifteen minutes, in the same spot, like a policeman directing traffic from the throne of his box … the chimes which tell him he must move; give the impression he is not a thief checking out the neighbourhood, that he has "business" here, at this intersection of Bay and Queen. But he must move on, before the black-dressed policeman, mournful in his uniform, frightens him, for loitering ...

But he is waiting for the lights to change, although they have changed ten times from the cold moment when he walked from corner to corner, for the first time, making his mind up with the question: "Go up the elevator?" And face the interview? And face the interviewer? And hear how much the elevator-man likes the sand and the surf of the beaches in my small country? And how he likes that dark Mount Gay rum? And the women? And, my god, boy, those women? Why would you want to leave that heaven, that Elysium? And come to this goddamn cold place? ...

"Or go home?" but "home" is not Barbados. I dream of laying-down under the next streetcar that comes. Under a coconut tree on the beach. Having the winds from the Caribbean Sea, and, if I am lucky, catch the wind off the Atlantic Ocean, which brings into port, dead crab, and dead sea-eggs, and dead fish ... and the freshness of new life in the breath of a bottle of astringent Limacol, to daub my face? ... to change my breath. To put a better smile of scent on my face?

I am nervous. I do not remember if I gave the secretary my curriculum vitae. I am not sure that I have cleaned the corners of my eyes. Inside? And out?

"What can I do for you, young man?" And he seems to forget what he has just said, and he calls the name of his secretary. And she comes into the room, and stands dutifully beside his huge mahogany desk. On the left side. Her hips touch the desk. On the desk, on the right side, is a dried coconut shell, cut by a beach sculptor, in the shape, in the artist's imagination, of a calypsonian; and he imagines that the head of the man is singing the calypso, rum and Coca-Cola; and he finds himself carrying the tune, and tapping his foot on the thick, rich, beautiful Persian carpet. There is no sound from the carpet. The vent brings in the cool air. Not cold. He thinks he smells perfume. Or incense. "Thank you," he says to the secretary, "for Mr. Clarke's CV ..."; and he flips each of its four pages, and on his face is no hint, no indication that he is enjoying the music in the room; nor, with the melody he has imagined is in the tune coming from the coconut shell. Rum and Coca-Cola. He wants this to be the song coming through the lips of the coconut shell ...

"So, what can we do for you?"

The room becomes quiet. I go over each detail of the way I am dressed. Earlier this morning. Did I drag the Lipsil over both my two lips? Did I wipe the corners of my two eyes? Did I rub enough underarm deodorant through the thick hair under my two armpits? Is my shirt buttoned up properly? None of my white vest is showing through the buttons, I hope? I hope my voice does not tremble when I have to answer a question he is sure to fire at me. What will I say? What will he ask me? Will he say he likes Barbados? That Barbados has the highest literary quotient in the whole world ... well, if not the whole world, at least the whole Third World ... which it has ...or which is what they say it has ...

He is looking at me. I wish he could take a cigarette from the silver cigarette case on his desk, and let the light from the glass in the window reflect on his face, to give me something to do, something to think of doing, some thing. A gesture. A smile. Anything to melt the military silence in the room. I wonder if the coconut shell sculpture will talk? Or, will sing? Even sing rum and Coca-Cola. Or, even "Beau-ti-ful, beau-ti-ful Barbados ..."

"You're from Barbados, I see. Beautiful place. I know it well ..."

"Yes, sir."

"Have you ever worked on a newspaper?"

"School newspaper, sir."

"Good. That's good enough. Now. Suppose. Suppose you had to cover a fire. How would you write it up?"

I had heard men in the Pilot Tavern talking about the four W's and the H, in the writing of news reports.

But before I could tell him how I would write the report ...objectively, using the four W's and the H ... or was it the four H's and the W? He interrupted me. "Good, good. Good." He buzzed his secretary. "Mr. Clarke will be joining us ... Timmins ... you'll arrange for his train ticket ... one way ... leaving tomorrow ... and temporary accommodation at the Timmins Motel ... near the ONR station. Well, welcome aboard!"

The handshake he offered nearly broke my fingers.

"Welcome aboard! And don't miss your train tomorrow night. Welcome aboard ... you'd better have a chat with my secretary ... and season's greetings! My secretary'll take care of the details ..."

TIMMINS! TIMMINS? TIMMINS! Did I just accept a job as a cub reporter on the *Timmins Daily Press*? In the frozen North? Cold? And free? And if you happened, at this moment of joy and happiness, to be passing the corner of Bay and Queen Street, and was attracted by the loud laughter of a black man, and you were watching him dance ... dancing foolishly ... by himself ... with no recognizable reason and cause of this merriment ... for there is no cause for this jollity you see, you would still have to wonder, "Is this black man ... this Negro ... this man ... has this man been just-released from one of the small holding pens, buried deep in the basement of City Hall?"

There is music in his legs. Christmas can come. There will be rum and presents and gifts ... and he will get to learn how to use the correct Canadian word for things ... with jingle bells for his daughters, and the scarf that his wife, on many window-shopping cold nights had stood with her nose pressed against the cold display window of the Eaton's store, smiling at Santa Klaus, under a shower of snow while listening to Jingle-bells, jingle-bells ... she had stood and had watched how the black, smooth leather — was it felt? — in the display windows of the Simpsons-Sears store had shown her the wrestling of bears, and how she imagined tickling them under their chins, and jumping on the backs of large dogs who carry casks filled with Mount Gay rum, exchanging the heavy, thick red Santa-Klaus robes for her lightweight raincoat, and she, and the children, and him, the four of them singing at the top of their voices, bursting their lungs, singing We Three Kings of Orient Are ... and remembering what Harry of Town Records had told me:

> There's a Black Man in the Ling
> In the ling, in the ling
> Yuh thinkn I mekking funs ...
> There is a black King, a black Wise man on a camel, carrying

myrrh to Bethlehem ...
We three Kings of Orient are
bearing gifts we traverse afar
field and fountain, moor and mountain
following yonder star ...

There are no stars for me to follow; only the telephone wires, and the cables of streetcars overhead, and the grey skies and the breath of the cold afternoon; cold and the grey clouds and the silence of the streets that meet me at Bay, tributaries; and the Old City Hall; and I move my right hand over the one-way train tickets on the Ontario Northland Railway, from this same street where it begins at the train station; and I think of the three wise men, and I substitute the black king and place myself on his camel, riding in a different rhythm, humpety-dumpety-dump; up and down until I become the third king. My hand is still on the smooth ONR train ticket; and I draw towns on it with my fingers, and I see rivers running beside the cold steel of the rails. But I have to remind myself that I am the third king, travelling in jerky majesty on the hump of a camel; with a box that contains myrrh, heading to the new destination in my life. To worship a king who is still an infant, just-born. My finger holds the stub of the train ticket more firmly. I must keep this train ticket forever, for a lifetime, to demonstrate my new success; to wave it, in victory, like a man not accustomed to victory, in her face, not disrespectfully, to let her face the sweet, soft breeze of my success.

My life changes now. I see things I have been taking for granted, things like the wombs and "wemms" of lashes delivered and taken as if they were rewards for indolence, and "bad luck." It must be my ascension to the throne, the throne of magic and imagination and luck, that is in my pocket, my side pocket, "on the left-hand-side, nearest to the heart, boy!"

And the streets that come now to greet me, as if I am a tourist, I pass them as if I am a real tourist, confusing history for beauty, like a man who has been walking with his eyes closed, and when they were opened, through accident or desire, all that he can grasp are outlines, vague, faded objects. But the touch of the hard paper of the train ticket on the ONR train, tomorrow … tomorrow? One day away? The material on which the ticket is printed, with my name on it, and my port of disembarkation, TIMMINS!

Where is Timmins? Where in the far North? Bears, whose skin is the same colour as mine: but more ferocious. And other wild animals that you trap and eat. And those that eat you: more easily; more often.

From this Thomson Building, here in Toronto at the corner of Bay and Queen, I open my right hand in my pocket, and I spread it flat over the ONR train ticket, and I feel the sudden thrust of that movement, the banging steel fitting into the joints of links, a sudden start of my journey up north. Timmins! And I get cold all of a sudden. My clothes feel wet. And thin. I think of mines; and falling into them. I think of bears. Why am I thinking of bears? Because I look like a bear? In size? Or, in attitude? Rrrrrr! Rrrrrr! I think of other wild animals … and I can't remember their names and their ferocity … wild animals which men hunt; and are unlucky and unrequited from sitting all day on a hole, as if they are sitting on the bowl of a toilet, exposed to the snow and the ice and the jaws of bears … and eaten alive … as if the dinner they were spying on through the hole; in the ice; and which I will be invited to help hunt, and catch a fish swimming below the mouth of the hole; and trap and trick the fish into the lens of our guns.

I am thinking of all this snow. Snow. Snow, snow, snow. I am thinking of the first afternoon, in a November when the first pieces of fur fell soft and light into my hair, and I opened my mouth and swallowed them. They had no taste. I thought they would have tasted — the snow-drops, that is — like an ice-cream cone, with its red-and-white sugared cones that sting your taste and make your hands wet and sticky. Snow. Rich, and royal; and thick like new friendships. And I think of losing my way back home, to the house I am renting, at the corner of College and Grace Streets, near Christie Pits, where the neighbourhood boys play baseball; and talk to girls; and I think of rubbing my hand, which is now sweating over the plastic ONR train ticket that will send me, one way, into Timmins. Three days before Christmas. To live in all that snow? To travel all that distance?

I imagine I am still following that star, pointing to Bethlehem, as I undertake this new journey, riding on the hump of a camel, bearing a gift of myrrh, in a box. I do no know what myrrh is. Or what it looks like. But I feel that as a black man in this city of whiteness and snow, the mystery of the origin of myrrh … I joke with myself and call it "mirth"; although I do not know the difference between myrrh and mirth … I turn left, and I face the recognition of the police headquarters, and supervising chief janitor; and the smell of disinfectant, and stale perspiration and the richness of background and illustrations, globes, maps of the world, the English world, painted red, to remind me and the supervising janitor that England "never, never-never-never shall be slave"; and I am passing the imposing building across the street from the main library, at the corner of "Sin George and College" that the sun shall "never, never-never-never set on the British Empire!"; and I clear my throat, just to be certain that there is no hidden rumbling deep into the thorax of my body, no clue to give them cause to test me a second time for TB…. Then there is Sin-George Street, and the Saturday-night "penny-hopping" dances where we danced to calypso old as last winter's snow; and ate badly cooked West Indian food; and we danced to the tinny music of beaten and battered old calypsos, "until morning come," and relished into the old calypsos. "Brown Skin Girl," and "Mr. Twirly and Mr. Twisty Were Two Screws"; and "Beautiful, Beautiful, Barbados," old and reliable as leather shoes, and Harry Belafonte!

So I turn left, to go home; along those alleys and haunts I used to crawl into during my first initiating days and nights in this city of Tronno … westward along College Street, including the whorehouse where I was dropped off. "It's a very nice place," the taxi driver had said. He had driven me from the King Edward Hotel, after the airport bus dropped me off there; and I had felt, for the second time, the excitement and the cool breath of winter air, I stood at the corner of Spadina and College, on the second floor of the sweet-smelling, thick red-carpeted spread of the runner, from my small room, to the room of the woman who slammed her door; and bolted it — I could hear the iron shriek as the key turned — and locked me out of her door, next door. She was unknown to me. I was unknown to her. We were silent. Next door. Adjoined. In our mutual silence.

There was no one to introduce me to her, in her locked adjoining red door. I do not think that I was waiting for her introduction, behind her locked door. And that was how I spent my first night in this country, in this city. In utter silence. And bewilderment.

And I awoke at six the next morning. No life came from the huge building, a men's clothing store, across from my room, across the street, on Spadina and the corner of College. The two-storyed building was shut. And silent. It was the coldest Toronto morning in my life.

And now, on this equally cold afternoon, three days before Christmas, I am to take a train and go to Timmins. Because I have a job. It is my first real job. In this country. I am a cub reporter. For the *Timmins Daily Press*. My salary is thirty-five Canadian dollars a week. I think that is what the man said. He might have said thirty-five. Or even forty dollars a week. But I think he said thirty-five.

No one knows that I have a job. I do not know what to do with myself. No one but that man at Thomson Press and his secretary know that I have a job. I have never had a real job. How does a man who has his first job behave? Visit a friend? Tell your wife? Buy new clothes from Honest Ed's? Or, second-hand clothes from Crippled Civilians? Buy three bottles of beer? But I have no money. That's why I am walking from the corner of Bay and the Old City Hall to get home. My home is the corner of Grace Street where it meets College.

Back home, in Barbados, I taught at a government secondary school: Latin and geography, English language and literature and The Acts of the Apostles, which we called the "Axe o' the 'Postles." And I remember it now, I laugh; but I become more scared that I have a real job; and I become scared, frightened, for I have no one to share my happiness with: I am not happy. Timmins! Timmins? I am scared to tell my wife I have a job in Timmins.

"Where?" She will ask this question when I tell her I have a job.

"Timmins," I will say, in a whisper.

"Timmins! Timmins?" These will be her two explosions at the news of my success. I can hear her shock and disbelief. And when I tell her that I have to leave tomorrow, she asks, "To go where?"

I can hear the tight timbre in her voice as she speaks these three words. I have no answer to her reasonableness. If she was not a

Christian-minded woman, she would, as a Jamaican as she is, she would have something to say about that.

"How are you getting to Timmins? How are we getting to Timmins?

"How are we getting there? What about the child?"

Howard Matthews and Archie Alleyne were roommates in a flat on College Street, just around the corner from Grace Street, where I lived, in a rented house. Around the corner, on College, was the best butcher, they claimed. Howard and Archie were good cooks. They were cooking steaks. And drinking red wine.

"I got a job!" I announced.

"No shit!" Archie said.

"No shit!" Howard said.

It was a Friday. They were preparing to go to the First Floor Club, on Asquith Avenue, which was run by Howard. On Monday nights there were jam sessions, at which all the up-and-coming musicians gathered to practise.

"Where?"

I cannot remember who asked that.

"Timmins …"

"Did you say Timmins? You gonna-be a railroad porter?"

"Shit!"

I think it was Howard who said that. Words flooded my mouth. I was talking. I was telling them where Timmins was; that I would be seeing them every Friday night; that I would drive back to Timmins on Sunday; even by bus, that it would be like I didn't leave Toronto. It was then that Archie took me by the hand and showed me the map of Ontario; and the dot that was Timmins, and he moved his index finger, down, down, down to the other dot that was Tronno … and I saw the long line that the Ontario Northland Railway would take, to take me to Timmins; and …

… when I entered the front door of the rented of the rented house on Grace Street, wobbling from the number of farewell glasses of red wine they had poured me, as my "going away, farewell drink …"

… and now, I have two days left. Before I depart to Timmins. I have postponed the trip for two days. Students are everywhere. The universities and colleges emptied on the cold leather seats on this ONR train. I am the only black passenger. I am the only Barbadian. And then, a porter appears down the aisle, holding a plastic tray, selling drinks and coffee and snacks. He stands alone. Like an inanimate statue. He is not alone. He could be a statue. I am sitting in the window seat. The seat beside mine is empty. It remains empty until we reach Timmins. The black man is selling things: coffee, snacks, sandwiches, and chewing gum; and he remains silent except to say "good evening," and "thank you" when a tip, a quarter or a dime, from the purchase is left with the change.

The porter does not speak to me. Not yet. He is too busy collecting his tips, and burying them, the dimes, the quarters, the lonely one-dollar bill, in his pocket. His pocket is hidden under his apron.

The porter has not acknowledged my presence yet. He is abreast of my row of seats now. "Brother," he says. It is almost a whisper; as if he does not want anybody to know of our relationship. The rumbling of the iron wheels fills the carriage, and then suddenly a voice announces "North Bay!" And seats are rustled, and bags and valises are cluttering, as passengers move to the exits. "North Bay!" a voice announces; and pandemonium reigns. The aisles are filled. New passengers now take up the vacated spaces. Young men and women settle themselves in the seats. I am still sitting, alone, in the seat beside the window. I am looking out into blackness. Blackness spotted by the white, thick snow. I am looking into the thick whiteness of North Bay. The train jerks. The wheels screech. It suddenly becomes silent in the rain. The snow is coming down. I stare into the desolate whiteness of the snow. I cannot see the porter. He is at the far end of the car. The two empty seats beside me are the only two that are not occupied. I look into the thick, white blackness, and try to imagine what life is going on in the silent, thick, falling snow. And then the car becomes silent. The passengers are sleeping … and some are snoring. I am looking into the whiteness of North Bay, going farther north, wondering what Timmins would look like.

The two seats, the middle and the end, are still unoccupied.

And out of the silence that now descends upon the car, comes the porter; and he sits in the aisle seat and says, "Want one, brother? Chewing gum?" And he pours two white gleaming squares into my left hand. They make a soft sound as they drop into my black palm, on my left hand ...

"Going to Timmins?" he asks, as if he knows, as if he has seen my ticket. "The mines?" He asks it as if he knows the answer. "Hold on. Coming back to chat ... to sit with you.... This is a long trip ... to Timmins. I'll be back ... after I clean up a little ..."

The two seats to the left of me are still unoccupied. And the distance and the time and the cold that seeps into the car, through the window on my right hand, are now like another passenger, and in this noise of iron wheels and the snoring, and the rattling of time and distance, and the pure whiteness of the snow which has joined the skies, a man emerges. I had not realized that the train had stopped. There was no whistle. No ringing of a bell. Just the heavy grinding of the brakes; and then the final snort, like a man waking from a deep sleep. And then out of the whiteness, a man emerges.

I can hardly make him out. The colour of his clothes, and the blueish colour of the snow ... I can distinguish no relief of colour in his clothes or the colour of the night. A man emerges in this light. Alone. With a bag in his hand; and then the bag is thrown over his shoulder. I follow the deep imprint of his boots. And I feel the silence. And I go back years and years and miles and miles, to place him, as the first explorer of this vast whiteness, and I think of Dylan Thomas's description of men and loneliness and devotion, and bravery and craziness; and love of adventure: this man of the snows is alone. And he has the thought-fulness, surrounded by a wall of white confidence. This white wall of confidence reminds him to wave. To say not goodbye. But au revoir. He waves at the windows with lights in them. He waves goodbye. His own goodbye to the world. Goodbye to the comfort and love of loneliness.

Would there be a woman, equally cold, at the end of his journey from the grumbling train, there, to meet him and blow warmer breath into his lips? He looked back one more time. And waved. And continued, as Dylan Thomas would say, into the holy darkness.

~

In all this time, my wife never entered my mind. Why was I, on this journey into the unknown coldness of Timmins, not thinking more passionately of her? Was it the fear of facing the unknown of Timmins? I wonder if I was erasing her from my present reality, and was like the man who left the train, and faded into the whiteness of the snow and skies, into a different consciousness? Was he a hunter? Or an explorer? To choose to walk in this white desolation and whiteness and leave a train, the only available transportation, and head into a white night?

I saw him drown in his sheet of pure whiteness; and when he eventually became invisible from the snow that ate up his body, I was listening to the slow, soft voice of the porter, now sitting in the seat beside me.

"Forty years … forty goddamn years I been on this run. Tranno to Timmins … and before that Tranno to Winnipeg. I love Winnipeg. Less racism … and I love them goddamn Indians. My people …"

And the rocking of the train, and the silence in the compartment where we were the only two persons awake, and the snoring of some passengers who would suddenly stop snoring, and then stammer in their sleep, as if someone had kept his fingers over their nostrils and held them there, for a while, to make the sleeping man stammer and cough, to make it seem as if bullets were coming out of his throat. And eventually he joined the other sleeping men and women in a deep unmusical snoring.

"I don't know if you have the same feeling as me … but my gut reaction is that the North is less racist than back-down South … where we live. I mean Tranno …"

I tell him about my job at the *Timmins Daily Press*.

"Where you staying?" he asked me.

He's staying at the Timmins Motel. "Porters are put up there." I am too. We promise to meet and have a few beers for Christmas. We never did.

"I had to look after a little business," he explained, after Christmas. "You know how things is?" I knew how things is.

I had never stayed in a motel before. This one smelled of Christmas; and was close to the railroad tracks. I walked from the train, which was breathing like a sea monster, giving off puffs of steam; coughing like a man with something stuck in his throat. It was easy to seek me out: I was the only black person, in addition to the porter, on the train. Tonight, apart from the railroad porter, I am only the second black man in all of Timmins. The other Negro, the second "permanent Negro" living in Timmins, teaches literature at the high school. I didn't know his name. No one ever thought of introducing us. Or, if we did meet, it was one time, one year, when we walked the same streets of this small town, when I was covering an event for the newspaper. We seemed to have carved out, with mutual precision, the paths and passages we would walk, without the similar desire or accident of crossing each other's path.

A high school student was assigned to greet me, to show me my office, to take me to the *Timmins Daily News*, and "register" me: give me envelopes with advance salary; Christmas bonus; weekly salary, and the most reasonable repayment of the loan of advanced salary. Five … ten dollars a week …

I called my wife, and arranged for her to come to Timmins from New Year's Eve until the day after New Year's Day. Janice slept on the floor, on top of two thick woollen blankets and covered by one. It is the best Christmas I have spent in this country. The very best.

With the arrival of my wife and daughter in Timmins, Mrs. Jeanne Larcher, a pianist of great skill, did everything to make our lives in Timmins a time of great happiness, and education. She used to refer to us, as "the black population of Timmins." She counted us on one hand. We were three and a half. She never explained to me who constituted the half. I have never been a member of such a small minority. But I am sure that Mrs. Larcher decided — to suit the circumstances — who would become the half, and who would be members of the larger group of three.

Mrs. Larcher had a popular programme on the local television station and every Sunday afternoon I was the invited guest at her luncheon. Mashed English potatoes with parsley and condiments, roasted chicken in a rich sauce; and washed down by a lovely white wine. And, of course, after Sunday dinner, we stood around the piano and sang the blues and jazz. Mrs. Larcher was a close friend of Sammy Davis Jr., so we sang his songs, too.

I remained the cub reporter for months. I shivered in the Timmins winter. As the junior reporter, my duty was to get coffee for the staff, all day; and this would continue until they had hired a more junior reporter. This never happened during my stay in Timmins. I had been putting off looking for a flat to rent. The comfort at the motel was so seductive. For weeks and weeks I prayed that vacancies did not exist in the whole of Timmins for a flat or a room. But decentness, as my mother called it, was so redoubtable, that I gave in and started, most seriously, to look for a place to rent. I found a flat with two bedrooms and a kitchen, in a house owned by a miner.

My wife, and Janice, and I lived in this flat. Timmins remained cold. The steep banks in front of the house turned one morning in warmer temperature, into spring. I was shocked to see that the high mounds between narrow passages through which we had been walking, in the middle of the street, were the gradual melting of banks of snow. In all this time, months now, I did not lay my eyes on the other black resident of Timmins' recalcitrant cold. But before the snowbanks melted, our landlord, satisfied that we were good tenants, opened the trap door in the floor of our kitchen, and showed us the flight of stairs that led from our kitchen into his kitchen. On cold-cold Friday nights, we paid the rent in warmth, and with a glass of homemade wine in the warmth of Timmins' redeeming comfort.

And then my wife rebelled. Would I go down the steps of the trap door, and pay the rent, on the next Friday night? The last time she had paid the rent, going down the sturdy trap door steps, it had taken her three hours to return to our quarters. I did as I was told. I learned what her reservation was. Our landlord, and his wife, and my wife, had been sitting round the table, drinking homemade wine. I welcomed the neighbourliness. But I did not last long in this new arrangement. I went through the back door, down the long, narrow passageway, knocked on the front door, and waited for hours, it seemed, until the landlord unlocked the two heavy locks. There were three locks on his front door.

In all these fortnights, I still never rested my two eyes, as my mother would say, on the other black resident of Timmins. Perhaps he had his own trap door, from his flat to the kitchen of his landlord?

And then I was sent to cover my first story. It was a Friday night. It was cold. Schumacher was always cold. The newspaper's photographer had driven me there. And left me there. The club members loved me. When they served me the second beer, I was seeing straight. The meeting of this service club was in Schumacher, a small town outside of Timmins.

When dinner was served: chicken and mashed potatoes and boiled carrots, and of course, another beer, I was in the thick of things. My notes were full. I reported every word the president had said. I took down every word of the disagreements of the members; and I even counted and noted the number of disagreements of the members. It was a brilliant reporting of the details of the meeting. My enthusiasm disregarded the length of the speeches. I wrote down every word, every nuance, every detail of the disagreement. It was a full reporting of the meeting. They even asked me to join the service club: The Lions of Timmins. And I did: I became a member of the service club. I forgot about the other black man in Timmins. There is, now, only one black man in this town: The new member of the Timmins Lions Club.

I think it was the president who drove me back to the newspaper office. I had to polish my language. And I did that. Five pages of the best English prose.

Looking back on that night, on that writing, I know now that I must have been sowing the seeds of the writer of fiction. Afterwards, I walked home from the newspaper office. The cold of Timmins' cold had had no effect upon my literary enthusiasm. I slept soundly that night.

From my chair at the back of the reporter's desks, I could see when the city editor held my copy up to his eyes. The look on his face was of great disturbance. Torment, even.

"Clarke?" He was summonsing me to his desk. And then he said, "Simms?" — meaning the senior reporter. "Simms?" he said, again. "Translate this, please, into journalese." And to me, he said, "Clarke, you spend the rest of the morning reading the *Globe and Mail*, and see how to write a news story ..."

I was transferred to the *Northern Daily News*, another Thomson newspaper in the region, in Kirkland Lake. As a general reporter.

Sadness descended upon me. In the loneliness of the first heavy snowfall in November, Kirkland Lake became a town completely barren of acquaintanceship. I had been the second black man in Timmins. Now, in Kirkland Lake, the only other Negroes were the railroad porters who came to town with the arrival of the ONR trains, and left when the trains went back down South, as everybody called Toronto.

Clothed in this loneliness, my wife and I would buy the weekend *Toronto Telegram* and the *Toronto Star*, and after dinner — no occasion for levity and relaxation with friends, as we had no friends, and we made no friends in the first few weeks — we turned the pages of these two Toronto newspapers and read the entertainment pages. And pretended we were attending the programmes written so enticingly. We read the names of plays, and became two members of their audiences. This was stronger than any mere pretence. We were in the audiences at the O'Keefe Centre; holding our glasses properly at the long stem with the cool white wine in them, in the lobby of the Thomson Hall. We attended, in our live imagination, all these social events: but they were no more real than imagined literary and social contact with the Toronto literary and social whirl. The literary gossip and the crossword puzzles were as exciting and real in our large appetite for "culture" that we imagined we were living in the realism of the small town, and not spending dollars to win the Lotto. We had never, in our lives before these times in Kirkland Lake, bought a Lotto ticket and sunk to our knees, and prayed to win millions of dollars …

So, we went to the exciting pages of the *Star* and the *Telegram*, and imagined that these two newspapers were in our hands; and that we were, through their pages, living real life. So, we lived in these literary and artistic phantasies, as if we were still in Toronto. And of course, when we did live in Toronto, we did not attend plays and literary events. Now, in the Northland, without friends, without even the evasive presence of the invisible third Negro who had lived in Timmins while we were there, I was thrown back upon my own devices to work out a *modus vivendi*, through the help of the weekend pages of the *Toronto Star* and the *Telegram* newspapers.

I had developed the facility of writing fast, without the use of shorthand; and this got me assigned to taking news over the telephone. The reports came from the newspaper's correspondents. You can imagine my shock, therefore, when I recognized the voice talking to me over the extension was that of a Jamaican.

"Rasta man!" he greeted me.

"Rasta man!" I greeted him.

He taught me many things. He told me many more things. His name was DaSilva. He was a member of council for the small town where he was assigned. He taught me how to "string" for the *Globe and Mail,* and the *Star,* and the *Telegram,* instead of spending my time, as other reporters were doing, drinking in the bar of the hotel which was frequented by the other reporters. The father of a Maple Leafs player, Larry, was the chief bartender of the popular hotel in town. My "countryman" showed me how to "rewrite" all the local stories that would interest the Toronto newspapers. I took his advice. Soon, I was making more money from "stringing" for these Toronto papers than most of the other senior reporters on staff.

Working for Thomson newspapers, you were taught to do everything: write advertising copy, take photographs, for every department, including advertising copy for the sale of used cars, cover the police beat, the local school board, and the Kirkland Lake RCMP.

Without noticing it, I was being guided into the realm of writing feature stories, which, in time, covered every conceivable subject. And I took to this like a duck to water. It was like being trained to be a novelist. And I marked my serious desire to be a novelist from this point in my life in Kirkland Lake.

I checked in with the RCMP twice a day. Including Sundays.

I was assigned to write advertising copy and take photographs of a second-hand Jaguar Mark V. The owner, who was also the owner of the largest garage in Kirkland Lake, asked me why I didn't buy the car, at the reasonable price he would offer me? I took his advice. I found my beat extended to include searching for hunters lost in the bush, miners swallowed up, by accident, in the Ramore Mine. And two times a day, driving my new second-hand Jaguar Mark V, I paid my respects to the RCMP.

And then, it happened. A Kirkland Lake woman was reported lost. Or murdered. Her red sports car was found in an Ontario town. Her father, a farmer, had photographs of his daughter. The story, with its new Kirkland Lake twist, loomed big. I visited the RCMP four times a day to get what news I could squeeze from them. I was checking, four times a day, with the Kirkland Lake chief detective. They said that this detective had a photographic memory. He never forgot a face. He had arrested a man from Kirkland Lake for a traffic violation; and that man had fled and then had returned to Kirkland Lake. But when he returned, the detective held him. Without bail. Until he could deal with the matter. And then he had him. The face came back to him. He was now in jail. Charged with the traffic infraction. And suspected of having a hand in the murder of the Kirkland Lake woman.

I had been making my daily visits to the RCMP, who by now had become accustomed to my persistence, the regularity of which peeved them.

"If I was you," the sergeant told me, "I would get in my Jaguar and drive to Timmins …"

I took his hint, as his word. I would drive to Timmins. First, back to my newspaper office, to get a camera, a notebook, all the clippings written on the murder case — which it had become — and drive straight to Timmins. It was now about midnight. When I arrived at the Timmins police station, the suspect, along with three detectives, were returning from showing the police where he had buried the body of the missing woman. The suspect was now charged, through his confession, with murder.

It was in the early morning of Thanksgiving Day. The detective sergeant had not forgotten the murderer's face after all those months. I spent that night, and three more days back and forth from Timmins to Kirkland Lake, writing stories on this case. It was the first time I was covering a murder case, for the *Globe and Mail*, as a "stringer."

It is more than fifty years since I drove up the long driveway of a farm, a few miles from Kirkland Lake, and knocked at the door of the farmhouse, painted in the black of shadows; and mourning; silent, except for the growls of dogs, which frightened me and made me wonder why I would have driven all the way from Timmins to Kirkland Lake, to that remote farm in the countryside of this thick black night. It is 1959. How would a white farmer receive me, a black reporter, at this inhospitable graveyard hour? To ask a question of great indelicacy: "Would you mind telling me about your daughter's disappearance?"

My indelicacy did not arouse his sleepy anger. It was, by now, almost three or four in the morning. He would have fields to plough. Cows to be milked. Breakfast to prepare. And a wife, in the kitchen, to whom he would have to explain my intrusion. And his own heavy grief to have to deal with and to explain to me, and to his wife, after I left. And what was this black man doing at their front door at this hour?

I tried to imagine the two of us in the American South. In this blackness? The South was in the news every day in these days. Montgomery. Texas. Mississippi. Alabama. Harlem. Detroit. It seemed to many of us, black and white, that the country at our Canadian borders was exploding. In our faces. Now, tonight, in a country lane, on a farm, on this dark night, at this graveyard hour, I have woken up a farmer, from his deserved and tortured sleep, to ask him about his dead daughter.

For some time, during these days, I had been assigned to write feature stories on all aspects of life in Kirkland Lake and the surrounding townships. And I must have done a reasonable job, for there was no aspect of life I had not touched in my feature stories.

"Why don't you write a feature story on the life of a library book?"

From the time it enters the library, and to the moment it appears on the library's shelf to be put into circulation.

It was at this time of excitement and fear and as the surrounding realities of danger, violence, hope, and hopelessness that began to point me in the direction of fiction.

But the fiction I had in mind to write was not "fiction." It was reality. Hard, cold reality. And standing alone that late night, knocking at the door of the farmer whose daughter had been murdered, me a black man on this black dangerous night ... he must have wondered if my presence at his front door, foreday morning coming like a photograph out of focus, he must have wondered ... and could have done so ... if this was the new reality he had to live through, for the rest of his life.

I returned to the newspaper office. I developed the photographs I had taken of him. Of his home. And a print of his murdered daughter, where you could see the beauty and the liveliness and the future in her strong blond body. I drove back to the newspaper office in a daze. Of doubt. Of astonishment. Of hope. As a white farmer he must have felt no danger, nor threat, at my arrival at his door, at the breaking of that dawn, that cold Thanksgiving morning ... no idea that his life would have turned out this way.

The *Globe and Mail* liked my stories. They offered me a job, to join their staff, as a cub reporter.

CHAPTER NINE

Looking for "Colour"

Robert "Bob" Turnbull, city editor of the *Globe and Mail,* never liked me. I never liked Bob Turnbull. He sent me to cover a fire at the Royal York Hotel, one night around ten. I walked the short distance from the *Globe and Mail* office, on King Street West, across the street from the Press Club (where I spent most of my time, learning to be a journalist), to the Royal York. I looked "up in the air" as we do back in Barbados: meaning I would look up to the clouds, to see if there was any smoke. I saw nothing. No fire. No smoke. There was no smoke, so there could be no fire. There were no people on the street. Nobody was jumping out of windows. There was no fire brigade truck. At least I did not see one. There was nobody screaming out, "Fire! Oh God, fire!" So I went back to the *Globe* and reported this positive news to Mr. Robert Turnbull. Mr. Turnbull was an amateur fisherman. He used flies. He looked at me, over his tortoiseshell spectacles, and he said, "You couldn't write about the colour?"

This cryptic statement of his worried me for days. What did he really mean, asking me about colour? In these charged days of tension and discomfiture caused by the civil rights problems in the United States of America?

Later that night, I finish my shift and leave the *Globe*, taking the last subway from King Street, and I get off at Bay; and walk along Davenport, past Jesse Ketchum Elementary School; past the fire station at Bellair Street; past Azan's Beauty Salon, owned by a Jamaican man. Azan is the first black man to have studied hairdressing at the Toronto School of Hairdressing. His "saloon," as we called it, served all the black women in Toronto, right up to Hamilton. There was no white hairdresser who would, or could, "fix" black women's hair. Those few who tried, could not do a proper job, as it was done back in the West Indies.

… Past a dry cleaners, and more art galleries on the north side of Davenport; come to Avenue Road; and more cleaners; past the street of horrors on which the Department of Immigration is located, shaking its finger in your face, threateningly; round the corner where three streets intersect; IGA grocery store, which sold the best fruits and lamb chops in Toronto; the LCBO on your right; come right along the west; pass private houses; pass Walmer Road, Lowther, Brunswick, Albany, and then … ahh!… just before Bathurst — where I have to turn left to go home to Vermont Avenue, Number 2 — there is a telephone booth.

It is cold. It was always cold in Toronto. It is late. It is late in those days, when midnight came. Toronto used to go to sleep, with locked doors, closed blinds, music turned off, at ten o'clock. I stop in the telephone booth, on the south side of Dupont, to light my pipe. And I make certain that the pipe will be lit from the two remaining matches I have in the box marked SWAN VESTA SAFETY MATCHES, made by Bryant & May, matchmakers to H.M., the Queen, on which there is a white swan almost as tall as Big Ben and the Houses of Parliament, in the background, in black. I pull the hood of my British Navy light-brown parka over my head, to shield the match from the wind. Out of the corner of my eye I see the police cruiser. I am by now accustomed to the identical colours of taxi and of cruiser. The cruiser drives slowly behind me. Following me. I have seen scenes like this in the murder mysteries on CBC television. The music rises. The tension becomes thick. The man being followed panics. There is usually rain falling. And there is a fog if you are watching this drama in a street in London. In Maida Vale, for instance.

The pipe is lit. On the first strike of the Swan Vesta wooden match. I throw the match into the gutter. The cruiser is still following me. I walk bold into the night. My pipe is blazing. We are still in the Christmas season. I turn the corner, at Bathurst and Dupont, to get home, not exactly "slap-dashingly." I have to walk to the first street, south along Bathurst, to turn right at Vermont Avenue. I pass the hairdresser's. Across the street on Dupont, there is the Beer Store. The Bank of Commerce is at the corner, the southwest corner. I pass the florist shop. And pass the convenience store, Naylor's Convenience Store, in which during the lazy hours of summer afternoons, I would stand with Bill the owner's son, and listen to Cannonball Adderley's "Somethin' Else," so many times, that in two weeks I had memorized all the notes in the solos played by Miles Davis on muted trumpet; by Adderley on alto sax; by the pianist Hank Jones; Sam Jones on bass; and my favourite, because of his attacking style in playing the drums, Art Blakey. This album is so frank, so brutal in its declaration, partially hidden, of its attitude to racial discrimination, so moving, so fast, so beautifully violent in its delineation of the blues, that Art Blakey — known for his fast driving rhythm and pulsing "high hats" — is reduced to keeping time. Keeping time. Keeping time comes into my mind, as the police cruiser is joined by another one. The solo that Cannonball Adderley plays in "Dancing in the Dark," with its sad, plaintiveness of love and pain, and fear, comes into my mind and into my body. The cruiser swerves in front of me. And cuts me off. Now I have to walk on to the sidewalk.

And it is now that I see the second cruiser, out of the corner of my eye. And I stand and wait for the explosion.

"Good night, sir. Where are you off to?"

"I don't have to tell you where I am going."

"Do you live in this neighbourhood?"

"I don't have to tell you where I live."

And then the occupants of the second cruiser come toward me. I immediately remember the advice of my stepfather.

Instead of answering, I take my ID card cockily from my pocket. And I offer it to the policeman. He reads the name of the *Globe and Mail* on it. He sees that I am a reporter. He saw my name. And he sees the embarrassment that had loomed on the horizon of my cockiness.

And I save him further embarrassment.

"Are you looking for somebody like me?"

"Yes, sir. A murderer. He looks about your size …"

The man he is looking for, is Lucas. Lucas Somebody. Notorious as one of the last two men to be hanged in Canada, at the Don Jail in Toronto. Back-to-back with a French-Canadian.

It would be years later that I rented a flat in the same house in which the murder had been committed, silently and skillfully, and clean, by the passing of a knife across the neck of the man who sold the drugs that didn't belong to him, and had thought he could keep the money from the sale, from the bosses back in Detroit. Lucas of Detroit. His face reminded you of Sonny Liston's, the World Heavyweight Boxing Champion.

Days and weeks afterwards, I would spend many hours looking into the mirror in the bathroom, wondering if the policemen saw a real resemblance; or if it was a case that "all o' you look alike!" I hoped that I was more handsome than either Lucas or Liston.

South Africa, for its apartheid policy, was in the news often those days. I was a reporter for the *Globe and Mail*. A demonstration was walking up and down in front of the South African Airways office, somewhere downtown. Richmond, or Wellington. A photographer was assigned to me. Reporters from the *Telegram*; from the *Star*; from the *Globe*; and from smaller newspapers, like *Contrast*, the newspaper that served the black community in Canada; and the *Financial Times*. And I was still on probation. But I was ambitious. And I wanted to impress Mr. Robert Turnbull. So, I walked up and down, alongside the demonstrators, asking them questions, remarkable for their foolishness; questions such as: "Why are you marching?"

"What do you hope to accomplish?"

This assignment was after the fire at the Royal York Hotel.

I was seeking "colour."

Mr. Robert Turnbull liked "colour."

And immediately, all the photographers from the other newspapers, except *Contrast*, started walking beside me, taking my photograph.

"He is a reporter. My reporter. He's a *Globe* reporter," my photographer told them, with some anger. "The man is a *Globe* reporter."

They had never seen a black reporter in their lives, so they mistook me for a black South African. They had "looked-over-me" in the Press Club, and if they had, had not considered that I could be a reporter, drinking Scotch and soda, Scotch and soda, after them. Apparently.

CHAPTER TEN

Harlem, 1963

When we had crossed the border at Fort Erie, that cold Friday night in 1963, searching in the darkness for a bar to celebrate our "entry into Amurca" with a rye and ginger, or a rum and Coke, in vain, for the streets were marked with signs we could not read for direction, since Genessee, Washington; Niagara Falls, New York, were useless street signposts, and the store boasting of duty-free liquors, emblazoned in fiery red neon lights, was on the other side of the border, the Canadian side.

And down the highway we went, arguing amongst ourselves, whether it would be five more hours, whether the sun would be rising when we saw the sign pointing to New York City, whether we'd see the Statue of Liberty, whether we'd have to go right downtown before heading back up to Harlem, which was where they had agreed to drop me off; and, like three happy tourists, willing to lose our way, in our exploration of this huge, entrancing, violent city we had read so much about, and had seen so much about, its dirty underclothes, and its sparkling white drill suits, on the black-and-white televisions back across the border, in Tranno.

"New-York-New-York!" we screamed, as if we were at a football game. "New York!"

"It's so goddamn big, and so goddamn important, and rich, and god-damn powerful, they had to name the motherfucker, twice! Two times! New-York-New-York!"

"If you make it in New York, you can make it anywhere!" I can't remember, apart from Frank Sinatra, who said that.

In the darkness we drove on, feeling like worms, or such animals, pests that burrowed into the ground to screw out a channel, a road beneath the road on which we were travelling in this exciting darkness. Lights from oncoming cars hit us in the face. High beams. Red spots like fireflies became smaller and smaller like cigarettes being extinguished, as faster cars pass us. The radio has picked up an American station.

"Georr-gia!" said the Trinidadian.

The Trinidadian said, "Georr-gia!" again, slamming his hands keeping rhythm into the steering wheel.

"Oh-God-oh-God! Ray, man!" he says.

And we tried to follow the song, and we tried to imitate Ray Charles's voice, and we tried to remember the words, to sing along with him.

"Georrr-gi-ah, Georr-giah!"

Ray Charles's voice carried me back to Georgia, back to Ole Virginny, back to the Island, on a soft pillow of waves, and I was once again, like the worm burrowing a lane through the tenebrous darkness, except for the high beams coming toward us, and becoming like the flickering cigarette stubs of red, in the disappearing distance; and all this I saw in the short interval of following the lyrics of "Georgia on My Mind" just before the night took me in an embrace and buried me in my own dreams. And when I was disturbed by the Trinidadian's voice, "Man, New-York-New-York, man! Wake up! Is New York-New-York, in your ass!"

The dream that had swallowed me in the monotonous humming of the tires and the swishing-pass of cars newer and better oiled than our 1948 Pontiac, showed me poets walking in long fur coats along the streets of Harlem that I had read about in *Ebony* and *Jet* magazines, and in the pages of the local newspaper, the *Amsterdam News*; and women more beautiful than any back in Barbados, or back in Toronto, with their hairdos shining in the same glitter as the black bodies of women shine in the sun when they come back out from the waves, on mornings and in the evenings, before the sun touches the same waves, to say good night. And I saw bars and clubs and places where they played jazz; and the names came back to me from those pages and in Technicolour snapshots of people moving faster, in greater hurry, conducting better and bigger business … James Baldwin and Duke Ellington; Langston Hughes and Count Basie; Charles W. Chesnutt and Errol Garner; Larry Neal and the Modern Jazz Quartet; Leroi Jones (later to be renamed Amiri Baraka), and John Coltrane; Richard Wright and Thelonious Monk; Harold Cruse and Errol Garner; Ralph Ellison and Fats Waller … and they were climbing a ladder whose steps were laden with books and musical instruments, to get into a three-storey apartment building named the Harlem Renaissance; and when I looked up, to count the number of them, they disappeared, and then were seen leaning on the stage of the Apollo Theater, and Ella Fitzgerald and Sarah Vaughan were singing and the place was jumping and I was with all these great men and women, eating Southern-fried chicken. And drinking Southern bourbon and Coke. We walked across the street and faced the Theresa Hotel. And we walked across another intersection, and were at the door of the restaurant-club that sold chicken and waffles. No one was hungry. We were all thirsty. And walking along Seventh Avenue, we saw men reading books about Africa, giving them their names in African languages and various tribes, and we walked up the street … "You wanna go east, or west? Brother? Red Rooster be west, Brother."

It was in a basement. For the three hours we stood jauntily at the bar. I heard the jazz played by Duke, Basie, Monk, Garner, Charles Taylor, Art Blakey, Trane, and Miles. With me at the bar, leaning, standing cool, looking around, a Salem at almost every pair of lips, of men and women; and Cutty Sark and soda at the same pairs of lips … and Charlie Parker, somebody said his proper name was Bird. Bird! A lover of chicken, a lover of the culture of feathered birds, once you have listened to "Ornithology" … "babba-dabba-boop-de-boop …" And suddenly, as if they had been delivered by parachute from the impenetrable clouds, in one drop, like a large soup spoon delivering dumplings into boiling soup, appeared beside me, all smoking, all with stubbed-and-cheap-glass in the left hand, the smoking was carried on in the right hand, covered by diamonds and glitterings that shone like diamonds, were James Baldwin,

Langston Hughes, Charles W. Chesnutt, Larry Neal, Leroi Jones, Richard Wright, Harold Cruse, Ralph Ellison, and John Henrik Clarke. And the man from a different Island from me, from Jamaica, Claude "If I should die, let me nobly die" McKay. Winston Churchill, in one of his most disrespectful acts of quoting from sources, without acknowledgement in order to make his language more effective in gathering allies for the Allies, quoted Claude McKay's poem, and forgot to say from where he got it. But its application, formerly in the specific context of slavery, and racial segregation and the civil rights movement, was now laid at the doorstep of international democratic resistance to the fascist threat of the twentieth century of slavery, of racial segregation, in the context not of civil rights, but of worldwide racial profiling — if you are not white and blond, and Germanic. Churchill, with the worldwide success he gained from this speech, could at least have brought the Jamaican into the picture as having given him grist for his pronouncement. But this is a small digression from the writhing contents of my dream ... and there, at the bar of the jukebox-jumping bar of the Red Rooster, with proper Negro middle and upper class moderation, I am dressed; and in the level of conversation, with cigarette dangling and the smoke blinding him, and his fingers of feminine grace in gesture and length, talking about "the immorality of silence," as James Baldwin began talking, in *The Fire Next Time*, to his nephew, "Dear James, I have begun this letter five times and torn it up five times. I keep seeing your face, which is also the face of your father and my brother. Like him, you are tough, dark, vulnerable, moody — with a very definite tendency to sound truculent because you want no one to think you are soft."

That explained, I think, the mood of the two letters written to me with not-so-glad tidings of great joy, by the registrar of Canadian Citizenship and the supervisor of CBC stagehands ... that I must have appeared and had behaved "truculent" so that crew chiefs and government officers, policemen, newspaper editors, and others, would not think I was soft.

"Jesus Christ!" The Trinidadian was driving more slowly now, in the thick Saturday-morning traffic along streets wider than I had ever seen in

Toronto, buildings higher, more people, more cars, and not knowing the name of the street, or avenue, as I had not looked soon enough when he said, "Look! Oh-Jesus-Christ, look!" … but it was New-York-New-York.

I was pulled from my dream, and Baldwin's face disappeared, and was never to be seen, alive and in the flesh, by me, ever again.

Baldwin has more to say about the citizens of his own country, in that letter written in 1962, on the "one hundredth anniversary of the Emancipation!"

> This innocent country set you down in a ghetto in which, in fact, it intended that you should perish. Let me spell out precisely what I mean by that, for the heart of the matter is here, and the root of my dispute with my country. You were born where you were born and faced the future that you faced because you were black and *for no other reason.* The limits of your ambition were, thus, expected to be set forever. You were born into a society which spelled out with brutal clarity, and in as many ways as possible, that you were a worthless human being. You were not expected to aspire to excellence: you were expected to make peace with mediocrity. Wherever you have turned, James, in your short time on this earth, you have been told where you could go and what you could do (and *how* you could do it) and where you could live and whom you could marry.

We had been following Castro. In the mountains of Sierra Maestra. In the newspapers, the *New York Times* and *Granma*. In the opinions of the Americans. In the more cautious witnessing of neutrality of the Canadians. But in my mind, I was with him in those Sierra Maestra mountains, fighting alongside a black general, General Maceo, whose statue stands large in the most prominent part of Havana, as you drive along the Malecón — I was nervous and excited during those days of "revolution," and I remember the tangos and the boleros I would pick up in the late nights on the Dutch "private set," the short-wave radio, coming in strong, then fading out, and you had to remember the words in Spanish which you could not translate, but the rhythm and the beat was black and was from Africa, years and years before Baldwin's brother's understanding of racial violence in his native America was ever pronounced, in poem and play, fiction and non-fiction. I could taste the bloodshed, on both sides. I could taste the *moros y cristianos* — black beans and rice. Slaves must have eaten this food. The poor, exploited, ill-treated *paisanos* under Baptista must have eaten this food. Fidel Castro ate this food. All black people should eat this food. And why, for the very first time, did I buy a large bag of black beans in the Kensington Market on the 30th of November this year — 2004? Which ghosts, which fleshless skeleton of my ancestor, slave and slave master, was breathing on my face? "Gimme a pound o' white rice. And a pound of black beans." I have never cooked black beans. But I know that they take a lifetime to cook. Most slave food takes a lifetime. Just like the slavery itself. I could taste the movement of women's breasts and legs and "body-lines" as they swept the floor with men, and swept the same floor with their flowing bolero dresses. Sugar cane. Sugar cane. And rum. They were grown in Cuba, and they are grown in Barbados, and they place me in the philosophical and culture maelstrom of General Maceo. I saw him, standing in glory and bronze, haughty as Othello, haughty as Hannibal, haughty as Toussaint L'Ouverture, in his pride and achievement of place, in 2003, in Havana, as I drove along the Malecón. "Ya know he was black!" the Cuban interpreter, a professor of Afro-American literature at the University of Havana, said. She said it in a way that meant she didn't feel she had to say it. Everybody knows Maceo's black. "*Todos. Todos el mundo.*" Yes, Maceo's black.

And yes, the world was following Castro. I started to enjoy cigars. Rabbi Feinberg, after a march, after a hearty meal at The Bagel Restaurant in Toronto, would take me to his friend who "rolled the best cigars outside Cuba!" My beard was ready. I learned the revolutionary catchword in Spanish: *venceremos*, meaning "we will overcome." And a few of us, from the Islands, added that to the greeting: "Be cool, Brother!" that all black people started to use. It was now, "*Venceremos*, brother. *Venceremos.*" The "pig" was not only in stalls and let loose on muddy soiled land in the South and the North, and in Canada: the "pig" was in Cuba; and in Chile, in Guatemala, Nicaragua, all over Latin America. Che Guevara became everybody's model. His posters were stuck in painters' studios, in writers' basements, in the offices of university professors, and sometimes one could be found, undisturbed, and without competing theologies of graffiti, on telephone poles throughout the City of Toronto. We were being "Cubanized": for we had formerly been cannibalized.

About this time, I began a correspondence with Andrew Salkey the poet, novelist, broadcaster, and pro-Cuban ideologue who was still living in London; and he ended each letter, written in a batch of sometimes three a week, with "Peace and Love. *Venceremos*, Andrew."

"Peace and love." I think he got that from Marcus Garvey. From his Jamaican beginnings. Bob Marley and Garvey and Bussa; and Bogle. The Cuban flag was pinned to the walls of witnesses counting the murdered bodies, as they came down like skiers who had lost their way and had succumbed to the suffocating jungle of the Sierra Maestra mountains — on both sides — waiting, as Dylan Thomas said, "for the explosion."

And it came. And Castro was our hero. We claimed him as a West Indian, living through geography and climate, though not through culture and ethnicity, as a Caribbean man. And many of us started to learn the *palabra* of Spanish, "*Sí, señor.*" "*¿Cómo está usted?*" "*Mi nombre es...*" And we gave the Black Power salute in greeting of the new "brothers" from our part of the world. Brotherhood, political and philosophical ideology now closer, symbiotic almost, than was our return, in our minds, in our dashikis, in our "slave bangles." Watusi and the tribes, linguistic and cultural, were too intractable to learn. Spanish was easier. Cuba, "power to the people, *compadre!*" was closer than Africa. It was in our own backyard. And then the extraordinary happened. Castro was made respectable. He was invited to the United Nations, to tell the Americans that their colonialism had failed in Cuba. After thousands of lives dripped in blood. And the suite at the Waldorf Astoria in midtown Manhattan, hundreds of feet up in the air, with the correct number of bathrooms and baths, room service to suit a king, and a television in almost every room, including I am sure the WC (water closet), bathroom, pissery, or banon ... Castro became nostalgic for the soldiers' camp and pillow of a rock covered in a sweat-stained army jacket. He chose the Theresa Hotel, in Harlem. The name has a certain Spanish ring. How many Theresas had Castro himself inducted into his ragtag army of revolutionaries?

The blacks in Harlem shouted for joy, at their victory, much more tangible than it was symbolic or subliminal. Castro had eschewed Manhattan's Fifth Avenue for Harlem, and for Harlem's men and women, revolutionaries in the Biblical army of Jesus, "marching as to war." Castro had most certainly read Baldwin's advice to his young brother, continuing to remind young James, that "you have been told where you could live, and whom you could marry. I know your countrymen do not agree with me about this, and I hear them saying, 'You exaggerate.' They do not know Harlem, and I do. So do you. Take no one's word for anything, including mine — but trust your experience." Castro trusted his own experience. And I followed suit. If Castro could live in the Theresa Hotel up in Harlem, during his visit to the United Nations, who was I not to follow suit?

I booked myself into the Theresa Hotel. Into a single room. With no bathroom. But with permission — "naturally, sir!" — to share a small one, "just down the hall, brother. Just down the hall." My first visit to the bathroom down the hall was short. I had made a mistake in my enthusiasm to be in allegiance with Castro. He must have been given a different room, on a different floor.

I did not have a bath in four days. My ablutions were conducted with surprising dexterity in the face basin, which looked out on to the street, and the street was always full, and I could hear the voices of Harlem's men and women; and see their swagger, and glimpse at their joy and happiness in the midst of the desperation in the country's urban ghettos, much like Harlem itself, engulfed day after day in flames, soaked in the blood of men and women marching "as to war" to sit beside a white man and a white woman, "integrating a lunch counter." Years and years after this second civil war, as Baldwin himself called it, as *Life* magazine called it in raging large print on its front page, years after we trembled at the thought of it happening, and sending the rising waves of blood north, against the natural flow of gravity, I was sitting in the restaurant of a Holiday Inn hotel in Miami, Florida, one afternoon, and I was about to order a dish of fried catfish — catfish is as Southern as lynchings! — when my host, O.R. Dathorne, chairman of African-American Studies at the university, leaned over and said, casually, "Boy, only twenty years ago, we got our ass bust, just to sit in this restaurant, to eat this kiss-me-ass bad food! That is something, eh? Only twenty years ago ... we got ourselves killed to eat bad food!"

I was trying catfish for the first time. I had read about it in Richard Wright's short stories, in some of Baldwin's heart-wrenching fiction, in the stories of Ralph Ellison, and in the blues, and as a boast of national tourism in the South, in the brochures that publicized the more delicate aspects of life in the South. I looked at the waitress, not a particularly young woman, not a particularly beautiful woman, not a particularly seducing woman, not the kind of woman as the wife of the panel truck driver in the South that Emmett Till had ogled at, and had been caught ogling at, and had been put in the husband's panel truck, and driven bound, kidnapped in rope used to tie a pig, out into the thicker bushes, and cut up as if the rope had turned him into a pig, and butchered him, and then lynched him; it was said he was raped, and not with a prick, either, sure as catfish is a Southern delicacy requiring a Southern sensibility. Raped. The catfish came. I can still smell its alluring fragrance. I tried to imagine the kind of man who would venture in the dead of night into Florida's swamps and lakes and seas that looked like lakes, to catch this fish, with a hook the shape of an anchor, thrown against a magnolia tree, to hook a rope on, to hang a nigger. I can still taste the delicate taste of the fish, and the quiet noise of the skin fried in a batter of flour mixed with ground corn, in muffled sensual excitement, similar to the noise that comes from a shattered skull, or a blow delivered with accuracy to the middle of a black man's back. "Only twenty years ago! Ain't that a motherfucker, as the Negroes say?"

But in Harlem, on this first visit, the chicken served in Small's Paradise, with waffles, was a bewildering combination of tastes, a wonder that became a natural marriage of chicken and flour. I think only a black man from Harlem, meaning a black man who was born in the South, could, in these times of torment, have come up with this combination. When I bit into the first piece of Southern-fried chicken, I could hear the voices of darkies in cotton fields, singing to make the labour more bearable, mixing their anger and their fatigue in a chorus that confused the men who enslaved them, into thinking that these were "happy darkies."

I was given permission to borrow a Nagra tape recorder from the CBC New York office. I remember the manager in the Rockefeller Center was

Dorothy McCallum. And I remember that she gave me a lesson on how to operate the Nagra. And I remember not wanting to appear stupid, so I told her I understood the working of this machine, whose fidelity was so good that it was used for the recording of the audio in movies … I told her I understood how to operate the Nagra. The Nagra is the heaviest portable tape recorder ever made! You can imagine, therefore, what it was like, in the hot weather, to walk about Harlem, with a Nagra, and a reasonable supply of twelve-inch audiotape, to match the emergency of a sudden interview with a man on the streets in Harlem.

The streets of Harlem were sleepless. Congested, romantic as in those fairytale days of the Harlem Renaissance, angry, black, and rebellious; with the new culture of nationalism, asking itself, "Who am I? Who am I? Who am I?" — repeated three times for emphasis and seriousness of identity; and sweet with music. Music in the speech which sounded like music played in bars, in night clubs, at the Apollo Theatre, and with a cockiness which even though they did not all stand and look up at Malcolm X, on his soap box outside Mr. Michaux's book store, The House of Proper Propaganda, at least they were injected by his voice and the rebellious, shocking, new thinking of blackness and Islam and discipline. Most of all discipline, and the amazing calling back of black masculinity from homosexuality, Harlem was now a picturebook copy of a street in Nairobi, in teeming Nigeria. Kwame Nkrumah in Ghana. Julius Nyerere in Tanzania. Jomo Kenyatta in Kenya. The colours of Africa, and the colours of Marcus Garvey's "back-to-Africa" bombast; women wearing dresses made in haste, by themselves sometimes, but with an African style, and a crown of black shining hair, the Afro. And men wearing the Afro, too. No one those days dared to suggest that black people were illiterate. And even if they were, even if a sizeable percentage were, they were all being schooled and unschooled bending over boxes of books, turning pages, yes, looking at the photographs of their "ancestors," recognizing these ancestors, through a scar on the face in Harlem, got in a knife fight, in Africa, a tribal scar deliberately got with a knife; and creating other ancestors, based upon nothing more reliable and authoritative than the cosmetic similarity to the flatness of a noise, the bushiness of hair, scars marching across the lower cheeks, at the eyes, teeth at the front with inordinate spaces … does it mean sexual appetite here as it connotes back in Barbados? And just in case ... just in case, you are really from Ghana, or from Nigeria, or from Kenya, you had better change your name; get rid of that motherfucking slave-name, Jack. Free yourself, brother! Power to the motherfucking people, Jack. Castro did it. Harlem can do it. Harlem judged your "relevancy," your "coolness," said you were "together," really hip. And all because of the size of your Afro. "Your 'fro, bro!" The glitter in your necklace made out of polished, cured beans. Any kind of beans, so long as they could be laminated. Lima. Red. White. Beans you did not know existed until you got some taste of brotherhood from Native Americans. And you adopted the "pimp walk" to match your new revolutionary ideology. You were black. You were a Zulu. You were a Kikuyu, all because you had heard of heroic acts performed by these tribes. And you wanted to be associated with, and to be publicly known to be related to these tribes. For ease, at the beginning, you were now X. Later on, as you grew comfortable in this alien identity cribbed from books, you gave yourself at your own re-Christening a real African name. Ali Kamal, Ali Kadir Sudan. The name, the sound of it, the country that bears its name, made you "relevant."

"And because you black, brother, you relevant! Power to the people! Yeah!" You're your clenched fist. Show your slapped palm. Show your beans, and ruffle your dashiki. Walk in your robes as if you are a priest, along the streets of Sweet Harlem, and you don't give a goddamn that the name, Harlem, comes from Haarlem, a place that enslaved those very ancestors you want to climb into the same crib with. Harlem is yours now. You can claim a territory, own it, simply because it has been transformed by your culture. Harlem is black. And the man doesn't mess with you, at this time of black cultural nationalism.

CHAPTER ELEVEN

Looking for Brother James and Brother Malcolm

Let there be no love poems written
until love can exist freely and
cleanly. Let Black People understand
that they are the lovers and the sons
of warriors Are poems & poets &
all the loveliness here in the world

We want a black poem. And a
Black World.
Let the world be a Black Poem
And let all Black People speak This Poem
Silently
or LOUD.
— From "Black Art," by Leroi Jones (Amiri Baraka)

Roi, as he was known in these Harlem days, when he started The Black
Arts Theatre in Harlem, the author of that poem, Leroi Jones, was regal.
A king. A lion. And you should have heard him reciting this poem, in
the musical and artistic vein and disposition that John Coltrane blew in
"Chasin' the Trane."

"Crane blow his ass off, baby! Trane!"

Now, he is Amiri Baraka. The King of Newark, formerly Poet Laureate. Those of us who know Roi, or Baraka, could only smile when he and the Mayor Rudy Giuliani of "clean-the-streets-of-black-mother-fuckers" fame, tried to engage in an intellectual argument with Roi, and naturally lost. But the bigger point was that Giuliani didn't know what "the motherfucker he was talking. It was all power with Giuliani. Power and unachieved privilege."

In these black artistic days, Roi wore the largest Afro, had the coolest African robes, suitable for an Imamu, had the space between his two front teeth, and he became a Sunni Muslim. His close ace-boon friend, Larry Neal, was contented to wear a brimmed felt hat pulled down in the same way as I had seen snapshots of his neighbour, Ralph Ellison, wear his; tweed jackets custom-made, button-down collars of shirts; and a constant smile that betrayed the poetical torment consuming his young body; and the gigantic talent it let out, in too few publications before his untimely death. I never did find out what he died from.

I first read an opinion piece by Allan Lomax, who came upon the scene of black intellectuals like a meteor, and in that same swiftness disappeared — like a comet. But he filled up the television interviewees in his time, more than any other black celebrity. But I was more taken up listening to the best blues played on a jukebox, and of course, Trane and Miles and Bird, and Billy Eckstein, and Sassy Sarah Vaughan, and, because it was proper, the Duke and the Count — neighbours I was made to understand of both Larry Neal and Ralph Ellison, these two giants of Sugar Hill, in the marbled vestibules, the wrought-iron concertina-like gates of the lift... in this part of the black world, you did not say, "elevator." The lift. Iron and marble, and red brick, built into the "brownstones," reminders of an earlier gracious, secure, wealthier past. The past of the Harlem Renaissance. But Harlem was wealthy, not only from an obvious visible and conspicuous materialism, not only famous for the longest Cadillacs and "Bruicks," and clothes fit for an emperor, leading the parade in men's and women's fashions and style, as they do today, but wealthy in the head, and in the mind. What other place, urban or suburban, country, Southern rural from the hicks, could boast of having in its midst at the same time, Marcus Garvey; W.E.B. Du Bois, Malcolm X, Reverend Adam Clayton Powell, Jr., Father Divine, Ralph Ellison, James Baldwin, Leroi Jones, Larry Neal, Ed Bullins, Robert Earl Jones (the father), and James Earl Jones (the son, the actor), and Miles, Coltrane, Monk, Sun Ra, Bird, Ellington, Basie, Errol Garner, Elvin Jones, Paul Chambers, Max Roach, Abbey Lincoln; Paule Marshall, John Henrik Clarke (no relation), and, passing through on his way to France, Richard Wright, Countee Cullen, and Langston Hughes? Arna Bontemps? What other city can boast of this quality of citizen. What about Charles Mingus? Cecil Taylor? Paul Chambers? And what then is the effect of all this "beautiful blackness" in one concentration, in Harlem, upon the mind of a young man from the Island of Barbados, wanting to be an author?

There are no words capable to do literary or narrative justice to the effect this "university of the street" had upon my development.

In this cultural and racial maelstrom, from the Theresa Hotel, I walked across the street to a restaurant, where I would bathe myself in the cuisine of the slave: grits and scrambled eggs, Canadian bacon (Americans showed taste in this regard!), hash browns, and innumerable cups of coffee, which in these days in the sixties, was extremely fine, anticipating the special coffee shops you get in upper-class neighbourhoods; and from the restaurant, I walked to the offices of the *Amsterdam News*. Here I know I would get help in locating James Baldwin, who was, after all the reason for my presence in Harlem. Somebody in the editorial department must know how to find Baldwin. I had already scoured the Red Rooster, day and night.

The man who would provide this information was the most unlikely one on the entire staff. He was probably also, apart from the office cleaner, the lowest-paid on the newspaper's staff. He was the telephone operator. The man whom every person who called in, had to talk to. The man who listened to every call: protest, complaint, congratulation, and, as an extracurricular activity, a bonus on the monotony of saying,

"Good morning, the *Amsterdam News*!," and when it was proper, and appropriate, "Power to the people, Brother!," making a date with a voice he speculated belonged to a body "built by Fisher," a woman who might turn out to be "foxy." Fred.

Fred accompanied me, after his shift ended at five o'clock, first to Small's Paradise, to have Southern-fried-chicken-with-waffles, and, of course, a double shot of Cutty Sark and soda water; then through the barbershops, where the gossip is more reliable than the news in the *New York Times*, where you got another lecture on blackness, where you got your shoes shined, polished so diligently that you could feel the blood coursing through your feet, with your shoes still on, and a haircut if needed, as you relaxed in the womb of black culture, second only to the so-called Negro Church. Here, in this barbershop, one of many along Lenox Avenue (I am 'membering from years past), is the uncle of the Right Honourable Errol Walton Barrow, prime minister of Barbados, from whom I learned everything about Barbadians and other West Indians living in Harlem, many illegally: their hardships, their successes, and their hostility toward American Negroes, as the term went, and their bragging that their "enslavement," which is not the name they gave to their colonization by the English down in the West Indies, was "better" than American slavery. This enmity begun then, perhaps earlier, certainly was crystallized between W.E.B. Du Bois and Marcus Garvey, and extended to a third proponent of black proficiency in occupations such as carpentry, masonry, and small-scale farming, to give the Southern whites a better image of the Negro, that he was not a rival for white jobs, that he was not an insurrectionary like Nat Turner, Booker T. Washington, whose motto, and modus operandi was "Head, Heart, and Hand." Perhaps Marcus Garvey felt that Booker T. Washington was reverting to the declared image of the American Negro, as a "fetcher of water." Head, Heart, and Hand! There is a privately run high school in Barbados that has "Head, Heart, and Hand" as its motto. Nobody knew its origin.

And across the street from Mr. Barrow's barbershop was another Barbadian, a bibliophile, a man who petitioned the mayor of New York, who wrote letters to the *New York Times*, for years, pleading, arguing, threatening, and eventually winning his case to have the officials of New York change the name for its black population, not only in New York, but throughout America, step by step, from "nigger," and from "Nigrah," from "coloured," from "negro" (with a common *n*), to "Negro" (with a capital *n*). And from "black" (with a lowercase *b*), to "Black" (with a capital *B*). From "Afro-American," to "Afro American," without the hyphen. From "black American," to "African American." But the appellation had stopped, satisfactorily at "Afro-American." And then the critics disagreed with the hyphenation, and settled, perhaps after this persistent correspondent died, for "African American." This man was Richard B. Moore, a man who liked the books he sold; and liked them better than the customers he served. He would refuse to sell a book that a customer asked for if he felt it contained a history of African culture, in which he was interested.

Mr. Moore lived in Brooklyn. In his bookstore on Lenox Avenue, there was hardly any room to move about between the shelves. In his home, there was no room, either. Books, books, and more books. And he gave the impression that apart from writing letters to the *New York Times*, he spent his evenings and weekends, reading.

A woman comes into the Frederick Douglass Book Center.

"Mr. Moore, boy, how?"

"How?"

"I looking for a particular book, boy."

"What's the name of this book?"

"I don't know. But it's about Africa. And the origin of names, and I trying to see if I have a' African name. You know how I mean? You know how it is, these days, boy…"

"How you mean, ma'am! I know how you mean."

"You could find this book in your bookstore for me? You think you could put your two hands on it, for me?"

Mr. Moore goes into the back, and I can see him, looking at the shelves that reach the ceiling, and miraculously he finds the book the customer is looking for. I can see him from where I am sitting in the congested store. And he dusts the clouds of particles from the book, front and back. And he puts the book away. And he returns to the customer. The customer is counting her chickens. But the news is sad.

"I sorry to tell you that I don't have such a book. I can find you a book that look similar, though, ma'am. But I will keep looking, ma'am. I will keep looking …"

"You keep looking," she tells him, encouraged. "Keep looking. 'Cause I want to find out if I am a' African. I tired with being called Negro, in the papers!"

And gaily, like a woman giving herself the promise that the lottery ticket she has just bought will bring in the "dookey" to her, she leaves the store, and swings back toward Seventh Avenue with a smile of emancipation on her black face.

"I couldn't sell she this book, man. This book is too important," Mr. Moore says, holding the book to his chest, with both hands.

The book is *Muntu: An Outline of Neo-African Culture*. It is written by Janheinz Jahn. It was published by Grove Press in 1961. It was first published in German in 1958.

I wonder how this woman, who, from the way she looks, if one can make such a generalization, is a simple woman; and whose language, in her short conversation with Mr. Moore, does not exhibit a post-secondary education, has become so intellectually fascinated with Africa and African names? But you know from her appearance, bright-coloured print dress, long to the ankles, with an African pattern, strong black features, as my mother would describe her, a mark like a tribal slash on her left cheek — probably an accident suffered in childhood, more than an initiation into womanhood, back in Africa — and fierce, black, shining hair coiffed into an Afro, and shining beads made of cured lima beans, painted red, black, and green round her promising, luscious neck, showing just that suggestion of sexuality round her breasts, you know this woman will get her way with Mr. Moore, and someday get her own copy of *Muntu*.

"This is philosophy!" Mr. Moore says. "Heavy reading! She couldn't understand what Janheinz Jahn is saying, anyhow."

I hold the book in my hand, and glance at the headings of chapters: SKOKIAN? VOODOO. RUMBA. NTU. NOMMO. KUNTU. HANTU. BLUES. And I read the opening:

"I. QUO VADIS AFRICA?

"Africa is entering world history. There is a flow of books and articles dealing with this process in its political, economic, sociological, and psychological aspects. But all these expositions have in common a single conviction; they are persuaded that one single pattern of cultural change is forming. Through the influence of Europe, it is believed, Africa is adapting herself, giving up her traditions and adopting foreign ideas, methods of work, forms of government and principles of economic organization. The time of transition, whether short or long, is thought to be a time of crisis which will confront all Africans with the decision either to accept modern civilization and survive, or to perish with their own traditions."

Mr. Moore was not a man who used profanities. But if he were, he would have said, "This is some heavy shit, brother!"

But all he said, was, "Coming up on Friday night? I making cou-cou and steam' red snapper."

That was an invitation I would not miss. And, during my stay in New York and Harlem, I would accompany him home, on Fridays, when he closed his store, holding a brown paper parcel, wrapped and sealed with Scotch tape, under one arm, briefcase in the other hand, and under that arm, a copy of the *New York Times* in which his pleas for a proper choice of name, by the *Times*, were printed.

"She wouldn't've been able to follow Janheinz Jahn! You think so?"

"Muntu is some heavy shit!" I say to myself.

I never did invite my new friend, Fred from the *Amsterdam News*, to Mr. Moore's brownstone in Brooklyn. This was family, something to be kept within the clan, or the tribe; something I did not want to share with a black American. But Fred did not mind: because he did not know. He shuttled me round Harlem, showed me which steps to take to get to Father Divine's temple; introduced me to some of the characters on the street, his friends included; and went with me, religiously, to the Red Rooster to wait like a detective, for James Baldwin to show up.

"Still looking for Jimmy, my brother?"

"This brother's from Canada."

"Canada?"

They did not think of Canada as a place that black people lived.

"Did you say Canada? Now, ain't that a bitch!"

"Brother's from Canada. Looking for Jimmy ..."

"Ain't that where there's all that motherfucking snow, Jack? Snow like a bitch, bro!"

"And when you find Jimmy, what you gonna do with Jimmy?"

They all laughed heartily. I could not understand the reasons for their merriment. But I knew something "heavy was going down." I would understand, later on.

"The brother works for the Canadian Broadcasting Company. Don't you see this big, heavy Niagara tape recorder-thing he's carrying?"

"Been wondering what the fuck this thang is!"

"Jimmy's in Greece!"

"Greece?"

"Been gone now ... two-three months! Holidaying with them Greeks! Ain't that a motherfucker!"

"Jimmy's gone!"

"Jimmy's gone."

"When's he coming back?"

"Jimmy may never come back. Giovanni's Room, brother. Jimmy's gone to Giovanni's room. In Greece."

"Thought Giovanni was Eye-talian!"

And Fred stepped in, and made a suggestion. It was said in such an offhand manner, as if he was not serious, as if he was posing the question because he already knew the answer, and the impossibility of bringing off this interview.

"Try to get Malcolm. Get an interview with Malcolm."

"With Malcolm X?"

The man of whom the New York commissioner of police said, with ironic prescience, that "Malcolm X is the most dangerous man in New York," because he was able to surround the precinct that "served" Harlem, with hundreds of Muslims, when the police had arrested a member of their Black Muslim Mosque No. 7; on a trumped-up charge, they said. And then they had to release the man. He was a member of the Fruit of Islam, the men specially chosen and trained to protect Malcolm X, and the Honourable Elijah Muhammad, the leader of the Muslims in America.

I had read many articles about Malcolm X. In the popular American magazines, especially *Time* and *Life*, and I had looked into the pages of *Muhammad Speaks*, the official organ of the Muslims in America. But I was not up to interviewing Malcolm X.

At this time, I was aware of a rivalry, and Malcolm's disgust for Dr. Martin Luther King, Jr., the leader of the biggest Negro organization in America, the NAACP. Malcolm's opinion of Dr. King was simple. King was "a pork-chop-eating nigrah!" This condemnation has great psychological implications as it casts aspersion on Dr. King's preferred dietary habits. The Muslims do not eat pork.

And it was the putting of this suggestion into a frame of possibility that I got a guided tour of Harlem. Fred took me to all the famous spots, including the storefront churches; and I sat in some of them and was "saved," and was pulled through with the power of the music and the singing, the preaching and the testifying. But it was the music that ripped at my heart.

And so, now in Harlem, on Wednesdays, Fridays, and Sundays, I listened to this redeeming gospel, spilling over me from the mouths of the preachers and from the words of the songs, which to me sounded like jazz, like gospel music, like the blues, like the voices of black people, like the "'memberings" of slaves. And in a very real way of its perspiration, its rhythm, its character, and its noise, in its "coolness," Harlem was not only a ghetto of the blacks, it was a plantation inhabited by slaves. Former slaves.

"Why ya don't interview Brother Malcolm, brother?"

The suggestion rang in my head, and it did not receive the boastfulness with which I answered Harry J. Boyle's question, months earlier, about my confidence to do the best interview the CBC would ever have of Baldwin. I was terrified by the suggestion. And even though I had read as much as I could about Malcolm X — who was already challenging Martin Luther King, Jr., for paramountcy among "the black masses," as some magazine labelled these inhabitants of the urban black ghettos — in *Ebony*, in *Life*, in *Newsweek*, in the *New York Times Sunday Magazine*, even in *Muhammad Speaks*, his own magazine, which I later found out he edited, I still did not feel I was up to this confrontation.

Fred took me into every storefront church he could think of, after we had visited the Muslim Restaurant on Lenox Avenue. This restaurant was historically singular. It did not serve anything made from pork. In Harlem? These dietary restrictions in Harlem? A culturally pork-eating society? Hog-maws, pork chops, barbecued ribs, the snout, the ears, the pig tails, the trotters — going to waste?

Who is this new Messiah? This new Deliverer, come to tamper with the fundamental backbone of Harlem's culture? This therefore explained the insult Malcolm X levelled at Dr. Martin Luther King, Jr. His face was always shiny. His face was always well-shaven in its healthy appearance. And this is why — and for other reasons, of course! — Malcolm X referred to Dr. Martin Luther King, Jr., as "that pork-chop-eating nigrah!" At the beginning, at the time I met Malcolm X, there was this clear enmity: an absolute despising of the man, for his celebrity status, perhaps; for his success in leading peaceful marches that turned out brutal for those marching, in the image and philosophy of Mahatma Gandhi. The Negroes, in their thousands, tasted the unwrapped, brutal, nasty violence of their "fellow Americoons," as President Johnson, who, like George Bush the Second, did not understand entirely the pronunciation of certain words. And in fact, if you looked clearly, and without the white-liberal perspective, you could see that white Americans regarded black Americans as coons. Take for instance, the statements of another distinguished white American, the novelist William Faulkner, at this time of civil rights and the peaceful Negro demonstrations for voting rights, particularly in the South. Faulkner lived in Mississippi, and, like most Southern whites, advocated a "go slow" support of these demonstrations, warning white America, meaning the white North, that if this Southern attitude of "go slow" was ignored, there would be riots in the streets; blood would flow.

And, he thought fit to add, "if it came to fighting I'd fight for Mississippi against the United States even if it meant going out into the street and shooting Negroes. After all, I'm not going to shoot Mississippians."

Faulkner was asked if he meant to suggest that Negroes were not also Mississippians, and whether he meant "white Mississippians."

Faulkner could not explain the confusion, and probably compounded it by saying, "No, I said Mississippians — in Mississippi the problem isn't racial."

I had got fed up with the political and racial implications of staying at the Theresa Hotel. The condition of the bathroom that I shared with residents on the same floor — perhaps not the entire floor, but four or five rooms — made me use the small sink in my room as a bath. I was having "sponges," as my mother would say. And I was using quite a lot of my stick of Ban deodorant. And worse, I was always tired. Fred suggested I should get a room at the Harlem YMCA, which operated as a kind of headquarters for some Harlem social agencies. There I met the husband of Paule Marshall, and some other "important" men who worked in the Y. And I came face to face with an aspect of my West Indian culture. The pork chop! I thought of Malcolm's derogatory remark about Martin Luther King, Jr. I thought of the clean menu of the Muslim Restaurant. And I thought of the pumpkin pie they served and how it had become a declared success there. But the pork chop was redeeming.

John Henrik Clarke was one of the "important" men I met at the Harlem Y. John Henrik was the editor of *Freedomways* magazine. I was impressed by the size and content of his library. The amount of books in his apartment rivalled the number in the bookstore owned by my Barbadian countryman, Richard B. Moore, and they rivalled those in the shelves of the House of Common Sense and the Home of Proper Propaganda. And the second thing that impressed me was that John Henrik was married to a young woman. Much younger than himself. I do not know why this impressed me.

Between meals, my new black friends, all of them middle class, and supporters of that time, of the integrationist movement of the NAACP, adherents of the "go slow" philosophy toward desegregation, publicly voiced a passionate dislike of Malcolm X. His history as a pimp in Boston and later in Harlem; his imprisonment as a small-time crook; and his belligerence in proclaiming the suitability of the Nation of Islam as the only saviour of the black man in America, both stunned these men (and their wives) who were the "important" supporters of the image of the Negro, especially in the northern ghettos like Harlem, Newark, and Detroit.

Amongst the "enemies" of the Nation of Islam were celebrities such as the actress Ruby Dee and her husband, the actor Ossie Davis (who, with irony of unbelievable and unspeakable vindictiveness, delivered the panegyric that Malcolm's assassination was identical and tantamount to the loss of "our manhood."); Harry Belafonte, who was a staunch supporter of Martin Luther King, Jr.; Sydney Poitier; in fact, almost all of the well-known actors and musicians were scared off from the Muslims. I thought they knew that they were being watched by the FBI; that they knew their careers could be tarnished, just as in the days when actors and screenwriters were accused of being communists in Senator Joseph McCarthy's investigations. And as contemporaries of Richard Wright and Paul Robeson, they knew what the FBI director could do to their earning ability. The exceptions were Leroi Jones, drummer Max Roach, and his wife, singer Abbey Lincoln. It can be argued, that at least through her interpretation of songs like "Mississippi Goddam," and "Pirate Jenny," and her other civil rights songs, that Nina Simone also, was more pro-Muslim. The conservative attitude of these modern-day Harlem Renaissance men and women underscored the possibility of the violence which they thought was near to the surface of things, and they still did not calculate the result of this violence, although they feared it would harm the relationship between black Americans and white Americans. As a matter of fact, soon after this period of broiling racial animosity, the cover of *Look* magazine bore the banner: "The Next Civil War." Everyone thought that the "fire next time" had already come. Malcolm X and the Nation of Islam were convinced that it was bound to come, that "the fire's" coming, and when it did, it was long overdue. "Chickens coming home to roost" was again applicable, though not desirable.

It was surprising, therefore, to have been aided by these middle-class, middle-aged men at the Harlem Y, in finding Malcolm X. Not that they no longer thought James Baldwin was a less worthwhile person to repre-sent the despairing mood in the black community of Harlem — but, in fact, to represent the mood of all the black communities of America. It was, too, a matter, of being there, being in Harlem, and the pragmatism of exploiting the opportunity. So, Fred and I, carrying the heavy Nagra tape recorder, and the bag of twelve-inch audio tapes on my shoulder, would walk throughout Harlem, stopping occasionally for Southern-fried chicken, chicken-and-waffles, the regular Cutty Sark Scotch and soda at the Red Rooster, meeting strange men and strange women for the first two times, and then greeting them after the fourth time in that week, a regular now, hailing, "What's happening, brother?"

"Ain't nothing happnin'!"

"What's happenin's happnin!"

"Power to the people!"

And, late at night, exhausted by the walking of the perimeter, looking for Malcolm X, worn out by the weight of the Nagra, by the effect of too many Cutty Sarks, and with the Gauloises unfiltered cigarettes cutting a channel in my throat, making me cough like an exploding car stalled in summer, I would fall asleep, late at night, at the table in a restaurant, recovering from the long day of interviewing. And I would nod. And the manager would come over, and growl, "Mafucker, not in here! Git! Not in here!"

Could I claim racial discrimination? We were all black. In a black ghetto. Could I claim ethnic discrimination? I was not talking loudly to Fred. We were both too tired from walking along Fifth Avenue and Lenox Avenue, right down to the Harlem River, tracking down Malcolm X, to engage in conversation. But Fred, a resident of Harlem, knew the manager. So on this third time that I — we — were being thrown out, Fred confronted the manager, who told him why.

"Mafucker's nodding, Jack! Don't want no junkies in here, man!"

So, we knew. And I knew. And after this, I would think of using matchsticks broken into halves, to keep my eyelids open whenever I entered a restaurant in Harlem after midnight.

I had seen countless men, some of them no more than boys, at street corners, standing up, or in abandoned lifts left over from the era of imposing Harlem residences in which black people lived, nodding. And one man standing alone, would carry on conversations with himself. Some carried on intense conversations with invisible listeners. I had seen women, too, in these soliloquies of contemplation, copying the attitude of monks and pilgrims from the East. These men and women were nodding. They were on drugs.

"On the heavy shit!" Fred explained.

This is the irony: the police and those who lived downtown, regarded Harlem as the centre of national sin. And here now, was a Harlem black man running a small restaurant, and proclaiming his disagreement with that attitude that brands all black people as drug addicts, because of colour and residence. This small businessman's attitude was a reflection of the image the Nation of Islam had stamped on Harlem: erasing the graffiti of self-destructive hopelessness scrawled on the tenements and apartments, from the face of Harlem. And it reflected, also, the new moral code that the Muslims were bringing to Harlem. This code was a clean mind, a clean body, a clean image. Harlem was being Muslimized. And, in the process, it was being given a new image. A new black image. Of heroes. And "brothers." And "sisters." Role models. Black men were becoming role models. Black men were redeeming themselves in front of their children, girls and boys. Black men were proud, were black nationalists, or "citizens" not of America, but of Africa, their new homeland.

When the head cleared, when the Scotch and soda was worked out of the system, and the long conversations into the night, that recorded a man's baptism on the road of his personal Tarsus, when morning came, I was introduced to Jimmy Yeargans, a painter, and a friend of the Toronto painter, Gershon Iskowitz, a man who walked with the reality of Auschwitz gouged in blue ink into his arm. Jimmy had two sons attending college, and a Jewish ex-wife living upstairs in a brownstone. Jimmy was installed in the basement, serving as apartment and studio. It was Jimmy who encouraged me to continue to track down Malcolm X. He used his own network to help me visit the Muslim Mosque No. 7 in Harlem. And I visited another New York mosque of which Louis Farrakhan, a former Trinidadian calypsonian, was the minister. At this time, Malcolm and Farrakhan were "brothers."

Malcolm continued to prove elusive. Not that he was hiding from me. He was out of Harlem. As I learned later, after the interview in New York, and later at my home in Toronto, Malcolm was a man who travelled all the time, taking Elijah Muhammad's "message" to the world. Malcolm was running the organization single-handedly.

I was getting tired: physically and emotionally. The Southern-fried chicken, the chicken-and-waffles, the late nights listening to jazz in the Harlem clubs and those downtown, like the Five Spot and Birdland, had already taken its toll on me. I was prepared to forget the interview of Malcolm X. I was going home. Home to Canada. On the new Underground Railroad, the Greyhound bus.

The question asked of me, in my search to find Malcolm X in Harlem, was the same, regardless of who asked.

"Why?"

I tried to explain to all of them: the waitress at the Muslim Restaurant, the man at the *Muhammad Speaks* newspaper office, the women dressed in long white dresses and white scarves, proclaiming a new, controlled, but nonetheless specific sexuality in this outfit meant to promote chastity and, at the same time, reverence of the black female body; and more than that, putting that black female body beyond the reach of the lasciviousness of the "nodding black man on the corner," and, in particular, from the clutches of "the man," meaning the white man who had had his fill of black women in various conditions of rape, of mistress, and of sadism. This new black Muslim woman, asked the same question.

"Why?"

I could have said many things. But I found myself claiming a loyalty to Canada, for the time being; a loyalty that spat in the face of American racial segregation, a loyalty that presented Canada, falsely, a moral superior to their "American cousins."

"We," I would tell them, mentioning multiculturalism in Canada, showing Canada as a symbol, Canada a neighbour, but superior to the United States, "we want to do an impartial interview with Mr. Malcolm X. We want to present him speaking in the narrative of his own words."

This seemed to please the waitress in the restaurant. This seemed to please the newspaper reporter. This seemed to please everyone.

"We'll get back to you."

It felt as if I were applying for a job advertised in a Toronto firm, where all the employers and employees were white. I gave up hope. I decided to spend the remaining time visiting Greenwich Village bars, sitting in the same seat Dylan Thomas kept warm before his historic night, breaking all records for the number of whiskeys drunk on this single seat, in that single night, and reading *The Village Voice*, and pausing to drag my feet in the three-inch-thick husks of peanuts on the floor, making a carpet; and dream of becoming a poet; and checking out Miles

Davis, and John Coltrane, and Count Basie, and Thelonious Monk, and Charles Mingus, and Paul Chambers, and Cannonball Adderley ... and hanging out at the Apollo Theater, back in Harlem.

But I was tired of Harlem. Harlem was too intense in its gestures of offering what it had to offer. The food was too rich. The watching of men and women on the street corner was too intense. It was not a diversion. It had never been a diversion. The soapbox speakers were proclaiming doom. The fire next time came through Baldwin's nostrils like a prehistoric monster breathing fire. Harlem was preparing a twentieth exodus back to Africa. All this feeling was like a too-rich curry, with chicken and basmati rice.

The two Yeargans sons were getting dressed to visit Basin Street, to hear Jimmy Witherspoon. I had never had too much love and appreciation for the blues. But I was keen to accompany them. As we were deciding on the time, the telephone rang.

"It's for you," the older son said. He was smoking. Taking puffs, closing his eyes, coughing a little, taking deep breaths, and when he opened his eyes, they were red. He talked as if he was catching his breath. "It's for you."

I took the telephone. I did not know anyone living in New York. I was not expecting a call from home.

"Are you Mr. Clarke?"

"Yes."

"Hear you're looking for Mr. Malcolm."

"Yes."

"Why?"

I became nationalistic. I became Canadian. I thought I would use the pronoun "we."

"We at the CBC in Canada, want to portray Mr. Malcolm X, impartially; and we will publish everything Mr. Malcolm X says in the interview ..."

"We'll call you tomorrow morning. Nine o'clock," said the man on the telephone.

It was a deep voice. It was a sure voice. It was an intelligent voice.

When I related the conversation to my hosts, there was general excitement in the large brownstone mansion. Even Mrs. Yeargans, whom I had glimpsed once, during the few days I lived in her house, came downstairs, and joined in the merriment.

"Congratulations, Austin!" she said, and went back upstairs.

"Let's have some shit, man!" the elder son said. And he offered what was in his tobacco pouch.

"I'll stick to Cutty Sark," I told him. I took my tobacco pouch from my pocket, and shook it, and got ready to stuff my Peterson of Dublin pipe. The Peterson was the same model that Sherlock Holmes and Harry J. Boyle used. My hosts, all three of them now, father and two sons, were disappointed by my refusal to be "communal," and urged me to "try some, this is some heavy shit, brother. From Latin America!" But I declined. I repeated that I got my kicks from Cutty Sark Scotch and Irish tobacco.

We are ready now. Friday night, out on the town! The eagle is flying, tonight, Jack! And the four of us drive in Jimmy's late-model Porsche with a stick shift, and zoom downtown to Basin Street.

My briar is going like a well-attended fire. And the three brothers in the cars are inhaling deeply and noisily. And saying, "Yeah," when no question requiring an affirmative reply is posed. "Yeah! Yeah, man!" Coltrane is in the tape player, and the automobile is filled with the fragrance of Youth Dew, which we all wear, because we have read it in a magazine that John Coltrane wears Youth Dew, that every great black musician wears Youth Dew. Somebody said, "Yeah, man!" And adds, "Because he's trying to kill the smell of this shit. Grass!"

We are going to check out Jimmy Witherspoon, at Basin Street.

"Ever'thing's Gonna Be Alright!" "I'm a Man!" And we become weakened by the power of his music, and at the same time, enervated, and we realize that he is talking directly to us; and I am in his thrall, but I feel like the little boy, facing Mother Horn at the Calvary Baptist Church, nothing more, nothing less than a storefront, with the question,

"Whose little boy are you?"; and I have no answer, just as that other little boy had no answer.

Jimmy Witherspoon becomes separated from his sweating face. We are in a congregation, musician and audience, clapping, shouting, rejoicing. There is a dismemberment of face from torso. Suddenly, the face is on a vinyl disc. It is revolving at thirty-three and one-third rpm. The shouting continues. The rejoicing. Tambourines are beating against thick, sweaty palms that have a lighter complexion from the back of the same hand, and the palms are tough leather, scarred and calloused; and hardened by manual labour in the winter. And my head is spinning, too.

Punctually at nine o'clock the next morning, the telephone rings. We are already up. Going back over the drama and the humour of the previous night. And the telephone is ringing. It does not interrupt our teasing. And no attempt is being made, by anyone else in the brownstone, to answer it. It seems as if they all know that it is for me. So, I go to the telephone.

"This is Malcolm X."

It is the same voice as last night's caller.

The shock, the punctuality of the call, the sound of the voice, almost cause me to drop the telephone. But it is the punctuality of the call, something I would get to know without falter. It almost causes me to drop the telephone. Although I am expecting the call, when it comes, it still comes as a shock.

I must have somehow impressed the voice of the previous night, that we — Canada and I — are not out to paint him in the demoniacal smear of a man who wants "separation from the rest of America," who hates white people; and calls them "devils." A man who with these precepts, comes to be known as the most powerful black man in America, representing the largest number of followers. And therefore, the most dangerous man in America.

It is the same voice that had called the night before. But this Saturday morning, the voice is indulging in nuance, and in linguistic trickery.

I thank him for calling. And for being punctual. Punctuality is part of the training prescribed by the Nation of Islam for its followers, particularly the Fruit of Islam, the paramilitary wing of the Nation.

"Can you come up to Harlem?" he asks.

I catch the nuance. I catch the stress placed upon "you."

I get my first taste of his ability to taunt, to confound, to humour me; and to be satirical, all in the same breath. I know I am going to be face to face with an intelligent man. A religious man. But a man of the world. And a very busy man.

I immediately remember I am bilingual. So I launch into my Harlem vernacular.

I had been picking up this Harlem speech; imitating it; rehearsing it to myself. I had been learning its comedic characteristic; and its dramatic and racial seriousness. Its pace. And its numerous linguistic meanings.

"I can give you ten minutes, sir," he says.

I would have accepted five!

"Can you meet me at the Muslim Restaurant?" he asks. And he repeats his nuance. "Can you come up to Harlem?"

He places the stress on the word "you."

I am not really bilingual: My Harlem speech he cannot follow. But I assure him, in my best black idiom, with judicious numbers of "Yeah," and "man"; and end with the egotistic saying, conscious of the humour embedded into it, "I'm cool."

He was apparently impressed. He was going downtown to meet with the editorial and photographic staff of *Life* magazine, to discuss the feature article they had done of his Hajj to Mecca. Malcolm had broken with the Muslims by this time. Some prefer to say that he was expelled from the Muslims. He had formed his own organization, more broadly based, and because of his experience in Mecca, he was no longer advocating the separation of the races. White people were no longer "those blue-eyed devils."

I was relieved when he chose to meet me downtown instead. I suggested the CBC studio in the Rockefeller building. I had become anxious about operating the Nagra tape recorder. Suppose I touched the wrong switch and something went wrong?

At the CBC studio, there were technicians, professionals, who could record the interview without a blemish of its levels. Also, they would relieve me of having to carry the heavy Nagra from the subway stop in Harlem to the Muslim Restaurant. But more than this, I knew that if I could get him in a studio, it would be more difficult for him to escape after ten minutes, even though he had promised me only ten. I could be devious and expand it to fifteen ...

"Ten o'clock, then. Monday morning. In the CBC studios in the Rockefeller building."

"Ten minutes, sir," Malcolm reminded me.

I assured him that I had taken his condition seriously.

Apart from his obsession with punctuality, his politeness in the way he addressed me, these were the two virtues of Malcolm X's that remain indelible.

He addressed me as "sir" throughout the interview.

Later, when I got to know him better, and could regard him as a friend, he still continued to address me as "sir."

The CBC studio in Rockefeller building is on a very high floor, above Sixth Avenue. It is a small studio. It is the size of the one used by Peter Gzowski for CBC *Morningside*. Apart from Ms. Dorothy McCallum, there were two technicians, a secretary, a receptionist, and perhaps one or two more persons. Ms. McCallum functioned as manager, and also producer. I reported to her that I would like a very good technician to record a five-minute interview with Malcolm X. At the mention of his name, she fell silent. Regaining a fraction of her former composure, she said, "That would be me. I'll be your technician."

I watched her line up the large reel of audiotape, large enough to hold a five-hour sermon. I watched her test the levels. I watched her place an extra tape on a second giant tape machine. "Just in case," she said. And then she left.

I went to the receptionist and told her that I was expecting Malcolm X, and that ... she had already started to breathe more heavily. She flicked her eyes shut; and then opened them; and then nodded her head … and then she answered the incoming calls.

I went into the studio, and checked that everything was in order, although I did not know what to do, or what to look for, to check that everything was in order. The clock on the wall in the studio where I would be conducting the interview, said five past ten. I walked into the control room where Ms. McCallum would sit, facing me, to give me instructions, in sign language: raise my voice; sit closer to the microphone; and the sign that I had one minute more. Thirty seconds … ten … five … four, three, one … NONE!

One minute in radio time, or one minute in television time, in an interview in a studio, is a very long time, particularly when you have nothing sensible to say, or to ask. But I did not fear this kind of constriction. I knew my opening statement. And I knew my opening question. And I knew what I would say to introduce Malcolm X. I had learned them by heart. My short, curtailed life as an actor, in television drama, when television drama was "live," had served me in good stead.

Seven past ten.

I would begin by asking him what was his reaction to the charge laid by all the American magazines and newspapers, "that you are bent upon forming a separate state within the United States of America?"

Ten past ten.

I had been always impressed, by the declared and reported obsession of the Nation of Islam, with punctuality. I would ask him whether these "states would be located in the South? And what would you do with all the white people living there?"

Twelve minutes past ten.

I was going to ask him if "the children of mixed marriages would be admitted to this black state? And would this black state, a total of six or ten Southern American states, still retain any relations with the rest of America, which presumably would be white?" This argument later proved not to have been so idealistic, when I put this question to him.

William Faulkner said that the problem in Mississippi wasn't racial, and Malcolm X's proposal to establish a separate black state within America, was to him not a racial matter, either.

Quarter past ten.

I telephoned the receptionist. And I asked her if Malcolm X had arrived. No sir, she said, confidently, Mr. Malcolm X had not arrived. But she would keep a keen eye out for him; and buzz me the moment he arrived.

I checked my opening statement to the interview. I must appear fluent, and assured. After all, this is my chance, my first chance, and probably my only chance to impress the executive producer of the Project Series, the famous CBC Sunday night radio programme. This is my first chance to storm the bulwark of what was at the time, an all-white CBC senior level of freelance broadcasters.

At this time, Barbara Frum was doing two- and five-minute fillers for Bill McNeil's midday show; and other small bits with announcer, Allan McFee. Howard Engel was editing small bits. Later he became a producer of one of the three literary programmes. It was a professional honour to have a three- or five-minute interview broadcast on CBC Radio. Many freelancers made a good living from these three- and five-minute interviews. The standard of interviews prepared by freelancers was very high; and the backbone of the CBC's programmes was freelance broadcasters.

Twenty-two past ten.

I went back in my mind to the U.S. immigration officer at the border, at Niagara, and wondered whether it would not have been wiser to return to Toronto, and bury my woes in rum; what was the point of trying the border at Erie, getting through what we called in those days, the Maginot Line, coming all the way down here, to New York, hanging out in Harlem, mixing with the "elders" of Harlem, and reconciling the disappointment of James Baldwin's flight to Greece, and nobody who told me he was in Greece knew that he was really in Greece, and not in Istanbul, which, because of what Istanbul is, is the more likely place Baldwin would have been; and coming this close …

"He's not coming, now," Ms. Dorothy McCallum said. "Try the front desk again, just in case. Perhaps, he got delayed …"

And I walked out to the receptionist, at the front desk, and glanced at the receptionist, who was chatting with another member of the staff.

Sitting to her right was Malcolm X.

Two stern men, in black suits, with bodies that looked as if they had just come from the gym, with heads almost shaven to a skin of their scalps, were his bodyguards, the Fruit of Islam. Sitting between the two of them, was Malcolm X. He looked as if he were waiting for his dentist to call him in for his appointment, as if he knew what was going to happen when he got inside, as if he had confidence in his dentist.

"I am very sorry to have left you sitting here, Mr. Malcolm X, but ..."

When the receptionist realized who was sitting so close to her, her countenance showed the fear in her reaction. But there was a more intense, though understandable, aspect to her fear. She had sat this close beside "this violent man," for about ten minutes, as she would have sat in a subway train, without knowing the danger they said she would be in.

I cannot remember what he said was the reason for his lateness. And I do not think he said that he was late. I think his manner was so compassionate toward the receptionist that he had remained silent about her inefficiency, and permitted me to apologize profusely, saying only, "It is all right, brother. It is all right."

Malcolm X, the two members of the Fruit of Islam, and I, walked into the studio. The receptionist was still visibly shaken. The technician was ready. And said not a word. I do not remember whether Ms. Dorothy McCallum greeted Malcolm X. The two Fruits of Islam, satisfied that Malcolm X was in no danger, retreated back to the reception area, and sat beside the receptionist, who seemed, at the end of the interview, to have regained her composure.

I knew that this would be the centrepiece of her dinner conversation, with husband, boyfriend, lover, or female roommate. "Guess who ...? My God, I could hardly believe my eyes when I found out who was sitting beside me! In the chair beside my desk! Oh my God ..."

What follows is a just a portion of the sixty-three minutes in which Malcolm X spoke with me. At the time of this book's publication, the full audio is available online:

AC: What are the aims of the [Nation of Islam] movement, the practical aims?

MX: The aims of the Honorable Elijah Mohammed, his reason for teaching us the religion of Islam is that it is the only thing that will solve our problems. It will clean us up morally. It will awaken us intellectually, mentally. It will show us how to stand on our own feet economically. It shows us also, it instills within us our independent desire to govern our own affairs, plot our own destiny, control our own future. One of the reasons it is so important for the black people in America to develop this kind of thinking, this kind of concept, you have to understand the religion of Islam. The religion of Islam teaches us to believe in one God, whose proper name is Allah. By believing in one God we believe in all of the prophets because we believe that there being one God, he only had one religion, and therefore every prophet who walked on this Earth had to teach the same religion. So once we accept Allah as God, the oneness of God, that means we also accept the oneness of God's religious message. And we also accept the oneness in the mission and the objectives of all of the prophets, the oneness of their source, the common origin that all of them had.

In accepting this, we also accept the Scriptures that were taught by all of these prophets and all of the prophets always mention that there would come a time when God himself would manifest himself in the flesh on this Earth and bring about the end of all wicked kingdoms and then establish a kingdom of his own that would be based upon freedom, justice, equality, righteousness, peace, love, and brotherhood. This would be heaven on earth.

AC: How close is the white man's kingdom? I mean, how close an association between a wicked kingdom and a situation of white prejudice?

MX: It is impossible to separate wickedness, corruption, slavery, colonialism, exploitation, and oppression from what we would call Europeanism or Westernism or Whiteism. Or, as they say, white supremacy. Only when the white man practises it he doesn't call it white supremacy, nor does he call it slavery. Today, he calls it colonialism. Colonialism was slavery. Colonialism was white supremacy. This was wickedness, this was exploitation, this was oppression, this was corruption, this is what it is predicted God himself would bring an end to at the end of time when he manifests himself in the flesh. When the prophets in the Scriptures refer to the end of time, they didn't mean by the end of time "the end of earth." They only meant the end of a system on this Earth that was wicked, or the end of a world on this Earth that was wicked. And most Negros in America, by having a limited narrow religious concept, when they hear the religious leaders say "the end of the world," they think this is meant to be the end of everything. But the Honorable Elijah Mohammed, our religious teacher, teaches us that God does not intend to bring an end to the earth, but an end to the world. And on this one Earth there are many worlds. The world of socialism, the world of capitalism, the world of communism, the world of colonialism, the world of Buddha-ism, the world of Juda-ism, the world of Islam, the world of Christianity; there are many worlds. When the religious reference is made concerning the end of time, Mr. Mohammed teaches us that this only means the end of time for a certain world, or a certain race, or a certain system.

As a religious people who have accepted the religious teachings of the Honorable Elijah Mohammed, we feel that we are living now in the last days of the white man's world, or at the end of time for the white man's world. Because we feel religiously that his time is up or that his world is approaching its end, its doom, its disaster, or its judgment, we have no desire to accept his belated offers of integration into a corrupt, outdated society that has been sentenced to doom and destruction by the God or lord of all the worlds, whom we refer to as Allah.

AC: If you are not willing to … let me put it this way, if you do not want to accept any of his crumbs or be in a partnership with him now because you think he's on the way out anyhow, are you in effect suggesting some form of apartheid? This has been one of the criticisms I have read of your movement.

MX: Apartheid is misunderstood unless you translate it into English with the proper counterpart. Would you translate the word — I think it's a Germanic word — *apartheid* into English under the word *segregation*? Does apartheid mean segregation?

AC: The existence of the two races independently of one another.

MX: Does apartheid then mean segregation or separation?

AC: Well, the apartheid we know of in South Africa seems to suggest some sort of segregation because the black man is not given all the facilities. In your case if you're going to establish yourself as independently of the white man I'm wondering if this cannot be termed some form of apartheid.

MX: See, apartheid has been used or translated or come to be known in the West now by something very derogatory because it's associated with South Africa. America practices apartheid, too, but she preaches democracy, but she practises the opposite. The reason I ask you for a distinct definition, we are against segregation, but we are for separation. Mr. Mohammed teaches us that the difference between segregation and separation is segregation is that which is forced upon inferiors by superiors. As you hinted. Separation is done voluntarily by two equals. The people of South Africa practise segregation. Apartheid in a segregated sense. We are against that, but we are for separation, which means the voluntary separation by two equals.

I have everything that I need to control my destiny, my future. You have everything that you need to control your destiny, your future. An example here in America: an all-white neighbourhood is never referred to as a segregated neighbourhood. It is only a Negro neighbourhood that is called segregated, because the white neighbourhood is controlled, it is lived in by whites, the economy is controlled by whites, the politics is controlled by whites, the society is controlled by whites. Whereas the Negro community here in America is also controlled by whites. The housing is controlled by whites, the educational system is controlled by whites, the politics of the Negro community is controlled by whites, the economy is controlled by whites, all of the businesses in the Negro neighbourhood are controlled by whites, the banks are controlled by whites, and this means that the Negros, even though they live in their own neighbourhood, are controlled by whites. This is segregation. And this is why a segregated neighbourhood is usually deteriorating, economically, politically, intellectually, and otherwise. But the white neighbourhood is separate, but they control their separateness, they're in command of what they have.

Now we believe, as followers of the Honorable Elijah Mohammed, that the white man should have his own and that the black man should have his own. The black man should control his own and the white man should control his own but we don't believe that the white man should control us politically, economically, religiously, intellectually, educationally, or otherwise. We believe that we should be in complete command of our own.

...

AC: Going back, Mr. Malcolm, to the subject of integration, and efforts to integrate certain institutions, talking specifically about Dr. Martin Luther King. How do you regard his achievements if at all you regard any of his actions as achievements?

MX: Our people in America have made no progress economically, politically, intellectually, or any way shape or form when you take into consideration the progress that America itself has made. This is a country that is supposed to be for freedom then why should black people … if this is a country in which the Supreme Court says that American policy is for integration, the congress says that American policy is for integration, the senate says that American policy is for integration, the president of the United States is supposed to be for integration, his brother, the attorney general, is supposed to be for integration. Now you've got these Negro leaders like Martin Luther King, who have to get down and allow themselves to be beaten and jailed and spit upon and they can't get integration? No, why, we haven't made any more progress in 1963 than our people were making in 1863. The whole thing is a farce; it's trickery. Not to solve the problem of black people in this country, but integration is just another political trick that the American white man uses to make black people think that we're making progress when we haven't made any progress.

AC: Your movement has been subjected to certain criticisms. You've been called a hate group, you've been referred to as violent, seditious Americans and instigating or advocating a black supremacy. Could you answer these charges for us?

MX: Number one, I don't see how anyone could accuse the Honorable Elijah Mohammed of teaching hate. He teaches black people to love each other. He teaches black people to respect each other. He teaches black people to work together in harmony and unity with each other. Now because he doesn't waste his time telling our people to run around here and drool at the mouth over white people, the white man jumps up today and accuses him of teaching hate. How can you teach black people in America to hate after we have spent four hundred years in a country that made us slaves? We have spent four hundred years in a country at the hands of whites who kidnapped us and brought us here and sold us from plantation to plantation like you sell cows and horses and chickens and bags of wheat. We have spent four hundred years in the hands of the white man who has lynched our fathers on trees, which is murder. We have spent four hundred years in the hands of a white man who has actually treated us like a beast, more cruelly than a beast would treat another animal. And in the past one hundred years the same white man has used every form of deceit to keep us from being recognized as human beings. Now, behind that kind of treatment, if black people in America don't hate the white man we would look like we were fools, we would be fools trying to teach our people to hate some-one who had done these things if they didn't hate them already. And if the black man in this country doesn't hate the white man behind what the white man has done to him, sir, I think that you can't teach hate to the black man.

So what Mr. Mohammed does is he teaches us love, but he teaches us to love our own kind and he says we would be fools trying to run around here and love white people before we learn how to love each other or before we learn how to love our own kind. Insofar as there's hate, too, the white man in America has a guilt complex. He knows that he is so guilty, he has blood dripping from his fingers, the blood of black people dripping from his fingers, he has the blood of black people dripping from his lips, from his mouth and he knows that if the black man had done to him what he has done to the black man, he would hate the black man. So it is his own guilt complex that makes him think that someone is teaching hate. Not only does the white man in America think that Negros hate him, he thinks the whole world hates him. Because when a man is guilty he knows that everybody should hate him. So this is Uncle Sam's complex that makes him put out the propaganda and project a religious man like the Honorable Elijah Mohammed as a hate teacher instead of a teacher of love, unity, and harmony among black people. And he accuses Mr. Mohammed of advocating violence, because the Honorable Elijah Mohammed says that the black man in this country should defend himself against the brutalities practised against us by whites. Because the white man is used to exercising brutality against black people without black people defending themselves whenever someone comes along and says we should have the right to defend ourselves, instead of the white man admitting that he is the one that's violent, he accuses the one who is defending himself of advocating violence.

It's like if someone was putting a rope around my innocent neck and I struggle vigorously to keep that man from lynching me, that man has the audacity to accuse *me* of violence and I'm his victim. This is, again, the trickery of the American white man. Every time a black man stands up and tries to defend himself against a brutality practised against black people in this country by white people. The white man puts out the propaganda that we are violent. He never says that these people in Mississippi who are siccing dogs on our people are violent. He doesn't say that the man who coils the lyncher's rope around our necks is violent. He doesn't say that the people who are bombing the Negro churches are violent. But when a Muslim says that it's time now for the black people to defend themselves since the government has proven itself incapable of defending us, it's time for us to defend ourselves, then the government puts out the propaganda that we're advocating violence. So, we're not a hate group, we're not a violent group, we believe in loving our own kind, we believe in defending ourselves. This other thing you asked me about hate and black supremacy was it?

Supremacy means to be over someone. To be supreme. To be over someone. Now, our whole philosophy is separation. We don't even want to be *with* the white man, much less over him. We believe the white man should be with himself, over himself. We believe we should be with ourselves, over ourselves. We believe that white people should be supreme over white people. We believe that black people should be supreme over black people. We believe white people should rule white people.

AC: Where would the children of mixed marriages fit into this?

MX: They're in trouble. If you notice, the white man always rejects children of mixed marriages. When you become of mixed blood you're never white. But you're always considered non-white.

AC: What is the degree of black blood you must have in order to be black?

MX: Well, as far as we're concerned, as long as we can tell that you have black blood, you're one of our brothers. When you get in that borderline where you can't tell what you are, or it's questionable, then it's best for you to get some papers, especially nowadays. Because you're going into an era today where the colour of your skin might save your life.

...

AC: Do you yourself experience any discrimination in New York?

MX: I myself don't experience any discrimination because I don't go where I can be discriminated. I know who I'm dealing with and what I'm up against and I know how to get around it. But you have just as much discrimination and prejudice and segregation in New York City as you do in Mississippi. The only difference between New York City discrimination and Mississippi discrimination, the white men in Mississippi who discriminate you are just like the wolf. He lets you know he's a wolf and he lets you know where he stands. But the white man here in New York City is like a fox. When you see the teeth of the wolf, you know what he means, but when you see the teeth of the fox, he holds his mouth in such a way you think the fox is smiling, you think he's your friend. But the wolf and the fox have the same motivation and if you take either one for a friend you'll end up in the same way …

Malcolm was saying these words as he got up from his chair beside me, because he was one hour late for his interview with *Time* magazine. He said these last few lines as he was going to the door, toward the secretary who had not recognized who he was.

Harry J. Boyle kept his part of the bargain. He had promised that if the interview (of James Baldwin, when the conditions were agreed to, with no handshake, or written guarantee — just word of mouth; trust) was acceptable, he would give me the regular fee; he would pay the usual CBC per diem; he would pay for the hotel for the time I stayed in New York; he would pay for a return ticket on Air Canada. Some of these fees were wired to New York, as an advance, and Ms. Dorothy McCallum was all smiles, because we had carried out some kind of a scoop; the interview was sent on the wire back to Toronto that same day; and snippets of it were used on "CBC Matinee" as teasers, with the full interview to be used on the Project Series, the most prestigious radio programme in the whole CBC. It was broadcast on Sundays. At the hour for dinner: seven o'clock. Its importance as the best commentary on social affairs in the country was so great that housewives and heads of households postponed the serving of dinner and listened to *Project* religiously.

It is not too extravagant to say that my career as a freelance broadcaster was made by this interview of Malcolm X. Harry J. Boyle was a fair man. And to demonstrate his fairness and his sense of justice and fair play, and to throw me deeper into the turbulent waters of competition with the other freelance broadcasters, he chose the toughest and most professional of all the *Project*'s producers to work with me on the interview. Fräulein Dita Vadron.

As time would illustrate, Dita Vadron had me on my knees, literally and physically. A piece of audiotape on which a comma was recorded, a comma which she decided had to be retrieved and used, in order to give the sentence from which it had been cut, by accident, the necessary balance and nuance, that she made me spend many minutes, during the preparation of the programme, on my hands and knees, searching for that comma, in the small cutting room.

My interview with Malcolm X was first copied, then rough cut, and then cut again. Then I wrote a script for it. And then and only then, when the piece was in the shape worthy to be "produced," did Fräulein Dita Vadron grace me with her professional presence, and started the routine, the regimen, the constructing of a programme, choosing music, listening to the tape so many times that I knew the entire interview and the programme into which it was made, by heart. And the searching on the floor, for the "comma," in the rising pile of cut tape covering the cutting room floor like a carpet, continued.

"We have to find that comma, Austin," Dita would say.

There were lots of commas on the cutting room floor. But Dita wanted the correct "comma." I was driven to the brink of tears, as any normal person would have been. I was driven to anger many times. And a smile, from Dita Vadron, and a wink, softened my malevolence. I knew I was being trained by a woman who was the best CBC producer of radio documentaries.

CHAPTER TWELVE

Aftermath

With the advance, a considerable amount of money in those days — and even in these days now, for a freelance radio broadcaster — I bought the things I always wanted to be able to buy. A pair of suede boots. A carton of Gauloises cigarettes. A silver Dunhill lighter. And three pouches each of Erinmore Flake, Condor, and Amphora, in a brown plastic pouch.

I could not hide my sudden good fortune from Fred, the receptionist at the *Amsterdam News*. And indeed, I did not intend to do so. It was Fred who had kept me walking through Harlem for days and nights, finishing the unfinished business of tracking down Malcolm X.

Fred was a part of my fortune. Fred had persisted in keeping me on the trail. He was almost like an agent. He had introduced me to Father Divine's temple, to Mother Africa, and many other Harlem characters. He knew the back alleys. And the entrances at the back of dark, foreboding buildings, where the concertina doors of lifts did not work, and where the floor retained its indestructible marble with patterns from Greek vases and gods and mythology. And it was Fred who opened the doors to my meeting many of Harlem's "leaders" and "role models" and pimps; and visiting celebrities from Europe and Africa, who were written up in the social and arts pages of the *Amsterdam News*.

One such personage of international renown was the Nigerian novelist Chinua Achebe. He is one of the few novelists I have envied, for writing a book that I wanted to have written before him. *Things Fall Apart* was a microcosmic treatment of all the ills in the world at the time. It represented, by its title only, the chaos into which America and its racial segregationist beliefs had thrown the world, certainly the world of liberal-minded, Christian people. And leaving the literary and the philosophical, if not the religious, *Things Fall Apart* grappled at the heart of the concurrent decolonization of African countries from the yoke of British imperialism, and the political, though not the economic, freedom, being talked about in the West Indian Islands. This coincidence with the "Africanization" of black American thought and customs was most ironical. Africa presented the image of strength and ancient culture that black Americans could never have hoped to boast of: just as black America envied the "history" of black West Indians who had come amongst them, legally as immigrants, and as stowaways.

"Wear your national dress!" But we West Indians, we Barbadians, did not have a national dress. Someone, with a Trinidadian sense of humour, suggested, "What about a grass skirt? Or a hot shirt, like in Carnival!"

When I was in second year at Trinity College at the University of Toronto, we West Indians suffered an inferior spirit, a disadvantaged image on those days when the University and the city and the country were celebrating events of national culture and importance. Dominion Day, as Canada Day was called. Formal black-tie dances in college. And the independence anniversaries of African — and even West Indian — countries, when the resplendence and the touch of superiority in the gait and the carriage of the robe, as it is flung over the shoulders, brings back images of other men of power who threw their robes over their shoulders to re-emphasize that power — the Roman senators! — the new African "senators" swaggered across the front campus, across the Trinity quadrangle, as they had swaggered in their rendition of High Life, a dance that brings out as much artistry and cultural richness as it brings out raw sexuality in the vibrating of thighs and hips and hopes.

We would have to import, or have our mothers send for us, through parcel post, a hot shirt, with the face of a tenor pan in a steel band orchestra. But this proved impossible. And we reverted to improvisation. Not improvisation because we had nothing to demonstrate our creativity on. We grabbed. We stole. We abrogated. We appropriated an African garb to go along with our Africanness. Africa became, in Canada, a noble image, a non-despised image different from the times when we hailed for Tarzan in the Hollywood narratives about black men dressed in grass skirts. And for years, for generations, we thought that the grass skirt was, indeed, the national dress of Africans. When this cloud cleared from our consciousness, and we saw the glitter and the embroidery in the robes worn by "real Africans," and noticed how disdainfully they regarded us West Indians, as they tossed their dark-red, gold-trimmed robes worn like togas over their shoulders, we could do nothing but try to imitate them. We began to wear Kente cloth. I am told, years later, that the robes we gloried in, and wore with manufactured dignity, were the raiment of the poorer Africans. The kind of clothes that a labouring man would wear. Communist irony.

Chinua Achebe is seen by me in this context. It was more than an interview that I wanted from him in 1964, more than a programme to be sold to CBC *Anthology*, more than a way of introducing this African novelist who was taking the world by storm, with *Things Fall Apart*, at a time when most of the countries and philosophies in the world were, indeed, falling apart. It was the recognition of a great novelist, a "brother" who had made his name, and who was accepted as a model on whom I could pin my own writing. I was jealous that he had written the novel I had in mind to write, first. Meaning quite simply that there were circulating in my thoughts, clouds of ideas, not defined, not really understood by me, and he had pulled it off first.

In these early days as a CBC freelance radio broadcaster, I functioned as an investigative reporter, tracking down leads as a detective tracks down suspects. I read the three daily newspapers, every day: the *Globe and Mail*, the *Telegram*, and the *Toronto Star*; and I continued this practice in Harlem, with the *Amsterdam News*, the *New York Times*, and the *New York Daily News*. And I supplemented this "research" with reading *Harper's*,

Look, The Atlantic Monthly, and *Ramparts*. I.F. Stone's newsletter came into my hands, through an American friend who worked for the *Financial Post* in Toronto. It is likely also, that through one of these sources, in addition to a word from Fred, that I knew that Chinua Achebe was on a Guggenheim Fellowship for Writing, and would be spending his residency in New York, in a men's residence of Columbia University. Harlem is, geographically, a part of Columbia University, "just around the corner in the next block," Fred said.

Chinua Achebe was not enthusiastic about giving me an interview. He did not know who I was. My first novel, *The Survivors of the Crossing*, had not survived from the critics in Britain, to establish me on his level. But I was persistent and he agreed to a five-minute interview. That was all I needed. To get my foot in the door, so to speak, and once there, I knew I would get the fifteen minutes I needed. And naturally, I had read *Things Fall Apart*.

The room was tiny. The room was hot. There was no air conditioning. New York in the summer, and living in a room the size of a prison cell, comes down in its representation, to a black face in shining pearls of sweat. Chinua Achebe was sitting on the bed. He looked like a black Buddha. He was not smiling. I do not think he even shook my hand. His irritation was obvious. I think he hated me. I think he considered me to be an intrusion. But I was a freelance broadcaster and my "subjects" did not have to like me. So long as his answers were clear, and spoken into the mike, I was satisfied.

He was wearing an ordinary white short-sleeved shirt. I had expected him to be dressed in an African robe. I think that this disappointment was the beginning of my own dislike for him.

The Nagra was heavier that afternoon. I had walked the two blocks from the subway. Now in his room, I sat in a low chair, a kind of easy chair, and with the Nagra on the floor that has no carpet, just the durable, tough floorboards made of oak, I turned the power on and fiddled with a few buttons. I did not engage him in frivolous chatter, as people do when they are fixing something mechanical, such as finding a station on the radio, or a football game on the television, on a weekend, filling up the interval of searching with small talk. I had felt from the beginning that Mr. Chinua Achebe was not a man for small talk. I continued to turn knobs and switches. Achebe continued to sit on the bed. The interval for small talk became tense. Achebe remained like Buddha on the coverlet. I managed to get the twelve-inch tape on. But I could not remember which stitch made the tape turn. And of course, I did not remember how to make the Nagra record. The humidity in the room made me begin to sweat. Chinua Achebe was furious in his silence. Imperturbable. Like a black sculpture made from a block of salt … like a sculpture of black salt.

If only I could get the tape to revolve, to give the impression that something was being recorded, I could then ask him my questions, and hope that since he could not see the face of the tape recorder, then he could not know that nothing was being recorded.

And then it happened. I turned the knob in its vertical position, and the recalcitrant tape moved; and I asked him about symbolism in the novel; about the meaning of "things falling apart"; was he thinking of the whole of Africa; and not only Nigeria; the role of the gods of the ancestors; and did the modern Nigeria suffer from a lack of religious deification of gods? And then it was over. And Chinua Achebe remained sphinx-like. He did not even say goodbye or thank me for the interview.

I returned to the CBC studio in the Rockefeller building on Sixth Avenue, faced with preparing a programme with no word recorded. I decided to prepare the programme from my notes, from my memory of the novel, from my impressions of the author. Reading the biographical notes, I was alarmed to read that "Chinua Achebe is director of outside broadcasts for Radio Nigeria."

I was now angry. Embarassed. Mortified. And hateful of this African. He had known all along that I was fumbling with the Nagra. For, as a broadcaster himself, and the director of "outside broadcasts," he would have been accustomed to using a Nagra. The technicians and machines in colonial Nigeria are not dissimilar to those used in Canada, or in Barbados, at the time. This was in 1964, in New York, in a student's room at Columbia University.

In 1992, I was writer-in-residence at Guelph University, in Canada. The office I was assigned to use was the office of Professor G.D. Killam, an authority on African and Commonwealth Literature. Chinua Achebe was his favourite author. Professor Killam's wife had died suddenly of cancer, and he had retired his position on the staff of the Department of English. And he informed the chairman of the department that I could take any book left behind in his office. I had a field day: I chose the best books for myself, and gave some to my students who showed an interest in African literature and in Commonwealth literature.

It was a Friday. Deep in the winter. Snow covered the quarter mile walk from my office to my lodgings, on the campus; and it was too far to the Faculty Club; and too cold to walk home, to an empty apartment, of two bedrooms, with a fireplace and a maid; so I remained in the office, and looked through the books I had not selected for my use. And then I found that in all this time, more than four months coming to this office, four days a week, my curiosity was not great enough to cause me to open this door. The door of a clothes cupboard.

Inside it, were boxes and large envelopes. On one large parcel was the name Chinua Achebe. Beneath it was the address of Guelph University. A line was drawn through this address. And an address in Nigeria written in. The Canadian postage, stamped in red ink by a machine, was still on the brown box. It had been someone's intention to send the parcel back to Nigeria. But, from the stamp on the parcel, that was more than eight years ago from this cold Friday afternoon, when the decision to "forward" the box to Nigeria was made.

Out of the blue, a man named James King called me to ask me if I knew how he could get in touch with George Lamming, the Barbadian author of the classic *In the Castle of My Skin*. "I am writing a biography on Margaret Laurence," he said, "and I have come across the name of George Lamming, quite often, as a lover of Margaret Laurence, and I want to check it out. I understand he lives in a hotel, in Barbados." I gave this stranger the name of the hotel, in Bathsheba, St. Joseph, where George himself had told me one Sunday afternoon, as we were on our third Mount Gay and soda water, that "if you look straight across this water, straight, you can see Africa!" We were sitting in the easy chairs in Enid Maxwell's Place, which served the best brunch in the whole of Barbados, frequented by Canadian "tourisses."

And the moment I gave the biographer the information he sought, I forgot about him and about George and about Margaret Laurence.

Mordecai Richler hit the airwaves and the literary pages of the *National Post*, the *Globe and Mail* and the *Toronto Star*, to say nothing of *Books in Canada*, and *Quill & Quire*, and all the CBC programmes that contended with literature, for his novel, *Barney's Version*, a very smartly written novel with an autobiographical hint. It had people talking. One of these was Constance Rooke, at the time vice-president of Academics at Guelph University; and it was Connie who subsequently reviewed the book on a CBC radio programme and predicted that it would win the 1997 Giller Prize, which it did.

Barney's Version was being launched in a fancy and well-stocked locale on Spadina Avenue and Richmond Street, on a lovely afternoon, when the heart was full of love and the birds were singing, and Mordecai was fresh from his triumph as writer-in-residence at Massey College.

The biography of Margaret Laurence had just been published, to much chagrin and threats of lawsuits and consternation from members of Margaret Laurence's family. In it, James King had mentioned his visit to Barbados, to Enid Maxwell's Place, where he tried to interview George Lamming, who told him that Margaret Laurence was "crazy." I felt that George, whether or not he had had an affair with Margaret Laurence, had not behaved gentlemanly in that personal opinion of her alleged predilection for love affairs. The biographer said that George denied any relationship at all, in the bluntest of terms. But what caught my eye was James King's suggestion that Margaret Laurence had followed George back to London, and would track him down in his favourite pubs, and even attended a party given by Mordecai Richler, at his London home.

Well, Mordecai, who had convinced the master of Massey College to stock single malt in the small bar in the Junior Fellows' Lounge, who had advised one of the beginning writers in his charge as writer-in-residence that he had absolutely no talent, who had developed a reputation for toughness, just like some of his non-fiction opinion pieces, Mordecai was there to bear witness to the "biographical facts" in James King's biography of Margaret Laurence.

I asked Mordecai if there was any truth in the story that Margaret Laurence attended one of his parties. Mordecai flatly denied that this was so. The other thing of interest in James King's speculation about Margaret Laurence's sexuality, her multi-partnered life, and separation from her husband, was that Margaret Laurence then went after "an African diplomat" stationed in London. James King says that Margaret Laurence confided to "Nadine the wonderful experience she had had in 'a brief but extremely sanity-saving encounter with one of the nicest men I have ever met — he is, (oddly enough) an ambassador for an African country (which shall remain nameless, but it isn't Ghana or Somalia!)'"

Imagine my surprise in 1992 to have fallen upon a file neglected in a drawer in Professor Killam's office, a file containing an exchange of letters between Chinua Achebe and Margaret Laurence! Was Chinua Achebe the "African diplomat" for whom Margaret had "fled behind" leaving her husband in Vancouver?

I am not suggesting, of course, that this is the case; that this is fact. I am merely giving the second dimension to this narrative.

From my reading of these letters, Margaret Laurence is the more doting of the two: there is more affection in her words than in his; and there is, in both, a guardedness, as if they were both speaking, through an interpreter, of their hearts.

And now for the third dimension of this story. In 2002, George Lamming was in Toronto to give the Dr. Cheddi Jagan Annual Lecture, at York University. George and I went up in an elevator with Professor Frank Birbalsingh, and I took this opportunity to ask George if he had seen James King's biography on Margaret Laurence, and how did he get along with the biographer who visited him at Enid Maxwell's place in Bathsheba. No, he hadn't, George said, scornfully. He was adamant.

He was so disgusted by the biographer asking him questions about Margaret Laurence that he "cut the interview off, got up from the table, and left!" James King did not have an interview that would have resulted in the statement George made in the book. James King's version of this aborted interview can be found on pages 418 and 419 of his book,

The Life of Margaret Laurence: ML's affair with George Lamming:

> When I met with George Lamming in Barbados in June
> 1996, he told me he had met ML at a party given by Binky
> Marks, the proprietor of The Co-Op Bookstore on Pender
> Street, in Vancouver; he thought they had perhaps seen one
> another one further time. Their conversations had been
> political in nature, centring on their mutual interest in Ghana,
> which he had visited. He did not recall that their relationship
> had ever become intimate, but when I asked him to deny
> statements by ML to the contrary, he refused to do so on
> the grounds that it was not his 'style' to comment on such
> matters. I pressed him on this point several times, since, I
> pointed out, it should be relatively easy — despite his "style"
> — to state something that had not occurred, had indeed
> not occurred. He refused to make any further statement.
> ML alleged to many women friends that she had slept with
> Lamming; shortly before she died, she mentioned her affair
> with Lamming to her daughter and named him as her lover.

What are we to make of this? Observe the moral: never sleep with a woman who is a writer. But there is a more distressing conclusion that can be made: why was Margaret Laurence so obsessed with placing Lamming in this light? And how great was the arrogance of James King to give more literary — is this literary? — significance to the mundane act of a man going to bed with a woman, inflating the act precisely because the man and the woman were writers of some reputation? Does it make the woman a better — or a worse — writer? Does the voodoo of the kind of "sex" Lamming is said to have indulged in with Margaret Laurence tantalize her mind, and her biographer's, to put such stress on a liaison that no one else seemed to have thought twice about?

The most important aspect of the episode of Margaret Laurence and George Lamming wrapped in a love affair that he denied ever having had, is its profound inability to stir us to interest and sexual arousal.

Chinua Achebe was being driven from his home in Lagos, Nigeria, by his son, on his way to a speaking engagement in America, when the car crashed, leaving Chinua Achebe in a wheelchair. The news hit me like a sledgehammer. And ever since that sad afternoon, when the accident was related to me by my friend Jan Carew, who had met Chinua Achebe in Nigeria, I have lived with the horribleness of my enmity, unrequited through the voicelessness of distance; and now it is too late to ask for forgiveness, and for redemption. I am in that wheelchair with Chinua Achebe.

～

And then there was Martin Luther King, Jr. He chose to spend the fifteen minutes I had asked his assistants for, had implored them for, and they had promised me that Dr. King would give me the five minutes, that he won't be a minute. Dr. King spent the fifteen minutes promised to me in conversation with the female staff. One of them was the young woman who had almost had a nervous breakdown when she realized that the man in the dark blue suit sitting beside her, that morning, was none other than Malcolm X.

But Dr. King was smooth. He left without mentioning my request. I thought of Malcolm X's words, "pork-chop-eating nigrah!" It was an awful thing to do. But I would have scored unchallengeable points by returning to Toronto, in quick succession, after the interview of Malcolm X, with one with Dr. Martin Luther King, Jr.! I would become what a columnist of the *Toronto Star*, Leonard Braithwaite, called, "an untouchable of Toronto." I never did understand what Mr. Braithwaite meant by that; whether it meant that no one could touch me, or no one wanted to touch me.

My pleading with the Reverend Jesse Jackson and Whitney Young fell on deaf ears. Neither was able to turn Dr. King's attention to my request.

Dr. King was in the CBC New York studio to revise his recorded version of the 1965 annual Massey Lectures. It was over a year after my interview with Malcolm X, in the same studio.

The animosity I carried that humid summer when I sat fumbling with the Nagra in the tiny student's room in Columbia University, is the same animus I held for Dr. Martin Luther King, Jr. I wrote about this animus in a pamphlet, "The Confessed Bewilderment of Martin Luther King, Jr. and the Idea of Non-Violence as a Political Tactic," was published by Al Kitab Sudan Publications of Burlington, Ontario. I began my salvo with this bitterness:

> During the hallucinatory climax of something called Integration, Martin Luther King wrote a book called, perhaps mistakenly, perhaps over-optimistically, *Why We Can't Wait*. More significant than the contents of this book, which dealt with Dr. King's misgivings and hopes for integration of the black man into American society, is the advertiser's blurb on the front cover of the book jacket. It refers to Dr. King as "the moral leader of America." (Note, not white America; nor black America: but America!) It also says that Dr. King was stating the case for freedom now. That was in 1964.
>
> Then as now, it is as much a presumption, if not a hallucination, on the part of a black man, to allow himself to be referred to as "the moral leader" of a country, which in its daily dealing with him, and others like him, is immoral in certain important functions of its genitals and its arteries. But this "presumptuousness" does not raise as many eyebrows of cynicism, as it raises the question, now very relevant, particularly when we consider the history of "immorality" in America since 1964. This question arises out of the results and practices of that "morality" which is concerned with the presence or absence of freedom that Dr. King has been talking about. Bluntly speaking, that question is, "What freedom, Dr. King?" Was it a freedom to eat at lunch counters with whites, the food at which counters was, in cases, worse than the grits and the cornbread and the collard greens that have been known, mythically, as the characteristic fare of some of those Americans of whom he is supposed to be the "moral" leader? Or was it a freedom to demonstrate against evil wrongs; and demonstrate non-violently; and

suffer violence from the white population of America, (of which he is the moral leader), peacefully? Dr. King made no gains of freedom, even with his nation-wide liberal support, and his emotional appeal to the conscience of white liberals, and black bourgeois liberals. The only significance of the NAACP, through which organization Dr. King came to prominence as a "Negro" leader, was that the violent suffering of black people, whom he insisted should suffer non-violently, was witnessed on television by the whole American nation, both black and white. The world saw the degree to which sections of American society are "immoral." In this respect only, was he ever a leader, a "moral" leader: he led a march of civil demonstration that brought out in the open, certain hidden and subconscious realities of American morality. But he was merely the present, coincidental agent. Those realities had to be faced, someday.

Another "reality" was facing me like a conscience. Riding me like a horse, at night into long-distance races of insomnia, and engaging in long, loud, and sometimes logical "conversations" while soundly asleep. I woke up each morning with a taste of the sourness of these nocturnal conversations — more regularly, soliloquies delivered in theatrical declamation — and the fear that I could have walked in my sleep, like Lady Macbeth attempting to wash the guilt of conscience from my nightclothes.

Why did I lash out at Chinua Achebe? And then at Dr. Martin Luther King, Jr.? And why did I think that this malevolence toward these two gentlemen would, in any way, weaken their appeal, and compromise their legitimacy in the eyes of their respective communities, and thereby give to me an acclaimed superiority over them, as a critic of their philosophies?

James Baldwin's fratricidal attack on Richard Wright, his former mentor, in *Notes of a Native Son*, was justified by Baldwin, in the most harrowing consolation, that the son must kill the father. And this is what Baldwin, devaluing Richard Wright's masterpiece *Native Son*, had done. I was shocked when I read *Notes of a Native Son*, a book in which Baldwin entertained his raw fratricidal assault, similar in my mind to Baldwin's criticism of the Black Muslim leader, the Honourable Elijah

Muhammad, in his mansion in Chicago, when Elijah extended member-ship in the Muslim community to Baldwin. It was not only a gesture of brotherhood: the Muslims were enthusiastic of attracting black men and women, celebrities in all walks of life in America — Cassius Clay became Muhammad Ali — so why not a writer of national lustre? This man, Elijah Muhammad, of gentle manner and vicious religious and political pragmatism, and threatening masculinity, still was, in Baldwin's mind, the father, the father figure whom he did not have in his stepfather, when he was growing up as a child preacher in Harlem. Elijah Muhammad was a more legitimate father figure than Baldwin's own stepfather. In the same way as Elijah Muhammad was a father figure to Malcolm X, his most distinguished disciple, whose natural father died at the hands of a lynch mob that threw him under the wheels of a freight train. But Baldwin had already chosen one other father figure, or role model, the black American expatriate, Beauford Delaney, who lived in Paris at the same time as Baldwin and Wright and others.

"Whose little boy are you?"

James Baldwin did not return from his holiday in Greece in time for me to interview him. So I returned to Toronto. Sixty-three minutes of Malcolm X on tape, clear and stridently controversial, speaking into the microphone, were played on the CBC, from coast to coast, awakening the black population of Canada to the philosophy of other black people like themselves, and to the justification of posing the question, "Is Canada as racist as the United States of America?" even if they did not have the guts and the honesty to answer the question, publicly. And so far as the white population of Canada was concerned, listening to the interview on national radio, they were made uncomfortable, and they continued to bury their heads in the sands of shame and denial; and they separated themselves from America.

I have wondered whether, had I been fortunate to catch Baldwin before his departure for Greece, whether the interview of him would have hurtled me into the same controversy and fame that my interview of Malcolm X caused.

Whether through naïveté, whether through the lack of malevolence in my unsophisticated nature, or whether through pure and simple ignorance, I never did grasp, immediately after my return to Toronto, the importance into which the Malcolm X interview had placed me. I was subconsciously putting distance and the danger of the theological and political association the interview had posed, between writing and broadcasting. I felt the danger, and the possibility that no difference between the two would be made by the Canadian literary establishment, newspaper editors, columnists, and the writers of opinion, in how they regarded the Black Muslims and me, the freelance broadcaster who had brought that threatening, dangerous, and frightening presence into their living rooms on that first Sunday evening, when supper was being thought of; but was postponed, in order to catch and be scared by each pronouncement from the mouth of this strange "prophet of false theology," called Black Muslimism. It was a situation of which I saw its raw ambivalence: to eschew this message; or to embrace it, in keeping with the new North American political liberalism towards racial integration that was now sweeping consciences previously convinced of the tactic of "go slow."

CHAPTER THIRTEEN

Election Campaign, 1977

Life had changed. Life was moving fast. Life was putting me into situations I had not bargained for: and one of these was the request for my opinion on all matters to do with race, racism, the civil rights movement, and the Black Muslims. I became an authority on blackness. Years later, when I campaigned for the nomination as the candidate for Oakwood, for the Progressive-Conservative Party of Ontario, I not only reaped the wrath of the New Democratic Party candidate, Tony Grande, but also suffered the shock and embarrassment and censure and downright dirty tricks planned and executed by the Progressive-Conservative Party, my own party. I was not, to them, suitable. But there was another, more dramatic irony: I was an official member of the Progressive-Conservative Party when I sought the nomination. It was during a meeting with one of the party's "bagmen" who asked me if it was true I had written the constitution of the Black Panthers. He said it was said that I had been a friend of Malcolm X. The information had come from two men, both black, one Canadian, the other American. Their function and service to the PC Party, was to inform on blacks, usually West Indian immigrants who were too vocal on the subject of civil rights for their taste and for the party's taste. But in these young days of political immaturity, and my characteristic naïveté, I was confounded to learn that there were two other men who informed on black people for the Progressive-Conservative

Party, feeding the party (and the government), and those Cabinet ministers who had thrown certain "bones" in their direction, "the goings and comings in the black community."

This "bagman" of the party, sitting opposite me in the Vines Wine Bar & Restaurant on Wellington Street East, in 1977, said to me, with a new air of confidence and fondness, as if we had been friends for years, showing that he was one who no longer questioned my suitability as a candidate, "We asked Dr. Dan Hill and Lloyd Perry what they thought of you as a candidate." I did not expect endorsement, nor glowing comment from these two gentlemen. To me, they were opportunists, middle-class men appointed to positions to assist the immigrant and the visible minority communities on how to deal with racism in Ontario. They mistook the danger in the situation; and did not know it was like a volcano, ready at the slightest next instance of racism, to explode as it had done in American ghettos. But I did not expect complete dismissal from the mouths of these two pillars of stability in the black community.

Dr. Hill is now dead. He was an American who had fled the segregation of the United States he suffered in Washington, D.C. He was appointed human rights commissioner in 1977. I think he was the first one.

Lloyd Perry, a light-skinned black Canadian, was, in 1977, the Ontario ombudsman.

I did not even have to ask what Dr. Hill and Mr. Perry thought of me. In the silent, seething animosity that existed between West Indians and black Canadians (and black Americans), particularly when the culture of class and colour is considered in this context of clenched black fists, reminiscent of the culture of black-on-black violence, and more appropriately, to the clash of Marcus Garvey with Dr. W.E.B. Du Bois with Booker T. Washington, this internecine animosity, the struggle of black men with black men, for the skimpy remnants of largesse and victuals and funds left over from white consumption, has its roots in the confused society of slavery. And even though I knew this, and have seen it illustrated in the interviews I conducted with figures of the civil rights movement in America, Negro leaders squabbling for individual paramountcy and white acceptance of their black protest, I was still not prepared to hear the declaration on my suitability to be a political candidate.

The "bagman" was now suggesting a "better wine," one that was full-bodied, and "goes well with the trout you ordered." He was ready to tell me what the two gentlemen thought of my suitability.

"I won't touch him with a ten-foot pole!"

We drank the wine, which was, in truth, full-bodied; and it went well, very well with the trout I had ordered. This was after we each had devoured one dozen oysters. Raw.

And what lesson did I learn? And what caution did I remember always to harken to, from this interview and lunch in the back room, sitting in the single booth at the Vines Wine Bar & Restaurant?

I learned to drink a full-bodied wine with trout. And I developed a taste for raw oysters. Nowadays, the Vines has a new name, Trevor Kitchen and Bar. These days I get my oysters at The Grand on Jarvis Street; at Bistro 990 on Bay Street; and at George on Queen Street East.

Willis Cummins, a Barbadian immigrant and I, two political amateurs facing serious elective politics, facing the Tory dynasty that had ruled Ontario for three decades, at the time, decided to tackle the "easy" task of registering the most members to the Progressive-Conservative Party, to support my nomination to run in Oakwood, "to throw our hat in the ring!" We had done our research, unprofessional as it was. Oakwood was 40 percent black: meaning West Indian, black Canadian, African, and others, living in this riding that had been held by the New Democratic Party, the NDP, for many years. But the important point we grasped was that the number of votes that the NDP got in each election was relatively small. Willis and I felt we could, when we won the nomination, get more people to vote for me.

Two very important events were taking place on the few nights before the nomination meeting. The first was that the miniseries based on the book *Roots,* by Alex Haley, was being shown on primetime television, every Sunday night. Perhaps it was a re-broadcast, but I cannot recall. Secondly, the NHL hockey playoffs were on. And a third, rain was forecast for the day after the Sunday. *Roots.* The NHL hockey playoffs. The rain. Three very significant factors to be considered when you are depending upon West Indians to leave their apartments and attend a meeting, any meeting, never mind a nomination meeting to support your candidacy.

I had given these social-racial determinants no attention. And I suffered fatally as a result. I paid the price of not knowing the tastes of the very persons whose support was essential to my victory. Perhaps, I knew about rain. As a West Indian, I had remained at home many mornings because the "rain was falling." But the rain fell many mornings, right up into the following morning. But few left their homes, many of which leaked through the roof, to go to work. Going to school on a rainy day was a treat. The masters gave us no work to do; heard no lessons set for homework; for it was as if we were all listening and in our listening, paying proper respect to the elements, to the natural works of God.

And now, remembering this attitude to rain, I see also that there were not any umbrellas or raincoats in our neighbourhood. Whether we were too unsophisticated, another term for being poor, to afford an umbrella — to say nothing of a raincoat! — or, whether we found a piece of newspaper over the head, or a piece of cardboard, would do the trick. It did not. And this is why not many of us ventured out when the rain was falling.

"What else the rain does-do?" a bright boy, who was always reading, and whom we detested because he was always reading and remembering what he was reading, said. "The rain can't fall up! All you have to say is 'it is raining.'" But who amongst us, excepting this boy who was always reading, would describe such a phenomenon of climate that sometimes lasted three days and three nights, and turned into a storm, or a hurricane, by using such spare words? "It is raining" is not the same dramatic experience as "the rain falling hard-hard-hard, man!"

Rain, rain, come-down! The rain falling buckets-o'-drops! This is a night-rain, boy! Like in the Flood!

Did the supporters of my main rival, Fergy Brown, a druggist, know this peculiarity about West Indians and rain, from his supporters who were West Indian, that West Indians do not leave home to go to work, and certainly not to vote in a nomination, when it is raining hard-hard-hard! Did Fergy Brown learn this from the West Indians in his camp, men and women now serving as recruits and as fifth columnists? Or did this privileged information come from Dr. Dan Hill, and Mr. Lloyd Perry, QC? Whatever means he had to gain this information, the party did not "touch me with a ten-foot pole!" Their strategy worked effectively. Even though, single-handedly, Willis Cummins and I signed up thirty more "members" to the party, than the sum total aggregate of my three opponents: Fergy Brown; Ben Nobleman, a counsellor from North York; and Arthur Downes, a well-respected long-standing member of the party, who was well-liked in party circles — we still lost the nomination. The Fergy Brown people, who were known to PC headquarters, and had staff members of headquarters working on their campaign, called my supporters (each candidate's list of signed-up "members" was made public), and told them that the nomination meeting had been postponed. Because the "the rain was falling bad-bad-bad-bad!" The West Indians could hear it raining. They did not need to be told. Rain, rain, come-down. It was their prayer. The rain falling too hard, to leave home. The hockey playoffs! And *Roots*!

Their plan was deliberately organized. And with a great, oiled machinery of dirty tricks.

For years afterwards, I felt that they had had some experience in these "dirty tricks."

Their plan was launched in the afternoon, about four hours before the nomination meeting was to begin. The telephones in my committee rooms started to ring, bearing the tidings in language and in dialects that were recriminatory. And they all seemed to be related to the three factors that prevent or limit West Indian attendance at school, at work, and at church. The rain falling …

The rain was falling. Alex Haley's *Roots* was at its most dramatic installment. All the black people in Canada, and in my riding of Oakwood, were glued to the television screen. They were learning about their "real racial roots" in Africa. And a hockey playoff game, in the Stanley Cup final, was about to begin. At eight o'clock.

The telephone calls that my supporters made were not seeking explanation for the "postponement" of the nomination meeting: they were accusing me of two-timing them.

"You come in my house. Every night almost, including Sunday nights. You prevent me from watching *Roots*. You prevent me from learning about my heritage. I tell you I voting for you. I disobey my wife's advice, and decide to vote for you to win the nomination. My wife had-tell me to-don't trust no Bajan running for the Conservatories. My wife, as you know, is a Jamaican. I is a Bajan like you. But you seeking political office for the wrong party, man. Why you went with the Progressive-Conservatories? You cause me to went-against my-own wife. I promise you my vote. And now, look how you disrepeck me! You postpone the meeting, and didn't have the decency to tell me, to my face, it postpone. Man, you wasn't man-enough to tell me the nomination put-off? How I could trust you? You isn't even elected yet! So, how I going trust you, when you get eleck to the Legislatures? You tell me!"

"Pin my hopes on a Barbadian immigrant, running for the Conservatives? What the rass is this?"

"Eh-eh, boy! You making-pappee show!"

We spent the critical hours, just before the time the nomination meeting was to begin, in a school somewhere in the Eglinton-Oakwood area, calling our supporters, pleading with them to come to the meeting; trying to convince them that the meeting was not postponed. And we discovered in our calls, from the mouths of those who had been tricked, that not only had the fifth-columnists said that they were calling from my campaign headquarters, we learned also, with fallen hope of winning, that the callers were instructed by people at PC headquarters.

My campaign headquarters now had many West Indians, Italians, a handful of Jewish supporters, in addition to Willis Cummings and myself; and things took on a serious aura of a political campaign office. But the die was cast. William Rashleigh McMurtry, a young corporate lawyer from Blaney, Pasternak, Smela, who was one of my advisers, who, like myself, was surprised at the turn of events — my supporters remaining at home, through the downpour of rain, through the playing of a hockey playoff game, through the cultural and racial significance of it, to the majority of them, the showing of another episode of *Roots* — all these shingles in the structure of my house fell off, and the ship began to sink. It was a *Titanic* disaster. And when it was clear, as an iceberg, that many of my 1,100-odd registered supporters had stayed home, sheltering from the rain, or watching *Roots*, or the hockey playoffs, when I "heard the shout," and when my competitor Fergy Brown secured the support of

Ben Nobleman and Arthur Downes; the results were announced. Fergy Brown was the candidate.

It was now the second time he was nominated as the candidate for Oakwood. In the previous election, where he had fought, primarily against the NDP candidate, Fergy Brown had got less than one thousand votes. In this present election, when it was fought, his votes numbered a similar stunning figure. This was the man the Progressive-Conservative Party had thrown their support behind. This is the man the Progressive-Conservative Party of Oakwood considered "suitable."

And then, William Rashleigh McMurtry, schooled in the propriety of matters political in Ontario, gave me the biggest shock on that sad night of nastiness. He told me I had to congratulate Fergy Brown on his victory.

Compliment the man who had defeated me: who had wiped my slate clean-clean-clean? As a blackboard? This was a most un-Barbadian act of political sophistication. In Barbados, you would want to curse this man. You would confront him and tell him he is a low-down, dirty, nasty fighter. You would tell him he has no character. You would promise to beat-him-up tonight; and the next time you met him; you would want to join battle with him the next time. You certainly would not go up to him, and say, "Congratulations, Fergy. You win. The better man win!"

"Better man, my arse!" my mother would have told him.

This nomination meeting was held in 1977. President Richard Nixon, and Deep Throat, and the culture of Watergate, and the break-in of the Democratic Party Campaign headquarters, and the suspicion that everyone who was not a Republican had his telephone tapped; and the FBI was still on the minds of most Torontonians who had a political opinion, in opposition to established conservatism. The right wng as a political sentiment and strategy was now rearing its head. When I wrote these words, in 2005, its head was like that of the mythological creature, the centaur or the minotaur; or the many-headed beast, with the head of Hydra.

In 1977, I was listening to the new wave of jazz, led by Miles Davis, and John Coltrane; and the singers, Sarah Vaughan, of course, and Nina Simone and Abbey Lincoln. These were the same black artists who had put their stamp on the civil rights movement led by Dr. Martin Luther King, Jr., as the other expression of protest, the protest in music at the debaucheries against the "American Negroes" that sought its most depressingly cruel torture and terrorist behaviour by any country, since the Nazi regime in Europe during the 1940s, until 1945, when Auschwitz became a metaphor of excessively raw brutality: snarling dogs we had seen in movies about the Nazis, ripping black flesh just as they had, in their literary context, ripped Jewish flesh; and water hoses that could, like boiling water, rip your flesh from your bones; and policemen kicking men and women, when they were already down ... this was the background ... not the background, the foreground to the context of my timid touching of the political water with my toes, on the winter landscape of Oakwood, the provincial riding, in the Ontario Legislature. Marvin Gaye, in an international hit, asked the question, "What's Going On?" But he never got an answer, either in a political speech, or in a ditty.

CHAPTER FOURTEEN

Georgia on My Mind

At the same time as I sought the nomination in Oakwood, I was writer-in-residence at Sir George Williams and Concordia University, in Montreal. I was making the journey by train: arriving in Montreal on the tick of time. I had fifteen minutes, if the train was on time, fifteen minutes left, for me to get to Concordia, by taxi; and walk along the unwelcoming buildings built in a time when Canadian architecture, because it has no tradition at this time, was the echo of the sound of brick and stone and mason's chisels and hammers echoing the structure of buildings erected in France, duplicating France's colonization, and cultural association with the French; and I would walk in this environment that remained dumb and unspeaking like a rude host, with no welcome, because I could not speak French. And never tried to speak French. I never once, in the academic year that I was commuting from Toronto to Montreal, said the French for "good morning" or for "thank you" — simple enough words to express basic courtesy. I was tongue-tied in Montreal, for the whole of 1977. In my mind, in my thoughts, in my body, I carried the plaintive question, "What's Going On?" Did I know the answer to Marvin Gaye's question which was more political and more accusatory than a rhetorical question?

It was not only the winter and the freezing of my blood that kept me in a straitjacket of English reserve, it was the architecture, the buildings, which placed me in France; in Europe; in England, perhaps. And I could not extricate my body and my mind from the narrowed channel of alienation, and from the isolation that ignorance of the language being spoken around you, in a tone and manner and voice of lightness so characteristic of French nuance, a turn of the head, a pout of the lips, a flash of the eye, and the hand, gentle and young and searching, on the stem of a long-legged glass that contains wine the colour of urine. I would leave Concordia University, which seems like a corner of a nearby suburb, and return to Montreal, to Sir George Williams College, in a taxi, more like a hearse because there was no relationship between me and the people who passed in silence, in the silent early afternoon. When you are lost; when you are feeling that you are lost; when you are in a strange place — Montreal from Toronto — there is the silence of terror and loneliness, as if you are in a state of solitary confinement, as if you are a tourist, inarticulate in the language and the mannerisms of the place you have been dumped by a tourist boat, or a plane. And I behaved just like a tourist. Every afternoon, after a quick drink of Scotch in a bar whose name I cannot remember, whose address has long been wiped from my mind, in this atmosphere of foreignness — French was spoken upon my entry, and dropped immediately when my gait and posture and the way I sat at the bar was diagnosed as "foreign" — when I found myself in the same bar, by glancing at the name on the matches for my cigarettes — Gauloises, of course! — my own touch of Frenchness, and even though there was a more relaxed feeling in this Montreal bar, I still was lost in the surrounding Frenchness of Montreal. I yearned for seven o'clock to come, when I could get back on the VIA train to Toronto, and live through, with vicarious indignity and some shame, the lives of men who had come before me, from the West Indies, to this same Montreal, from the United States of America, to work on these same trains as porters, as cooks in the galley, as men who cleaned shoes and laid them out like shells for cannons, and who made beds, and who cleaned spittoons, twenty raw years ago, and did not make a trip "on the road," two times a week, to teach creative writing to white Canadians, at two campuses.

Whenever, in those days, I thought of trains, I thought of the song, "Georgia on My Mind." Ray Charles, whom I was listening to in these years, has a way of playing with the scansion of the word, something like deconstructing the word, "Georgia," at the beginning of the song. "Georgia" is pronounced in a shortened vowel, as if he is accusing Georgia of something terrible. And those of us who have lived through the Georgias of the civil rights movement, understand why this scansion must be employed. It is the second pronunciation of the word, long and romantic and passionate, demonstrating a romantic association with Georgia, a state of mind and of artistic brilliance — a reflection of the attitude of "American Negroes," their ambivalence, if not their schizophrenia, toward America. The second Georgia is drawn out, suitable for a song that is really the blues. Whenever I think of trains, I think of Georgia, the song — certainly not the place, where "they had the most slaves, and the worst slave-drivers," contends Mary-Mathilda in *The Polished Hoe*.

One night, arriving in New Haven on the last train from New York, where I had spent the day, at a friend's, Tony Best, a Barbadian journalist, watching the Super Bowl, between New England and St. Louis, on which I had bet twenty dollars, Canadian, that St. Louis would win, the taxis that came late, and that picked up all the white people waiting for transportation before they picked up a young black woman and me ... it is she who told me that this was going on before my eyes, not seeing this ploy; and she recognized it was a ploy, the taxi driver asking where you are going, hearing your destination, and then telling you he was not going in that direction ... and I was reminded, in 1980, by my friend Professor Robin Winks, who was responsible for my appointment of Visiting Professor at Yale in 1968, that I should use "a little care" in where I was about to stay. It was a short visit to Yale to give a lecture on "Bob Marley's Lyrics of Violence and Revolution: The Distance Between Its Message and Its Lyricism." Robin had said, "Yale has changed since you've been teaching here."

This warning comes back to me, this late night, only about eleven-thirty, for after all, I was in America, I was not in Toronto. It was 2002.

I was still working on *The Polished Hoe*. It was useless to protest. Besides, I had the company of the beautiful young black woman. And she took the insult and the act of racism as one who has lived through these rebuffs from birth tends to do. I had lost the bet on St. Louis. I was no longer in a competitive mood. And it was a warm night. On my mind, was not the excuse and the chastisement the next taxi driver would give; not even a mental note on New Haven's racist disposition. I had lived through that, with the corroborating evidence of the black students who were admitted to Yale in record-breaking numbers, between 1968 and 1972, when I left to teach at Williams College, in Northern Connecticut.

A taxi came. We said nothing about the "tactics" of the previous taxi drivers. We gave our addresses. And we were driven off in silence.

"Be cool, brother!" she greeted me, as I got into the taxi. And immediately, we were buried in the blackness of the back seat of the rattling taxi that took her home and me to my hotel.

And before the clerk at the desk of this very rundown-looking hotel was finished registering me, I asked her the question that was on my mind. I think the hotel was in the Holiday Inn chain. The lobby looked like a part of a high school gymnasium. Coats and books and things were thrown into cupboards and lockers, whose doors were ajar.

"Could you direct me to the bar?"

"There's no bar here, sir."

"No bar?"

I was booked into the wrong hotel. The Department of African American Studies, who had invited me, probably to check me over to offer me a job ... the second time around ... were probably not aware of the "changes in New Haven"; or else, it was a matter of budgetary constraint ...

"But across the street is a restaurant," a woman, the receptionist, said. "And they'd give you a drink."

I left my bags with the receptionist. I walked with uncertain gait, across the street.

New Haven had changed. I had never visited this part of New Haven. I had never trespassed into this tough, informal section of the city. Between 1968 and 1972, when I lived in New Haven, it was "on campus" Across the street from my friend John Hersey. John was Master

of Pierson College, on Connecticut Street, "in a safe neighbourhood."
The first time that he invited me to dinner in the Pierson Master's House,
I addressed him as Mr. Hershey. He did all his best not to explode.
Hershey was a despised name in all Ivy League colleges — because of
the Vietnam War.

"No relation, thank you," John Hersey had said.

He returned to his beer — Heineken — which is the only alcohol I
ever see him drink; and I returned to my bourbon and branch water, something I had copied from Robert Penn Warren, in the Yale Faculty Club.

But here I am, in the year 2002, I think; tired and disappointed; walking
across the street from this Holiday Inn motel, I think; thirsty for a
drink to drown my sorrows; and the loss of the bet, and the nagging
reminder of racism that I see, each time I am in New Haven, hoping
that they make martinis … the light is soft and golden, for the night
has probably passed very slowly and expensively; and there are just a
few heads I can see from the middle of the road I am crossing; and I
can hear no sound of voices, for the door is closed; although it seems
to be of glass and mesh wire.

But I open it. And the room is silent. There are about one dozen
patrons. Men and women. They all look tired. Fatigued. Worn out, from
the dramatic commentary of the Super Bowl game. In this smallish,
screaming celebrations of the winners, and the moaning disappointments
of the losers. They had not backed the right horse.

A woman is talking to a man. Another woman is sitting beside a
man, not talking. Two men are playing a game of pool, with the same
desultoriness as the men sitting at the bar. The barman is nodding.
About to fall asleep.

"Who did you bet on?"

The question takes me by surprise. The question is directed to me.
New Haven has changed. Who, in the period of 1968, at the height of
the civil rights movement and the torching of urban ghettos, Harlem,
Detroit, Watts, and Newark, would pose such a question to a black man,
on the night of the Super Bowl, after the game has finished?

"I hope you didn't bet on New England!"

Was I in New England, as a geographical point of reference, and as metaphor for liberal political thought, even liberalism in the "race relations," whirring through America like a vibrating wire?

There are some questions, when posed in a belligerent voice and tone of confrontation, that do not require much intelligence to determine the right answer, the prudent answer, the answer to save your soul, or in this tense, run-down bar-restaurant, to save your arse. For the moment the question was asked, I imagined myself in the Deep South, regarding a game played by a Southern football team, and a team from New England.

"St. Louis," I said.

Cheers all round the room went up. We were all losers. We were bound in friendship by our misfortune.

"Come on in, fella, and have a drink. Those fucking New England Patriots!"

For some time, respectable in its length, and in its quiet, I watched the two men play their game of billiards; and I watched the women talking and drinking with the men; and the room was peaceful, with a tension that was like the feeling of unease in which the black woman and I drove from the New Haven train station in the back seat of the taxi … it was the same one that had refused us, that had asked "Where you going?" and that had pulled off when our address was not acceptable to him.

And then, as in these uncertain cases that lie between violence and ignoring, a man went to the nickelodeon, stubby and sturdy in a corner, and lit up like a Christmas tree that appeared on the front of the machine, the moment he dropped the quarter into the slot, and out came "Georgia."

The room became silent. The room became respectful. The room became sacred, like a church. Like the sacredness at Communion, up in the chancel, when the reverend is mixing water and wine to feed the congregation whose number and whose thirst he had not calculated correctly. The room became respectful. As it used to become, when "We Shall Overcome" was sung at political gatherings for racial integration, with lustiness and visible and vocal determination. "Georgia …"

I had never witnessed anything like this. This acknowledgement of the music, the lyrics, the voice, and the meaning of the song. "Georgia on My Mind." I could not really understand what was happening. This group of white men and women, whose attitude toward me was, at first, so tricky in a Southern way, a way that greets you at the door of a run-down lunch counter, when you are not sure, if before you had presented "your black ass," your shadow, your spectre at this door, if a black man had ever entered these same doors before. That uncertainty.

We listened, in silence. And in love with the voice, and with the song, and with the man singing the song. Ray Charles. "Geor-giah! Georggg-giah!"

"Ray Charles!" somebody said.

"… moonlight through the pines …" a man said.

"This is our national anthem," another person, a woman, said.

Years later, for it is now 2005, and Ray Charles is not only a figure of importance (some dare to call him a hero, a role model), but Ray Charles is now the name of a movie, nominated for five Academy Awards. And former president, Jimmy Carter, stood beside a white blues singer, Willie Nelson, singing "Georgia on My Mind" and smiled, and became black in his association with Ray Charles, a "citizen of Georgia," previously a banned, drug-using addict, born in Georgia. And when the Georgia Legislature welcomed him "home," the power of the song I had come to love, even before its performance in the run-down restaurant in the "tough section" of New Haven in 2002, I had already been imbued with the power of reconciliation that is a theme of this wonderful song.

It comes close, in my estimation, to the rendition of "Strange Fruit" sung by Billie Holiday.

But I'm back in 1963. And I am still in Harlem; and Leroi Jones has become Amiri Baraka; is directing the Black Arts Theatre from a the-atre in Harlem, is wearing robes with an African touch of style. The Brooks Brothers sports jackets, the turned-down cloth hat, and the but-toned-down shirt collar, are all things of the past. And in more significant ways than the changing of a suit of clothes. This is a new cultural and racial image. The image of blackness.

The Black Arts Theatre not only was promoting "black plays," but was devoted, through principle, and through what used to be called "the reality of being a Negro" in America, the bolstering of other forms of writing by blacks: poetry and the novel and the essay, into a "black arts movement," dedicated to the liberation of all black Americans. Leroi had moved from the culture of the Greenwich Village avant garde intellectual, in the company of Allen Ginsberg, Frank O'Hara, and Charles Olson, writing mainly a poetry that had come to be known as "beat." But Leroi, I use the name deliberately to show the effect of his new disposition of defining the black American through his literature and his music, changed his name into an African name. Not in the same frame of mind that caused Malcolm Little to become Malcolm X, and Cassius Clay to become Muhammad Ali, but a personal transformation of a more clear and professed religious rationalization. Leroi changed his name from Leroi Jones, first, into Imamu Amear Baraka. And never did he have the same reliance upon a Muslim theology to justify this "awakening," as he couched his "redemption" into cultural-nationalist justification. And, as if renouncing the presumption that he was more bound by religion than he was by black cultural nationalism, it seems that he got rid of the "Imamu," whose meaning would have brought him face to face with a religiousness, similar to James Baldwin's storefront religiousness, when the thrust of his concerns was buried deep into what he came to call "black cultural nationalism."

"The black writer, or the black artist, cannot afford to be interested in art for art's sake," he told me, just before I left Harlem, following my interview of Malcolm X in 1963. I waited a moment, to see if he would complete the conviction by criticizing the proponents of that literary theology, the French Existentialists. But he did not. He felt that I could make the connection on my own. And I did, in my mind. I was a writer at the edge of stepping off into the great blue yonder without a map, without a compass, without a briefing of the wind currents, brewing storms, empty-handed, and devoid of a "model." What model? Who in Toronto, writing at this time — and most of the writers at the beginning of their careers — was interested in writing poetry?

Very few were considering beginning their careers with the novel. Some had tried the short story. But I was a man in a desert with no idea of the geography of the surrounding landscape that was so barren as the desert itself. But Leroi was himself, probably at this stage, in the same questioning uncertainty about what direction his plays and poetry were going to take, having renounced the beat generation's way of looking at literature, which I myself regarded as dead, and nihilistic, since, in my lexicon, "beat" may carry that connotation of the airy-fairy, not facing the surrounding harsh reality of racism, violence, and cultural brutality against the black American.

"The black artist has the moral obligation to make sure that everything he produces, is intended for the liberation of all black people." This was the way he finished his thought. I went through my mind, evaluating the works of the black American writers I had read: Langston Hughes, Richard Wright, James Baldwin, Lorraine Hansberry, Paule Marshall, Ralph Ellison, Maya Angelou, Larry Neal, and a few others, like Toni Cade Bambara, John O. Killens, to see whether their work honoured Leroi's prescription. "The black artist can't afford to be elitist," he went on to tell me, "not in this time in America, with the way blacks are treated by the white man."

Leroi himself had experienced this treatment of blacks during the Newark Riots, when he was bloodied by the revolver and the billy club of a Newark policeman, and this closeness to the "revolution," the revolution of black demand for justice and equality, caused him to make the next step in the logic of his new black cultural nationalism, to say, "We are all connected to the nigger in the street." Making the unspoken chilling reality that black people throughout the world understand in a most palpable way, that the policeman does not ask you if you have a degree, or if you are poet, before he shoots you, or breaks your skull with his billy club, or aims the high-powered water hose at your naked body, already stripped naked by the force of racism.

"We are all niggers to him!"

Around this time, in 1963 Leroi Jones wrote *Blues People: The Negro Experience in White America and the Music that Developed from It.* In this book, he laid out his philosophy and his analysis of racism against "American Negroes." In the first few chapters of *Blues People*, he comes very close to the analysis made by Frantz Fanon in *Black Skin, White*

Masks, published in English in 1967. It explains, also, the psychology in the white American's racialism against the "American Negro." Leroi said:

> Colonial America was the complete antithesis of the African's version of human existence. This idea seems to me one of the most important aspects of the enslavement of the African: the radically different, even opposing "Weltanschauung" which the colonial American and the African brought to each other. Each man, in whatever "type" of culture he inhabits, must have a way of looking at the world — whatever that means to him — which is peculiar to his peculiar culture. It is extremely important to understand that these diametrically opposed interpretations of life would be in conflict normally in the most minute human contacts. But when a man who sees the world one way becomes the slave of a man who interprets the world in an exactly opposite way, the result is, to my mind, the *worst* possible kind of slavery.

It is 1968, and I have left Harlem and the receptionist at the *Amsterdam News*, and the Apollo Theater, and Abbey Lincoln and Max Roach behind; and Paule Marshall my hostess; and the Harlem Y, and I am now in New Haven, at Yale; and it must have been the weekend, for I have made plans, from Sunday night, to escape the barren culture of New Haven, and its little hostility toward black people. At this time, New Haven is a little caught up in the net of what Frantz Fanon called "Negrophobia." I would escape to New York, and Harlem, and Greenwich Village; and listen to Thelonious Monk, wearing his pork-pie hat (later to be replaced by a Muslim-looking cap, like a Jewish yarmulke, only bigger and covering the entire head); and Miles Davis and Jimmy Witherspoon; and visit the Red Rooster with Larry-Neal-the-poet; and I would have tracked down Leroi Jones at his home in Newark, a large house which served, or so it seemed to me, as his theatre and his study and his private quarters. His wife was there, though in the background, giving us privacy to talk and to have the interview recorded without background noise, except the constant humming of the stereo player, dispensing John Coltrane, and John Coltrane, and John Coltrane. I learned everything I know about jazz, and about John Coltrane, from Leroi Jones.

So, in 1968, down from Yale, to breathe the healthy, easier air of Greenwich Village and visit Small's Paradise, to remind my soul and body of the taste of chicken and waffles ... and Newark was like some streets years ago, in Beirut; and today, like many streets in Bagdad, the neglected aftermath of the riots following the assassination of Martin Luther King, Jr. I have always wondered why, considering his greater image in the North, there was not the same outpouring of anger and frustration and suicidal "psychoexistential complex" animosity for white America, at the assassination of Malcolm X.

We sat down in Leroi's second-floor drawing room, in easy chairs, with the smell of bullets and gunfire coming up the hill into our company, for the painting of desolation, over and above the dilapidation of some streets in Newark, which seemed to have been chosen as a battlefield on which white America was bent upon reminding the "Negro" of his everlasting inferiority, we sipped lemon, listened to "Chasin' the Trane" and I began the interview, using the borrowed Nagra — which I had now mastered, and could operate it, as my mother would say, "with my two eyes closed!" — and asked him this first question.

"Leroi, when I was talking with you the last time, about a couple of months ago, you hinted at some new intensive search into religion, a special interest in the East. I am wondering whether in the search you have explored, even if only intellectually, the Black Muslim religion?"

"I have always been interested in religion," he replied. "I think a black man has to be very brainwashed to consider himself completely free of religious tendencies, and I've always studied religion. When I was younger, I studied Christianity and then Buddhism, but I think that religion is, finally, the most admirable attempt that man makes to shape his life. I know that, because of what we may call 'priest-craft,' religious ideals can often be twisted by the people who are supposedly keeping those ideals alive. A lot of times, the ideals are distorted to further the worldly, non-religious ambitions of the priests.

"This is especially true of Christianity, where it is all 'priest-craft' and no religion. The black man who is an Oriental, and Eastern man, is naturally a religious man, just as most people from the East are religious. Religion comes out of the East. Even Christianity comes out of the East. It's an Eastern religion and Christ, or Esonumarian, was an Eastern man. Our whole tradition has to do with religion rather than with the speculative philosophy of the Western mind."

"Do you think that by going back and searching out this religion you could begin to know yourself better than if you had done it through philosophy or through politics?"

"It is not a matter of going back so much as it is cutting through the mass of lies and distortions we have been subjected to here in the West.… We can find the substance of our real life-force. And then, once we know the powers we have, we can find out who are the gods that we are really supposed to worship. Then we'll understand we cannot possibly be a subject people, because our gods won't allow it.

"Most of the Negroes and the 'niggers' — and I use the term because that's what they are, self-admittedly so — they pray to a god who allows them to be slaves. Now if you pray to a god who allows you to be a slave, you are a fool. When we say you should find out who your god is, it means going back to a time when the black man was *powerful*. Because then (if one finds that ancient god) the god he worships extends power to him, not subjection, not a kind of diseased humility — because humility in the right context is desirable.

"Take the Black Muslims, for instance. As I said, I have always been interested in Eastern philosophy and, although I certainly understand the wisdom of a great many of Elijah Muhammad's teachings, I am not a member of the Nation of Islam. I am an Orthodox Sunni Muslim."

It was at this point in his religious and intellectual re-evaluation that he became known, first, as Imamu Amear Baraka. From then, and until his death in 2014, he was Amiri Baraka.

CHAPTER FIFTEEN

A Walk from Asquith Avenue

The townhouse on Asquith Avenue, joined like a Siamese twin to Number 44, which houses an old man, a retired policeman, and a younger man, a commercial artist, who wears thick, black-rimmed glasses and wears only white shirts, and black trousers, as if he is practising and studying to be a priest and does not quite have the nerve to go on, and wear a black cassock and a white surplice, and who never goes next door, westward, to the French restaurant, whose afternoon preludes of cooking onion soup has to hit him strong, first, before it rides with the wind to my rented townhouse, number 46, this man "looks after George." George no longer now wears his billy club and his revolver. But he sits in the main room, downstairs, amongst piles of paper and boxes and things to be delivered by special delivery, and in Metro taxis, and he says, and goes on saying, "Hello, Austin!" even when I have walked out of his eyesight. And then, "Afternoon, Austin," and then, "How's the writing?" And then I know he has not fallen off into that good night. Pleasant in his retirement, secure and safe, and "well-attended-to" by this much-younger man, carving out and painting out his career as a commercial artist. And suddenly, I want to become a commercial artist. And upstairs, up the narrow, steep stairs, is Gord. Gordon Peters, another commercial artist, whose speciality is "retouching" photographs, and images of men and women, and things, on paper, and sending them back by special delivery and in Metro taxis, with a fine covering over them of paper that looks as if it has been dropped, but only for a moment, and watched with eagle-eyes, in water that contains something to make the sheet look like silk, and that almost can be seen through. Gordon Peters became a successful, famous painter of watercolours; but that is another story.

So, from 46 Asquith Avenue, before the Reference Library was thought of, before Raymond Moriyama became nationally famous, before The Bay came and blocked my view of Bloor Street and Grand & Toy, and the small coach-house-looking house where Dora Mavor Moore told young men and women how to stand, how to talk, how to walk on a stage so that, one day, soon, before the money for their acting fees ran out, they might stand in better posture and better position on that stage, on Stratford, before all this "progress and development" that churned up the landscape like a construction site of sewers in the suburb of Scarborough, and had us walking through mud the colour not of mud — brown — but off-white like clay; and witness before our horrified eyes the beauty of red brick and yards and green lawns behind houses, and the quiet of voice and manner, and a tree, across from number 46, under which a man could sit during the day and dream of Barbados where there are more trees that produce shade, and under which, during the concealing night, a man and a woman could sit, and hold hands, and lean closer together when no one was looking, and "steal" a kiss; so I shall walk to Bloor, and cross the street, like a yacht in a sea of traffic, tacking in and tacking out, to reach the shore of the south sidewalk, and turn left and reach Church Street, and turn right, and continue in the canal of the street with the banks of houses — I almost said, private houses, exposing a meaningless extravagance: for most houses along Church Street, going south from Bloor, were private — walking to the CBC Radio Building, at 354 Jarvis Street, to discuss "story ideas" with Harry J. Boyle in charge of the Project Series; and with Robert Weaver, for *Anthology*, *The Best of Ideas*, and to peddle a short story on him, in case Alice Munro, his favourite, had not already taken up his entire budget. And just walking, and humming a song to myself. There were no Walkmans or iPods in those days. No men and women walked with their ears bombarded by the various noisy music of their choice; and if there were Walkmans, I certainly was not in the position to own one. Besides, I despised as a point of snobbish principle following too close on the heels of the latest fad. What was the fad at this time, in 1964 and 1965? Apart from the fads in fashions? Bell-bottoms? Blue jeans? The Afro — for black men and black women? The jumpsuit? Painting of the body? The smashing and the curving of spoons and forks to make bangles for jewellery? The dashiki — for black men and some white men; and for black women, and some white women? The obsession with silver — and not gold — to be worn as rings and bangles and sculpture to decorate the "pad." And the favourite colour in which the "pad" was painted. BLACK. Everything was black in those days. Everybody wanted to be black. For to be a black American was "the cool currency of cool," in a new civil rights motto, and metaphor. No! It was not really the civil rights movement that came up upon this metaphor. It was a combination of ideas, floating around in the American air, in the South and in the North, to say nothing of the West and the Black Panther Party — it was Malcolm X; and Stokely Carmichael and H. Rap Brown;and the Imamu, Amiri Baraka; and John Coltrane, *Live at Birdland* and elsewhere in the world: in Toronto on a small street named Asquith, and in London where Notting Hill came to have another meaning, beside the address of poor, black, cold, shivering, out-of-work West Indians; and Miles, Miles Davis, *Someday My Prince Will Come*. Black is beautiful. Black is beautiful, baby. Yeah! Black is beautiful.

If Phyllis Sommerville is in her office, I might stop by and sell her an idea for her programme, perhaps, snip off a piece of the Leroi Jones interview and sell it to her. She is a poet. And from rumour in the basement cafeteria, she is about to enter the Anglican ministry. (Imagine how life goes round and round before it expires. I attend the weekly sales on Thursday, Friday, and Saturday, between noon and five o'clock at the Toronto Reference Library, on the first floor, past the three commissioners who smile at me, and say "Cold enough for you?" in winter; and "Damn humid today!" in June, July, and August; and immediately attend to the next person coming through the security line, in case he has sneaked a library book in his shoulder-strapping back pack. One of the twenty books I had bought that Saturday, was, I couldn't believe my two eyes, as my mother would say, I almost dropped dead as I recognized the author's photograph. I recognized part of the biographical note of Paule Marshall. I recognized the date. But I did not believe that I was holding in my hand, the book written by the woman, who was at the brink of her career, as I was on mine. But she with more sureness and succour and success, possibly through privilege, than was my case. But my love for her, as a fellow artist, contradicted those feelings of jealousy, and I went back in my mind to those afternoons, when we chatted lightly, skirting over and beside our ambitions to be writers, published writers, and went back to devote our time to the making of programmes and of making money.

But I am not even close to her office on Jarvis Street. I am still on Church: and Church has a few run-down restaurants, dives; and the reliable hardware store, which we all buy things from; nails; and light screws, and screwdrivers — when I was a CBC stagehand, I bought my first hammer from this hardware store; and passing mansions and remembering what I was told in casual conversations at the Pilot Tavern, and elsewhere; and now, look how things have changed, for the worse, women have now taken over the streets, and Church is known as Whores Row, and we haven't reached Jarvis Street yet! Nondescript is the word to describe Church Street, south from Bloor, just passing Isabella. I know Isabella. Bert Hilckman, the Dutch fellow, lives in a basement, not a basement, but a space he literally dug out in the basement of a rooming house, owned by a woman who does not work in the house, doing housework, and by a man who does not work, in the house or outside. He likes beer. And he drinks his beer slowly, so no one knows how many bottles of Molson's … including his wife; no one keeps count … he has put away, "this unemploy son of a bitch sit down, down there, all day and drink!" He took me once to the tavern, on Hayden Street, along with Bert, who was a stagehand, too, the first street south of Bloor, running between Yonge and Church. And we sat in the room filled with round tables on which were small bottles of salt, and a small bottle of vinegar, and ashtrays made out of tin, and covered with white paint and the name of the donor, and with three places to rest your cigarette, Players Plain, they could cut out your guts they were so strong, and we drank draft beer, establishing our social status as "slobs" or "men on the dole"; and the waiter who smoked as he served us, served us the three remaining pickled eggs that were in a large see-through jar, like fish in a fish tank, dead to the bottom of the putrid vinegar water; dead to the world.

If there were a woman with us, if his wife were with us, we would have sat in the better section, named "Ladies and Escorts." But the hard-boiled eggs there, were the same as in the proletarian section where we sat, and where the painter, Kenneth Seager, dressed lugubriously day after day, year after year, in a black baggy corduroy suit, red round-neck sweater, desert boots, and thick black-framed spectacles which warned you that Ken was near-sighted; and in this room, where it is said, for breakfast, lunch, and dinner, he ate hamburgers all day, "well done, with chips, no mustard and heavy on the ketchup," every day of the year — except when his sister invited him for a meal on Sundays — and where he found his inspiration for his huge paintings in oil, of imposing buildings that gave off a scent of religion. He painted the front of the chapel of St. Paul's Anglican Church, on Bloor Street, a building made of stone that reminds you of a coach house. Perhaps, this is where the assistant acting vicar lives. Kenneth Seager likes to paint buildings that are more sturdy than his weak and delicate frame and constitution, healthier in their architecture of proud boasting stone. How can a man who lives on well-done hamburgers, for breakfast, so they say; for lunch and dinner, so they say; and at Christmas and Easter, and who paints the brown-black meat with the thick red of ketchup, live to paint the city's architecture and leave behind for us, the generations that follow after him, the correct idea, the correct and recognizable brushstrokes of our cultural wholesomeness? And he did this, before the city got cocky and turned its attention to, and asked for the authenticity of, "real-estate developers?" The mayors of this city, from 1963 until the reign of David Crombie, did not like architects and town planners.

I walk music-less in these streets, Hayden, then Charles, Isabella, then Gloucester, then Dundonald, then Wellesley, buildings with apartments in them. But there is one off this street where Bert lives, in a hole in the ground, a hole he has transformed into a palace and that caused the landlord, between sips of Labatt Blue, to bargain: "Would you fix up our place if I charge you half the rent?"

Bert gives us hard, dark, blackish, Dutch chocolates every fortnight, when his father, who makes chocolates, sends him a parcel of chocolates, and a pouch of Dutch tobacco for me, for which we run to the Charles Street post office, to collect. The rich, wholesome smell of the chocolate struck our nostrils the moment we entered the door. The parcel had been wrapped by an employee in Bert's father's chocolate-making firm. He could not have known, the pungency of the power of scent, under the arms of the postal clerks in Toronto.

Maitland, Alexander ... turn left here, and walk beside the elementary school, and turn a short left, and I am beside Studio 7 where the big live shows are done. Eugene Onegin, all the Chevrolet Sunday Night dramas, *Wayne and Shuster Comedy Hour,* and the small nook of a studio, beside it, where Barbara Hamilton and the *Howdy Doody* crew read their lines from cue cards. We called them "idiot cards." And where Percy Saltzman, every night, except Saturday and Sunday, changes a plain black board that is green, into a work of art, with the hieroglyphics of modern, abstract art, making an art of giving us bad-weather stories, and tossing his chalk into the air as the punctuation mark to mark the end of his spellbinding presentation of foul weather that is digested by all of Canada every night during the week, as if to tell us, "You ain't seen bad weather, yet! Wait till I talk about Quee-bec!"

I am travelling all this time and in this place, from Asquith Avenue to Alexander, and it would be easier if it was not the winter. In Toronto in these days, winter was winter: snow piled high to the knee, climbing over snowbanks and falling into them, and receiving a smile of understanding from the woman who waited for you to fall before she tried her dexterity; and cold wind blowing straight from the Arctic into your bones, ripping off your underwear you're wearing, your pantyhose and your long johns, and exposing you to the curse and the vow, that "this is my last year in Toronto, in this winter!" But winter in Toronto in days gone by, were days of adventure, of romance, of dressing up and going to parties where food was cooked and served, and where men and women danced after dinner, no matter how small the house was. We danced to all music, even though we did not know the steps. After all, we were having a "love-in" with ourselves. Harry Belafonte's "Day-O." Nat King Cole's "Unforgettable." Miles Davis's "'Round Midnight." Even the Beatles. And Bob Dylan. And "Both Sides Now." And this walk, this morning at ten in the deepness of winter, I left the house on Asquith Avenue, with a song in my mind. It was an ordinary song. Not a song I would listen to, intentionally. Not a sound I would buy from Harry's Records and Used Books. Not from Sam the Record Man. Not a song I would turn the volume up on if it came over CFRB, or CHUM.

I do not listen to CFRB, because of Lister Sinclair and Betty Kennedy. I do not listen to CHUM because it plays the Beatles and Elvis Presley. There is a tune moving about in my head. It came there when I stepped down the single step of the front door of 46 Asquith Avenue. And when I turned the corner, at Park Road and Asquith, and cast a glance at the Oscar Peterson School of Jazz, at the corner of Church and Davenport, I remembered to put the tune out of my head, and think that in all the years I have lived on Asquith, so close to Oscar Peterson slamming black and white keys on a Steinway, with Ray Brown and Ed Thigpen, and teaching young "musicianers" to play in similar beat and time, I had never cast my two eyes on Oscar Peterson. Never saw him "live."

Across the street on Asquith, from my house, was the First Floor Club. Sonny Rawlins played there. Art Blakey played there, and broke three drum sticks. I caught one and put it in my study like an object to worship, for years; to give me the inspiration to play that driving, heavy bebop beat. Philly Jo Jones, Elvin Jones, and Max Roach. I wanted to be a jazz drummer, when I caught that stick, that night in the First Floor Jazz Club. But I was too shy to approach Mr. Peterson's house that schooled young "musicianers" in the swing of the times. Before that, I wanted to be a trumpeter. Miles Davis got into my blood, under my skin, and I even bought at the Goodwill (now showing more goodwill than when the same store was called "The Crippled Civilians") ... I even bought a chair made of cane, and with an iron frame reinforcing the cane. Miles Davis sits in a chair like this, on the cover of his album, *'Round About Midnight,* wearing a shirt made of a material that looks like the blue-jeans cloth, so cool, the shirt open almost down to the middle of his chest. I tried to be cool like this. But I had only the chair. It was easier being cool, than going to the Oscar Peterson School of Jazz, and listening to the hollers and the shrieks and the mornings of first experience on the trumpet. I forego the trumpet, and think of the trombone. So large, so clean, so sliding like okras on the tongue, so simple, you blow into it, you slide the shaft out, you slide the shaft in, and you are in the holy presence of J.J. Johnson … Rob McConnell was still jamming on Monday nights at the First Floor Club, learning his instrument. And so was the Japanese musician Nobby … the trombone became less attractive. You could not get women playing the trombone. It was the tenor sax … Coltrane … then, the alto sax … Charlie "Bird" Parker, Jackie McLean, and Phil Woods; and P.J. Perry, "in from out West … blowing his ass off, and the asses of older musicianers, this cat … ain't he still a teenager?… kicking ass!" and kicking it, still; and once I really listened to Louis Armstrong and I wanted to play the trumpet like him, feeling that if I listened to him, and liked him, and imitated his antics on stage, I would be like him. And then one night, during my years teaching at Yale, I returned to Toronto on a weekend, and stopped off at the Embassy, famous for its steaks, at the corner of Bloor and Bellair, where exactly the tailor shop is, Harry Rosen's, where Louis Armstrong was playing. It was a sad day for Louis Armstrong; a sad day indeed. The lounge where jazz was played was empty. There must have been at most, eleven of us. I was ashamed for my city and the insult it had given, symbolically through the absence of audience, to this great musician. I thought I would go up to him, and tell him how happy I was to see him playing in Toronto. The Embassy was not like the Colonial, or the Towne Tavern. It was hidden away on Bloor Street where nothing happened. Not even Yorkville Village was exciting in those days. The artists, famous for having no money, and prone to spend four hours over one cup of espresso coffee and a Danish, playing chess, were recently chased off the streets of Yorkville by Toronto policemen on horses. But nobody seemed to notice. Not the mayor. Not the counsellors. Not the people who spent their time writing letters to editors of the city's four daily newspapers, complaining about everything they disliked about Toronto. I think that the only person of stature who raised a voice, except those ineffectual pleadings of the artists themselves, was Pierre Berton. So, Louis Armstrong the great trumpeter was more or less relegated to a second-rate place to play his music. The deeper tragedy that visited him that night, apart from the small audience — but it was an audience of jazz enthusiasts! — Louis Armstrong's sister had died that same day.

I was listening to "Mack the Knife" and "Saint James Infirmary," and feeling in Louis's playing the pain and the sadness at the death of his sister. He did not announce it to the audience. He was proper. He was elegant. In a black suit. Very expensive. And well-tailored. He was private. With a silk shirt, buttoned all the way to the neck. And in his breast pocket, his talisman. The white handkerchief. Like an orchid. Growing out of his pocket, in four furls, or leaves. I can still hear small rock-stones and the gravel in his voice, bereft, of sorrow for his sister, back in the States, Georgia, Manhattan, Brooklyn, Harlem, and Louis Armstrong, up here in Toronto cold as a tundra, warming our hearts with his trumpet.

He confessed his sadness to me as I stood beside him, reaching to the level of my eyebrows, to have a photograph taken with him. He is grinning his famous, and infamous, historical grin. All his teeth that are possible to see, are "skinning," as my mother used to say, about laughter that was so expressive. She didn't like me laughing too much. "skinning your blasted teeth, boy! Every skin-teeth isn't a laugh, boy! Remember that, long's you live!" I am dressed in a three-piece black suit, with a fairly, fiercely long Afro, wearing the tie of Berkeley College, Yale, where I took dinners, and not smiling, except with my eyes. Beside me is Louis Armstrong, skinning his teeth, disclosing both top and bottom teeth, and Betty Clarke, skinning her teeth, but displaying only her top teeth.

Three streets are left still to cross, before I turn left and walk along Carlton — why does one street have two names, College and Carlton, when it reaches Yonge? College is West, Carlton is East. The east of this city, has always been looked down upon, like a resident in Rosedale looks down, along with school teachers and principals, upon students who live in rent-controlled apartment buildings in Regent Park, put up by the city — after passing Wood Street, and Granby Street, and McGill Street…. Who would have thought in that passing McGill Street on this morning in 1965, I would, twenty-five years later, without warning, without planning, call McGill Street my residence? I say this is fate. Destiny. Voodoo. Something invisible and unknown that is guiding my footsteps. I keep coming back to the spot, to the point of view, to the belief, to the landmark, geography, and argument, from which I started. Not in a straight line. Journey is not so calculated, so drawn with slide rule and computer. My journey is a circular one. Circuitous. As if I am a lion walking around my prey, measuring and hypnotizing him, before I sink my teeth and my ambition deep into its soft flesh, to see the blood of its life spurt from its claimed body.

In my head, from the time I have stepped out of 46 Asquith Avenue, as I started to tell you, there has been a song in my head, a silly song, an extraordinary song considering the songs I like. "It's a Man's World." "April in Paris." "No Woman No Cry." I want this one to be sung at my funeral, in the St. James' Cathedral Church, whilst the congregation — not the mourners! — with their lips to the bottle of Jamaica White Rum, passed from lip to lip, touching the flesh, as at Communion; and followed by ice cubes in coconut water, flown fresh that afternoon, from Barbados. What could beat this sending off? The heavy breathing of the organ in the Cathedral, the plaintive strings of Bob Marley's voice and its imprecation and the soothing stimulant of a white Wray & Nephew! To complete this farewell, all that is needed is a bowl of Barbadian cou-cou, turned mellow-mellow-mellow, with green okras like sentries and an okra-slosh to help the meal-corn slide comfortably down the throat…. But I was carrying a tune in my head when I left Asquith Avenue, a tune of no personal significance, except that if I am thinking about it, and not being able to call to mind either its tune or its lyrics, or why it is that this piece of music that has entered my head. "Somewhere Over the Rainbow." Why this? There are other more profoundly significant songs which bring back heartache and the sorrow of love: "I Will Always Love You" by Whitney Houston; or "Evening Shadows Make Me Blue," sung by Ella Fitzgerald, even before I saw a photo of her on her album, sung in the dusk and tricky double light of Barbados, after six-thirty on an evening; and, as with matters of the heart, it is always on a Friday when these tormenting pangs and reminders take over the heart, and sadness like the sadness that visits a man condemned to die by hanging, until he is dead, dead, dead, enters his body like his thinned blood; and in spite of the benediction of the chief justice who dons his black cloth hat, as he intones, in deeper lugubriousness, "… and may the Lord have mercy upon your soul," I am pretty sure that this does not subtract from the heaviness upon that man's heart, nor change his blood back to thickness. Life not yet lived, not even imagined, suddenly visits the poor present with gripping cancelling of the future, which suddenly becomes like a mirror, like a memory, of the present. Present and future become one. That is the feeling I suffered in the hour just after the sun had changed the green waves from golden yellow with red stripes in the shape of a semi-circle, into the darkness, the gloom, the smells of boiled chocolate and the leaves of nutmeg, oily and made substantial with the addition of "flour-drops," soft dumplings, and Ella, like an artist far away in America, adding to my small personal torment of lost love — but was it ever there? It was all hope and fantasy and longing — as her voice anointed the song with greater sadness; and loneliness. "Evening Shadows Make Me Blue." The shadows that fall over Barbados, at dusk, with the certainly of a shroud the undertaker puts over a body, snow-stiff with death and disappointment, are blacker than the shadows in Toronto. "Somewhere Over the Rainbow." This is Sarah Vaughan, isn't it?

But now, continuing this small journey, from Asquith Avenue to the red brick building of the Canadian Broadcasting Corporation, at 354 Jarvis Street, where now stands the National Ballet of Canada, without the antenna on the small news studio, which makes your head spin when you look up, into the snow, into the mist, into the clouds, into the sun.

I have no Walkman to make my walk easier to take, especially in the winter. So, I memorize the song I want to hear. "Flamenco Sketches" from the album *Kind of Blue* by Miles Davis, I have memorized, especially the solo by John Coltrane, every note; and I would skat along with Trane, in "So What" and in "All Blues." It was this ability to remember all the notes that Coltrane plays, and the solos of the other musicians, Julian "Cannonball" Adderley, Paul Chambers, Jimmy Cobb, Bill Evans, and Wynton Kelly played, that caused me to think that I could become a bass player, or a saxophonist, or a trombonist, or a drummer, without attending one lesson at the Oscar Peterson School of Jazz. I was sure I could learn the keys and the notes by heart. And when I realized that this was wishful thinking, I decided to become a sculptor.

I was helped along in this delusion by the power in John Coltrane's 1963 record, *Coltrane Live at Birdland*. The same power in Coltrane's "sheets of sounds" as Nat Hentoff stupidly called Coltrane musical effervescence with notes, not much dissimilar from Charlie Parker's speed, it was this power, this control over the material being used by these great men, instrument and clay, that drew me to the busts of the Jewish artist Jacob Epstein. I imagined myself as the Black Epstein. And I did something about it. Something realistic. I sought help. First, I had an appointment with a real sculptor, a real Canadian sculptor, a woman named Pauline Fediow. She lived in the Village, which at the time was a small street between Bay and University Avenue, on Elm, in a small house filled with her sculptures and clay vases and works by other Canadian painters — all of them unknown to me — and near Mary Jane's Restaurant, which catered to the nurses in the nearby hospitals, Toronto General, Women's College, Mount Sinai, and the Children's Hospital. At Mary Jane's you could get Hungarian goulash, meat loaf, and a pork chop with mashed potatoes, and still have money left back from your ten-dollar bill.

"So, you want to be a sculptor?"

CHAPTER SIXTEEN

Mother's Precepts
and Commandments

"You're like a racehorse, boy!"

"You are going to hurt your eyes, with all this reading you reading, boy?"

"You know what you want to be when you grow up? If you don't know, right now, all I going tell you is be the best o' whatever you choose to be. Even a garbage collector, then! Be the best, in the whole Island — if you know what I mean."

"Pass the iron over the seams in your grey flannels, boy! Always look your best! Not as if you went-through a pig's mouth!"

"Always remember to dust your two arm pits with powder and a drop o' Limacol, or Bourne's Bay Rum, one or the other."

"When you are eating, whether in or out in company, 'specially out in company, always keep your tools on your plate, if your knife-and-fork not carrying food."

"And, always, you hear me, always hold your head up! Never walk and look-down in the gutter. You not looking for coppers. So, hold your head up, high! Only wurrums, dogs, cats, and centipedes walk with their bodies touching the ground. But you isn't one o' them ... mammals! Is that what you call them, at Cawmere School?"

"And remember. Manners maketh man. Manners maketh man. What manners maketh?"

I was inculcating my mother's precepts, preached to me every day, in the mornings before school, and in the evenings after school; and sometimes, late at night, after I had dusted the grains and the dust from my feet, before I climbed up on the bed.

"What I say manners maketh?"

"Man!"

"Yes. I want you to be a good man."

"Yes, Ma."

"And wherever you happen to be, here, Amurca, England, wherever … go to church! Sunday is the day you must always put aside for God, hear?"

"I hear."

"You hear, who? Who you hear?"

"I hear, Ma."

"Good!"

This conversation, containing ten precepts, as if they were Commandments, comes back to me, on this Friday afternoon, the 4th of March 2005, as if it had been conducted between my mother and me, yesterday, and not sometime in 1939, when war was raging around us, and the Island was resembling more of a county in England, than a carefree colony in the tropics, and we were all little black soldiers fighting for His Britannic Majesty, George the Sixth, and when he died, suddenly, we continued to fight, but for Queen Elizabeth the Second, our new Britannic Majesty, our Queen. Not the Queen of the Commonwealth. But the Queen of Barbados. And Barbados was very proud of this loyalty, and heralded it, in a cablegram, during the war, to Winston Churchill, entreating the prime minister that "Go bravely ahead, Big England, Little England is behind you!"

I was stunned to be told by school friends who went to university in London, and Oxford, that the cablegram, sent by Grantley Adams, premier of Barbados at that time, and knighted later by Her Majesty, who turned him into Sir Grantley, does exist, in the British Museum. It was a moment of national pride. Of loyalty. The flexing of undeveloped muscles in a physical boast, like Charles Atlas smiling from the comic pages of the *Barbados Advocate* newspaper, as he brags of bigger muscles. Canada and Australia and Africa might be large countries, able to swallow

Barbados like a lion swallows a rat, but our voices and our singing of "Rule Britannia" were expressed in the same boastingly patriotic way as it was being sung up in England. And we argued, strong-strong-strong, that since we hadda-been train by English teachers who formed glee clubs, and by English organists who could make an organ roar and groan as deep as any organ in Westminster Abbey, or in Coventry Cathedral … we did always feel that Westminster and Coventry wasn't really no match for the powerful organ instal in Sin-Michael's Cathedral Church, in Barbados.

And so, when I see myself in those years in the Island, I accept the image of myself, not the character or the philosophy, for I was not so introspective, even if I was spending most of the day alone, "by myself" as my mother would say, I see this little boy, "by himself" in a world that was kind and safe, and that assured success, since it was driven into me, by word and by lash, from the beginning, that success comes only one way. From hard work. But we worked hard without really being obsessively conscious that we would succeed. It was more a behaviour that was second nature to us. Everybody — or almost everybody — in your neighbourhood, in your school, and in your church, worked hard. We saw the result of hard work all round us. And we never had to be lectured about role models. The term did not exist in Barbados, certainly not when I was growing up; and it never was given the heightened moral and cultural significance that it seems to have in this city, in particular, during Black History Month.

It is 1953, and we are studying *The Canterbury Tales* by Geoffrey Chaucer; and we are imitating the accent and the pronunciation the English master, an American from Harvard, Harry J. McNiff AB, AM (Harvard), is using; and we are enjoying our imitation, and being preposterous, and extravagant in our scansion of the words, showing off our mastery of this fourteenth-century English language, in this hot, small colony, instructed by a twang-talking Yankee. Mr. McNiff (Harvard) was the first American to teach English literature at Harrison College. Our disdain for this presumption turned to adulation, not only at his skill, but more so, at his splendid wardrobe. We started to count the number of shirts he owned — and gave up counting — and we tried to pin down the number of socks he wore, and gave up counting; we started on his trousers, with the same result. And we settled on liking him, as it was he who introduced us to American literature. Hemingway and Faulkner. We had already been washed in the poetry of T.S. Eliot, but we did not know he was not born in England. We assumed that since he was on the curriculum set by the English examiners, he was an Englishman. His works had been in our texts for generations! And nobody told us differently. So, we roamed the playing field, as the cricketers shot the red leather ball through the covers, and knocked down wickets with their fast bowling of in-swingers and out-swingers, and "bumpers" that could knock a man down just as easily as the ball knocks down the five pins in a bowling alley. There was no bowling alley in the entire Island. But we had seen photographs of one in an alley in Brooklyn, in a magazine called *Ebony*. It was a black bowling alley. And this stunned us.

> We are the hollow men
> We are the stuffed men
> Leaning together
> Headpiece filled with straw. Alas!
> Our dried voices, when we whisper together
> Are quiet and meaningless
> As wind in dry grass
> Or rats' feet over broken glass
> In our dry cellar ...

We could see ourselves in this predicament, as a variation of our colonial status, of our being despised, as men with voices that could not yet be heard in any rendition of our future and our ambition, even though we were young men in the Sixth Form. We embraced T.S. Eliot as if he were a West Indian politician guiding us by the hand, from colonial dependency into some form of polite, and gradual "responsible government," ruled over by a governor appointed up in England, but sharing out, because of our "political maturity," a few insignificant ministries that did not illustrate the same "political maturity" the colonial office had deluded us into believing we possessed. But it was a start. And so, we continued, in our sixth form classroom, which was the reading room of the college library, to recite "The Hollow Men." We thought of men of straw, doll-babies sold in the stores in Town, with faces resembling those of minstrels we laughed at, and ridiculed as they were American — they were not us: we were English! — and we found their antics degrading. These minstrels, and the people they represented in their caricaturing of black people, were not Barbadians. And we thought of Guy Fawkes Day, the fifth of November, and of other straw men. But most of all, we roamed through the bookshelves crammed with other religions and ideologies of England and English civilization, singing, just as the language of Chaucer had to be "sung":

> We are the hollow men
> We are the stuffed men ...

And as my mother said, "one thing led to another"; and we used Chaucer's language of the fourteenth century to daub the personality and character of our colleagues sitting beside us, in the Modern Sixth, at Harrison College. And we gave them longevity and their idiosyncrasies wider scope. And we went through the list of pilgrims, from the General Prologue, and transferred from them, to our colleagues, the identical narrative description that Chaucer had used.

My best friend, Rawle "Briggs" Archer, because the Knyght:

> and that a worthy man,
> That fro the tyme that he first bigan
> To ridden out, he loved chivalrie,
> Trouthe and honour, fredom and curtesie.

But since Harrison College was an all-boys' school, we had no girls on whom we might pin the language of Chaucer to describe their oddities. But we chose the sister of one of our colleagues, and branded her thus:

> Ther was also a Nonne, a Prioresse,
> That of her smylyng was ful simple and coy:
> Hire gretteste ooth was but by Seinte Loy ...

These character sketches were my first ramblings into creative writing. I enjoyed writing these capsules of character; and I became good at them; and they made the literary magazine which we edited and published, in the long tradition of Sixth Form boys editing college magazines. But I never did consider them to be the practice necessary to becoming a "real writer." I wanted to be a barrister-at-law, and use words in a more practical and significant manner: getting a man off from the gallows after he had committed murder. And making lots of money; and driving a black Humber Hawk; and walking about Town, in wig and gown, with my "man" walking behind me, holding a cloth bag of royal, deep blue, a string tied through its mouth, containing briefs, to be introduced by me, in court, in the court of the grand assizes, and in high court, in appeal court, even before the highest court in the British Empire, the House of Lords.

> Muh Lud, I cite in support of my argument, the case of Rex versus Chesterfield in the High Court in which the Learned Judge, in the majority opinion stated, and I quote, Muh-Lud … if it pleases the Court, allow me, without prejudice, to remind you, Muh-Lud, that this majority opinion was written by yourself, Muh-Lud …

The language of the law, "of the Lawe," similar to the language of Chaucer, heavy with the weight of logic and still light of narrative in it.

My shock was insurmountable when I picked up a book about Geoffrey Chaucer, recently, and found it talking about rhetoric, and rhetoricians, and how to present a human being, stating that it was "a technique or figure known to them as *descriptio*, of which there were at least three doctrines, equally explicit, which were current in the Middle Ages." The first was Cicero's, taken from his book, *De Inventione*, I, xxiv. The book in which I was shocked to see this skeletal technique of writing narrative, was published in 1956, although I did not see the book until January 2005; but it is still relevant. Cicero said, *"Ac personis has res attributas putamus: nomen, naturam, victum, fortunam, habitum, affectionem, studia, consilia, facta, casus, orationes."*

In translation, Cicero was saying, "We hold the following to be the attributes of persons: name, nature, manner of life, fortune, habit, interests, purposes, achievements, accidents, conversation." But Cicero gave us more: a paraphrase of these eleven attributes— one more than my mother's precepts and commandments for the Bringing Up of Young Black Boys into Men — which we may refer to, when necessary; that is to say when we, as novelists, attempt to build a character from a smile, or a hat, from scratch, and are held up in our construction, through doubt, or ignorance. I wish I had known of this formula, when I was writing *The Polished Hoe*, for I might very well have drawn the characters of Mary-Mathilda; her son, Wilberforce; Sargeant; and the Constable; to say nothing of Mr. Bellfeels; in sharper poignancy and focus. But I might have described them, too.

Cicero's formula, which it seems Chaucer followed, is:

Nature — Includes Sex, place of origin, family, age, bodily appearance, whether bright or dull, affable or rude, patient or the reverse, and all the qualities of the mind or body bestowed by nature.

Manner of Life — Includes occupation, trade or profession and the character of the person's home life.

Fortune — Includes whether rich or poor, successful or a failure, and rank.

Habit — Includes some special knowledge or bodily dexterity won by careful training or practice.

Feeling — A fleeting passion, such as joy, desire, fear, vexation, etc.

Interests — Mental activity devoted to some good subject.

Purposes — Any deliberate plan.

Achievements — What a person is doing, has done or will do.

Accidents — What is happening to a person, has happened, or will happen.

Conversation — What a person has said, is saying, or will say.

I won't argue that in my painting of the characters, Mary-Mathilda, Wilberforce, Gertrude, the Constable, Sargeant, and Mr. Bellfeels, in *The Polished Hoe*, that I have used the same brush that followed this Ciceronian formula in order to draw the shapes of these "human persons"; but at the risk of being immodest, I feel that I have come close enough to give the impression that I acknowledged Cicero's warnings. I can now say that I agree with the analysis presented by Nevill Coghill of this aspect of the rhetoricians' *descriptio*. But this analysis is based upon the belief expressed by William Blake in "The Mental Traveller," a belief that I have always held, but could not have expressed so precisely, that "For the eye altering alters all." Neville Coghill, to give the *descriptio* full significance, enlarged upon William Blake's truism, telling us that "Chaucer thought the work of a writer to be something like that of a reaper, and it is with a wondering smile that we hear him say that all the corn of poetry has been reaped already and that only the gleanings are left for him after the great poets have done their work." I sometimes feel this way when I read the novels of William Faulkner, Ian McEwan, and James Joyce, and the poetry and the "tales" of Chaucer himself.

I have dawdling thoughts concerning the best way to construct a character, in a novel and in a short story; and I have, without benefit of Cicero's "formula" achieved I would think a fair satisfaction with the character of Mary-Mathilda, in *The Polished Hoe*, without knowing the fundamentals essential to creating the balance suggested in Cicero's *descriptio*. This makes me believe, and believe after many incomplete and detouring journeys, that a writer can end up at the correct destination, even after many digressions, detours, and wrong turns. There is something within the writer's body, some gadget like a sensor, like a piece of metal which attracts other pieces of metal, or complimentary other metals, that rings a bell announcing destination. My thoughts on this subject are written in *Prize Writing: The 10th Anniversary Collection*.

CHAPTER SEVENTEEN

The Green Door House

I find myself sometimes, at odd moments, with no preparation for my recollection of song, nor any indication that the words of the verses have still remained in my memory; but when these snatches of memories come to me, like a spasm of history, I recall most of the lyrics, and certainly that part which must have struck me as relevant, or personally touching, when first the 'membering of the tune struck me. Whitney Houston's "I Wanna Dance with Somebody."

This one grips me by the heart, and throws me back into a moment of love and love affairs when "I was free and young and used to wear silks." Back to times of sweetness, times when the spirit and the body knew that they were each an operational part of that love affair. This is Whitney Houston singing, soon after she woke up the entire nation of America, one afternoon at a football game, when she sang the national anthem. That anthem was never sung like that before, and since. Whitney's rendition sent shivers of deep emotional love through the body, and her rendition changed the way future singers would approach the anthem. Whitney's interpretation was not given to the world exactly in a time of racial pleasantness in America: it was sung like a challenge to that racial animosity which made white Americans retreat from the urban centres and delude themselves that they were living in a different country, in an all-white country. The same racial animosity overcame black

Americans, whose cultural antics, like a kind of chloroform, made them feel they were living in Africa, or in some segregated part of South Africa during that country's period of apartheid; or in the Southern States, those ten states that the Black Muslims had argued for, as the homeland of Negroes, "since Uncle Sam doesn't want us living amongst him, anyhow," so said Malcolm X, in the interview I did with him, in New York, in 1963. And the irony of Whitney Houston's singing "The Star Spangled Banner" was similar to the feeling I had that night in New Haven, when in the rundown bar-restaurant, I listened with the few white clientele, to Ray Charles singing, "Georgia on My Mind," and how the song drained whatever racial animosity there had been in the breasts of those white men, and transformed me into their "brother," which is what they called me, and therefore christened themselves with; once more a black American was showing the light to the vast, overwhelming white America, who had to confess that in the matter of this popular culture, they had to defend themselves precisely in these terms of black popular culture.

"I Wanna Dance with Somebody" is about more than physical love, although it embraces that, too: this is about patriotic love, national love, a respite from the bull whips, the high-powered fire hoses, the beatings, the spilling of blood, the terrorist behaviour of the white American man, during Selma.

It was always in May, before the coming of summer, but enough of a change from the stranglehold of winter in the joints and in the mind, that I would pass this house on a street in Toronto, conspicuous for its green-painted door, cut vertical into two halves, so that only half opened to let you enter; and this house has stood out in my attention because of the way the lights settle on it, in a soft sensual sensation. This house pulled me toward it, in a trance-like communication, to face the spirits and the myths of my history. Following a visit to Italy, in the northern city of Vicenza, I saw that the most important element in Italian paintings of the landscape was the light; and the way this mesmerizing light was manipulated by the artist. It was as if the light controlled the way the artist used it: and not the other way round. And so, this old two-storey house in the dilapidated section of Toronto, close enough to Regent Park to give no comfort; butting-and-bounding with derelicts, drunks, prostitutes, addicts, and with a park that is filled day and fore-day morning with pimps and drug-dealing users, who move stealthily, making no noise on their bicycles the size of children's training bikes, moving over the snow, over the grass, over the mud of spring in pools of brown water, this house stands out in the new light of life, as spring claims the park, as the sun strikes it at the four o'clock angle of romance and seduction. Always on a Saturday afternoon, and a Sunday afternoon. Perhaps it is that I travel this street only on the weekends, returning from a sleepless night of poker in a rent-controlled townhouse where the tenant — who is also the host — plays and cuts the pots to face the landlord early on Monday to pay the rent controlled by the City, which he finds to be beyond his control to pay. This weekend slant of the sun on the house intrigues me. The sun shines on this house, only.

But the light in Vicenza was painted on fields, and lines of cypresses, rigid as guards of honour, and on the wall of the palazzo, built according to my memory of Roman numerals, in MXLXMII — the year Christopher Columbus "discovered" me in Barbados, and others like me, in the Caribbean. In 1492.

One afternoon, as I walked through the wicket gate of this house in Vicenza, built in 1492, when the waves in that sea, the Caribbean Sea and that ocean, the Atlantic, were the colour of blue, the same waves took me to Cuba, many years after Christopher Columbus's "navigational error," which caused me to be branded "Indian" — from the West.

In Cuba, in Havana, I am being driven along the Malecón, which has the water on one side, and a line of buildings on the other side. The Malecón is noble; and you know that when the sea is rough, that the Malecón could be tragic. We who live on islands have a different respect for the sea from the daring masculinity of North Americans. On the other side from the sea, there is still the stately and impressive architecture, apartments from a more blessed and favoured American past, the era of dictators, stately even, though a more recent hurricane of wind and turbulent water from the sea had combed the delicate grandeur of these same buildings, like a mother combs the hair of her child. But the tidiness

and the majesty are still observable in the decay. These five-storey buildings that line the Malecón, look out across the water, the same water that
Christopher Columbus travelled, the same water that is the Caribbean Sea,
that is part of the Atlantic Ocean. These beautiful buildings, crumbling
from neglect and from political "embargoes" and national poverty, are
like old men, former elders, now stripped of their dignity: their trousers
no longer fit, even though they wear leather belts to keep them up; and
their frayed shirt collars have collected dirt each time they scratch their
hair and their brow to suggest thought and intellectual consideration of
their situation, but these men are remembering nevertheless, a time when
time was pride and style, and the profits made from the Atlantic trade
that came across the Atlantic Ocean, that England, France, Holland, and
England had their hands into, and from it, became wealthy.

And soon after this, I find myself in Venice. "See Venice and die!" is
a saying I heard first, and used first in Barbados. The saying fit. Barbados
was our Venice of the West Indies. In Barbados there are no castles.
There is a hotel that is called Sam Lord's Castle. But there are no castles, palazzos, or five-storeyed apartment buildings. Or Italian villas. In
Barbados, everything is flat. You do not "see Barbados and die!" But in
Venice, with Shakespeare on the mind, with Portia and Shylock, justice
and racism returning in the camera lens with more dramatic irony than
on a stage at Stratford in Canada, I see the "Bridge of Sighs." And I
hear the lamentations of women forlorn for husbands lost in prison and
bent out of shape on racks; and I walk through the thickening crowds,
tourists from Mississippi, Selma in Alabama, Washington and Harlem;
and Canada, buy fake leather from illegal African immigrants waiting to
be branded with the new curse as "refugees" — refugees from the slave
trade, buying postcards that show you in worse light, exactly what you are
seeing, as they repeat the sorrows and sighs of Portia, sighs that bring the
Square into my hand, as I am surrounded by the magnificence of palaces,
and palazzos and Palladian villas. And built on water! Contradicting the
ground rule of common sense and elementary architectural science,
and the wisdom of the Old Testament. "Build your house on a solid
foundation." But by another wisdom this is contradiction of the building
trade. And I am, by this stubbornness against wisdom, back in Barbados,
moving over water, scummed with dirt as the water of a harbour is:

dead bodies of small animals, and dead bodies of men, and fishermen, travelling over these waves that have no current and do not move. And I see the Barbados Harbour Police, dressed in the times of Lord Horatio Nelson's British Royal Navy, pulling the same oars, taking men across the waves of this journey that history gave a different name to, from what tourists call it by.

Where did all this Venetian wealth come from? From how many Shylocks? Or, how many Brabantios? Venice, to my mind, does not manufacture Ford SUVs, nor does it have an assembly line of Pontiacs. Venice has no iron ore. Venice has no coal mines. The wealth that floats brazenly around, on the stagnant water, conspicuous as the naval uniforms of the gondoliers, the spitting image of the Harbour Police of the Island, moving into Carlisle Bay in boats that move with oars, was obtained in trade and through trickery. And trade and trickery over these waters that move hardly enough to give birth to a wave from the oars, and carry the songs that the gondoliers sing, in a language that I do not understand, that trade and trickery "was the slave trade."

This magnificence of the buildings surrounding, was obtained from the sweat of slaves and the lash on black bodies. "The Trade. The trade in slaves": and also the Pyramids and the palaces of Venice. But this is speculation. I do not have papyrus and old tomes to check against my fancy, and my fantasy. My narrative is built upon the strong foundation of myth. But there is the same pull, the same importance of light, the same hidden spirits in the buildings that surround me, in Toronto; and on the Malecón, and here in Venice. Who has the ownership of this history? And who — meaning the descendants of slave owners — would wish to divulge one bone of guilt, from a skeleton preserved in a vault with the silver, ill-gotten from bargaining and bidding and auctions; and the handshake of a gentleman's agreement?

My next journey had taken me, surprisingly, to France. "Boy, go to France!" This exclamation expresses precisely that. It also means, go to hell. What lie are you telling me? Get lost. But the handshake that France offered, in the city of Bordeaux, was like the embrace given to a prodigal, a man who had been lost, who had lacked direction, but who is coming home now, to a house he did not know existed before his departure seeking adventure; seeking escape from family; seeking loneliness.

A barbaric veneer on my sensibilities during my first visit to France, and my four-day stay in Paris, might be reasonably used to explain why in the two days before Bordeaux and Toulouse, and the two days after I had visited those cities, with the courtesies extended to me, the choice of hotel and the choice of address of the hotel, across the narrow street from the Sorbonne III, Paris; and in the district known worldwide as the Latin Quarter, an area similar in its ambiance and its smell, its pace and its excitement, to Greenwich Village in New York during the early 1960s, or Church Street in Toronto, with all this applause and celebrity, recognition, and friendship, I did not feel the "cultural need" to visit a café in the street next door, or walk farther along the main street, to sit in a café and watch the French women pass, and dream, of conquest and of love; and compare "anthologies": my choice of drink, and my choice of chair where it is positioned and placed, for better vantage; what postcards to buy and write on and what notes to declare of my "arrival"; and whether Paris could ever be my home. Paris is the romantic home of many writers, significantly and dramatically, writers who have no relation, culture, geography, frame of mind, to France or to Paris. But I did not enter Paris with this kind of baggage, with this kind of anxiety about appropriate tourist attitude. I do not have the language. But in my lack of "civilized" sophistication, I carried the English sense of superiority regarding language and the speaking of a foreign language in the company and in the country of that language, this is an ironical egotism; and I believed without being arrogant or egotistic, to state to the strangers around me, that I speak English, because "English is the language of the universe," meaning the civilized world. I still do not, even if I harbour such thoughts of superiority and priggishness, behave like the ugly Canadian in the company of my host. So, in a way, equally ironical to the presence and the history of black people, artisans and artists fleeing their countries, America and the West Indies, and seeking and consoling themselves that they have found peace and freedom, and respect, in this country of France, France who had one of the most repressively violent regimes of slave plantations (witnessed and written about by C.L.R. James in *The Black Jacobins*), whose treatment of Haitians seeking political freedom in the mid-1800s, Toussaint L'Ouverture and others, was abominable, yet I still did feel, in the four days I existed in

Paris, that I was home. Home in the sense, that when the café is closed, when the last Armagnac cognac is served, when the napkin large as the tablecloth is removed and thrown into the bin with the other dirty, soiled things, and there is no one else left to talk with, when the lights are dimmed in civilized anticipation to urge my departure, and I get up, uneasy on my legs, I feel that I can walk, or take a taxi, and pass all these foreign reminders on the landscape, streetlights, statues, the name of a street or a building that goes back in history, I still can feel that I am home. I am home in Paris because Paris reflects a relationship, that, in spite of its viciousness and its inequalities, it was a relationship that involved me, in presence, in colour, in voice, and ironically, in labour and the profits made from my labour. So, even if I may be regarded unimportant in my invisibility, the enormous, record-breaking profits, shekels, pennies, pesos, francs, pounds (shillings and pence), render that invisibility hypocritical. But the hypocrisy observed in my presence, in history, in European cities of power, has been as characteristic of my existence and the attitude to me, as the cruelties that have marked my black skin in my "captivity."

So, I think of the most foreign and unusual cities, as home. Havana. Toronto. Venice. Manchester. Bordeaux. Toulouse. Amsterdam. Paris. Never New York. Never Atlanta. Never Boston. Never Selma. And definitely not any city or town or county in the United States of America. But, Paris. And this conviction arose in me, as an intellectual consideration, before it gained fruition and was a passionate sentiment.

The "welcome" of Toussaint L'Ouverture in France was so unwelcomed, and so regarded beyond the shores of France, that the English poet, William Wordsworth, was moved to explain the heinousness of the deception that brought Toussaint to France:

> Toussaint, the most unhappy man of men!
> Whether the whistling Rustic tend his plough
> Within thy hearing, or thy head be now
> Pillowed in some deep dungeon's earless den! —
> O miserable Chieftain! where and when
> Wilt thou find patience? Yet die not; do thou
> Wear rather in thy bonds a cheerful brow:

Though fallen thyself, never to rise again,
Live, and take comfort. Thou hast left behind
Powers that will work for thee; air, earth, and skies;
There's not a breathing of the common wind
That will forget thee; thou hast great allies;
Thy friends are exultations, agonies,
And love, and man's unconquerable mind.

My host is a professor. A Frenchman. He is the man who told me to meet him in the Bordeaux train station; that he will be under the sign, Pont de Rencontre. I did not meet him under that sign. I met him under another sign outside. Men's toilets. He was lost. He lives in Bordeaux. I met him under a sign that said these other things. It turned out to be the public urinal.

Driving me from the train station, with the water on my right — river or lake or sea? — certainly a harbour, with ships that look like luxurious hotels, or like castles built on water, to cross over the Atlantic Ocean, carrying the new "slaves" of pleasure back to the Caribbean, to sit on beaches and turn the body over one time every fifteen minutes, to face the sun and turn it the colour of lobsters, and turn the pages of a fat paperback novel, which make us admire this scenery, and wish we were on them. It is almost Mediterranean in its beauty. The light that the artist depends so heavily upon, hits these buildings, and the hotel-boats, in the same way as it lands on the green-door house. These Bordeaux buildings, matching in magnificence the palaces in Venice, and the dilapidation of the Malecón's architecture, are built from the same blue print of a disposition, from the same state of mind.

"There is a house in Toronto with a green door," I say to the professor. "The way the light hits these buildings we are passing, reminds me of some on the Malecón, in Havana. It makes me feel I've been here, before. And I know I have not been here before. In a different sense. But I also know I have been here, before. There is something about the light, and the way it strikes these buildings. There is something about this light, and these buildings. They make me think of Venice. I bought the house I was telling you about. And I added a green awning over the green door."

And then my host, the professor, said, without prompting, something that took me by surprise for its frankness. I was shocked also because of its presumption that he could, and did, read my mind. He said, in the most non-dramatic voice, "These buildings you're seeing, all along this way, are the profits from the slave trade. We in Bordeaux admit it, fairly openly. But in Toulouse, where you're going after your lecture here, they are a bit more embarrassed of their past."

Into my mind comes the architecture of a building in Toronto. The St. Lawrence Hall. This was the meeting place of abolitionists, in council to debate, and to glance at the black faces which lined the neighbourhood, and which surrounded the landed gentry, just as today the drug dealers surround the homeless and the tenants and owners of the Victorian and Georgian townhouses. This neighbourhood, rotting and decaying like bad teeth, is now called, officially, the Garden District of Toronto. Some garden! The Garden District is no garden. It is inhabited by the homeless and the hopeless — most conspicuously. And I am thinking that this house, the one with the green door, built in 1863, could have been the residence of a man who fled to Canada, on the Underground Railroad, and who became "a shoemaker." And I turn the pages of history and of speculation faster, in order to get to the narrative of myth grounded in truth. And to see whose truth I am using; and whose truth it is. The man in the house with the green door is more than a "shoemaker."

"These buildings in Bordeaux haunt me," I tell the professor. "I feel that I have been here before. When I bought the house with the green door, not because it had the green door … incidentally, Indians love the colour green!… It's religious, isn't it? Or cultural?… When I bought the house, and entered the door for the first time, I felt that a black man had lived there, before …"

There was a very strong presence of this man. Like a lingering smell of perspiration coming from a woollen undershirt that was soaked in the sweat of labour; or like the smell of incense. The man back home in the Island, who drove the iron drill into the coral stone in the rock quarry, from six until six, had this smell, this smell that was like the smell of a man's breath. Not a sour breath, or a sweet breath, just the smell of a man's breath. And it was after these thoughts of remembering and going backwards, that I found the framed Xeroxed page, a narrative taken from a page in an archive that was recognized to be more reliable than speculation, a narrative saying what it said about the first owner of this house built in the year 1863. The year of the signing of the Proclamation of Emancipation. And this was what caused me to take the presumptuous position that what had been drawing me to this house, with the light on its green door, making the green emerald, a precious stone, a valuable rock mined in places with quarries where slaves came from, the association of the building of the house with the year of Emancipation, made me sure that when I stepped inside that door, the first time, there was a spirit from my past inside the house, appointed to greet me.

There have been previous owners of the house. But they were not spirits. The spirits that greeted me were inhospitable to those previous owners. Those owners were incapable of reading the signs that tied them to myths and narratives and drums and shouts and "shants"; and the blues. I could feel the spirits. I could hear them. I could talk with them. And in time, when it was important, they would talk to me. And I knew that I was wise in purchasing the green-door house.

But there are other houses whose front doors are painted green. Arthur de Smet, young Dutchman who is translating *The Polished Hoe* into Dutch is very intelligent, intense, and sensitive. And he is taking me this morning in 2002 on a tour of the canals of Amsterdam. There is something about the light shining on the three-storey apartment buildings on the canal. They look like the ones in Havana and Venice and in Bordeaux and in Toulouse. Some of the buildings are four stories. But in this canal where we are now, travelling in a boat that looks like a launch, with a transparent roof through which you can see the tops of buildings; where you can drink beer, the smell of the water and the way the light strikes the buildings, standing majestically along the canals, some with doors painted white, some that are blue, some that are black, one that is green, this sightseeing takes me back to the

Wharf in Bridgetown, in the Island; to the Venetian gondoliers; to the ships entering the Malecón in Havana; to the ocean-going, floating apartments that look like tourist cruisers, along the river (was it a sea?), in Bordeaux. All this history and history of architecture here in the Netherlands is bound up in slavery. "Bound up" is the ironical, intransitive verb. My history touches all of them: buildings in which I was tied up and flogged, but in which my spirits lived on. So, each time I enter the right-hand half of the green door of the house, built in 1863, I think of all those other houses in Cuba in the Caribbean, in Bordeaux in France, in Venice in Italy, and in Amsterdam in The Netherlands, erected from the help of my sweat and floggings, from the bones in the basements with the skeletons, in such present-day magnificence whose cargo, the source of that trade, has been wiped from the conscience and the moral responsibility of those sea captains, sea-dogs, buccaneers and merchants and investors, and ordinary citizens.

It takes me five minutes to walk from my house to the St. Lawrence Hall, which I have to pass to get to the St. Lawrence Market, which is my destination. Years ago, before 1873, when the house was built, and after 1492, my future and my present disposition were discussed and quarrelled about in this St. Lawrence Hall. I walk past the St. Lawrence Hall now, to buy pigs' feet, ham hocks, plantains, okras, and pigtails in the market itself. And nowadays, I go to the St. Lawrence Hall to receive the Trillium Prize for Literature, and to drink wine and eat thick slices of cheese at other functions — weddings, book launches, and dances. When I pass the post office, midway to the hall, reputedly the first post office in Toronto, and I pick up snippets of history from the neighbourhood newspaper, I add to the "facts" of that history, the real truth, the "narrative" coached by the spirits and the myths, and I conclude that the man who lived in this green-door house, in 1876, three years after it was built, was a slave — whether in chains still, or "freed," or manumitted, or spared the hangman's knot thrown round a branch of a magnolia tree — if there are no magnolia trees in Canada, then I still say magnolia tree, to denote the symbolism, for it doesn't matter.

The slave's profession is gouged out in history as "shoemaker." He lived in this house from 1876, until 1880. More than a hundred years after emancipation. I have been passing this house for fourteen years. Then, I bought it. Not for any historical or racial, or cultural reason. Not even for its archival benefits. Could the "shoemaker," deliberately, and from the grave, have sent those spirits to alert me, and have me join them?

The shoemaker's name is Lamb Jno. Lamb is his Christian name. A Christian's name. His spirit, whether from a body sold in America or in the West Indies, continues "to ride me," as my mother, who knows more about slavery and ghosts and skeletons and witchcraft than me, would have me believe, referring to matters that pester her for solution. And the shoemaker's spirits ride me across the Atlantic Ocean, to the Malecón, to Venice, to Bordeaux, and now to Amsterdam.

CHAPTER EIGHTEEN

"Invisibility"

The dreams I dream of the Malecón, of Venice, of Bordeaux and Amsterdam, are dreams scotched in my mind in Barbados, in the board-and-shingle house, at the front window in the front house, looking out on to the white road, the colour of its gravel, and the ownership of its construction, "studying my head." Or acting mad, "with a turned head" (… young men looking and walking old…). But on those afternoons between three o'clock and five, when the sun is ready to skip below the hill into the sea that is the conveyor of mysteries and surprises, bringing in bones washed clean of flesh, like seashells gathered from the sandy beach, by children, there is a madness in my head. The sea to me, as I sit here in Toronto, trying my best "'membering things," as my mother would put it, I am always quite concerned by my ability to write, as if it is a gift from God; and I have told the young writers who were my students in the master class of Fiction, when I had students, when I had a job, to regard their gift, whatever its standard, as a valuable gift from God. And I am surprised, adding to the concern, that there is Biblical confirmation of this: "The Lord God hath given me the tongue of the learned, that I should know how to speak a word in season to him that is weary, he wakeneth mine ear to hear as the learned." And, as many times as I have held this as a precept, so too have I warned young writers, that they stand in danger, through sloppy writing, and dull narrative, of putting the reader (and in the oral situation, the listener), to sleep. I have also warned them, that there are certain societies in which dull narrative could end in tragic circumstances — a gun to the head of the author-reader.

The dreams I was dreaming in 1963, just after my return from Harlem and Newark and Greenwich Village — from Amurca — had nothing to do with wanting to be a writer. I wanted to continue being a free-lance broadcaster in radio, for the CBC, as this was a secure means of earning a living, and was something that was tangentially "artistic and literary," while at the same time existing on the fringe of the tremendous cultural vitality coursing through the city and the country. But there was more to it than this: a deliberate intention to separate the energy and the commitment necessary to be a good freelance radio broadcaster, from the insecurities and frustrations of being a writer of short stories, and, eventually, of novels. At this time, there was an emphasis on the publication and sale of short stories: finance, or fitting into the available editorial space. And there was no stigma attached to being a short-story writer only; and no extraordinary glory attributed to being a novelist. If there were any laurels associated with the mere division of this "artistic labour," it was to be found in the writing of poetry. The poets at the time, those who were labelled as representatives of the times, were Leonard Cohen, Al Purdy, Earle Birney, Irving Layton, and the three other members of the Montreal Group, with Phyllis Webb on the sidelines with Margaret Atwood and Dennis Lee, ready to pounce upon the landscape and the canon of poetical critics, and gain acceptance. The poets were to the art scene in the 1960s what the painters of the Pilot Tavern were, to the entire canvas of Art and Artistic expression.

And so far as I was concerned, there was no "model" against which I could place my thinking about being a writer. In these days of excitement about wanting to become an artist — and some of us dressed as we imagined artists to dress and to behave; for we had as evidence of this artistic behaviour, all of America and the hippie movement. Mode of dress and manner of behaviour, social and sexual, were already established, and to some extent worshipped and ingrained in the sensibilities of anyone wanting to be "an artist," and placed upon an altar of acceptance like a commandment.

The Survivors of the Crossing was my first novel, published in 1964. It is a novel I do not have any affection for: it is too tentative and unrealistic; and it paints a picture of fiction about a place and an attitude, which, even taking into consideration the literary licence of a writer to disregard. But, as I said, there was no model in Toronto against which I could match my intention. No Canadian writer, in 1963 — and even today, there are very few — had dealt, in a realistic way, its limitations notwithstanding, with the "presence" of black people on the Toronto landscape of whiteness. Not even were black characters placed, unspeaking, and "invisible" upon the pavements of Bloor Street West; not even down Spadina Avenue, the meeting place of blacks at this time; not even in dreams. Even Harriet Beecher Stowe had outstripped us, by the presence of black characters — no matter how despicably and racially drawn — in her novel, *Uncle Tom's Cabin*. We black people, as characters and presences on the landscape of the city, were "invisible" precisely in the context of the term as it is used by Ralph Ellison, in *Invisible Man*. I had to look elsewhere: to Richard Wright and *Native Son*; to James Baldwin and *Go Tell It on the Mountain*; and to Ellison himself. These were my nearest models, so far as geography and a veneer of cultural-racial context were concerned. My more real, "literary ancestors" had to be found elsewhere: across the Atlantic, to Great Britain. And this caused me to hesitate since I had lived in a British colony, Barbados, and to seek literary succour amongst the colonizers, even though the "colonizers" were black men like myself, seemed a bit retrogressive. But I could not ignore the contribution that these "black Englishmen" had made, not only to West Indian literature, but also to Commonwealth writing. George Lamming, Samuel Selvon, O.R. Dathorne, Jan Carew, Wilson Harris, Edgar Mittelholzer, John Hearne, Andrew Salkey, V.S. Naipaul, Victor Reid, Edward "Kamau" Brathwaithe, and Derek Walcott. There are others who were writing at this time of what I like to call the Renaissance of West Indian Literature, 1955 to 1975. But the theme of this literature written, though conceived back in the West Indies, dealt too strongly with a pleading sensibility to acknowledge the West Indian character, the West Indian personality, the West Indian narrative history, as the lot of the colonized man. I saw a sharp discord between this "message" in those novels, and the message of harshness, of toughness, of threat and the threat of retributive violence … there were no significant "motherfuckers" in this West Indian literature written at this time in London, as there was in *Native Son*, and *Go Tell It on the Mountain* and in *Invisible Man*, written in America. I could not use the West Indian novel written in London as a model. For this would have been to accept as realistic, to time and to place and to geography, the omission from the literary landscape of Toronto, that the Canadian novelist (and short-story writer) had indulged in, from 1955, when I arrived in this country, and for decades afterwards. The "feeling" of *The Survivors of the Crossing*, therefore became an enforced realism, a fraudulent exploitation of tension, racial and social, a conflict between "them and we" and between "we and we." Not even the contention that fiction is able to bear the most imposing burden of unreality, the fiction, and therefore the narrative of *The Survivors of the Crossing*, were too extraordinarily unreasonable.

But how ordinary is it for an author to write about his work in this dismissive way? And how morally obligated is he to point out the errors, or misconceived aspects of the book, after it has been discussed in various ways of intellectual significance, and discussed in comprehension? What right does the author have in repudiating a conclusion already laid down and believed in, from the number of persons who have followed that delusion? The critic and the book reviewer are, I believe, free, and intellectually on solid ground to dispute the interpretation of a narrative even though the author might very well contest such an interpretation.

The Survivors of the Crossing is therefore a novel I would like to hide from; a novel I would, at the same time, like to write over from the first sentence: "Rufus looked up from the ocean of young green sugar cane plants and saw the threat of rain, painted grey and black in the skies." Right down to the last sentence: "For a purpose — a good purpose —"; not because I think that *The Survivors of the Crossing* is a literary disaster. I would like to recreate it because I have just learned how best I could have dealt with the material I was using — as plot, as narrative, and as political purpose. I would have lessened the burden of social and political tension that the character of Rufus has to bear — and irrelevantly so — and I would have given a more detailed treatment, emphasizing the way in which Rufus's disadvantaged, stunted vision from being a cane field labourer, affected the way he saw his world, the world of the Plantation and the Village, not as two hemispheres, but as structured parameters of a well-structured society, a symbiotic reality of personal sorrow.

I sometimes refuse to acknowledge that *The Survivors of the Crossing*, though published a year before *Amongst Thistles and Thorns*, in 1964, was actually written afterwards; and I think that my reservation about giving the correct order of the writing of the two novels the significance it deserves, is my belief that *Amongst Thistles and Thorns* is a better novel, and the author likes to feel that his writing is on a line of progression and improvement; that each succeeding novel shall be better. I cannot remember why I held *Amongst Thistles and Thorns* back. And I do not even think, on reflection that I thought that *The Survivors of the Crossing* was the better novel, the flagship, so to speak. Now that the disclosure is made, I have to admit however, that I do not have the obsessive insecurity about the second novel that I suffer from the first. I would not, if I had the time, write over *Amongst Thistles and Thorns*. But what I would do, if I did have the time, is to take out the expletives in the "dialect" that the characters use. And let me explain my corrosive usage of expletives. It was simply the way I heard men and women — but mostly men — speak in the neighbourhoods in which I grew up, in St. Matthias, in Dayrells Road, along the Bath Corner, which we later called the University of the Bath Corner, and finally, in Clapham, on Flagstaff Road. I indulged in it, because I found it more poetic than offensive. There was drama, violence, and tension in the way these men used the Barbadian "dialect" or nation language, which rendered their narrative poetic and legitimate. But I would still take out the explosion of expletives. And the reason is really more monetary than literary. These first two novels have never been taught in schools in Barbados. The "censors" in the Department of Education, and those on the school boards and the committees of the CXC, Caribbean Examination Committee, have refused to expose schoolchildren to this "use of bad words," even though the very members of these distinguished bodies hear these "bad words" and use them, themselves, not only in the privacy of a game of dominoes or the playing of poker on Friday nights. I would indulge myself as a copy editor and remove all expletives, just so that young Barbadians in primary and secondary schools could experience through reading about it, that their great grandfathers lived in the same villages and neighbourhoods that they inhabit today, and that they used these "bad words."

Apart from this, there is nothing in these first two novels that I am dissatisfied with, that I would want to change, in order to embellish my reputation. But looking back to 1964 and 1965, brings me now to remember the context of my life at this time, before and after.

Harlem and Newark and Greenwich Village, and New York, the glorious jazz clubs of the early sixties, were now behind me. I had to concentrate on making a living, as a freelance broadcaster. Even with two novels and some short stories in my pocket, I was still very insecure about a future in writing fiction. I had seen the flattery given to a few writers, most of whom lived in Toronto — the "giants" of Canadian literature, at a time when the term was used with some duplicity. For we were still engaged in fierce arguments, private and public, about the meaning and the "place" of Canadian literature, which I regarded as a colonial literature, in the scheme of things, meaning the Canon, which as a true colonialist mentality, meant primarily, if not entirely, England. And American literature came second. Those few were Dennis Lee, Margaret Atwood, Graeme Gibson, Morley Callaghan, Robert Kroetsch, Farley Mowat, Margaret Laurence, Leonard Cohen, Irving Layton, Earle Birney, and some other members of the Vancouver School, and the Montreal Group. I have not mentioned all those who deserved to be called "giants" of Canadian literature at this time; and the reason is that I cannot remember all of them; and I know that there are more; so it is not the prejudice of selection, but rather, not mentioning those whom I did not know. There are always others. For years and years, I withered in the ranks of the unmentioned and probably the unmentionable. Times were the occasions too many to number when the list of Canadian writers was published, to the exclusion of the name of Austin Clarke — and of all other black writers in the country. And I always wondered who compiled those lists: and resented the exclusion of my name. Even today, after the Giller Prize, names of Giller winners are mentioned, and the hand of invisibility, similar to the tongue of silence, is characterized by the omission of my name. Now, after I had won the Giller Prize, it is easier to take this literary slight. I ascribe a new reason to this "invisibility." Years ago I called it racism. But it could have been, innocently, an enumeration based upon an honest placing of talent made from an honest evaluation of that talent.

How did I live with this omission of my name from the Lists? And how did I deal with the implied egoism in thinking that my own evaluation of my work justified my name on these Lists? And how does the author, at whatever stage in his development and acclaim, justifiably argue against his omission? And to whom does he vent his animosity? We, authors and critics, are prone to dismiss the blowing of one's own trumpet of idolatry, as just that: idolatry. I know the punishment the Establishment, which is a secret, silent vindictive agency of putting one in one's place, can do to such excessive egoism. Years ago, after *The Meeting Point* was published to fairly good reviews, I was interviewed by Kildare Dobbs, who like me, worked for the CBC, in radio, most frequently as the host of CBC *Anthology*, the prestigious literary programme, of which Robert Weaver was the executive producer, and who later became my friend. Kildare used the headline, "An Author to Watch," signalling to the Establishment that I was coming into my own as an author. During that interview, I made the remark that I considered myself to be one of the best writers in Canada. I do not now feel that it was more egoism, than it was a declaration that I wanted to become, and was working toward that end, to be one of the best, if not the best writer in Canada. I do not think, that considering my upbringing in Barbados, and the precepts of my mother, the obsession with success drilled into me like a book of manners, that I could have said that I wanted to be the worst writer in Canada, or one of the mediocre writers, if I was not serious. The statement was made. I did not at that time, and still do not, know who read my comments; but I am aware of the reaction the statement caused and how that reaction was translated into neglect, resentment, and most importantly, a turning off of the tap of freelance assignments and the drastic reduction in the amount of stories I was able to sell to the literary programmes and magazines. It took some time, about six months, before I was able to redeem myself from that the precipitous remark.

But I conquered that setback, as I have overcome each obstacle and controversy put in my path, beginning with the "court martial" on the windy hills of Walkers in the country district of Barbados. Since that Saturday morning, there have been abrupt "terminations" of most of the jobs I have held: the post office Christmas temporary help, when I refused to be the supervisor's "slave"; the *Timmins Daily Press*, as a reporter, when I could not learn how to write a news story, but presented my covering of a Lions Club meeting, as if I were writing a short story; from the *Globe and Mail*, who hired me — I did not apply for the job — as one of their young, bright, college-educated reporters, an innovative move initiated by Clark Davey — along with Warren Gerard, Barrie Zwicker, and an American, a graduate of Princeton, or Harvard — who had me fired for not getting a story right, when I was sent to take over from the reporter who covered metropolitan politics. I was not briefed about the meeting that dealt with religious education taught in elementary schools, and I confused an amendment to the motion, for the motion itself, and said so, in one of the most beautiful leads ever written by a *Globe and Mail* reporter: "North York came within a hair's breadth of having religious education wiped irrevocably from its curriculum." I hope my memory is correct in this. It was a minister in the Unitarian Church who wrote to the editor, who caused Bob Turnbull, the city desk editor, to challenge me, and my accuracy. I told him that I wrote what I heard. I have forgotten the context. But I have not forgotten the gist — if not the words — of the Unitarian Church minister. "I have been a reader of the *Globe and Mail* for forty years, and I have always been impressed by the accuracy of its reporting. I was at the meeting reported in your paper, and ..." It happened before the end of the six-month probation. And then there was my appointment as assistant editor of *Canadian Nuclear Technology*! I did not even know trigonometry! I did not get beyond simple equations.

But the job was "given" to me when I threatened Maclean-Hunter, then at the corner of Dundas and University, that I would take the case to the Human Rights Commission. So they gave me a job. And the job was such that they knew I could not last in such shark-infested waters; that I was out of my depth. After Maclean-Hunter, there was Industrial Sales Promotion, in Don Mills, driven to work by the editor Dick Flohil, now an impresario of the blues. Dick drove me in his Morris Minor — or is it a Mini-Minor — with blues coming through the 8-track player, educating me in this music, which I had thought was derogatory to black people. In these days, blues was listened to mostly by white people. We blacks listened to jazz: Jimmy Smith, Duke Ellington, and Count Basie. To Miles and "them motherfuckers of bebop." The publisher-owner would send me down to Toronto, a considerable distance in those days, to write articles on subjects that he chose. And he liked me doing this because I could take photographs, a result of having worked for Thomson Newspapers, where reporters are taught to do everything on a newspaper, including fetch coffee, and lay out advertisements for the sale of cars and houses. I would write these articles and hand them in to the publisher. And this went on for some time. Then, one Monday morning, having survived the drive in the Puny-mini, and the sadness of the blues, the publisher's wife handed me an envelope with a window in it. I opened the envelope, and there was a cheque in my name, in the amount of $150.00. In those days, $150.00 was an amount not to be scoffed at. I announced my good fortune to the office. The publisher heard. And came to me, took the cheque from me, and said, "This goes into the company." I contacted a friend of mine, a commercial artist, Kenny Craig, that same day, and asked him to design some calling cards and a letterhead for me. I was now going to be AUSTIN CLARKE ASSOCIATED LTD, FREELANCE WRITERS AND PHOTOGRAPHERS. And Kenny called the office when the job was done to ask for me — "Austin Clarke, president of Austin Clarke Associated Ltd." You can imagine what words, what epithets he had to have used to describe me, when the boss told him he had the wrong number. Summarily, I was terminated. And it was this that caused me to be a writer, having vowed never again to work for any man — white or black. But the point about a black employer was moot. You could count on one hand with three amputations, the black employers you would want to work for. There was *Contrast* newspaper and *Share* magazine; one real estate broker; and a few hairdressers. And to be honest, you didn't want to work for any of them. You had heard about them. And about the life and health of "black business."

I went on the dole instead. Twenty-eight dollars a week, every Friday, down at the Richmond Street unemployment office, which you got only after convincing the unemployment officer that you had religiously spent the previous four days relentlessly looking for employment. It was impossible for me to get a job. Not only because of racism, but because I really did not want a job. I told them that I was interested in getting an executive position that dealt with the "Econometrics of Supply and Demand in an Undeveloped Country, as those Econometrics affect a Developed Country." Who had the last laugh? I would get my twenty-eight dollars every Friday afternoon — I think it was a cheque! — and my first expenditure was on a case of beer, which in those days cost about six dollars. The rest I gave to my wife. I was earning regularly, every Friday — twenty-eight dollars. It was degrading, "you on the dole, man!"; and the officers made no bones about letting you know you were the scum on Canada's unemployment rolls. And then, there was the CBC stagehand crew. I think the CBC is the last employer to have hired me, and to have fired me.

But what was my resentment to these terminations? Were any of them justifiable? Regardless of my sentiment at the time, I never allowed the disaster of my employment history to crystallize in my mind, sufficiently to make me reckless in my self-pity. Each seemed to have been a determination to go on to another adventure, for I must have regarded living in Toronto as an adventure which would end the moment I got enough money to move family back to the Island; or slip across the border; or take a boat to the Mother Country, where I felt I would be welcomed, and be more successful. I still feel that way. This was before the Notting Hill Riots, number one and number two, and the Brixton Riots.

It was as if these terminations were water off my back. I did not even try to philosophize about them. I did not allow them to make their definition of me, to coincide with the way I valued myself, as such adversity is defined in Psalm 31:

I was a reproach among all mine enemies, but especially among my neighbours, and a fear of mine acquaintances: they that see me without fled from me.

I am forgotten as a dead man out of mind: I am like a broken vessel.

For I have heard the slander of many: fear was on every side; while they took counsel together against me, they devised to take away my life.

I can hear my mother's voice remonstrating against my puny plots of vindication, reminding me that, "God don't like ugly! If a man unfair you, or do you an injustice, leave him to God. God will fix him." But even though this delegates the exertion of retribution to God, I sometimes wonder if God does always give one the satisfaction of being vindicated. The more I think of this, and the more instances there are of persons who have "unfaired" me, the more I believe in this divine intervention. "God don't like ugly, boy!" But it seems to me that it takes great personal durability, since the same God "works in a mysterious way," and this entails, if not implies, the pleasure of God's patience, in giving me the "satisfaction " as I "become a reproach because of mine enemies, and especially unto my neighbours."

One morning I returned from a trip and left the front door open. As I lugged my bags upstairs to the second floor, I heard footsteps in the house; and then saw the fleeing shadow of a black man going back down the steps three at a time, and I in underwear — it was summer — running after him, down McGill Street, Church to Gerrard, down Gerrard, crossing traffic and red lights, right into the park, where men sit all day and dream and drink from a brown paper bag, and swap cigarettes and jokes and adventures. I saw him give the ghetto blaster to a man, and run off, into an alley, east of Sherbourne Street. And another neighbour, Mike Thompson, driving a BMW, saw me in this wild and demented state, in the middle of the road, in underwear, barefooted, shouting, "Thief! Thief!" attracting no attention, for in this park there are all thieves, and which one was I picking out?

"Austin, boy," my neighbour said, "lemme drive-you-back-home, and put on some clothes. We-going-go-after the fucker!"

And we did just that. Retracing the same route of escape and the same geography of pursuit. And we found him. Cowering under one of the huge trees in the park, and we rushed after him, in the car, to cut him off. But thieves are clever, and creative. And he made his calculation like a mathematician: he saw that the BMW was an older model, and too large to enter the alley he had chosen for his final escape. We watched at the mouth of the laneway as he sauntered off into the declaration and the promise that I might entertain him one dark night, armed with knife or gun, against my wish. The item he took was a ghetto blaster that belonged to the son of a friend of mine from Barbados, attending the University of Waterloo.

"Can you describe the ghetto blaster?" the investigating policeman said. We were on the street, in that section which is the ghetto.

I described the ghetto blaster.

"I would advice you, sir, that it doesn't make sense to go after a thief of that sort, just for a ghetto blaster."

The black man could have blasted my head with a gun. Or stuck a knife in my guts. For a ghetto blaster? Is it worth it? A man in your position?

I had no position. I was no longer a member of the Immigration and Refugee Board of Canada, earning about $100,000.00 per annum; I had made no preparation for my re-entry into the real world of the writer, the world of poverty and near-penury; and my frantic applications to the Canada Council and the Ontario Arts Council fell on deaf and I suspected, "prejudiced," ears and conscience and evaluation. I was faced with the predicament that writers face every day: wondering if I had talent, whether my talent had dried up, whether I had been wasting my time since November 1964 when *The Survivors of the Crossing* was published and gave notice — in spite of the fact that another black man was daring enough to call himself a writer on this precious soil of Canadian literature.

At this time in my writing career, I had to acknowledge that I was a man with little talent, unable to compete with the kind of writers who had superseded me in an application in 1996, for an Ontario Arts Council Grant. Of all the names mentioned in the document, I knew only Dionne Brand, my friend; and the juror Catherine Bush. It was difficult for me to justify the phrase "the range of applications within the program" with seven of the names mentioned. But I am not making any other point: except that the letter rammed home the insecurity, the defeat that my life characterized at this juncture. I found the letter in an old rare Oxford dictionary I had bought in 1996 when things were good. I am looking at this letter written on the 6th of February 1996, and I am reading it today, the 27th of March 2005. On the 7th of February, I was giving a reading in the University of Toronto in their series, "Conversations," a symposium of internationally famous writers. I mention this entirely as if it is an entry in my journal.

CHAPTER NINETEEN

The Culture of Chains

When the schooners from the Leeward Islands and the Windward Islands, from Trinidad, Cuba, and Dominica came into the Careenage, I would stand up on the city side of the wharf and watch the men, lifting huge crocus bags of things, with perspiration pouring off their backs like black sweat, and try to imagine these vessels piercing through the blackness of night, through the unknown roads of the waves and oceans to enter this small harbour safely, in the bright, sweating morning light. I do not remember what a man, who knew the sea, told me about the flags and pennants running down the main mast and the smaller masts like kites children fly on Easter afternoons; or if all the ships that entered Carlisle Bay to get to the Careenage flew the Union Jack. But there were many Union Jacks flapping loud and unmusical in the wind. They probably flapped with that pride, because on the land, not more than twenty years away, was the hero of their seamanship and valour at sea, Lord Horatio Nelson, standing in one-arm majesty and oldest loyalty, on a pedestal of bronze turning green with age and looking like a sore that had gathered gangrene. But tall and looking out to sea, to the entrance and the exit of the Careenage, probably whispering to himself, "England expects every man to do his duty." I liked sailing ships and schooners even though I cannot swim: never learned how to; never was taught; never was thrown into the waves at Gravesend Beach, when I was one, and left to float or sink; never wanted to learn to swim, after my mother told all those sad, frightening tales about my uncles, white men, light-skin men, black men, all men from the parishes of St. James and St. Peter and St. Lucy, country men, who were fishermen, who could not swim, who drowned in number disproportionate to the number of fishermen to boats, to uncles, to men who knew the land and the mud of the fields in the country districts, more than they ever learned the ways of the waves and the sea; and who still wanted to be fishermen. They were all Christian-minded men: they read the Bible, and not only on Sundays, or when a cousin died. They had understood the meaning behind the slogan, "I shall make you fishers of men"; and they drew the conclusion that "fishers of men" was a simile for "fishermen." That's probably why they never learned to swim. They presumed the efficacy of Christ's protection from the raging waves outside Carlisle Bay and the Caribbean Sea.

In Toronto, for many successive years, in the summer, there used to be a display of "tall ships." This display made me uneasy. These were ships, sailing across the Atlantic with cadets being trained to be members of the navy of certain European countries, countries whose history of sailing took in Africa and the West Indies, and whose cargoes contained presumptions of my history: sailor and slave; captain and driver. And I lost interest in sailing ships and schooners. Some of the recognizable schooners that entered the peaceful harbour at Bridgetown were also from Nova Scotia and Newfoundland and New Brunswick and Prince Edward Island, PEI, famous for sending "Irish potatoes" that were rejects from the best crops which Canadians ate; and which I ate for the first time, in 1955, when I came to Canada. Yes, sailing ships and schooners have always fascinated me, even though I cannot swim; even though I did not get the training to be a sea captain, by joining the 1st Barbados Sea Scouts, because I could not swim, and you had to be able to swim before you could join the Sea Scouts, and look like little black sailors dressed in the similar uniform as Lord Nelson's dutiful men. My fascination probably covered other aspects of ships and schooners. The tall ships that docked at Toronto Harbour, with their pennants and flags sluggish in the breeze that was not like the playful teasing laughter of a West Indian wind, were like cards an actor who has not remembered his lines, needs; and as I looked at them, the one time I went out of curiosity, they reminded me too much of the ships that Captain Bligh and Captain Newton and Captain Cook, sailed. And we all know what they were up to: "a thing up to which we would not put!" I imagined that the first cargoes of these "tall ships" were not "Irish potatoes" and saltfish, which were stuffed into the holds of the schooners from Nova Scotia, Newfoundland, New Brunswick, and Prince Edward Island: scabrous saltfish and PEI potatoes with roots and things growing out of them, because of the length of the journey from Canada in exchange for first-rate rum and molasses and raw brown sugar.

The stain of history had remained high as a stench from the holds, from the ropes, from the colouring of the wood of the decks, and from the "hollers" of the men and women and children crammed into the lowest class of accommodation, with the greater smell and stain of feces, spit, vomit, and curses. There was nothing romantic in the tall masts of the tall ships.

And I travelled over many seas and seas turning into oceans, and I arrived in Amsterdam, in Holland, which I had met years before, coming through the speakers of a secondhand Philips radio, short-wave and strong enough to bring distance into the front-house of the grey-painted house on Flagstaff Road, early in the morning, when the only people awake in the Island were gamblers and fowl-cock thieves, and young men learning to be poets. I knew Holland from those sleepless nights. Now, I am in Holland. It is 2002 and my latest novel, *The Polished Hoe*, which deals with sailing ships and schooners and about slaves, is being translated into Dutch, and I am invited by my publishers, De Geus, to spend a few days in Amsterdam. And here, through the canals and other waterways, I am given a tour of the city of Amsterdam, penetrating it in such a way that I feel I am going through the intestines of a city that fed upon the land and upon the people that came from islands in my part of the world; and in this shocking realization, I am not angry, I am not ashamed, I am not feeling as if I am a victim. I feel I am a partner. A senior partner. It was my "wealth" of skin and sweat and culture that made the "wealth" of Amsterdam and the Netherlands. I like the word, Netherlands. It has a more awesome, mean-spirited meaning underneath its obvious etymology.

I am in a tour boat that has a roof of glass to afford a panorama of the canal system; and the water is foul, in colour and in smell — what wharf is not? — and I in the company of Arthur de Smet, my translator, who ties the knots in the history of the Netherlands and the Island, to sustain meaning and the history of that meaning.

Before us, in resplendent and dramatic force, the force of an apparition, is the *Amsterdam*. A sailing ship as big as a monster. Resplendent also in the choice of colour used to embroider the mean-spiritedness of a ship such as this, rolling with the waves and with the punches of Abolitionists, over the Atlantic Ocean, and turning north instead of south, where plantations in Curaçao, Aruba, and St. Maarten were already established. I could imagine myself looking out a porthole at the wonders of fear and bigness, at canals and tall-tall buildings, and the deadening cold. The cold. The cold. How do people live in this reversed hell, this cold furnace, and remain healthy, and remain kind, and insist on being devout Christians?

I am looking at the *Amsterdam* from the rear, at the rudder, with three markings to identify cargo and ballast; and from the water to the deck, is the height of a four-storey building, with two rows of windows, seven in each row; but it is the colour of the paint used to decorate this portion of the ship, yellow, green, and red, and reddish-brown that is ironical, as if someone is playing a joke and purposely has used the colours of African Liberation movements, the colours (excepting the reddish-brown) of Marcus Garvey's Universal Negro Improvement Association, UNIA. Before the launch taking me on this tour of Amsterdam's canals turns to evade other traffic with tourists, I see the two figures: on the left is a man who looks like a farmer about to plant seeds, and beside him is a large fowl or a duck, white as the skin of the man; and on the right is another man, holding a trident in his left hand; and beside him, on the ground is a white horse; and climbing farther to reach the level of the deck, is a lantern, and below the lantern is a crown and below the crown, an oval-shaped crest, in bright red, with three crosses in the shape of the symbol for an incorrect answer. But when the launch turns and approaches the *Amsterdam* from a closer vantage point, I see the figure on the prow of the ship, a lion: the tip of his tail is golden yellow, and his knees and the soles of his feet are golden yellow, and his skin is a rich brown, something like mahogany, with his raging mane, yellow, the colour Serena Williams used to wear on tennis courts; the colour of some white people's hair braided on the excitement of a one-week holiday in the West Indies, from Canada's cold. Is the decorator, or the owner, or the city of Amsterdam making a point of racial harmony, a point about the history of this "harmony" in the markings of this ship, which is still redoubtable and seaworthy, able to cross those waves all the way from Africa, and down into the West Indies, searching out Curaçao, Aruba, and St. Maarten, where the cruellest and most repressive regimes of slavery existed in these three Dutch colonies? (I heard some of this history on the Dutch "private set," on the wireless radio, from Hilversum, in Holland!)

So, I was more interested in looking at the ground plan at the bottom of the ship, the "pen" where the slaves were chained, at closest quarter, living in their shit and eating in their shit until the cold dowse of water from a bucket was tossed upon their filthy bodies. If the *Amsterdam* was ever an ocean-going ship whose cargo was slaves, there would be one of these "pens" in its steerage. I saw a replica of one in the Slave Museum at the Kura Hulanda Hotel where I stayed in Curaçao, shortly before my tour of the Amsterdam canals. The hotel was once a slave plantation; and the present owner, Dutch, I think it was said he is, "renovated" the property without damaging its historical and architectural cosmetic value, so that you get the impression, in spite of the fact that there are statuettes now and not living slaves populating the grounds, in various attitudes of labour and recreation, you are given the distinct impression that you are living amongst this era of enslavement. To bring more history to the gaze of the tourist, not a person, characteristically, to be moved by the fact of this history of enslavement, there is the museum: spanning the entire period of the slave trade, and ending with the present-day segregation and violence visited upon black Americans, culminating in a pristine outfit of a "sheet" worn by the American Ku Klux Klan. I was made numb by the display of chains. Chains seem to have been the metaphor for slavery and the robbing of freedom, even after the Emancipation. Chains seem to have been like an adornment of misery upon the limbs of the black men and women and children caught up, and caught in this trade. And chains worn today by American rappers, their heaviness of link, their conspicuousness on the body and as part of the costume — but a costume with what metaphor and fashion aesthetic? — chains on the body of rappers and other young black men in America and in Canada, to say nothing of the United Kingdom! — is an ironical demystification of a symbol invented purely for its degrading effect and effectiveness, and used today in the same way of declaring a new cultural nationalism, in the change of the "slave" name, such as Austin Clarke, to a more "suitable" and "noble" name, such as Ali Kamal Al Kadir Sudan. Or, more simply, but equally effective, "Austin X."

When therefore, toward the end of the tour of the museum, walking underground now, in a symbolical sense, really walking through a tunnel beneath the ground on the grounds of Kura Hulanda Hotel, on whose premises this museum is built, signs declare in bold print:

EVOLUTION
SLAVE TRADE/MIDDLE PASSAGE
WEST AFRICAN EMPIRES
KINGDOMS OF BENIN

This museum is situated in the capital city of Curaçao, Willemstad. I was swallowed up — the deliberate intention of the planners of this museum — in the culture of chains. I had never seen so many chains employed to control a way of life — not even in the culture of Auschwitz was this reminder of domination and imprisonment of a despised class, a creation of an underclass, demonstrated so conspicuously. Chains and iron. "Iron chains" as my mother would christen this relic of degradation. "Iron-chains." Chains for the ankles; chains for the arms; chains binding the arms and the legs in a contortionist dexterity that no slave was strong enough to escape from; chains that declared the ineffectiveness of a Houdini; chains that formed the outline of a human body, that were used to control him, subdue him — if further restraint was necessary, was essential — in the Curaçao sun at midday, with the accompaniment of stinging bees to keep him awake from becoming drowsy and fainting in this debilitating tropical climate. Chains left in a pile, an added emphasis of the pervasiveness of this culture of inhumanity.

And then, now walking with bended head, as if I were back in Toronto, in the basement of the house with the green door, in the basement to turn the washer on, I have to bend my head, because of the cramped space between ceiling and floor — I pass the piles of iron-chains and enter a door, bending my head as the slave must have been forced to bend his head, and his entire body, like a miner living under-ground for most of a day of twenty-four hours, or like a man doing the limbo dance, torturing his body in the shape of a spider — Anancy; and then I am, without preparation, in the hold of a ship built to the specifications of a ship on which Captain John Newton was master, on which he wrote nightly love letters to his wife, back in England, in which he told his wife about a child that was crying, breaking into his concentration upon the correct word of love and assurance that he wanted to use, to express to his wife the love he wanted to show, and how he could not, because the black child was crying, and he could not tolerate any more crying of the slave child, so he went down into the "compartment of the coloured," the slaves, ripped the child from his mother's arms, and tossed it overboard. The roiling waves ate it up like a shark would snap its head from its body. The blood that soiled the deep green waves, was black. This same Captain Newton, who gave us these equally poetic and romantic stanzas of a hymn, replete with dramatic irony each time it is sung by black Americans, each time the singing is joined in by white Americans:

> How sweet the name of Jesus sounds
> In a believer's ear!
> It soothes this sorrows, heals his wounds,
> And drives away his fear.
>
> It makes the wounded spirit whole,
> And calms the troubled breast;
> 'Tis manna to the hungry soul,
> And to the weary rest.

But I doubt that the emotional effect of this hymn on the spirit of black people can ever be reproduced onto the consciousness of white people. To them, does it feel like a confession of guilt; collective guilt of the white race?

This hymn, number 176 in *Hymns Ancient & Modern*, standard edition, used by Anglicans, which I sang in the choir of St. Matthias Anglican Church, in the neighbourhood of St. Matthias, and later at St. Michael's Cathedral Church in town, is "Amazing Grace."

The epiphanic effect in Captain Newton's verses does not convince me of his sincerity, of his falling on his knees, as Paul did on the way from Tarsus, setting out to murder Christians in Damascus, for Captain Newton's path was taken in a journey of seas turbulent for their life-threatening danger and even more dangerous for the journey itself. The Middle Passage, whose physical aspect, navigation, weather, the prevalence of seasonal storms, all this was painted too thick in too garish colours to be "washed in the blood" of confession and of redemption.

Captain Newton became as skilled in the writing of hymns as he had proved in seamanship, through wealth and promotion; and after he left the captain's cabin, and had retired to England, the contribution he made to English civilization lies in Hymn 626, "Approach, my soul, the mercy seat"; Hymn 527, "Come, my soul, thy suit prepare"; Hymn 545, "Glorious things of thee are spoken"; Hymn 690, "Great Shepherd of thy people, hear"; Hymn 551, "May the grace of Christ our Saviour"; Hymn 691, "Quiet, Lord, my forward heart." Six hymns in all he composed. Six hymns in which the pleading for grace is being asked for, ironical for a man who offered none to so many hundreds of men and women, and children — because before his descent into requesting grace, seems, in its asking, to be incomprehensible. But white people, masters, segregationists, governors of states in the American South, have always been capable of using great brutality on black people, and then afterward, with a change of context and environment, declare their epiphanic redemption.

In this black hole, in this replica of a slave ship, in the most cramped quarters, with the chains, the "iron-chains" left on the floor of the compartment, as if the slaves had just been unlocked from their transatlantic journey, you could smell the filth of their conditions, the insipid taint in the air, vomit, expectorate, or puke, shit, tears, futile self-mutilation, and the sores that festered before they were attended to, the deterioration of beautiful black bodies, at a time of life when hope and ambition and love are at their highest potential.

"How sweet the name of Jesus sounds!" But to whom? In whose ears? Apart from Captain John Newton's obsession for redemption, proportionate to his excesses of emotion and of violence, his emotional calling out for grace, the requirement to be washed in God's grace to purge him of his predisposition to violence and infanticide, these aspects of his journey across the Atlantic Ocean, similar to Paul's change of character in his journey on the road to Damascus, this Pauline redemption, nevertheless, strikes me as being hollow.

CHAPTER TWENTY

Allies

Whether in the Black-Irish tension of the movie, *Gangs of New York*, the poetry of Amiri Baraka, libelling Jews as absent from the World Trade Center on September 11, or the tendency of the Irish Republican Army to align itself with the Palestine Liberation Organization, the images of the past few years feature antagonism between separate groups. This differs markedly from the way that the groups themselves previously constructed such relations.

Blacks, Jews and Irish regularly associated themselves with each other in an appositive sense to a much larger degree than we now suppose, while their external critics lumped the groups together in a negative sense. Racist pseudo-scientists of the day regularly viewed all of them as inferior races, and would jump from one to the other often on the same page or even in the same paragraph. Correspondingly, Black Nationalist thinkers liked to invoke the Zionist movement as a positive model for Africans or African-Americans, and leading Zionists paid tribute to the leaders and strategists of Irish nationalism.

This is how George Bornstein introduced his commentary in the

Times Literary Supplement, March 4, 2005, under the title, "A Forgotten Alliance — Africans, Americans, Zionists and Irish."

I have been trying to think, in varying degrees of seriousness, at irregular periods in my life, of my own association with Jews, in the years when I organized marches and other protests, during the mid-1960s on the issue of civil rights, which touched all of us, each of us, in peculiar manner, related directly to your race, colour, colour of opinion and of prejudice, with no reference to ethnicity. For the struggle around civil rights was a universal plea for justice: justice in all its real and cosmetic and metaphorical manifestation.

And when I think of my "forgotten alliance," I think first of my friend, Rabbi Feinberg. And I think of those nights when I lay on the cold pavement in front of the U.S. Consulate General, on University Avenue, protesting the war in Vietnam, supporting the fleeing of young American citizens north, fleeing the draft into the Vietnam War, and fleeing to "freedom" in Canada, in a modern-day Underground Railroad.

For nights, in the cold, shocked that my system had become conditioned to Toronto's inhospitable cold weather after December has passed, wrapped in this brotherhood of protest, in the warmth of bodies of Jews, men and women, we sat, some prostrate, with the hope of success that kept us warm, and from catching pneumonia; and walking in parades, in marches, and in picket lines, coming closer and closer to the expression of violence imitating the raw brutality in America, many times I wondered what was the purpose; what was the purpose to have placed myself so close to the violence — the violence of the system and the violence of the individual, and whether there was a purpose in this; a purpose that was more pragmatic than I had thought. There is, and was, a distinct naïveté in the actions and spoken ideology of black nationalism that raged throughout America, and which oozed north across the border, and infected our more paltry and conservative approach to the desegregation of the two systems, American and Canadian. This naïveté was the disregard by the black leadership, that their business, the speeches, the demonstrations, the sit-ins, the private correspondence, were all sacrosanct from the eyes and the ears of the Federal Bureau of Investigation, from the Central Intelligence Agency, from spies, many of whom were themselves black men and black women, in other words, the black leadership did not themselves place the significance upon their political position, that the establishment invested it with, a fact of lamentable significance when it was eventually known that the FBI and the CIA had both infiltrated every significant and non-significant black organization seeking integration and an end to racial segregation.

Although I never had any official organization — except *Ebo Voice*, a four-page stencilled or Xeroxed pamphlet which we called a journal, concentrating more on literary matters than political and racial — my naïveté about infiltrators, telephone tapping, infiltrators which we called "house niggers," and all systems of spying on me — if I was of such importance to the Canadian authorities! — exposed me to the easiest "watching." I was a target for any amateur intelligence officer. My life was an open book. And I had opened the pages myself. It did not occur to me at the time that the Americans in Toronto, through the agency of their consulate general, would be interested in my writing, or my writing of articles on racial discrimination; and even after I returned to Toronto with the first serious interview of Malcolm X in 1963, did it cross my mind that I was some kind of "security" risk. And the fact that I was — from my learned sophistication about telephone tapping, and from the mouths of infiltrators and other brands of "house-niggers" — of more than passing interest to American and Canadian authorities, was explained more from the nervousness that ran through those organizations, tempered by racial guilt, than any significance on my part, that I had anything important to divulge. Years later, when I learned the reason for my rejection of Canadian citizenship by the minister of citizenship, and the refusal by the Americans to grant me a visa to teach at Yale University, it was based entirely on "information which is confidential" and "not in the public interest to reveal." Unless there is more "confidential" and "public interest information" buried in the vaults of the ministry and the U.S. Consulate General in Toronto, my rejection was based upon a letter of complaint written to the Canadian authorities by a white woman, who objected to the sentiments I expressed in the article published in *Maclean's* magazine, under the headline, "Canada's Angriest Black Man." I was not even permitted by this unknown white woman — and here lies the danger: the unknown informant — to be "angry," after all the insults and indignities I might have suffered, and was suffering in the 1950s, on my arrival here as a student, by an immigration system, and an employment system, irrevocable as a gentleman's agreement, which sought to keep me numbered amongst the underclass. Canada had to have an underclass, because it was a racist society, and each racist society needs to have a class, usually visible so far as complexion is concerned, to kick around. I would say that this is the basis of the success of capitalism — this worker class, this gang of immigrants who are janitors, cleaners, car-park attendants, elevator operators, sweepers, and taxi drivers. In early times, in this country, this underclass emptied spittoons, toilets pits, vomit and faeces from hospital wards and rooms.

I believe that I was "watched" and my telephone was tapped because I am black and a writer whose writing was radical in comparison to the sentiments expressed by other writers, both white and black, who had no conviction to take a stand against racism. And I mean to suggest that I was a target because Canada was racist: and did not, to put it quite bluntly, like black people; particularly black people who were not afraid to speak out. In these days of the fifties, this city and this country showed no inclination to embrace the black strangers living amongst them, in a way to suggest mutuality of decency and civilized social intercourse. There have been individual cases of such mutually beneficial relationships; but as a "policy," not a public declaration by a government, but rather an "understanding," a code of behaviour and of etiquette, even something suggesting the term that came to be used, "multiculturalism," there was nothing of this social and behavioural intermingling and "understanding" that we now take for granted, for instance, by the fleetest glance at the landscape of Toronto.

The change in the attitude and in the comprehension of the social, racial, and political inter-relationship amongst African, African Americans, Jews, and Irish that exists today, had repudiated, perhaps scorned the "linking of Black, Jewish and Irish suffering and oppression."

When former slaves like Frederick Douglass invoke the words in Psalm 137: "By the rivers of Babylon, there we sat down. Yes! We wept when we remembered Zion," he was indulging in more than the similarity in the echo of racial suffering and oppression: he was showing the symbiotic nature of the two codes, or appeals, or ideologies.

Here is part of a letter that Douglass wrote to William Lloyd Garrison on February 26, 1846, regarding the question of slavery, and the moral need to abolish it. But in this letter, George Bernstein suggests that Frederick Douglass was showing his surprise at the "degradation of Irish oppression," which led him to take a new interest in the anti-slavery struggle:

> Of all places to witness human misery, ignorance, degradation, filth and wretchedness, an Irish hut is pre-eminent ... without floor, without windows, and sometimes without a chimney ... a picture representing the crucifixion of Christ ... a little peat in the fire place...a man and his wife and five children, and a pig ... a hole ... into which all filth and dirt of the hut are put ... frequently covered with a green scum, which at times stands in bubbles. Here you have an Irish hut or cabin, such as millions of people in Ireland live in...in much the same degradation as the American [Negro] slaves. I confess that I should be ashamed to lift my voice against American slavery, but that I know the cause of humanity is one the world over.

But relations between blacks and Jews, and blacks and Irish, have not always been hospitable. Remember that some of the worst race riots in New York involved the Irish immigrants and the American Negro. Remember that Stokely Carmichael issued an edict banning Jews from taking part in the demonstrations organized by the Student Non-Violent Committee (SNCC). And remember that here, in Toronto, Mayor Givens extended an invitation to Governor Wallace, at the height of his declaration of "segregation (in Arkansas) would be forever," to speak at Maple Leaf Gardens. This was in the mid-1960s. Remember, too, that in 2004, the mayor of Toronto, Mel Lastman expressed his consternation about travelling to Africa with the Toronto committee seeking to attract the Olympics to this city, that he did not relish the possibility of being boiled in a pot. There was no apology, no attempt to assuage the impropriety of the two instances I have mentioned: Mr. Givens's invitation to George Wallace, and Mr. Lastman's allusion to Africans' cannibalism. I cannot remember the attitude of Mayor Givens, but Mr. Lastman regarded his statement as a joke, saying he was not serious, that he was not a racist.

This indelicacy is usually not regarded as damaging, or even as expressing a change in the close relationship that the three oppressed groups, Jews, Irish, and Negroes, used to honour. But when the shoe is on the other foot, for instance, when Reverend Jesse Jackson, in a lapse of judgment during his running for the U.S. presidential nomination, was stupid enough to say in a speech in Harlem, that New York was "Hymie Town," and the wrath of the accusation of anti-Semite fell upon his head, and upon his political campaign. His statement ended any realistic chance of acceptability — even by those Jews who had no political intention to vote for Reverend Jackson.

Consider now, Amiri Baraka (Leroi Jones) and his poem about the 9/11 attacks on the World Trade Center, "Somebody Blew Up America" written while he was still the poet laureate of New Jersey, and in which he enumerates the massacre and oppression of black people in America, Leroi (which is what I call him), refers to "five Israelis filming the attacks; and asks in the poem:

Who knew the World Trade Center was gonna get bombed
Who told 4000 Israeli workers at the Twin Towers
To stay home that day
Why did Sharon stay away?

The governor of New Jersey, James E. McGreevey, asked for Leroi's resignation, "because of the poem quoted above, which Leroi read at a poetry festival," Leroi believed, and said so, that "Israel had advance knowledge of the September attacks." Leroi refused to resign.

In 2004, the same governor resigned from his office because of a homosexual incident, in which he feared his lover would expose him.

The duel between Leroi and the governor struck the inhabitants of New Jersey as surprising, since the state has a poetic tradition that includes Walt Whitman, William Carlos Williams, Allen Ginsberg, and a turnpike rest stop named for Joyce Kilmer. The *New York Times* commented that Leroi said, "superfluously that he dislikes poetry as 'decoration.' He likes strong stuff that rattles people. 'If they resent what I am saying, I can resent their resentment,' he said, 'but I'm not going to censor them.'"

When we came here to Toronto, in the mid-fifties, as immigrants and as university students, very ordinary, nice, mature, and Christian-minded men and women like Mr. Mel Lastman, wondered aloud — at times, in our presence — whether we black people, immigrant and student, "had tails," and some of these men and women inspected our backsides, surreptitiously, of course, as Canadian propriety dictates to see if we had tails. Some wondered if we "lived in trees," and some, still with a disquieting curiosity, wanted to know whether it was true that we ate one another. And some of these Christian-minded men and women called us monkeys.

Many times, on subway and streetcar, small children, barely able to talk, exclaimed with the gratification that their recent fluency with words afforded, "Mummy! Look, a chocolate man!" Those of us who had studied literature, West Indian or African, recognized immediately that the child's own literary preference lay in Little Black Sambo, enhanced perhaps, by some homespun soliloquies coached into his brain, by mother and father — if only subliminally. Perhaps, the child was read a new kind of bedtime story, different from Dr. Seuss, or Hans Christian Andersen, and that *Uncle Tom's Cabin* was selected instead.

We could not refuse to admit to the possibility that this small child had received instruction at home, in secret, of racial curiosity (and intolerance) about the sudden, strange, presence of so many black people upon the geographical and psychological landscape of Toronto's absolutist whiteness.

Toronto in 1955 was a plateau of lily-whiteness, remarkably intolerant as if this was metropolitan or provincial policy, and its disposition toward black people ventured on the truculent in the white-black psycho-existential complex, that is to say, the physical closeness of blacks to whites, all of a sudden, and without preparation, created the mutuality of distrust based upon race.

In the late fifties, when accommodation at Ontario resorts in the cottage districts of green grass and chilly lake water, which were not then rented to Jewish persons, in these days when the Granite Club refused membership to the Jewish wealthy, when Jews were restricted to quotas in certain professional courses at the University of Toronto, a very ordinary, nice, mature, and Christian-minded man, very much like Mr. Mel Lastman, but by the name of Mr. Pierre Berton, exposed this racism in housing — and other anti-Semitic discriminations — in a series of articles in the *Toronto Star*. We from Africa and the West Indies applauded Pierre Berton's courage and decency, and we formed in our minds an allegiance with him. His and our appeal in the mid-sixties to racial tolerance and integration was a common plea. (I was disheartened to watch the ceremony of readings and toasts and panegyrics that flowed at the memorial service held for Pierre Berton at the CBC, and which was televised, perhaps, to the entire country, for it presented Mr. Berton in a "whitened" state of consciousness and opinion. Mr. Berton, to me, has done more than most politicians and bureaucrats in Toronto and in Canada, to rid our society of racism and prejudice. His series of articles on the woes of Jews and blacks, during the 1960s is one of the most impressive commentary and analysis ever done in this country. So, when I saw the omission from the ceremony of this significant aspect of his life, I was disheartened, but I was not really surprised. For Mr. Berton's career and his "acceptance" into the Canadian Literary Establishment — whatever this is! — has only recently been vouchsafed. I remember the days, in the sixties, the seventies, and the eighties, when Mr. Berton was not taken seriously as a writer. Yes, his articles, and his appearances on television programs, debates, and *Front Page Challenge* showed him to be more entertainer than writer, or historian of popular culture. So, even though my distress at the exclusion from praise of Mr. Berton's understanding of the treatment of Jews and blacks in Canada, and their allegiance in the fight for equality, I was nevertheless gratified to see his work re-evaluated and his character come through a revision from its previous, pervading rejection — the ignoring of his talent. He has emerged from being a "hack writer" who churns out books, to commentator of the flesh and bones, the skeleton, of Canadian sensibility toward honesty. Pierre Berton made simplicity and honesty a revisited Canadian virtue. I was pleased, in spite of the attempt to "whiten" his literary and social persona, to see that he was honoured.

Pierre Berton presented, through debate, the rawness of Canadian racism. In his interviews and commentaries, on radio, on television, and in the *Toronto Star*, he challenged our prejudices. (He was after all the first serious Canadian journalist to interview Malcolm X.)

In the early sixties, when we black people in Toronto (and Canada), were buoyed by our false sense of racial tolerance (or euphemistically, by our smallness of racial intolerance), and we displayed a superciliousness in our attitude of superiority towards those "racist Americans" — high-powered water hoses, bombings of Negro churches, murder, rape, and savage police beatings of suspects; more palatable demonstrations of truculence and of racial animus, than a little girl's naive inquiry after "a chocolate man, Mummy"; a very ordinary, nice, mature, and Christian-minded man, a charitable man, Rabbi Feinberg — and I — marched in demonstrations and took part in sit-ins, to protest segregation and racial discrimination in American cities; against the assassination of Medgar Evers, against apartheid in South Africa, and the equally vicious racial soliloquy of Mr. Mel Lastman; and, before his time, during the pass-book riots by black South Africans in Johannesburg that exposed the cruelty of white South African police, up stepped Mr. Garfield Weston, president of Weston Bakeries and of Loblaws, with his own soliloquy concerning his belief that "every black piccaninny or black mammy can call on the government for solutions to every social problem." Jewish men and Jewish women joined our insignificant ranks in these protests against Garfield Weston's sentiments. Our ranks were thin, but the new alliance of Negroes and Jews revitalized our ranks.

It was always assumed that Jews shared the "psycho-existential complex" with black people, that their suffering and oppression, their present racial nationalism came out of that experience of persecution, which is, arguably, of the same "complexion" as slavery. There could not be two more symbiotic political sensibilities to fight expressed racial hatred.

The mutually beneficial alliance of "Negroes and Jews" was fashioned many years ago upon moral principles, including in America, the WPA projects of the late 1930s, based also upon the similarity in political philosophy that caused members of the two groups to be affiliated with socialism, if not communism. In these days, socialism was almost synonymous with racial and political freedom. The psychology that exists at the bottom of this affiliation lies in its fascination with Russian Communism, and with Trotsky and Stalin, and the Russian Revolution. It is based also upon the more realistic and symbiotic tribal closeness of the two groups who are victims of racial animosity and persecution, who had a common history in the 1930s.

We come now to the year 2001.

I have been puzzling, since 1955, on the reasons used to defend racial intolerance. I have considered the economic reason, the environmental reasons, the sociological reasons, and still, with each time the head of racialism is reared, I have to go back to Frantz Fanon, and see in his explanation, the most feasible reason. Fanon believed that the Negrophobia that exists in Canada, is dermatological. It is a disease. Lingering in the blood. In the veins. "Bad blood," my mother used to say. And if it is in the blood, then this is the best interpretation to apply to Mr. Mel Lastman's truculent behaviour, in spite of the advances in "race relations" that we have made in this city, and this province, especially in this city of Toronto.

But blood is blood. And blood will have its say. Now, this question of blood brings to bear the corollary, "racial collective responsibility."

Mr. Lastman's soliloquy brushes all of us who are black. But it does not miss those of you who are "white." It diminishes both black and white. James Baldwin argued that racialism does not corrode the mind of the victim, only: it also eats away at the mind of the man who created the victim. Victor and victim are destroyed. And if this is so, it really is a point of great moral virtue and astonishment to recognize and to be deafened by the silence of those elected white people, who normally are radical and moral, conscious and outspoken on all matters that are not directly related to, and that have no clear, direct identifiable connection with racialism, to voice an opinion. Baldwin also had a term for this convenient sudden inability to voice an opinion, for this convenient silence. He called it "the immorality of silence."

Where then, in the passing of wind, the passing hurricane in the wind of Mr. Lastman's word that wrecks years of piling brick upon brick to construct a statue of multiculturalism are those conveniently "periodic radical views?" Where is the premier of the province? Where is the attorney general? Where is the Human Rights Commissioner? Where is the police chief? Where are the mayors of towns surrounding — all except Mrs. Hazel McCallion?

Where were Councillor Layton and his radical partner in the crime of politics, Ms. Chow? And where is — even if it is not proper for him to voice an opinion publicly in this matter that transcends the jurisdiction to contend with the separation of law from politics?

I have never met Mr. Mel Lastman, but I worry that the span of similar years, 1955 to 1975, did not expose him to the bitterness of racialism of the sixties, both here in this city and elsewhere in Canada, and to the struggle of good men like Pierre Berton, Rabbi Feinberg, Roy McMurtry, and others, but most importantly, to the pride that some of us, can, justifiably, wallow in, and say that in spite of the silence on important racial matters, in spite of the interminable, gnawing, and destructive eroding of racial harmony from the spirit of some of us, Toronto's summers have never been "long and hot" in the same way as Watts, Chicago, Newark, Detroit, Selma, and Harlem have been. No Canadian author has had the inspiration to label his or her forecast of the racial situation in Toronto and Canada, as "the fire next time." The unrelenting persecution and racism, as silent and sophisticated as it is, has not, as it ought not to have had, theoretically, brought about a revolution. Not even a revolution of black political thought. We are all integrationist conservatives; and still are able to be hypocritical about the silence with which we endow that conservatism.

Do we dare argue that Toronto is not, in spite of the former mayor's statement about the fear, the threat to him, of black cannibalism, a very racist city? The mayor's statement has hit us hard here, as it has, for generations, hit those who live in Africa.

The mayor offered a weak argument to postpone — I use the word, advisedly — to postpone his resignation from office, by attempting to confuse the number of ballots cast in his favour, in the election, as the statement of overweening popularity — but who were his opponents? — with his intrinsic, innate inability to say a racist word. His argument is puff, is straw. Unless he can show that those who voted for him in such numbers, assumed that when they cast their ballots, that he was going to make racist statements in their behalf, then surely he cannot now claim umbrage and electoral sovereignty and personal innocence with those very votes.

And those who voted for Mr. Lastman must certainly feel some discomfiture that their votes, cast in ignorance and disbelief of this development, are now being manipulated to keep him hanging on to the girth of a moose.

It has done something else. It has caused me great shame. It has reawakened my reservation against trust, and challenges the conviction of the "niceness of Toronto," and has added a taint to the honours which Toronto and Canada have given me — Member of the Order of Ontario and Member of the Order of Canada.

I am, morally, and virtually balancing, with a feather bearing the determining weight, between "yes," and "no," of returning my Order of Ontario, along with the Order of Canada. And seeking refuge elsewhere, perhaps in Brixton, London, in England.

I wrote this note of censor against Mayor Lastman's rabid offensive comments, as a means to encourage debate on the subject, but the Toronto sensibility is so conservative on these matters, so immoral in its silence, that I left it unfinished. Its enthusiasm melted like the snow in May, and the "silence" because indifference and individual satisfaction which in wiping out the injury to self and to race, rendered the problem no problem at all. Toronto went back to is placid contentment. "No prab-lem, man! No prab-lem!"

Many years ago, almost twenty, I was in Vancouver promoting *The Origin of Waves*, and saw this sign, painted in blue-black spray, in capital letters, taking up three lines, on a white wall. I cannot remember if the wall was the wall of a house, or of a store, or of a public building. In the photograph that I took, there is the sky, blue with white clouds, and on the right-hand side, is what looks like a metal staircase, leading up to the blue and the white in the skies; and on the ground are more metal pipes, and sharp pieces of rock, and the ground. It is an aesthetically unpleasing portrait of a street, of a neighbourhood, of a city — of Vancouver:

> OUT WHITE MANS
> CANADA NOW FOR
> ASIA PEOPLES

There are serious problems with the syntax of this sentence, which is perhaps not a sentence at all. It is not a declaration. It is not a summons. It is more like the intractableness of a new testament. It is both a declarative statement and a plea.

It is chilling.

And my next curiosity is to define the author of these sentiments, to draw his picture, to see his face, and to see whether the way he looks and the way he talks and the way he walks, is similar in its lumbering, its awkwardness, to the difficult language he is learning to use, in his plea for political and geographical belonging; and status.

And the harder I sprain my brain to paint a picture of him, one that is true, and is not based upon the effect of the sensational gnashing of teeth that surrounds his written testament, the more he is a figment of my imagination, a man walking in the thick mists and low clouds of Vancouver's weather. A man in the mists. Impossible to capture on canvas with paint.

I wanted to find it to send to Mayor Mel Lastman at the appropriate time. But I had misplaced it until this very moment. And now, for three reasons, it is too late.

CHAPTER TWENTY-ONE

Audience with the Queen

In a colour photograph, with dimensions of seventeen and one-half inches by eleven and one-quarter, is Her Britannic Majesty, Queen Elizabeth the Second, sitting with calm, and stoic determination — impossible through her Britannic power to ever feel that numerical smallness leads to being in the minority! Herself alone, amongst forty-seven men; and not one other woman in the photograph! Some of the men are cut off at the shoulder, others at the neck, in order to be accommodated within the cropping of the photograph. The photograph shows the Queen in the middle of the first row, sitting in that row, with the four officers, members of the 1st Battalion of The Argyll and Sutherland Highlanders at Howe Barracks in Canterbury. The Queen is surrounded with barely detected smiles on the faces of the officers' sternness. Not one of them is smirking. This is serious business, spit-and-polish such as I had seen on the countenance and the black boots of the Guards officer, on the eighth of March 2004, a Monday, at 12:40 p.m., when I arrived, chauffeured in a Mercedes-Benz, at the main entrance to Buckingham Palace. I was having my audience with the Queen. It was the last symbol, acknowledgement — the cheque had preceded it, so too had the congratulations from around the world — of my having won the Commonwealth Writers' Prize for having written the best book in the Commonwealth in the year 2003.

The whole week was full of enthusiasm, of reminders of the British Commonwealth, which in a way has really not ceased to exist, but is still burly and contented, satisfied with its girth of influence and power; and revisiting old themes, old castles, old shops, old roads that bring back their only memories, it was almost like going home, going home to mother, and to the Mother Country. And I was in the midst of this, as an honoured writer, but in a real sense, even if I did not absorb it, beginning with Commonwealth Day, which was observed in its lingering taste of history, my history, the history of colonialism, this history it was that defined me and my presence amongst the powerful and the wealthy of the Commonwealth.

Commonwealth Day was observed with a late afternoon service at Westminster Abbey.

On Sunday afternoons, late and before the bells of St. Matthias Anglican Church, climbing the hills in the fading presence of the humidity, which left the land just as dusk was descending like a chastisement, to remind us that in one hour, Evensong and service shall start with the organist, Mr. Williams (nobody dared remember his Christian name, or called him by it, he was such a musical genius — some called him Bach, and some called him Palestrina, not even knowing who they were — that it was unspeakable to claim equality with him), he who got the organ to breathe like what we were told in elementary school, whales breathed like, "parading on the pedal organ which breathed like a sea monster," the single speaker of the "private set," its aerial a piece of fine wire given to my stepfather (I shall call him Father after this, for he behaved and treated me as a father would; and did), by the neighbourhood joiner, and tuned to Hilversum, in the Netherlands, religiously from nine o'clock this Sunday morning, and all other Sunday mornings so long as I lived in the grey-painted house, with white trim, windows, doors, eaves and gate, named "Macon," after a town in the American South in which the "private set" pinpointed a religious sermon by a Southerner whose accent my father could barely understand; a place whose geography no one in the neighbourhood knew, or could find out about; and the men in the neighbourhood, policemen like he was (he was a private and remained a private for most of his life; and then turned lance corporal, with the Distinguished Service Record, the best in Her Majesty's Royal

Constabulary in the Island, for having not arrested one man, one criminal, one suspect during the twenty-four years he walked the beat). So,
carpenters, joiners, fishermen, and the man who drove the iron drill
into the coral stone, in the rock quarry, and thought of his wife each
time he tore up the palms of his hands, and the soft flesh between his
thumb and index finger, from five until six, standing alone in this quarry,
his kingdom of rock and dust and pebbles and marl, every day except
Sunday, they all — meaning the men; the women were wiser and kept
their silence — said that my father was mad, crazy, "crazy as shite!," that
"you loss your fucking marbles, man"; and to his face, they called him
"Foolbert," meaning that he had passed the limit beyond possible saving.
And when they called him "Foolbert," I did not laugh in agreement
with them, because he who had begun as my stepfather one year after
I was born, had now become my father, in word, in love, and in deed;
so, together, son and fathering-stepfather, around six-thirty, with the
heavy sound of the organ from Westminster Abbey whose choir we in
Barbados did not think could "sing as sweet as we," but which we listened
to, religiously; going down the hill where the stone cutter worked alone in
the hot sun until midday Saturday afternoon, payday, through the fields
of sugar cane and Indian corn, hedgerows of pigeon peas, like fragile
guardians to protect the boys in the neighbourhood from stealing the
young, sweet canes, or digging up a hole of eddoes, or sweet potatoes to
sweeten the pot, their roots and fragile limbs to serve as dams to prevent
the rain water from washing the fields down the hill, and into the sea;
cross the Brittons Hill main road, near the Tank, a hill built out of grass
and dirt, like a fort made out of the ground, owned by the Marine Hotel,
but claimed by us as a cricket pitch to play firms on, during the week,
and "Tess Matches" on Saturdays and Sundays. Then, down the incline,
walk along the gap where I began my life, into St. Matthias Village,
passing Mr. Edwards's cows who did not observe Sundays, and the pigs
quarrelling at five minutes to seven on a Sunday evening, precious as a
wedding, and as loud and as dirty and as smelly, as during the week, but
reminding us of our order of black pudding and souse made and delivered by Mistress Edwards, we turned left, under the streetlamp with the
forty-watt bulb that burned from six till five the next morning, in front
of the reddish-brown painted house, a one-roof-and-shed-roof, with a

six-foot galvanized paling, like a moat, to prevent fowl-cock thieves from climbing over, to grab a Leghorn or a Barred Rock pullet, this galvanized paling painted glossy black, guarded this house tidy as a Scottish cottage, where George Benn lived with his aunt, and across the white gravel road, passing five more houses like this, but which are painted grey, the St. Matthias Elementary School for Girls. Then, the large wall-house with breadfruit trees, Julie mango trees, sugar apple trees, golden apple trees, and a dunks tree in the backyard, making Africa and jungle of this special verdancy; and one bougainvillea tree at the front, beside the six cement steps you have to mount to reach the latticed front door, to press a bell the size of a cent, to bring Mr. Morrison, the retired headmaster of the boys' elementary school, who wrote with a Waterman fountain pen, grey and black and white, where he lives with a wife no one has ever seen; and a servant, a woman who walks the road as if she is Mistress Morrison, his wife. Mr. Morrison lives here, in Labour Blest, the name he christened his house with. Writing with a nib pen into his thick ledger book, lined in red and black, with blue-black Quink ink, the entries of the Savings Society, "a penny a week," and having it marked by his italic handwriting in the ledger book, like a secret, that you were "paid up — clear, just in case you dead suddenly, you paid up, and your survivors could get a nice 'turn-out' from Mister Corbin the Undertaker …"

You walk up the path of the East Gate, with the bougainvillea and the mayflower and wisteria blowing into your face like the handkerchief of a woman whose love for you is dipped in No. 4711; and you know, as you are walking beside your stepfathering father, that you cannot steal a glance in the direction of any girl; and you understand the sacredness of stone and coral stone, and rock in these surroundings, for the graves, tombs and slabs of marble with the names of Englishmen on them, in gold, are not to be disturbed, so the same silence of your passage over all this history that died in the Island centuries ago, will remind you in whose presence you are; and it is the same as if you are in Westminster Abbey, in the presence of the Queen of England, of prime ministers from the four square corners of the world, and by the world, because you are a black Englishman, you mean the Commonwealth. The Commonwealth is the successor of the British Empire. It is the remaining decaying anachronism and metaphor contained in "Rule Britannia."

I had never been in such presence of the mighty, the high and the low mighty. The swath of former Empire swept wide. The Speaker of the Legislature of Ontario, a Jamaican by birth, the Honourable Alvin Curling, was present. Bishop Tutu was there. But I mention these two only to give scope and wideness of theology and politics to the service of benediction, and of praise. One more must be singled out. Three is a good number, a lucky number back home in the Island. Three is a female number, a woman told me once.

Westminster Abbey is larger than either St. Matthias Anglican Church or St. Michael's Cathedral Church. But the feeling that you are in the presence of saints and holy men and wealth and power and the correct way to behave, and the silence of finger touching lip. From their posture and gait, from the way they held the Hymn Book, from their enthusiasm in singing the hymns, slightly off key, slightly too loud, except for those with good voice and pitch, I concluded that the English in Great Britain, are of lusty voice, unashamed to contribute to the ritual and hymn-singing of this great abbey. It is as if each one of them knew exactly the year in which Westminster was built, how many bricks were quarried in its construction, and the first year it opened. And that somebody in the skeleton of their history was an artisan, if not a "straw-boss," if not the architect, stonemason, artist who created the stained-glass windows. I could compare this splendour with the sugar-cane fields of my own Island; artisans, women and men who spent most of their waking hours picking weeds from the rich, rewarding soil, bent almost in half. But here were English artisans working in stone and mortar, cement and wood, beams hewn from trees whose bodies were stout like hearts of oak, understood before their time, looking into the future, how to make a whisper in a church, in an abbey, and have it resound like the amplification of microphones. This they knew, and gave us the simile that means absolute silence, and referred it to the church mouse. Quiet as a church mouse.

And then, from somewhere in the deepness of the abbey, incense and rich deep-coloured velour, from choir stall, from chancel, from altar, from pulpit, came the third important personage I have enumerated, known to me. Courtney Pine. Dread-locked "like a lion from Zion."

I was dread-locked, too. And I claimed immediately a brotherhood of cultural understanding.

In this quiet came the Lion, with tenor saxophone, meandering through nave and aisle, walking along each aisle like a needle with fine thread, sewing the geography of his art; for it was as if, not only the saxophonist, but what he stood for: Bob Marley, Ras Tafari, all black men in England and in other places, back in Jamaica, was making a claim of possession, if not a claim of associated ownership. For Westminster Abbey this late afternoon was turned into St. Matthias Anglican Church, and into St. Michael's Cathedral Church, and into Charlotte Street in Port-au-Spain, on Carnival day.

"Redemption Song!"

The irony is as dramatic as is the appropriateness of the song.

I closed my eyes and allowed Courtney's saxophone to water the words that Bob Marley first planted in 1980, almost a quarter of a century ago. Would he have thought that his "Redemption Song" would be played at this Commonwealth Day, in the presence and hearing of queens and kings and prime ministers and dictators, with the Queen present? And princes, too? I kept my eyes closed and I was now hearing John Coltrane and his management of keys and sharps and chords, and the multiplication of notes in the furious expression of the blues content in "Redemption Song."

I opened my eyes, expecting this Commonwealth congregation, including Bishop Tutu, to scream, "Yes, Bob Marley. Yes. We shall help sing these songs of freedom." For indeed, when you took us out of the abbey, when the taxi, bus, private motor car, or chauffeur-driven diplomatic limousine has delivered us to our destination and address, we might very well be in need of some redemption. Our true natures will have been exposed to the police or the skinheads, or just the mean-spirited. This is why I closed my eyes and imagined other things, as Courtney Pine walked down the aisles of the abbey, serenading Queen and prime minister, bishop, and speaker of the house.

The dignitaries in the abbey in full beautiful blast of Courtney's saxophone, moved in their personal redemption, were too dignified through custom and class to break out in clapping, to applaud. But you hear the beating of their hearts and their palms, in silent applause. It was left to the hoi-polloi, the witnesses without invitation embossed by Commonwealth insignias, not restricted by that protocol, to clap their hands in a joyful appreciation of the clear, piercing, precise notes, the daggers of his artistry being plunged deep into their hearts. In full appreciation. "Won't you help to sing these songs of freedom?"

We walked, as if in a slight rain, although no rain was falling, but we walked as if we were being drizzled by the water of tears and applause from the notes of "Redemption Song," to a reception; ushered into a room that was small and that had more than fifty persons standing with drinks, recalling the way the saxophone's notes went through their hearts. These I had not seen in the abbey. They had better seats than I had; but we were all members of the same family of the Commonwealth, and we knew this by the quality and the amount of champagne being poured into our flutes.

On a chair, away from the press of people and the passing waiters pouring drinks and champagne, was Bishop Tutu and his wife. I had heard everything about the Bishop, had disagreed with him sometimes, had agreed with him sometimes; did not agree with him and his court of reconciliation. South African whites should pay for South African whites' brutality to South African blacks. Here he was, with his wife, jovial and happy and wise. Just one month before, in an American city, promoting my novel *The Polished Hoe*, a woman came up to me, and said, "Oh, gosh! I mistook you for Bishop Tutu!"

I was not sure there was a compliment intended. I think South Africa's whites should do penance for their treatment, all these years, of South Africa's blacks. I remembered each time my appearance was associated with a South African black: Chief Luthuli, Nelson Mandela, and one South African coloured whom I helped to get out of South Africa, at the height of the atrocities of apartheid, and my friend who attended McMaster University in the sixties. He gave me his pass book. He gave it to me, to make me know, from reading the restrictions with my own two eyes, how deep in the marrow of a black man was the insult slammed into his face, like a rotting pie; that was his daily experience. This pass book is one of the most precious gifts I have. So, I was pleased to meet the Bishop, and to introduce myself to him; and to his wife.

"If you do not mind, sir," I said, having by now had three flutes of champagne, which I am sure loosened my tongue to make this approach. "I must tell you that people mistake me for you, and say, 'You look so much like Bishop Tutu.'"

"They make a mistake," he said, smiling. His wife was attending.

"Why do you think so, sir?"

"You are much more handsome than I!"

His wife nodded her head. I was not sure whether it was an acknowl-edgement of the truth, or of her husband's diplomacy.

He told me he was drinking water.

And then I was beside a beautiful black woman, standing beside her husband; for she was an English Olympic star, and her husband was a Dutch Olympic star, and they introduced me to Sir Bob Geldolf, known for his financial assistance to African countries. And then, a voice of warning, of diplomacy announcing that Her Majesty the Queen was about to pay us a visit and we fumbled for a few moments about what to do with our glasses, white wine, red wine, whiskey or champagne. Would there be offence, to be in the presence of Her Majesty, holding a glass of champagne? But a few brave, accustomed hands held on to their drinks, and Herself was introduced to those of us, with preference in the order of our standing — or should I say, those with standing in the order of Her preference ...

"Your Majesty, may I present Mr. James, this year's winner of the Commonwealth Best Book Literary Prize?"

I bow as I have seen men, in the presence of Her Majesty, bow.

"Good evening, Mr. James."

I have just risen from my bowing.

"Your Majesty ..."

And behind the Queen, is Prince Philip, who is told, "... May I present Mr. Clarke?"

The little mistake about names is corrected.

And the Prince and I shake hands. And Prince Philip moves on. There are many hands to shake. And it is the Prince of Wales's turn, in the order of preference, and the introducer, a man from an African country, Ghana perhaps, judging from the beauty and embroidery on his white robe, tells the Prince, "May I present Mr. Clarke." And I stare at Charles as much as I can under the circumstances, knowing that a commoner does not stare into the countenance of royalty, but I had to take account of the man punished in the opinion pieces of the British press and the press of those countries who deal in gossip; and I saw his eyes, and the proper cut of his collar, and the size of the knot in his tie, admirably outfitted. But it was his shoes, and the sheen of the shine. No ordinary hands could have achieved this professional brilliance on the Prince's black shoes. And the same must be said of the shoes Prince Philip wore. Someone told me, years ago, that you could tell a man's character by looking at his shoes. If a man's shoes are not shined, then there is a reasonable conclusion to be made: the man is sloppy, and not only in dress. I have always hidden from this declaration, since I wear only suede shoes; suede shoes because I think they make me look like an artist. Black shoes and brown shoes make me look like an undertaker or a civil servant. Or a businessman. I wear black shoes only with a "monkey suit," and at funerals. And the times I am called upon to wear my "monkey suit" are infrequent. The shoes! And the sheen in the polish of the shoes.

Someone took a photograph of my introduction to these three members of the Royal Family, Elizabeth II, Prince Philip, and the Prince of Wales. In this photograph, the African diplomat who introduced me is standing in the centre like a referee, like a judge not certain that the behaviour of the man he has just introduced will meet his high standard. There is a certain undecidedness. An anxiety. But when I look more carefully at the photograph, the smile on the African diplomat's face is reassuring. He has swallowed the "boo-boo" he made of my name to the Queen, and is relieved that no one, not even Majesty, will be disposed to the suggestion that the Tower of London is a better address for this diplomat than the VIP Room of the Commonwealth House.

The Queen is resplendent in her dress, the colour of salmon. My grip of her hand is firm, but not challenging. My silver slave bangle, a fashion statement of the sixties at the height of black nationalism, is conspicuous. And the Queen is wearing black gloves. And she is smiling. Perhaps, she has already known that the diplomat has made an error with names; perhaps she already knows that I am Austin Clarke, only for the reason that she has been briefed, and knows that I am the author of the memoir, *Growing Up Stupid Under the Union Jack*. Perhaps, she knows I am not "Mr. James." Perhaps, not.

There is one item in this photograph that puzzles me. A half-pint crystal tumbler, with something the colour of gin, or sparkling water, and with a slice of lemon in it. And whether it is the cleverness of the palace photographer, or the accident of this kind of candid photography, I cannot tell whose hand holds the glass with liquid sparkling like water. Or is it, thinking of the Queen Mother, a "spot of Beefeater Gin?"

The white intricately embroidered white robe of the African diplomat, has a charming but eerie gloss, that has a tinge of gold seen through a pale of clear, resplendent water. The smile on the Queen's face is genuine.

My dread locks are as long and verdant as Courtney Pine's.

The sparkling black Mercedes-Benz comes silently into the narrow parking space of the Royal Over-Seas League House, at Park Place, St. James's Street — a stone's throw from St. James's Place — and from the letterhead on the stationery, I read, of the hotel's pedigree: "Patron H.M. The Queen, Vice-Patron HRH Princess Alexandra." The Mercedes-Benz is a 2004 model.

In the car is Colin X, a member of the Commonwealth House committee, who will present me at Buckingham Palace, "for your Audience with the Queen." At twelve-forty in the afternoon, on Monday the eighth of March 2004. The car comes for me at eleven-thirty, to take me to Commonwealth House, to meet the other officers, and to get the lay of the land, so to say; and to have a gin, to settle my nerves, an assumption made by Colin, proven to be correct.

Colin's right hand is bandaged with white dressing, is bulging, is painful, is eventually conspicuous in the official photograph requested by the Queen, to be taken to mark in history that this day existed, because his little finger was broken in an accident, and had to be broken a second time to get it back in place.

The car takes us through London's busy streets, to the Palace, passing places I have been seeing in photographs in newspapers and in news on BBC television; and introduced to me first, earlier, in the Island, in textbooks, in *Punch* magazine, in the *Times* newspaper, which trickled into Barbados, and in the reading room of the British Council, many months out of date, but still contemporary in a colony; and from the description of these buildings, monuments, in the pages of novel and memoir written by West Indian authors who lived in England from the 1950s.

And then, the Palace. I had the same disappointment seeing it close up, as I had when I first stood in front of the White House, in Washington D.C., looking in. It seemed to me that Buckingham Palace and the White House have a more dramatic and architectural aesthetic power when shown in a photograph, or in a television news report, than they have when you are standing at the wrought-iron gates, looking at them; when you are a tourist. And the disappointing thing about this is that they look more ordinary, and without the power, both real and symbolic, that you have been brought up to think that they have. So, this afternoon, as the black Mercedes-Benz moved toward the entrance to Buckingham Palace, slowing down to accommodate the press of people, tourists come to see the Changing of the Guard, to peer in, unsuccessfully because of the tinted windows, to see who the important personage in the car was, as a bonus for the delay in the Changing of the Guard, I suddenly felt the power of the Palace, and the significance of my presence here. And miraculously, the Palace became grand and imposing, and was like the Palace made out of glass and diamonds in a children's book of fairy tales, inhabited by a beautiful queen, and it took on a swell-head enchantment from my being so close to its mortar and wrought-iron fence, and its glistening windows and winding staircases made of glass.

The Mercedes-Benz is directed to the main entrance of Buckingham Palace. A member of the Guards is waiting to greet us. I can see the brilliance of his black boots, in blinding shine, equal to the black shoes the Prince of Wales wore the night before. Spit-and-polish, I remember my father saying, as he spat on the thick-leathered ugly black boots issued by the Royal Constabulary of the Island; and when he was finished with them, they were like the ones I am looking at now.

All of a sudden, I am nervous. Has the Queen been told of my cynicism in the title of my memoir: *Growing Up Stupid Under the Union Jack*? And if she has, will she mention it, even in passing? But the Queen is a queen, polite, diplomatic, intelligent, wise, and worldly. And I am still nervous. The Guard ushers us to a long couch against the wall, on which are oil paintings, fields and castles and pastoral scenes of English country life; paintings I have seen before, in films and newspapers, and the *Illustrated London News* magazine.

The colour of the palace is a yellowish brown. But I am colour blind.

A delegation is waiting before us, to be presented to the Queen. Last night returns, with its colours and its races and its beautiful women, and African princes and kings in robes just like the diplomat who introduced me by the wrong name. The King of Morocco! Is there such a title, such a man? But this gentleman stood out in my memory because of the tantalizingly beautiful woman beside him, wife, queen, daughter, or lover?

This same king and his wife are sitting in the delegation waiting on my left hand. And another Guards officer goes up to them and ushers them farther along the long anteroom, on the ground floor of the Palace, and up the stairs, and into the silence, out of sight. Only the paintings, of Sir Joshua Reynolds, of J.M.W. Turner, remain to remind me of the dances and dinners and cocktail parties that have been pitched in this room, years ago.

"When we go in, you will bow. The Queen will speak first. We have ten minutes. You do not initiate any conversation." It is my friend, Colin, with the bandaged hand, instructing me on protocol.

The blindingly polished black boots of the Guards officer … I forgot to pay attention to the pips on his shoulder telling me his rank; but I think he has at least, two pips. His back is straight. Erect as a tree trunk. Spit-and-polish. And well prepared; well trained; well spoken. And kind.

"The Queen will initiate any conversation. The audience will last ten minutes. Unless the Queen prolongs this audience. You will be shown where to sit by the Queen. When the audience is ended, the Queen will press a button, which is inconspicuously placed on the table beside her, to indicate that it is over. She will stand, say goodbye to you, and you will leave, walking backwards, with a bow …" This is the Guards officer speaking. "Naturally, there will be no photographs taken. Unless the Queen orders one …"

We are led up the stairs at the end of the long room. I pass animals on English lawns and fields; and a woman is walking with a basket in her hand; and the beautiful woman from last night, walking beside the King of Morocco, comes down the dramatic stairs that shine as much as the boots of the Guards officer, and leaves her husband the king and the other members of her delegation, breaking rank, and comes up to me. The King comes too. They congratulate me; and shake my hand; and tell me when I am in Morocco, remember to call on them.

Colin with the white-gloved bad hand knows them. They have come to him, not to me, to pay greetings. But I accept my share, too; for I remember when they arrived in the black Rolls-Royce, and about ten men and women, bodyguards crowded round and hid them from view except by those who were entering the same door of dignitaries, which is when I first rested my two eyes on her flowing robes.

We are in a second floor room, a waiting room, with more paintings I have recognized from former times, but do not know the names of the men who painted them, or the names their painters have called them by; and the Guards officer cannot remember either, "although I have seen them many times." And we sink into this satisfaction and self-confidence, aware that we are in the household of the Queen, for "Her Majesty" — which is how the Guards officer addresses the Queen. "Her Majesty has decided to have your Audience in her private apartment." This says something. I am not such a commoner that I do not grasp the significance. "And she has asked that a photo be taken of you when you enter," the Guards officer adds.

Colin with the sprained finger is smiling. He wants to give me more history, and place me in the context of this history.

"Very good," he says, like an Englishman telling you that what you have heard, or what you have just spoken is very good, meaning in the language of an American, or a Canadian, "fantastic, super!"

The only other winner of the Commonwealth Writers' Prize to have had his audience with the Queen in her private apartment is Peter Carey, the Australian writer. I know Carey. I met him once at Harbourfront International Festival of Authors in Toronto. I take a cursory glance at my clothes. I straighten my tie. I inspect my fingernails. I pull my socks up. I wet my lips. I hold my right hand in my left hand, not tense; but relaxed. I look at Colin's white bandage, like a soft boxing glove, and I ask, "How's the hand?"

"Little pain."

"Good," the Guards officer says.

And as the words leave him, we are summoned to present ourselves. The door of the waiting room opens, and I hear the yapping of dogs. The Corgis! Did not one of them chew a small dog to bits, recently, in the London tabloid newspapers? I look down a hall, on my left, and there they are, royal dogs behaving like hungry dogs. There are about four, but they could have been six, all the same size. We are at the door. And everything changes. My world has come topsy-turvily on its head, around one hundred and eighty degrees, in my 'membering journey from the two-roofed and shed-roof, grey-painted house on Flagstaff Road, Clapham, St. Michael, in the Island, in the British West Indies, with its name, "Macon," on it, to Buckingham Palace, in the private apartment of Her Majesty, the Queen. I know now what it means to win the 2003 Commonwealth Writers' Prize for the Best Book. And I wonder how long it will take her to hint at the title of my memoir, *Growing Up Stupid Under the Union Jack.*

Colin sits across from us, ushered to his seat by Her Majesty.

I sit beside Her Majesty, almost knee-touching distance apart, with the round table separating Queen from "old Colonial" and with the discreet buzzer on the table, to alarm the guards and the Guards, to announce the end, to require a cup of tea, to have a martini brought into the company and the conversation, to say, "time's up!"

In the presence of kings and queens, as in the presence of dictators and cruel criminals, what is said, either to you, or by you, is not usually remembered afterward, there is no indelibility in those words spoken. The place swallows the meanings of words, and becomes the meaning of the words themselves.

Colin introduces me to Her Majesty, calling me by my right name, Mr. Clarke. And Her Majesty smiles. I take the chance, for she has spoken first, to say, "I was introduced to you, last night, as "Mr. James, ma'am." And the moment the words fall out of my mouth, I realize how stupid a thing it was to say, when so many other important, witty things could have been said. I could have commented on the Corgis, whose barking and playing I could still hear. The Queen is sympathetic, and says, "Those things do happen."

I am dumbfounded, can think of nothing more to say, and Colin, his bandaged hand no longer painful after Her Majesty has inquired of his injury, fills the discomfiture of the moment with light conversation.

"And what tie are you wearing, Mr. Clarke?"

"Harrison College, Barbados, Your Majesty."

"Oh! My trainer, Michael Stoute, is a Barbadian. His father was Commissioner of Police, I think."

I am uncertain of the word, "trainer," and I must have shown my mild curiosity, for I take the liberty to glance, most prudently, knowing she will not detect my curiosity, to see whether there is obvious evidence that Her Majesty the Queen of England has time from her impossibly busy schedule of appointments, with personages more important than myself, to jog around the gardens of Buckingham Palace; or even run up and down the stairs, with the Corgis trailing and encouraging.

"Horses," she says.

"Oh," I say, "I know Mr. Michael Stoute. He and I went to Harrison College."

Mr. Michael Stoute was no longer Mr. Stoute, but was Sir Michael Stoute. It was an afternoon, at Bigliardi's on Church Street, in the company of Barry Callaghan, drinking wine and martinis and betting on the Triactor races, in which Callaghan is a master, the best I know, that the name Michael Stoute came up; years ago. "Ain't he the Bajan who trains the Queen's horses? Who won the Derby for her?" This was the man; this was the Knight. Sir Michael.

I take the opening offered me, not deliberately, perhaps only casually, and expand on the history, and the connection, between the Island and the training of horses and knighthoods, and imagine the ring and the sound of "Rise, Sir Austin Clarke." — if only I liked horses, even to bet on them! I think it was a reasonable expansion on the skeleton of a common history, if not a common culture between Sir Michael and me.

"As a matter of fact, Your Majesty, Major Stoute was the Commissioner of Police, and my stepfather, who was a police constable, was his driver ..."

"Is that so?"

"As a matter of fact, ma'am, I had a photo of my stepfather being given a medal, Distinguished Service Medal, by Major Stoute."

"Really?"

"And the dean of the church I attend in Toronto, St. James' Cathedral Church, is the brother of Sir Michael, your trainer!"

We are, after all, in her private apartment, and the nature of our conversation is relaxed, informal, cordial, something approaching the exchange of ideas between two friends; two old friends; and the demand for formal decorum was not required. And I felt so. And when I look at the photograph she asked to be taken, from her face, and from her smile, a stranger looking at this group of three persons, so diverse, in background and place and position, there is no conclusion that they are not three friends. And you will pardon my impropriety in this expansiveness.

I look at the two fingers on her right hand, touching her engagement ring; as we stand to leave, for she has, without my knowing, without Colin knowing, touched the buzzer on the table beside which we sat, and we stand to leave, and I see the beauty of her yellow dress, which I call gold, and the light in her eyes, expressing some joy, happiness rather, some enjoyment at what is being said amongst us. I cannot recall what it is we were talking about, as we stood, just before leaving, to pose for the photograph. But her visage — I use the word, advisedly — is more that of a happy grandmother, and not the stern, reserved, thoughtful expression she has sitting amongst the members of the 1st Battalion of the Argyll and Sutherland Highlanders.

We had talked of other things, too: IBM Selectric typewriters as against IBM laptops; and how I had lost the first five hundred pages of *The Polished Hoe* and went to the grave of a depression; and now the irony of it; and children; and books; and the computer, which we, at our age and with our taste, had not much regard for; and we bid Her Majesty goodbye, remembering to bow and walk backwards; but the length of my courtesy is not imposing, for the Guards officer is there, smiling, happy that the audience went so well and so long; and he congratulates me; and he tells Colin he will see him again, sooner than he will see me, "But who knows?" Colin is walking on thin air, and I am beside him on a cloud of confusion — happy at my success, happy at my recognition, and, at the same time, like the victim, like the "old Colonial," who cannot help but remember colonialism, and who questions the singling out of me and of my work, for this success; wondering if the success is real, if the adoration and praise is honest, when I should be wallowing in the idea and in the event and in the act, instead of being crushed by this historical burden of doubt that Empire and Commonwealth had instilled in me, and in all of us, of my generation.

Her Majesty is not smiling in the photograph with the soldiers, published in the *National Post* on the 10th of November 2004.

On the 8th of November 2005, Caryl Phillips was one of ten internationally known authors invited to "Conversations: Writers and Readers in Dialogue: the Literature of Africa and Its Diaspora," sponsored and organized by the Department of English, the University of Toronto. The other authors invited were, in the order they appeared, Erna Brodber, Tayeb Salih, Linton Kwesi Johnson, Lorna Goodison, Kofi Anyidoho, Austin Clarke, George Elliott Clarke, Olive Senior and Ngũgĩ wa Thiong'o. Caryl had just won the 2004 Commonwealth Writers' Prize for Best Book. The novel is *A Distant Shore*. He understood that meeting the Queen in an audience was part of the recognition of the prize. His prologue was a well-directed barb fired in my direction. He had no intention of meeting the Queen who represents all that he resents; and as a person growing up in England in the fifties and sixties, he knew what racism of the English kind was: and he proceeded to read from a paper he had written on the subject.

I am in Willemstad, the capital of Curaçao. I have been here, once before, in 1955, coming from Caracas, Venezuela, where I spent a summer vacation with my cousin, Douglas, before coming to Toronto for university; and when the ship, the SS *Antilles*, a French steamer as we called it then, stopped at Port-of-Spain, up came on the gangplank behind me, to thunderous applause, which I assumed was meant for me; one of my favourite actors, Peter Ustinov, fresh from his triumph in *Quo Vadis*. But I remember Curaçao more than I remember Trinidad, because the humidity there could not match the humidity of Willemstad, where you could hardly breathe, and wanted cool water in any amount. And you wondered what the price of ice was, for the people born there, who had to live and work, "out in the hot-sun."

I am sitting beside a black man much younger than I am, on a sunny morning with the humidity of an afternoon in Guyana, or Trinidad, or even Toronto in mid-August the last few years, when our weather might well have been West Indian. It is the 31st of October, a Friday, in the year 2003. I have been in Curaçao since the fifteenth. My left arm is round the shoulders of this "brother." To my right, are two other "fellas," as my friend Samuel Selvon would describe these personages. Behind me, and slightly elevated because he is standing in a garden filled with ducks or swans, and where a man is playing the piano, is Louis Armstrong. The two men on my right are younger than Louis Armstrong and me, and they are dressed elegantly in white striped pants, one in a bright blue jacket, the other in red. Both have that smile, that "coon" smile, that "idiot-smile," as my mother calls it, the "smile of Foolbert," that smile that was associated with Louis Armstrong himself, the grin of the empty-headed, and the Negro. I am in the company of the inanimate, dead members of the garden statuary. These are objects. And I wonder why, even in their role as *objets d'art*, they are represented in such a servile characterization? Looking at them, from the photograph that was taken by a friend, their image mocks me, and I go back years to try to remember if in real life, in Barbados, and elsewhere in the West Indies, this sculpture's conception of black people, even during slavery, which these men stand for, was so realistically inhuman? Louis Armstrong, in his statue, is dressed in white, resplendent and fashionable, his left hand on the microphone, and his right hand holding the characteristic large white handkerchief, and his trumpet at the same time. These statuaries are in the main garden area of the hotel. And when I leave this spot, and walk to my room, I pass a short phalanx of these men's cousins: dressed in hats and helmets that mock their dignity, coloured or painted black; blackened to suit the Curaçao humidity, standing all at attention, as if they are waiting for orders from their master to serve the dinner, or stand guard. Against the light yellow of the walls along this narrow lane, these men scare me, and are not companions, but watchmen, observing my next act of sabotage, of dislike for their plantation-hotel world. Why would the owner, a Dutchman, name his hotel with a Dutch name, and retain this history of oppression in the figurines of these seven men who stand guard on the yellow painted wall, along the way to my hotel room?

There is a more pleasant vista and surroundings when I leave my room to walk to the restaurant, and the Slave Museum, and to attend the meetings, a cobblestoned pathway that is greyish blue, with walls washed in yellow, trees overhanging the fence and barrels that look as if they contain rum and molasses, and palm trees and carriage lights over doors, and I wonder which of the seven mock-men, or the other three with whom I sat many humid afternoons, had the duty to light these carriage lanterns; or sweep this laneway; or empty the garbage, both household and personal? The abiding character, the lasting personality of this hotel, Kura Hulanda — for I think that a hotel, like a person, has a personality — is its presumptuous identification with a past of slavery, and, at the same time, seeking to attract the abolitionist liberalism. The yellow walls remind me of the hot sun in the Islands. They suggest life. A good life, even if it was one that was observed from a distance, the distance of the colonized man, and the slave, the labourer working on the plantation. Kura Hulanda is a slave plantation in spite of the "artifacts" of its inhabitants, the "fellars" drawn in black wood, with faces punctuated by wide white eyeballs, stiff in their clothes, standing without a hint of life, in their historical posture, the postures of labourers. Servants. Slaves.

Beyond the Sculpture Garden and the images of slaves, Rasta men who resemble Bob Marley, beyond the mention, in three lines, written by the Guyanese poet, Martin Carter. "I Come from the Nigger Yard." The excerpt is three lines. But it is a mouthful of history:

> I come from the nigger yard of yesterday
> leaping from the oppressor's hate
> and the scorn of myself.

Martin read this portion for me, in 1965 in Georgetown, Guyana, when I interviewed him for a radio documentary for the CBC Project Series, produced by Harry J. Boyle. Martin's exhibit, if I may call it that, is mounted against a wall, and illustrated by three examples of the irons used in the "nigger yards." Without the three versions of the symbol of oppression and colonization, the three lines quoted from Martin Carter's poem do not have the same frightful effect upon the mind and the body as they would if there were no illustration.

I am thinking now, today, Tuesday, of what it means to go on this journey, bent upon digging up the past, 'membering the paths taken in that journey, over land and over sea. But wherever the journey takes me in my 'membering my passage is made easier through song. And the song could be jazz or the blues. Popular music sung by black artists, or calypso. I am listening at this moment, on this Tuesday, to Abbey Lincoln. I may, to stretch the relationship slightly, call Abbey Lincoln a friend. I met her in 1963 through Paule Marshall the novelist, who introduced me to Abbey and her husband, Max Roach, as brilliant subjects to interview for my programme about the Harlem Renaissance and the succeeding artistic enthusiasm taking over Harlem at this time. Abbey Lincoln had collaborated with Max Roach in the composition of *Freedom Now Suite*, which was banned at that time in Canada. They gave me a copy of the studio tape of the composition. Abbey and Max in turn introduced me to Nina Simone. Abbey cooked dinner that night; and Max had to go on a gig; so I went along with Nina Simone, Paule Marshall, and Abbey to the Apollo Theater where a friend of theirs, a woman who sang the blues, was performing.

Can you imagine the effect these three beautiful powerful talented women had upon me? I do not remember much about that night at the Apollo Theater, except that I had a lot of fun. I do not even remember the name of their friend, the woman who sang the blues. But I remember the laughter, and the happiness and the enjoyment. Abbey was wearing an Afro. She had been fired from gigs in downtown New York supper clubs because the Afro was regarded by white managers and owners to be too aggressive and symbolic of violence and of cultural nationalism. Abbey covered her Afro under a wig, until she could no longer stomach that compromise and "went natural." Not many women and men who were entertainers had that courage, in those days of the 1960s.

I sometimes marvel at the endurance of black men and women who are in the arts, at their ability to stomach this insult to their persons, this devaluation of their talent, to suit a white appearance of acceptability, and still are able to remain creative. And more than that, are still able to remain alive. To me, this makes their art more valuable.

And so, listening to Abbey Lincoln today, and yesterday, and tomorrow, I remember the chilling interpretation she took with her voice, the

scream of a woman in torture, her child taken from her, her man emas-
culated, and lynched, in her presence as the Southern (and Northerner,
too) white man stands unmoved by his own violence. *African Now Suite*
is the precursor of what I am listening to, at this moment — her CD,
Wholly Earth, and the cut, "Another World":

> Within some walls of stone,
> another world is
> waiting for its own.
> Another World,
> another time,
> another World.

This song, "Another World," is haunting and it makes me sad, and it
makes me happy at the same time; and when it is not her plaintive voice
and the dramatic delivery of word and voice, and emphasis, it is the
meaning of the words. "Within some walls of stone" makes me imagine
the chains and irons hanging on "those walls of stone," which are walls
built in castles in African towns and in plantations in the West Indies.

You would question my sanity therefore, if I admitted that I have
been listening to one song for twelve hours now, non-stop, from nine
o'clock this morning, until now, nine o'clock this evening. And I listened
to it six hours, last night.

What is the solace I find in this kind of music? What is the cultural
connection?

It was probably that night at the Apollo Theater, in 1963, summer,
a beautifully humid night in which your clothes were sticking to your
skin, but in a soothing manner, for there was music in the air; and
it was that first night that I saw Nina Simone in the famous fishnet
jumpsuit, which her admirers said was worn without panties and
other underwear. Nina's fishnet is on some album covers; and it is
a white outfit. Here now, I am, admiring Abbey Lincoln — (I have
her name written on a cassette tape, as "Abby Lincoln"; and I could
have sworn that this was the spelling I saw on other record albums).
But nonetheless, I am talking about beauty and style here; and I was
touched to see that Abbey has chosen a fishnet for a shawl, which

is brown matching the brownish-red long dress, a robe, she wears, conscious of Africa as she has always been; and the fishnet is wrapped round her body, and the image and the symbol and the myths and the meaning are all obvious. Abbey Lincoln is a beautiful woman, with a compelling voice, frighteningly real, especially when it is exercised in the *Freedom Now Suite* and on some songs in *Wholly Earth*. But more than the stature, there is the voice. Plaintive and punishing to the soul in a cry for freedom; the personification of determination to choose "another world."

For "another time is here." But this "time" I am in London, in 2003, taken around to sign books and to book parties in a taxi and hired cars, and following me like a shadow, or a detective, is the image of a black man dressed like an infant, with a white bonnet ending in a flowing bow and two strings tied under his chin; naked from the neck to the waist, wearing what looks like a pair of white diapers. The black man's hands form a rough triangle, holding up a sign on which is printed: WHAT'S YOUR GUILTY SECRET? The man is encased in a telephone box that is made to look like a coffin, so the man is not only standing up in the telephone box, he is lying on his back, with his eyes open, and a pacifier — which looks like spittle on his white thick lips — is in his mouth. The other writing on the coffin, reading from the top to the top of the black man's head, is WINNER OF BEST MUSICAL. JERRY SPRINGER: THE OPERA. And at the very bottom, is CAMBRIDGE THEATRE. I spent about a week trying to remember my camera to take a photo of this advertisement; and I would see the ad, in places like Soho and Covent Garden, and I would not have my camera with me and vice versa. But I was determined to take the picture. And worrying about my opportunity, and talking about my obsession with this advertisement, all the people with whom I talked about it, my publisher, my agent, the taxi drivers, none of them could see any irony, any insult, any compromise in its publication. This indifference to the true meaning of the sign, the meaning below the first layer of comprehension, reminded me of years before, in London, in Maida Vale, famous as the location of murders and mysteries in film, and in books, at the home of my editor, David Burnett of Heinemann, I came upon a large billboard advertising tea. The image used to seduce the English into purchasing and drinking this tea, was a golliwog. A face similar to the face of the man advertising the Jerry Springer opera. Round face, large red lips, bulging eyes with enlarged whites, and the hair done in what came to be the dread-lock image. To me, coming from Toronto, in 1965, this was an insult. David and I would walk out from Maida Vale and stand at the bus stop. Above our heads was the golliwog. A week went by, and David had not looked up to see the golliwog. It was part of the landscape to which he was accustomed. And it had taken me about a week to get the confidence to bring it to his attention, when I was certain that he had not noticed it. In the same way as we do not notice the details of things and people who make up the landscape on which we trundle every day. The Notting Hill Riots were still on our conscience and our consciousness, a stain on the character of the English, a contradiction in behaviour of the true Commonwealth. It seems to us as if Caliban had ventured into Prospero's streets and was punished, dehumanized, for his uppitiness. And to demonstrate the English displeasure at this intrusion, black people were called "wogs." Here now, "in another world, in another time," is the same wog: in 1965, a female wog, and in 2004, a male wog; one advertising a special tea; the other, a special opera. It is ironic to me that the opera the wog is advertising, is an American production. American wogs come from the nigger yards of yesterday — and of today.

But that morning in 1965, when I brought the huge billboard to David's attention, he sincerely had not "noticed it" before. David is a good man. A bright man. An educated man. A man of honour. I trust David. And during my two weeks in London promoting *The Polished Hoe*, I made a point to seek him out, spending four weeks, from Toronto, tracking him down. You go to such lengths to contact a real friend. David and I had dinner at the Royal Over-Seas League house where I was staying. I did not bring up the advertisement of the Jerry Springer opera. David was a shadow of his former ebullient self; an assured Cambridge University graduate in English Literature, with a career in publishing; and now, from his lips, he has "given up on women, given up on sensuality." He was living apart from his wife. He mentioned her by name, once; and that chapter, that entire life, was hermetically sealed. I did not consider it prudent to pry. But I was saddened by his disposition; and the claret which he chose tasted flat, as if its true body had been squeezed out of it. I looked silently and with fear, at my own life as I sipped the wine, and I wondered what turn of luck, what love that turned into disaster, what failure and rejection of a book, what "experience" I could have to cause me to be so intellectual and sexually monastic. David never struck me as being religious, sticking to dogma and ritual, of any denomination.

He no longer needed a telephone. I found this out in the difficulty my English agent had in tracking him down. He was now living the life of a man he had read so many times as an editor of fiction. He was now a fiction man. A man of fiction. Which of his authors he had chosen to pattern his later life after his novel; and when he was reading that particular novel, did he have already his plans for "retirement" drawn, to be followed as he had followed the development of the character in the novel?

I could choose, and did not like, any of my male characters that I would follow out of the book, off the page, and into my everyday life. Had David chosen a character from Compton Mackenzie? From Olivia Manning? From Helen MacInnes? Or Anthony Burgess? There was something of the deliberate dismissal of passion, similar to Hamlet's nihilism, in his gait. All that was left was his good manners; and manner.

David had been vindicated: he had taken me on as a writer of promise in 1964. This was now 2003. I had won the 2003 Commonwealth Literary Prize for Best Book. Olivia Manning had written this blurb, about my first novel, *The Survivors of the Crossing*, published in 1964, on the jacket of my second novel, in 1965, *Amongst Thistles and Thorns*:

> Austin C. Clarke seems to me an outstanding writer — outstanding, that is, not only among the brilliant novelists who appeared during the last decade in the West Indies, but outstanding among the writers of the English-speaking world. He has a wonderful ear for the speech of Barbados and a wonderful gift for reproducing it with wit and poetic force.

Unlike most writers with this gift, he can also tell a story and construct a novel which is compelling in the delicious revelation of the deviousness of the human heart and the painful humours of the human condition. If he does not hit the reading public like a tornado, I'll eat all the pineapples Mr. Clarke cares to provide. — Olivia Manning.

This was written, as I said, in 1964. Olivia Manning was at the height of her career as a novelist. She was married to Mr. R.D. Smith, a producer of the *Third Programme* at BBC; and it was Mr. Smith who organized a panel consisting of V. S. Naipaul, Anthony Burgess, and me, to discuss Imperial literature. The afternoon of this radio program, I took tea with Olivia Manning and her husband at their home in St. John's Wood. In the discussion, Naipaul who had a strong liking for the whiskey (the BBC was civilized in their treatment of you in the green room: you could drink and smoke, even during the radio discussion), Burgess was smoking mini-cigars; and Naipaul defended imperialistic literature. He praised Rudyard Kipling. I cannot remember what I said, except that I objected to Naipaul's obsessive appreciation of Kipling's novels about India.

But regarding the eating of pineapples, and the prophesy, I am sorry that it took from 1964 until 2003 to have Olivia Manning's declaration of my ability come to pass; and more sadly to report that in the long wait for acknowledgement that she saw in 1964, she had died before the cup could be passed to me. This is why my dinner engagement with David, at the Royal Over-Seas League dining room, was such an important event in both our lives. He had at last seen the fruits of his labour; and could now bear witness that Olivia Manning's testimony had been spread on fertile soil of expectation; and also could claim, that Olivia Manning knew her pineapples.

But just as David, forty years earlier had not "noticed anything" in the billboard with the golliwog, so too, in 2004, forty years later, no one but me seemed to have been offended by the advertisement of the Jerry Springer opera. I was offended by the erosion, the dulling of my triumph (for to be in London for those two weeks was a recognition; and the recognition was a triumph), the corroding of my image by the reminder that someone sees history in terms of many Notting Hills, and that subliminally, there is still the image of the golliwog. When I look carefully at the photograph of the black man dressed in diapers, with bonnet and pacifier, it is a golliwog I am seeing.

Thinking about this London golliwog in the advertisement, it has just come back, suddenly, after fifty years, back in the Island, attending Harrison College, the headmaster (acting), Mr. Medford, a graduate of Oxford University in Classics, who taught Sixth Form Classics, and was a brilliant master and scholar, and who, important to state was white, was nicknamed "Golli," shortened from "golliwog." And we boys, both black and white pupils, called him "Golli," not exactly to his face. But we knew, from the fact that other junior masters also called the acting headmaster "Golli" meant that "Golli" himself had accepted the nickname as a term of endearment.

You wonder then about this thing called racism, and whether it is not the context and the interracial environment in which it is expressed and spoken, that cancels out any intention of racial spitefulness.

I do not think, however, that the advertisement for tea, and for the opera, placed in popular places in London, during Notting Hill, in 1963, or today, in 2003, is the same thing as calling a white man, living in Barbados, "Golli."

Perhaps, Mr. Medford, a Barbadian, got the nickname "Golli" from English university students, when he came up to England to enter Oxford University!

CHAPTER TWENTY-TWO

The "Loyalty of Negritude" in Sport

Austin Husbands, the most beautiful sprinter to watch, as he sliced seconds and seconds off the existing records of the one-hundred-yards dash, and the 220 yards — also run by him as a "dash," was also my nemesis. He was a sergeant, I think, in the Harrison College Cadet Corps, when I was "court-martialed" at the end of the Walkers Summer Cadet Camp, in 1950.

I knew, the moment I "went through the wire" and over to Harrison College from Combermere — a wire fence separated the two schools, who were not friends, or friendly during my school days — I knew that I had to beat Austin in the one hundred yards, in order to finish Sports Day as Victor Ludorum. And to make matters worse for me, Austin had a bigger brother, John, who was equally good, but not as beautiful in his stride when he came round the last bend in the 220 yards. Girls, from our sister school, Queen's College, packed the grounds and the small pavilion, just to see Austin. And Austin was one of the first school boys to wear running shoes. Most of us ran barefooted. The natural way. I would watch Austin in his running shoes, and dream of the time when I would be able to wear the soft black leather shoes with the "sprinter's spikes" in them, and blaze the track.

We were not friends. We were not close. Although we were in the Modern Studies Sixth Form at the same time, Austin doing English language and literature and history; and I doing English language and literature and Latin. Austin was a prefect; and the next term, was Head Boy. I was a prefect, and even when I was the most senior prefect — the others having left school — the headmaster, John C. Hammond, Esq, M.A. (Cantab), who was not a friend of mine, and vice versa, refused to give me the expected honour of being Head Boy.

I am thinking of Austin now, because I had been thinking of Ben Johnson, who to me is the best sprinter Canada has ever had, and will ever have, for a long time, as I do not see anyone on the horizon, so to say, who could replace Ben Johnson. Ben Johnson is a much better sprinter than the other Jamaican; and I lost all respect for Donovan Bailey, when he "dissed" Ben Johnson, just before the 1996 Summer Olympics. It was an unkind cut: unwarranted, in the circumstances. And the circumstances revolve around the fact that Ben Johnson set the pace for all future black Canadian sprinters. This outstanding quality, performance and personality, this comparison Austin Husbands had with Ben Johnson.

In the obituary notice of Austin's death, is this paragraph: "And as his brother, Mr. Justice John Husbands recalled, 'I don't think Tom Clarke ever forgot that he was beaten by Austin in the 100 yards...'"

My name in Barbados is written as Austin "Tom" Clarke, with "Tom" as a nickname; but more than a nickname, for I am addressed, formally and informally, always as "Tom." And it is true that not only have I not forgotten that Austin beat me in the one hundred yards more times than I beat him, Austin's brilliance at this distance caused me to have nightmares the week preceding Sports Day at Harrison College. I have carried this memory for sixty years. And there was a time, after I came to Toronto, when I could not bear to watch athletics on television, and would turn my eyes away when the half-mile race was being run. I was less reminded of my final failed performance in that race, at Kensington Oval in 1951, whenever I watched the one hundred and two hundred metres than the half-mile.

What we used to call, in Barbados, during the thirties and forties, "decentness," is a characteristic which is sadly missing from professional sport, and without belabouring the point, I attribute a dramatic amount of this to Donovan Bailey.

In 1997, on the 4th of June, there were some responses published in the *Toronto Star*, concerning Mr. Bailey's comments on the aborted

150-metre race, promoted as a challenge to settle who was the better athlete, Mr. Michael Johnson or Mr. Donovan Bailey. A convincing majority of persons who responded to the question, "Do you think Donovan Bailey's comments about Michael Johnson being a coward were in poor taste?" — 56 percent as against 44 percent — said, among other things, quite pointedly, "Donovan Bailey should run with his legs, not his mouth." This is the sentiment I held, when Mr. Bailey "dissed" Ben Johnson, publicly, concerning Ben Johnson's offering technical help for Mr. Bailey's upcoming 100-metre race in the Atlanta Olympics. The race was not only arranged to decide who was the better athlete, it was obviously, and perhaps, primarily set as "nothing more than a publicity stunt that gave both men a healthy wallet."

There was a quarrel that erupted around this aborted race.

Michael Johnson's coach, Clyde Hart, according to the *Toronto Star*, said that "From the accounts I've read in the Toronto papers, Dan Pfaff [Bailey's coach] ordered Donovan to go take him out hard and you'll get him hurt.

"I have very strong concerns that their runner was instructed to do that. That's very unprofessional ..."

The irony about this dispute lay in the fact that Michael Johnson went back to Dallas where he was getting "two-a-day treatments" for the pulled muscle that Bailey did not think was legitimate: and soon after, Bailey himself was sidelined with a pulled muscle. It can be said that this was the last we heard of Donovan Bailey, except as a literary critic.

Regarding the match race between Michael Johnson and Donovan Bailey, there are three interesting views that correct the misconception that I am biased against Mr. Bailey:

"I realize that Donovan Bailey was rude, but then we are not the ones to who went through all that training, pressure and finally getting cheated by the track configurations. We are not in his position or shoes, so we have no clue how he felt and hence do not know why he reacted the way he did," wrote Deepti Rampal of Toronto.

Henry of London, Ontario, said, "Why is it that Michael Johnson can run off at the mouth when it comes to hurling insults at Bailey and his fellow Americans praise and support, while Canadians turn on their own, claiming Bailey's comments were in bad taste? Surely there are other things in the world to worry about than whether or not the fastest human in the world was a 'polite' Canadian."

The last word goes to Judy Brydon of Milton: "Donovan Bailey indicated to everyone watching on Sunday that he is no sportsman. He may be an athlete, but to command respect and admiration, one must also practise good sportsmanship. He is obviously unfamiliar with the concept."

Professional athletes, wrestlers, boxers, runners, and hockey players use various tactics, bravado, and antics to "psych out" their opponents. This was not a case of that less abrasive taunting.

Living in a country like Canada, where there is a division, or a difference in point of view, amongst white Canadians and black Canadians — perhaps, I ought to have said, non-white Canadians, a peculiarity, or a point of view that comes out in the watching of sports, principally, and those sports in which historically non-whites have not been known to excel at, this gnawing feeling that I am looking at sports through the eyes of colour and race, and not looking at the competitions from a purely athletic point of view, appreciating the brilliance of the particular athlete, is of some concern to me. I think this is the case more in a society like Canada, and certainly in the United States, than it is the case in Barbados. In Barbados, we were brought up on a diet of cricket that was absolute, and that became a culture of cricket.

You could hear the crack of the cricket bat when the red leather-bound ball, bowled at lightning speed by the fast bowler, was struck, full, sharp as a cannon-shot through the covers to the boundary. The "covers" is the name of a position on the field. A cover drive, crisp as a fresh soda biscuit. Four runs! You could see the style of the batsman, brandishing his cricket bat, his "willow," shining from an oiling with linseed oil, which must have added to the clarity and the sharpness of the shot. I can easily see that in the manner the batsman held his "willow" was, metaphorically, a gesture of manhood, a gesture of sexual prowess. He had held his cricket bat, after having driven the ball to the boundary, the way he would have held his penis in another similar act of having scored a boundary. As a matter of fact, in Barbados, the "willow" is the colloquial term for penis.

So, you would hear the applause of the spectators, men and women, sitting in the pavilion, (if there was one), but mostly sitting on the warm grass of the cricket ground, on benches; a few men on English-style walking sticks, a few reclining on English-made lounge chairs. These men and women, watching a game of Saturday-afternoon cricket, and who were supporters of the home team where the match was being played, would applaud the shot made through the covers by the batsman on the opposing team, as vociferously, as enthusiastically, and sincerely, as they had been clapping at the brilliance of the bowler, a member of their team.

On this Saturday afternoon, in this game, the bowler is a black Barbadian. The batsman, who has just executed the brilliant cover drive, is a white Barbadian. These attributes, "black" and "white," that relate to colour, are used here, only because I am writing this reminiscence in Toronto, and also, only to define status and colour and ethnicity, as they relate to Canada, in other words, putting them into the Canadian context. These two attributes were not used back then in Barbados to denote excellence at cricket, or the enthusiasm of your loyalty and support for the batsman, or for the bowler. Those two adjectives were not used to define your support, or your hailing for the particular cricketer, because of his colour; or even his social status.

In Canada, however, watching sports is, for me, a more personalized and psychologically serious occupation, based upon what Frantz Fanon calls "a historicity" that applies to black people who are "immigrants" or who are, by race, different from the majority of the people in the country where they live. This is particularly the case if the person watching the sport is not white; but is black; and if the athlete he is watching is white. Fanon was a West Indian from Martinique who studied psychiatry at the Sorbonne in Paris. His views on this subject relate specifically to French colonialism and the brutality the French government of Charles de Gaulle used in its attempt to defeat the Algerian struggle for independence. And these views are contained in *Black Skin, White Masks: The Experiences of a Black Man in a White World*.

If you are a black person, to be watching sports on television, "ain't no sport at all, boy!" A black man watching sports on television, such as golf and tennis, finds himself in addition to watching, analyzing, and interpreting more than the serving of aces, and the sinking of birdies, becoming obsessed by the new racially significant expression of excellence in these two sports, which cut across, diametrically, the formally acknowledged cerebral ability of the black tennis player, and the black golfer. It challenges that presumption and the absence of mental expectation of superiority at these "white" sports, a superiority that is attributed normally and historically to white athletes.

Therefore when I watch Venus Williams and Serena Williams at Wimbledon, or the U.S. Open, or the French Open — as a matter of fact, in a tournament of even less stature, it ceases to be a moment of casual relaxation. It is war. A war of nerves, a war of expectation, and hope, and more than that, the demand, conveyed telepathically, that they win. A war of racially motivated and induced expectation of victory. "They got to beat those white girls, boy!"

You want Venus to win. And you pick out her victim based upon her race, and her attitude, and her subliminal superiority. And this vindictiveness in the spectator is made all the more malevolent by the comments in the commentary of those commentators who remind us that Venus and Serena win because they use force, serving aces at more than one hundred kilometres an hour. And they contrast the sisters' style to that of Martina Hingis, "who uses her head." So, I like especially to see Venus and Serena beat Miss Hingis. Venus therefore stands in the minds of some, for Africa, and blackness, and brawn. Miss Hingis for Europe, and whiteness, and cerebral sophistication.

But most of all, I want the Williams sisters to demolish Capriati. I wish this on Miss Capriati, because she has the most obvious "class," "style," if you like, of all the women players. And although to me, Miss Capriati is identifiably European, she carries nevertheless in her European gait and posture, the anger and demonstrativeness that powders a tinge of blackness on her personality. It must be because she is Italian!

So, in each event, first round or quarter-final, I want Venus, or Serena, it doesn't much matter, to defeat Miss Capriati, in all their head-to-head bouts (I say "bouts" deliberately, as to me, they are no longer "matches"), because in my mind, Miss Capriati "looks" black, but of a "high yaller" colouration; and I want the glory to be blacker than that, blacker than a light-skin woman who could pass for white. I want the victory to be black.

The significance of this kind of black victory, of this way of looking at a tennis match which ceases only to be a match, and becomes a fight, a struggle, a demonstration, lies in the "historicity" of race, and is erupted from the steaming, oppressive vortex of slavery; and of any other kind of colonialism made more complex by racialism.

When it comes to watching Tiger Woods play golf, it is the phenomenon of having black people united in a sudden attraction — and affection — for a game considered by them, perhaps through exclusion, as a rather childish pastime — hitting a little white ball. Another reason for this almost universal black attraction is that Tiger Woods has not only broken the racist barrier which characterized golf, by integrating the long-standing clubhouses in the American South, but that he is so reliably good at hitting the little white ball to suit his impulse and his technical knowledge of his game.

There are millions of black people who are cognizant of the socially segregationist history of golf. And the young-enough and the healthy-enough are now invading Canadian golf clubs — and elsewhere in the world where there are black people with their clumsy, unprofessional clubs in their hands — and imitating the swing and the putt of every ball that Tiger Woods strikes, with the same racial cohesiveness and racial intensity as fans who are black, who watched Joe Louis, and Muhammad Ali and Jack Johnson symbolize by their fists the desire of the black man to excel. And to beat his white opponent, publicly, in a way that he could not achieve, through the same racism, in other social endeavours. What goes through the mind, the veins, the spirit of the black man, especially his or her living in a predominantly white society, when he watches Joe Louis fight Max Schmeling for the heavyweight title of the world? On whose side, really and psychologically, is the sentiment and the hope for victory in a boxing match between Muhammad Ali and Floyd Patterson? The irony is that although Floyd Patterson is black, he is "white" through the overwhelming support he had from the white society. And this was caused because Muhammad Ali, previously Cassius Clay, came to represent an extremist philosophy and antagonism; and Patterson, white middle-class "decency." And who can forget the history of racism that exploded, physically, against Jack Johnson, when he fought Sammy Burns in Australia on Boxing Day in 1908? And the blatant racist opinions of Jack Johnson, of the fight, published in international newspapers, including the *Sydney Bulletin* and the *New York Herald*, in 1908. During the fight, the arena was filled with shouts of "coon" and "flash nigger" writes Joyce Carol Oates, in a review of *Unforgivable Blackness: the Rise and Fall of Jack Johnson*, "the hatred of twenty thousand whites for all the Negroes in the world," as the *Sydney Bulletin* reported, yet the match would prove to be a dazzling display of the "scientific" boxing skills of the thirty-year-old Johnson, as agile on his feet and as rapid with his gloves as any lightweight. I have not gone so far in my sentiments when I watch Venus Williams playing against Miss Hingis, or Tiger Woods playing against the rest of the world. I have simply put my money on Tiger, metaphorically speaking. But I have always been sensitive to the taunts, delicate and sometimes subliminal, that must greet, and must have greeted Venus and Serena, at the beginning of their remarkable appearance on the scene of professional women's tennis. And how they bore those taunts and slights, including the bounce given to Venus by a European player, is a compliment the high standards with which their father and their mother brought them up, in America.

To taste this discomfiture caused by social integration, I offer my feelings of unease the first time I entered the Yale Faculty Club, in the company of Robert Penn Warren, who invited me to lunch, irrigated with Wild Turkey Bourbon "and branch water." Yale had recently opened its doors to a significant number of black students; and the history of Yale as we all knew, the names of colleges reflecting the names of Southern segregationists, like Calhoun College, of which I was a Fellow, and the presence of black men and black women, most of whom were in manual jobs, kitchen help, janitors, workers in the Yale post office, all these reminders of a segregationist past were not too distant 'memberings to make this sudden social and academic entry into the ivied halls of Yale, the same as going to a Baptist church in New Haven, for the same time. We have already heard of the racist taunts and harassment of black players on the Boston team, by Boston fans.

Joyce Carol Oates says that "Jack London, at that time the most celebrated of American novelists and an ostensibly passionate socialist, covered the fight for the *New York Herald* in the most race-baiting terms … transforming a sporting event into a 'one-sided racial drubbing that cried out for revenge.'"

Jack London had this to say: "It had not been a boxing match but an 'Armenian massacre' ... a 'hopeless slaughter' in which a playful giant Ethiopian had toyed with Burns as if he'd been a naughty child. It had matched thunderbolt blows against butterfly flutterings."

Jack London "was disturbed not so much by the new champion's victory, as by the evident glee with which he had imposed his will upon the hapless white man.... A golden smile tells the story, and that golden smile was Johnson's."

Unforgivable Blackness is a title pregnant with symbol, metaphor, and the truth of racial sentiment. And what was unforgivable in the title, is, according to Joyce Carol Oates, "in Johnson's boxing wasn't simply that he so decisively beat his white opponents but that he publicly humiliated them, demonstrating his smiling, seemingly cordial contempt. Like Ali, at least more astonishing than Ali, since he had no predecessors, Johnson transformed formerly capable, formidable opponents into stumbling yokels."

Joyce Carol Oates sees the "trickster" in Jack Johnson, as she saw the "trickster" in Ali, both of whom "believed in allowing their opponents to wear themselves out throwing useless punches."

"To step into the ring with a Trickster is to risk not only your fight but your dignity."

So, my wanting the Williams sisters and Tiger Woods to always win might be regarded not really as vindictiveness, but merely a non-violent respectable expression of a disposition crystallized over many years of racial disaffection in other functions of a system that has nothing to do with tennis and golf. It is the "historicity." So, the vindictiveness that might be perceived in the desire for the Williams sisters and Tiger Woods to win each time they compete against white competitors, is merely the respectable expression of a state of mind of "getting even" that has crystallized over years of racial disaffection.

Underlying this expression of racial solidarity, of this wish, rests the unspeakable and unrealistic hope that Tiger's victory on the links could be transferred to a larger victory of black success in the wider society, in the wider world of business, government, and science. Success not only at golf, and at tennis, but success in everyday endeavours: in the workplace; on public transportation; at university; and during all aspects of social intercourse. This attitude relates to a wish, a simple wish to be a man amongst men. And this wish becomes an obsession because of the nature of the society in which we live.

Back in Barbados, it was only the expertise, the professional brilliance of the sportsman that prompted our admiration and adoring. He was a brilliant batsman. Whether he was white or black; whether he played for the team we cheered for, our home team; or for a visiting team from Trinidad, or England, we applauded his brilliance. And it is an aspect of the game of cricket, played first by the English, our colonizers, and later learned by us; and at which we superseded our former masters and instructors. It is the natural characteristic of playing the game of cricket, that you are bound, "as a gentleman," to applaud the ability of your opponent. And you never ever ridicule the shortcomings of your opponent.

"Well played, old chap!" you say, in as civilized and sincere a manner, albeit a borrowed sophistication.

The English had taught you manners: not to imitate the vulgar shouts and screams and fights of persons who watch hockey, or baseball, basketball, or football. You were taught to applaud in a proper English — ah-hem! — understated civilized manner. "Old chap" had just dispatched your best fast bowler through the covers for another boundary, four runs — similar to a grand slam in baseball — and the game is in great danger of being lost by your home team; and still you applaud, because a good shot is a good shot, and this after all, is cricket, a word that conveys special irony and symbol and declared standards.

With Tiger Woods, however, you watch with clenched fist, or with your hand tight round the bottle of beer, certainly in clenched emotion and anxiety, silent teeth covering your nervousness, writhing with each extension of his arms, feeling and living through this young black man's concentration, vicariously, at his tension as he addresses the small, white ball, not much larger than a freshly laid egg from a Leghorn hen. And you hope and pray that every other golfer would make a bogey and open the door for Tiger Woods. Because he is black. And you never applaud this white player, and imitate the enthusiasm of the commentator who says, "Now, that's a very good shot!" when this opponent sinks a birdie. Only Tiger Woods is supposed to make that good shot.

In the same way, only Venus Williams, or her sister, Serena — when they are not playing against each other — is deserving of this racial "hero worship" in the serving of aces, serving with the speed of lightning, keeping the opponent at six-love. And every ball, whether it is "in" or "out" — in spite of the machine that checks its accuracy — must be called "fair," otherwise you accuse the umpire of being biased — well, at least, a little racist.

Not that this allegiance to the Williams sisters and to Tiger Woods, is based upon dishonesty, so much as it represents our acknowledgement of the change in the fortunes of black people, their emerging more frequent and greater presence in occupations and avocations, on national television, and the sight of one of them beating a white opponent, who might not personally have regarded the particular sport, tennis or golf, as their natural-racial province, but who, whether he knows it or merely accepts it as privilege, still does stand for the former attitude of black people playing tennis and golf. So, that by extension, when the black players defeat the white player in a game that distributes rewards inappropriately according to talent, and disproportionately according to disadvantage, this enthusiastic and natural-racial applause is therefore explained.

Such a win is a catharsis of the "historicity" that cannot be vented and is not experienced in the world of everyday social intercourse and interaction of white and black Canadians.

But why this almost absolutist obsession on the part of the black person watching sports on television to desire and hope for total black victory, at every competition, against the white opponent? Or, in other words, a victory over the white society? The answer is simple: it is because the white society, a society such as Canada's is perceived to be by most black people, reflects a system that does not reward professional sports ability, impartially and fairly. "All I want," the dislocated black man says, "is to be a man among other men."

The symbolism that lies in this kind of victory, therefore, is the thing, is the point. For a game of sport represents a basic cultural microcosm of the way the entire society is structured. This slice of Sunday afternoon leisure becomes, in its symbolism, much more than "making sport," or "watching sports." It takes on an importance similar to *panem et circenses* in the time of the Romans, when games were institutional and were made to represent an institutional, deliberate echo of the cultural and ethnic structure of Roman society, and sports became a symbol of Roman cruelty, and of its bravery; and a reflection of Roman obsession with valour and cruelty.

When the slave in that Roman society entered the garlanded and heralded arena, on a Sunday afternoon, and managed somehow to defeat the best fighter that Roman aristocratic society could throw against him; when that slave killed the mightiest Roman centurion, one of those giants chosen for his cruelty and his ability to inflict deadly wounds; when that slave managed to outfox the most ferocious lion let loose against him in the arena, the blow that dealt death to the centurion or to the lion, was a blow intended to be landed against the entire Roman state, a blow for freedom, if you will. And the blow executed by the single, frightened slave in the vast arena, that blow was delivered in the behalf of all the other slaves waiting their turn to be decapitated or devoured for the entertainment of the dignitaries in the arena.

And so it is, with black people in Canada, sitting down on a Sunday afternoon, watching Tiger Woods play golf, and the Williams sisters play tennis, in a golf course, in a court, that is similar in its meaning, to the Roman arena. Performance is expected of them. Performance and the expectation of blood and violence.

Now, what are the reasons for this way of watching sports, through eyes that see race and colour first, and athletic prowess, secondly? I can find only one convincing explanation for this "loyalty of negritude." And it comes from Frantz Fanon.

"As long as the black man is among his own," Fanon writes, "he will have no occasion, except in minor internal conflicts, to experience his being through others." This sentiment was written in 1952 in the French edition of *Black Skin, White Masks*, and published in the English edition in 1967; and it applies today to the spectator in Barbados, or in Toronto, watching a cricket game in which the players are both black and white — but who are all Barbadians, or Trinidadians, or Jamaicans.

Fanon is talking about the self-assurance that racial homogeneity provides. This black Barbadian spectator can therefore cheer for any member of the two opposing teams without taking a racial stance, as I would do were I watching Tiger Woods; and this absence of the "loyalty of negritude" is the case, even although one team, the home team, might be, in fact, his team. No assault to his "crushing objecthood," his being seen by the other as an "object" and not a Barbadian, is possible. Certainly, no attention given to him by the other spectators is able to detract from his "personhood," so long as he is "among his own."

In the case of the black spectator watching Venus Williams, or Tiger Woods, at a bar, in the presence of white fans, the black man's real feelings of racial identification with Williams and Woods remain stifled, held obsessively within his wishes, and are never voiced.

Fanon says that, "The black man among his own in the twentieth century does not know at what moment his inferiority comes into being through the other," that is to say, through the white man. It is therefore reasonable for the black spectator watching tennis or golf to ward off this assault of inferiority through the other, by leaving his seat and inhabiting the body, the political psyche, and spirit of the black player, and living, by inhabiting, more than vicariously, inside the body of that black player, and becoming that player, for a period longer even than the duration of the match.

The black sports fan relates to the play and to the outcome, replaying it in his mind to savour its brilliant shots, and drawing a lesson from them — even to teach his children the meaning of aces and birdies — and to experience and exult in his own personal vindication of the "inferiority that comes into being through the other." And he does this not only for the sake of historical reference, but as a catharsis, a purge from his system of the sense of "inferiority" imposed upon him by the attitude of the white man. This history of tennis and of golf gouge out in the mind of the black spectator the relationship he has, and will have, with the white man. "For not only must the black man," whether he is spectator or as citizen, Fanon says, "be black; he must be black in relation to the white man."

In spite of the criticism that might be levelled against Fanon's proposition, he maintains his position on the ground that "the black man has no ontological resistance in the eyes of the white man."

This obsessive "colourization" or "loyalty of negritude" that comes into play when a black spectator is watching blacks compete against white athletes, particularly in tennis and golf, two bastions of racial segregation presumed years ago to be sacrosanct, is "based upon the black spectator's knowledge of legends, stories, and history that defines him; and above all, historicity," Fanon adds. It is the "historicity" in the act of viewing that cleanses it of any propensity to violence; or even to oral vindictiveness, even in spite of the violence that prevails in the other stands.

Venus Williams and Serena Williams, like Tiger Woods, become heroes, models of excellence that transcend the games of tennis and golf, and they become instead role models. The lamentable sadness might very well be that they themselves do not know, or care, if they are to be role models. And to whom? Blacks, only? But this is something much bigger than their individual achievement. We shall be reasonable and leave them to the playing of tennis: and we shall ascribe the status of role model as we watch their continued brilliance.

In the case of another kind of black hero, the gang leader, hero worship tends to take on a more short-lived course; and tends also to be restricted to a younger age group. But this kind of hero worship is neither so pervasive throughout the black community, nor is it sanctioned as adulation like that given to sports heroes. Nevertheless, the member of a gang would himself be impressed by the excellence of the Williams sisters and of Tiger Woods; and he would identify with them. Venus and Serena and Tiger would be held to his chest puffed in pride, because the three of them "fucked up the motherfuckin' system, Jack!"

We know then, that with the help of Frantz Fanon's examination, written in 1967 at the height of segregation and lynching, which also corresponded with the greatest successes in the civil rights movement, that the fact of blackness and the "historicity" of the Negro and his recognition of this way of seeing sports in a place like Canada will persist because "spectators in this context have discovered their blackness, their ethnic characteristics, intellectual deficiency, fetishism, racial defects, slave-ships, and above all, 'Sho' good eatin'.'"

And if we really want to know how serious a matter this is, put the very expensive Adidas shoe on the other foot, and walk into a locker room with Venus, or Serena, or Tiger Woods, the first time, and observe — not even like a fly on the wall — but observe the reception with which the three of them are welcomed ...

CHAPTER TWENTY-THREE

"A Writer's Life"

My life, remembering it now, with the small victories and gigantic sur-
renderings, was marked by the good fortune that winked at me, on
Fridays. On Friday afternoons around twelve-thirty. There are certain
times of the day that I remember, and make a point of remembering;
and all of them coincide with the arrival of the postman at my door
on Brunswick Avenue, bearing tidings of no joy. Notices of businesses
intent on suing me; reminders that the Hydro was not paid, that the Bell
Telephone Company, the most heartless so-called public company — or
a public company providing service to the public — serving the needs
of Torontonians, but which, certainly in the black community, had an
atrocious image of racism and oppression, and a profound absence of
understanding. Your service will be terminated and the arrears must be
paid in full, in cash or by certified cheque, "within five days from the
date of this letter" and you wondered if the Bell knew that, as immigrants in Toronto in the 1950s, when loneliness, unemployment, racism
in housing, and the cold months of October, November, December,
January, February, March, and April, the immigrant cannot, because of
the factors mentioned above, have the kind of life of poor happiness
and joy he had back in Barbados or Trinidad or the Bahamas, compared
with the more materialistic life he now has in Toronto, a life of more
money, of better steaks and lamb chops, and a communalism which he

lives in here, a way of life that is different from the colonialism he knew back home; so long as he had the ten dollars that the millionaire pays for a choice cut of steak; and the Bell does not understand that in his loneliness bordering upon mental breakdown, that he has to reinvent his society back home right here in the seven months of cold and desolation of the spirit, and bring his family to meet him in the cold apartment, or flat, or room, or basement suite. The Bell did the right business thing, but crucified the immigrant by doing the insensitive thing — cutting him off from his roots. For Toronto was inhospitable.

And then, during those seven months, the notices were more frightening, more dangerous to the health, more deadly, and they drove a stake through my guts, labelling me as an indigent man incapable of providing the basic requirements of a household: heat in winter. Winters in the fifties were longer and more depressing than they are today. They were colder and more snow fell, and it was always dark, certainly after four o'clock. And this continued for seven months. It took two months, May and June, to recover from the chill that seeped into the bones. I do not know whether the prevalence of tuberculosis, or TB, for short, or consumption as we more graphically called it in Barbados, was caused by the unrelenting seeping into the bones of the chill of Toronto winters; but I do remember that between 1955 and 1960, people talked more frequently, and openly, of other persons whose lungs were being eaten out by consumption. When you passed in front of the doors of the TB Laboratory on College Street, west of St. George, you did not cough. Or if you had a tickle in your throat, you made sure to pass the TB Lab, walking west to reach Spadina Avenue, when you could cough to your heart's and lungs' delight. Or you made a little *ugh-ugh*, looked round to see if anybody heard, covered your face with a handkerchief, or a Kleenex, and pretended there was no disturbance in your chest. I always thought of consumption when the cheque to Roma Fuels bounced, or when they grew angry at my late payments, and put just enough oil in the tank to start the motor. And of course, when they did not come at all.

There is no greater joy, when your furnace is not working, when you dress yourself in all your sweaters and your winter coat, with two pairs of thick socks, and a hat on your head; and you walk up and down the hallways on the second floor, from the kitchen to the bathroom, shuttling electric kettles of hot water, saucepans and pots, to put life and warmth into the bath tub, in which you shall have to put your five-year-old daughter, beside your three-year-old daughter, and your wife, helping you in this demonstration of personal failure, and you cannot even run, just run out of the house, as you could do, would do, were able to do, had you remained back in Barbados, where there is no winter. But there is no escape here.

When I made the decision to be a writer, and gave myself one year to see if I could be a writer, and when I decided to remain home and look after Janice and Loretta, aged three and one, I did not know what I had decided to do. There was logic in my decision. But I realize now that I was brave, and reckless, self-centred, and perhaps a little irresponsible to have thought of this "temporary abandonment" of wife and girl children, at a time when to be black in Toronto was, as my mother said, "a horse of a different colour." And I think that my mother understood the pun intended; and that was intended.

To whom could I go to tell me what a writer was ... or is? To whom could I go to "discuss writing?" Where could a young black man, wanting to be a writer in Canada in 1962, go to hear other writers, and talk with them about plot, theme, hours sitting in a chair, pounding a Remington Rand Noiseless? And when and if he managed to write something, a story, a poem, where could he go to get it read, and edited, then published?

It startled me that no one, critic, reviewer, professor, has seen the real point, the explanation, in this solitary journey embarked upon in a state of mind, on a landscape that was like a badly drawn map, which showed just the dot of destination with no route to that destination. They do not know. For many reasons. They do not know because they have never had a serious interest, and did not promote in the fifties and the sixties, a developmental interest in the writing of a black man from the West Indies. Not that I felt that this was part of their literary obligation. It must have been strange for them, and for Canada, to have been faced with a novel written by a black man amongst them. It was, after all, only 1964; and in 1964 racism was widespread, was publicly stated, was engaged in without apology. They had no black men born amongst them who were writing — even if they were not writers. I think the distinction is important. For even if there had been blacks writing, the so-called literary establishment did not automatically and necessarily regard them as writers, even a "Negro-Canadian writer." This establishment is more stupid than it is racist. So I absolve it of its manifold iniquities. I have always been granted absolutism to this so-called establishment, mainly by ignoring it, and refusing to admit to its influence. It is a shifting disposition, with no guidance to the writer, certainly the beginning writer, in his own literary uncertainty. I have always felt that the recognition or the status conferred upon a writer by the establishment was based upon matters other than literary. It gave me the impression from as early as 1964 when my first novel, *The Survivors of the Crossing*, was published, that the establishment had been like a small room made of thick cement, with no ventilation of windows and no jalousies, and no means of entrance. It is a cell, a cellar, from which beginning writers, especially "visible minorities," are excluded. What is inside this unventilated structure no one knows. For when the contents or the inhabitants are disclosed, we are left in awe of the establishment's method of selection.

I understood how difficult it would be for a beginning writer, a writer who is black. And knowing this, I decided from the beginning not to tie my person, my hope, my disposition, and my character to the uncertainty of acceptance, of appreciation, and of being a favourite. And this separation of the actual writing from the person doing the writing, saved me from the anxiety of neglect and the disappointment of my writing being misunderstood by editor and by reviewer and by critic. It was too new to them. Unexpected. Unappreciated. Too foreign. Problems with the usage of dialect; problems with the themes dealt with in the fiction, problems with the interest asked of the Canadian reader to be taken in by this new literature. The establishment was unprepared to deal with this "new voice." And the establishment did what establishments faced with a new virus of writing does best: it pretended that the new writing was irrelevant and did not exist. There were a few reviewers and critics who, in their broad-mindedness, gave this new literature a chance: Kildare Dobbs; William French; William New; and one lone intellectual, a professor of English at York University, Stan Fefferman, writing in the *Telegram* about my third novel, on May 27, 1967, who, even if he did not understand the portrayal and the "function" of the main character, Bernice, wrote that "the first twenty-five pages of Austin Clarke's novel,

The Meeting Point, convey the familiar morally superior attitudes of the Negro observer of white society. The Negro observer in this case is Bernice Leach, a West Indian woman who works as a domestic for a Jewish family in Forest Hill. Bernice's view of the Burrmanns' household is a stereotyped Negro parody of a white family."

My question to Professor Fefferman, not really to him personally, but to the attitude he represents is this: How would he know what the Negro thinks? It is an old presumption that "others" know what the Negro thinks. Many white intellectuals have presumed to be able to "think" for the Negro. It is a bulwark of the psychology of racism, and a characteristic of colonialism.

Two of my friends joined Professor Fefferman in this attitude of presumptuousness: Norman Mailer, who wrote a piece for *Look* magazine in which he confessed he was thinking for the American Negro, if I understand the article correctly. But Mailer had the fortune or the misfortune of presenting this thesis to an audience of students and faculty at Calhoun College at Yale University one night in 1969; and he earned the wrath of the few young black students, recently admitted to Yale in the university's program of recruitment of black students. The other friend, Robert Penn Warren, novelist, poet, and professor of creative writing at Yale, asked the question, "Who Speaks for the Negro?" in the title of his book, and left us with the impression that he was not asking a deliberative question, but was, by innuendo, stating that he knew who spoke for the Negro, and by extension, offered himself as candidate for that authorship, or authority.

But Professor Fefferman does not deserve complete chastisement. He acknowledged what I consider to be the first steps in literary reasonableness, that the novel he was asked to review for the *Telegram* in 1967, *The Meeting Point*, "has more in common with Sherwood Anderson's *Winesburg, Ohio* and Margaret Laurence's *The Stone Angel* than it does with James Baldwin's *Another Country*. Which is to say, it is an original book."

Those five last words are the point. The writing which the establishment faced in 1964, 1965, and 1967, with *The Meeting Point*, and continuing with two more novels, *Storm of Fortune* and *The Bigger Light*, in 1973 and 1975, respectively, resulted in misunderstanding of the point. Before

I leave this point of the presumption that white critics and intellectuals "speak for the Negro," and to give it an international context, I must add the names of William Styron, author of *The Confessions of Nat Turner*, and Irving Howe, the critic who presumed to educate Ralph Ellison that he had the wrong image constructed in his novel, *Invisible Man*, by comparing the main character in *The Invisible Man*, with Bigger Thomas, the main character in Richard Wright's *Native Son*. Ellison wanted the comparison to be made with other writers. I shall let Ellison make the point himself in his essay "The World and the Jug":

> Let me end with a personal note: Dear Irving, I have no objections to being placed beside Richard Wright in any estimation which is based not upon the irremediable ground of our common racial identity, but upon the quality of our achievements as writers. I respected Wright's work and I knew him, but this is not to say that he "influenced" me as significantly as you assume. Consult the text! I sought out Wright because I had read Eliot, Pound, Gertrude Stein and Hemingway, and as early as 1940 Wright viewed me as a potential rival — partially, it is true, because he feared I would allow myself to be used against him by political manipulators who were not Negro and who envied and hated him. But perhaps you will understand when I say he did not influence me if I point out that while one can do nothing about one's relatives, one can, as an artist choose one's "ancestors." Wright was, in this sense, a "relative," Hemingway an "ancestor." Langston Hughes whose work I knew in grade school and whom I knew before I knew Wright, was a "relative"; Eliot, whom I was to meet only many years later, and Malraux and Dostoevsky and Faulkner, were "ancestors" — if you please or don't please!

I have never presumed to give reviewers, critics and professors of English advice. I have never, before this, discussed what professors of English, critics, and reviewers have written about my work. Not that I have not noticed and read their views. But my view is an echo of Ellison's evocative advice to Irving Howe: "Consult the text!"

Ellison, as was to be expected, by his claimed "ancestral" connection to Eliot, Pound, Gertrude Stein, Hemingway, Malraux, Dostoevsky, and Faulkner, was branded an Uncle Tom, a traitor to the Negro literary establishment, fawning over white writers, like Saul Bellow, his friend. It was, after all, at a time when the civil rights movement of Dr. Martin Luther King, Jr., black cultural nationalism advocated by Leroi Jones (Amiri Baraka), and SNCC demonstrations against segregation scratched the character of American society, and this I feel caused Ellison to explain this "ancestral" literary connection to, and praise of, the "ancestors" he enumerated.

> Do you still ask why Hemingway was more important to me than Wright? Not because he was white, or more "accepted." But because he appreciated the things of this earth which I love and which Wright was too driven or deprived or inexperienced to know: weather, guns, dogs, horses, love and *hate* and impossible circumstances which to the courageous and dedicated could be turned into benefits and victories. Because he wrote with such precision about the processes and techniques of daily living that I could keep myself and my brother alive during the 1937 Recession by following his descriptions of wing-shooting; because he knew the differences between politics and art and something of their true relationship for the writer. Because all that he wrote — and this is very important — was imbued with the spirit beyond the tragic with which I could feel at home, for it was very close to the feeling of the blues, which are, perhaps, as close as Americans can come to expressing the spirit of tragedy. (And if you think Wright knew anything about the blues, listen to a "blues" he composed with Paul Robeson singing, a most unfortunate collaboration!; and read his introduction to Paul Oliver's *Blues Fell This Morning*.) But most important, because Hemingway was a greater artist than Wright, who although a Negro like myself, and perhaps a great man, understood little if anything of these (at least to me) important things. Because Hemingway loved the American

language and the joy of writing, making the flight of birds, the loping of lions across an African plain, the mysteries of drink and moonlight, the unique styles of diverse peoples and individuals come alive on the page. Because he was in many ways the true father-as-artist of so many of us who came to writing during the late thirties.

But what has this to do with Professor Fefferman? Absolutely nothing. Except as a caution to the reviewer, the critic and the professor of English, not to minimize the importance of "consulting the text!"

But I was talking about Fridays. If you had lived through the four preceding days, and Fridays came and you did not receive a notice that your last cheque was NSF, if there was no letter delivered by the postman saying that you had five days from the date of the letter now in your hand, in which you did not pay all the arrears of the bill, Hydro, Bell Telephone, mortgage, Roma Fuel, your subscription to *Maclean's* and the *Atlantic Monthly*, then you could breathe more easily on Friday night, and invite friends to dinner — white rice and oxtail stew, with West Indian potatoes, avocado pear, and canned peaches cut into halves, and filled with sour cream — and play calypso music (as I played many times for my former editor and publisher, Patrick Crean, when he lived down the street from me, on Brunswick, beside the French high school, Loretto College), and talk into the night, until the blob of blackness in the black night changed into the grey outline of a man, Sibelius, in Jean Sibelius Square, where a girl was raped and stuffed into a refrigerator on the second floor of a flat, and the man who did that has not been found and caught yet. Patrick responded to my dinners with dinners of his own, "silvers and crystals licking-down the place, and antique furnitures" in greater profusion than the window of Britnell's Antiques, up the street from Britnell's bookshop (somebody told me he was his brother), near the corner of Yonge and Dupont, across from the Masonic Temple lodge, where rowdy dances and speeches by visiting West Indian politicians were held, religiously. So, if the clarion call, and being reminded of bounced cheques — I have always hated this term, it is so crude and so accusatory! — could be left until Monday to face the music, not lessened by the intervening weekend, then we could have a discreet, modified, Friday-night party. Six bottles of beer, Labatts; one bottle of rum, bottled by the LCBO; a bottle of white wine, Graves; peanuts in the shell from down in Kensington Market; cashews, and roasted walnuts from an Italian man with a cart who sold the best walnuts in the whole of Ontario. When we — my wife and I — changed the menu. It was beef stew. I had convinced the butcher I went to, most often, that I had a large dog who liked beef bones; and the butcher would give me a large parcel wrapped in brown paper, filled with parts of the cow that had as much meat as bones, and I carefully cut the meat to the bone, and had not only enough for a stew, but sufficient for the yellow split-pea soup, with dumplings and pig tails, fit for a king. In these early days of Kensington, which was called the Jewish Market, the butchers gave away beef bones, pig tail, the worst part of salted cod from the Grand Banks of Newfoundland, because the population of Toronto in the 1950s was of a culture and ethnicity that did not stomach what we in Barbados, called "the leavings" from the best cuts of the meats, pork, beef, lamb, veal, and saltfish, served at the tables of the wealthy and the white, which at some period in Barbados, was the same thing.

So, Fridays had their hours of relief: going to the Kensington Market and leaving with bones and beef on the bones; peanuts in the shell; vegetables and fruits at prices more suitable to the budget of a writer who had no budget, and all this made possible by the absence of letters and telephone calls and threatening form letters promising doom. But there was never, upon my soul and spirit, a feather of despair, for I always felt that this was a period of testing my longevity: my longevity in the sustaining of hardship.

I used to feel, in those days, that I did not have any right to expect Canada to be more hospitable to me, in life, in employment, in civil rights, in public decency, and that I did not have the moral or the political right to attempt to inflict my Barbadian culture and morality upon the Canadian character, no matter how oppressive and racialistic it became with significant frequency. I felt then, that I was the one to adjust to Canada, not having Canada moderate or modify its "way of life" to accommodate me. And I felt this was the case because I showed no allegiance to Canada. I did not want to be known as a Canadian. I did not desire Canadian citizenship. If Barbados had the nationalistic presumptuousness to declare war on Canada, I would, naturally, fight for Barbados. But this might very well mean deportation or departure back to Barbados. I did not even want a Canadian passport. And the reason for this is that Barbados was still the natural and cultural navel string of my spiritual and artistic ancestry. Canada, and Toronto, were unable, at that time, to infiltrate and diminish the strong links that birth in Barbados created to define me, in character, as a Barbadian.

The irony that explains this startling nationalism, and an almost contradictory dismissal of a country in which I had lived, at the time, for ten years as a visitor, foreign student, foreigner — never "immigrant" — is that I became in time, officially in 1985, a better Canadian, whatever this term implies, than if I had, as some "immigrants" do, rejected my own country, or had minimized the contribution of that country, as some "immigrants" have done, from countries they have fled because of race, poverty, unemployment, political upheaval, and as in recent times, racial massacres.

Did I know what no UIC supervisor could, with the year I had given myself in which to prove to myself whether I could write a novel? Or a short story. Or a play. Anything. Anything worthy of being published. And published in the literary magazines that existed in 1963: *Tamarack Review*, run by Robert Weaver; *Canadian Literature*, edited by William New; the *Queen's Quarterly*; and one radical magazine, *Evidence*, edited by Kenneth Craig, from 471 Bay Street, a quarterly whose price was four dollars a year. Kenneth warned writers seeking publication that "manuscripts will not be returned unless accompanied by a self-addressed, stamped envelope."

Volume one of *Evidence* magazine published the following writers and artists, most of whom drank almost every night in the Pilot Tavern, on the corner of Bloor and Yonge, on the northwest corner, north of the Canadian Imperial Bank of Commerce. They were:

William Ronald — Toronto abstract expressionist painter now living in New York and exhibiting with the Kootz Gallery.
Ray Jessel — Well-known writer of songs and sketches for Canadian revues. Latest revue soon to be opening in New York.

Austin Clarke — Young fiction writer from the West Indies. Just completed second novel and has published his poems widely in Canada.

Kenneth Craig — Editor of *Evidence*.

Gerald Gladstone — Toronto-born sculptor and painter exhibiting at the Isaacs Gallery.

Lynne de Ceuleneer — Young advertising artist who is a promising painter. [And was, at the time, Kenneth's "lady."]

Joyce Wieland — Toronto-born painter represented by the Here and Now Gallery.

William Ronald was concerned about "ideas," and in his piece he wrote:

At a certain stage admirable ideas seriously worry the well disposed life of such people as kings, statesmen and religious leaders. Weakness stands fluttering her alternating banner. Upset and entranced these people engulf something far more serious than we may imagine.

Ray Jessel's piece, "How Many Miles from Gil to Bill?" begins with a strong statement of historical categorization:

Since the goings-on at Minton's in the early '40's crystallized into a handy reference point for the Jazz Critics, history has been nice enough to hand those indefatigables yet another "era" on a platter.

Gerald Gladstone advises us that:

A great piece of sculpting is the road, at the corner of King and Church Streets, just in front of the Royal Bank of Canada, Main Branch. It's been ten years in the making — every type of person has helped make it — it expresses the complete wordless statement of a built city that is decaying into a completed sculptural whole.

And he ends by offering this assistance: "To make a modern piece of sculpting, just take two of anything — break one into two pieces — put them together and you're finished. It's that easy. Nature does it all the time."

Following my contribution — a very wordy poem that has no title, a poem which abuses all the rules of writing that I have subsequently warned my students not to commit — is a very interesting advertisement for Irving Layton's collection of poems, *A Red Carpet for the Sun*, published by McClelland & Stewart, for $3.50: "cloth, Paper $1.95, with two blurbs for 'the collected poems of one of the most powerful poets writing in Canada today.'"

Roy Fuller regarded Layton as "This mature and excellent poet."

Hear what Robertson Davies said: "These poems are the feelings and thoughts of a man who pierces through triviality to something that is enduring," prophesying in 1964 what Layton would become.

Here now, is my poem, untitled, bringing shame upon my head, to read it now, in 2015, fifty-two years after it was composed; written at a time when I imitated Dylan Thomas and found no literary consolation in Irving Layton, or Earl Birney, or Alfred Purdy, or Margaret Atwood, or Dennis Lee, or Robert French, or any of the Montreal Poets … there was no one living Canadian in whom I could entrust my flimsy and tentative verses, for inspiration and for strengthening, and for width. And for relevance. For I never thought there was a relevant model amongst Canadian writers on whom I might base my work. And even today, more than fifty years later, I have not found among our writers a model that speaks to me in the same way as I speak to my readers, meaning the people whom I would like to read my novels, and who do read my writing.

I have never held the obsession that the reader of my work is the important force in determining what I write. I write with a profound ignoring of the reader, and his taste, and moreover of any influence I might think the prevailing fashion, or style has upon the writer. I am therefore a loner in this sense of being unacquainted with a particular school, or style of writing, so far as a Canadian model is concerned. And I have never held a Canadian writer as a model of my own work. This is simply because the theme and the style of Canadian literature are irrelevant to my work. I do not therefore see any connection, in the sense of "literary ancestry" to my writing. I am alone, singular, peculiar, and foreign to the establishment that governs and controls Canadian literature.

This singularity is both a benefit and a disadvantage: it allows me to experiment, to discover literary territory in the same way as seafarers and sea dogs like Drake and Hawkins "discovered" countries and West Indian islands, widening the scope of my journeys into unknown waters, and it disclosed from my penetrations the limits and the vastness of boundaries that I might have tried to imitate.

But there were models. These models had to be West Indian, black American, African to a less degree, and some of the classics, so far as the experimenting with language and "voice" are concerned. However, I never attempted with theme. For the narrative I wanted to present had to be pure in its relation to the narrator and the narrative itself. So, I found solace in William Faulkner, tasted the concentrated narrative of James Joyce and recoiled from its thickness and its virulent taste; and embraced Geoffrey Chaucer and tried to retain the lines of Shakespeare. And something of T.S. Eliot's irreverence with tradition.

This is part of the poem that was published in *Evidence* magazine, in 1963, in Volume One:

> In my barefoot days, under the sun, blackened
> By miles of walking, and moons of coming, and never going,
> In my bastard days, young and pure; before
> I saw everything, but innocence in the girls,
> Browned and cocoed, on the beaches, marbly
> Under the sore foot, and lazy as my native-cousins
> Stretching in yawns till moonshine come;
> In my first days of growing with the canes
> On the two sides of my upbringing
> Flogged-out, and repaired
> In the booted days, when the tamarinds, new-cut,
> And cutting into the havoc of my ways of living,
> When the church-bells, tolling for dinner and mass
> Roused me from the rascals, propping the corner
> With sailor-jokes, and the tales dribbled by mother
> And grandmother ...

And it goes on for seventeen more lines, justifying Robert Weaver's stinging reprimand of my effrontery to submit it first to the *Tamarack Review*, telling me that "poems enclosed showed no poetic value" and advising me that I should, perhaps, turn my literary attention to other things; but more important than Weaver's chilly commentary, is my recognition of T.S. Eliot in some of the music and phrasing, and Dylan Thomas's echoes in the other lines. It is obvious to me, fifty-two years after this was published, what I was reading, either for pleasure, or for instruction.

Thirty lines before I came to a full stop. How reminiscent of the opening sentence in the short story, "When He Was Free and Young and He Used to Wear Silks." I wonder what influence the one, the poem, had on the other, the short story; and why I was so attracted to long, breathless, unpunctuated salvos?

Fridays then signalled a hiatus in which I could breathe some relief from the imprecation of debtors; and this would become a feature of my life as a writer for a very long time: the evading of the jabs of penury by the dipsy-doodling of prescience, knowing when to duck, when to run, when to breathe. I indulged in all pleasures late on Friday afternoons, all of Saturday, the beginning of Sunday, moderated by going to church and thinking of going to church, and not going to church very often; and by five o'clock on Sunday nights, when back in Barbados I would be listening to the choirs of King's College Cambridge, to the service from St. Martin-in-the-Fields, and to the mellifluous tones of Southerners who mixed the Bible with personal psychology, growing out in their rich molasses voices the hard, cruel, brutal character of their other lives and livelihood as members of the Ku Klux Klan, at least as racists, when I should be sitting close to the "private set" from Hilversum in Holland, so close that I could hear the waves of distance coming through the speaker, and not, as was the case in Toronto, at this hour of dusk in the good weather, darkness for the seven months of winter, preparing for the harshness, the realism of the week, which began for me on Sunday night, in sleepless twisting of the body, instilling in my anxiety and limbs, the planting of insomnia. But insomnia is part of the life of the writer.

In 2007, Margaret Atwood gave a talk at a dinner at which she was guest of honour. She called her talk "The Writing Life." And she talked about writing. Pierre Berton, at the end of his life, wrote a book on this subject. I have not read Berton's book, so I do not know if his views agreed with what I consider to be a very casual title for a life of hardship, a life of uncertainty, a life that results very often in ruined family and broken promises of money and of love, and of charity. The Writing Life! The title so chosen is usually expressed in terms that remind me of the frivolousness of sports. The Sporting Life! No matter that the Sporting Life, with its similarity in title with The Writing Life, can never be so synonymous in its nature, to "the writing life" that Atwood and Berton unfortunately suggested.

For me "The Writing Life" does not reflect the burdensomeness, the instability of life of a writer, the torment that is the characteristic of "The Life of the Writer." I do not think that this change in title (epithet and subject) suggests a similarity as it appears at first glance, to do.

What have I ruined in my life, personally and in association, in my relentless craving after becoming a writer? In 1963, I thought I was too old to embark upon this uncertain body of water, over which to chart a career, water that is always shifting, with currents that were not always flowing in the desired destination, rudderless because of personal disposition and also because of the evaluation of my work, what little it was, through whim and whimsy, and what was being written and was fashionable. And race. Race has always featured in these considerations. No black man, no immigrant in living memory, meaning no living immigrant in the second half of the century had ever expressed the thought, the experiment, of wanting to be a writer. It must have been as startling to be heard, as it was for my wife when I announced to her that Friday afternoon that I was not going back to work, but would "go on the dole" for one year; and after that year, in failure or in success, I would return to work, and cease being a financial liability on the Canadian society. My life on welfare lasted six months, when to my astonishment, and to the shock of others, my first manuscript, *The Survivors of the Crossing*, was accepted by McClelland & Stewart. I would have to work with an editor, and if the revisions and the editorial changes were satisfactory, I would be published. Heinemann in London was the co-publisher.

What was the atmosphere like, when I started out? What novel could serve as my model. Who, as Ralph Ellison said, were my "literary ancestors"? And who were my "literary family"?

There was no black Canadian writer. There were three West Indians. Wallace Collins, a Jamaican, who came over from England and the raw rise in racism, and the Notting Hill Riots. Clyde Hosein, from Trinidad, who specialized in brilliant short stories, published primarily in England. And Lloyd Brown, a reporter at the *Globe and Mail* — the first black man to have been hired by that newspaper, a graduate in journalism from the University of Western Ontario — tormenting me by its presumption that you could be taught how to write, even non-fiction, and journalism, and graduate with a degree! — and who was now writing plays.

Charles Roach, a Trinidadian, who later became a distinguished lawyer representing blacks against the police and other acts of discrimination, was at this time, in the early 1960s, writing poetry.

Ernest X, an immigrant from the Bahamas, who was writing plays.

All of these young men were at the beginning of their careers. The only other writer with a published book was Wallace Collins.

This then, was the atmosphere. The writers who "had made it" in fiction were Arthur Hailey, whom we envied for the huge amount of money he made from *Airport*, and other works, turned almost immediately into television dramas and movies; and a gentleman named Robert Mirvish, the brother of Honest Ed, who, when I met him in the drawing room of the Kilbourns in Rosedale, advised me, "Don't mind what they say, Austin. Write things that sell, and make money. Don't get trapped in fancy fiction."

But it was Arthur Hailey, not for his literary style who would impress me, and lots of beginning writers, both black and white, but the amount of money he made, from everything he wrote, that drew us in that direction, unsuccessfully, but which caused us to be looking up in the sky, to see the shape of airplanes.

If I were going to pick a model for my fiction it would be Hugh Garner, who wrote about a socialism and realism that I wanted to address. But Garner lived and died in utter, deep neglect, from the critics, reviewers, and the establishment. Canada was not ready for him. It is his honesty, and his raucous language, so similar to the rasp in his voice, like a shout into an empty barrel, a hoarseness caused by his chain-smoking of unfiltered green Macdonald's cigarettes.

And suddenly it is a Friday afternoon, and I am in the front row of seats in Varsity Stadium, looking east, to the red brick building where I had lectures in statistics by Professor Triantis; in economic history by Professor Karl Helleiner, in which the brightest student was George Ramsay Cook, himself a professor emeritus now, at York University; and in political science, by Professor C.B. Macpherson, who made good socialists of all of us West Indians, and whom we remember even today with affection and gratitude for his understanding of us, black students, from the West Indies. On this afternoon, Varsity Stadium is overrun with people, people in numbers greater than the crowd of a homecoming football match between Toronto and McGill; but with the difference that on this afternoon, the stadium is not dressed in the colours of supporting allegiance, in the blue of Varsity, and in the red of McGill, but in the multi-coloured mufti of white liberals. It is a "teach-in." America has just killed another black man for demonstrating his civil rights. Or a Southern sheriff, or a Southern governor — Wallace or Faubus — has just brought out the cops and national guards of their empires of violence to stop a child from entering an all-white school or a lunch counter. Something more violent than the disgrace we have been living through for the entire month has just happened. Michael Ignatieff organized this "teach-in," and, knowing of my activity in civil rights protests, invited me to speak. I would have drawn a comparison between the horrors taking place in America, and the threat of those horrors crossing the border like illegal immigrants. There were beautiful women on the pasture, sitting. There were always beautiful women at these civil rights demonstrations. Beauty and social conscience, and liberalism went hand in brassiere, hand in waist, in those days that corresponded almost with the political dogma, "Make Love Not War." We were all beatniks and hippies. Weird people in the eyes of everybody else who were not "beat." To be "beat" held a certain honour. Pot-smoking, soiled, dirty, colour-loving, drug-loving, jazz-loving, hillbillying, bearded men, and women who wore dresses that showed the beauty of their physique and breasts, loose-dressed women.

I cannot remember what I spoke about, but I do remember the applause, the kind of applause that any kind of speech defending Negro civil rights in Canada; any kind of harangue against the apartheid regime in South Africa under Verwoerd, against racism in Rhodesia under Ian Smith, and especially racial segregation and racial violence in the United States of America; any declaration of sympathy for the Black Power movement, and to make the appeal international, any collaborative opinion of showing that racism was international, was greeted with applause, for these were the days of liberalism: a struggle engaged in by Jews and blacks. So, my speech, similar to the opinion pieces I had been writing for the *Telegram* and the *Toronto Star* newspapers, had to bring a large crowd, and bring the house down, for there was vocal, public declaration of sympathy amongst these white liberals, and a few socially conscious blacks, that gave the civil rights movement its moral strength. More than that, it showed, for a short time in the late 1950s and 1960s, how Jews identified their own status with that of the Negro.

"You are cordially invited to attend a Reception for Mr. Stokely Carmichael, on Thursday, December 8th, 8 p.m. to 11 p.m., at the Home of Mr. & Mrs. Ed Creed, 74 Donwoods Drive, Toronto 12, Ontario."

As I arrived at the imposing home on Donwoods Drive, after Stokely Carmichael had given a rousing speech at Convocation Hall in the university, as the door was answered, and I entered the large hall, with the art and artifacts that declare and demonstrate wealth and taste, while I was wiping my feet and taking off my black, cheap, ill-fitting plastic rubber boots with the zipper in the middle, from toe to above the ankle, and which was broken on both feet, down the ornate swirling staircase came a black woman. A "domestic servant" — if you'll pardon the repetition. One of those West Indian women permitted to enter Canada as house servants, under a two-year contract, after which they automatically became landed immigrants.

She smiled. I could see my mother. She said good evening, and immediately I knew where she was born. I remember this woman in all this time, from that cold night in 1963, because she reminds me of another woman, one created in fiction; and I must have remembered the dignity of the way she moved her body, as she came down the polished spiral staircase, the grace and sexuality with which she moved, and I must have been thinking of this woman, forty years later when I was writing the character, the physical and spiritual character of Mary-Mathilda, the strong, powerful, independent woman in *The Polished Hoe*.

The irony in this invitation is that a Jewish millionaire with a West Indian domestic extended the invitation to Stokely Carmichael, and also, that it was Stokely Carmichael himself, as head of Student Nonviolent Coordination Committee (SNCC), who had recently in public speeches rejected the moral co-operation of Jews in demonstrating for SNCC, and their monetary contribution the SNCC's programmes.

When Stokely arrived, after me, he walked straight up to the West Indian domestic, embraced her in the manner black nationalists greeted one another, and called her "sister."

The air in Varsity Stadium was getting close; and as I looked around I thought that the clouds were coming more and more lower, almost touching the field; and then I realized that it was smoke. From cigarettes and pipes. And from marijuana. Applause and cheers, and cries of "Right on!" and some lesser enthusiastic shouts of "Power to the People" were as common at rallies of this kind as the smoking of pot. One went with the other, in a kind of symbiotic relationship of liberalism. Handkerchiefs tied around the head, or around the waist, or wrapped around the hips of women, were worn as badges announcing you were "cool," you were "with it," and that you "had your shit together!"

"Like, man, you were like, hip."

And in this "hippie-ness" following the ranting of another speaker at this Varsity "teach-in," I completely forgot that I had another appointment on this Friday afternoon, miles from the corner of Bedford Avenue and Bloor Street West, miles away, up in the Hickies of Scarborough, out on the highway leading to Oshawa and Kingston, a journey not taken normally except if you were going to Montreal by Greyhound bus. I was travelling to CFTO-TV. To go on a program, one of those popular in this time of games and of singing the mournful folk songs of Josh White and Burl Ives; games that disclose cleverness and spite, idealism and Christian charity. The game this Friday afternoon was about ten survivors, men and women, on a raft, drifting from their sunken ocean liner, with limited water and food, and anticipating that they would drift to an island, where there would be enough food for only two persons. They were locked in a game of deciding the fate of which one — by seducing him or her, to jump overboard and commit suicide — would be left to live and to carry on the race, since it was assumed that the two remaining persons on the raft would be a man and a woman.

This program was filmed live, in the days when almost everything shown on television was live.

When I eventually arrived, the program was in progress, and I was urged by the director to "swim" to the life raft and climb aboard. I knew all the men and women taking part in this parlour game. I was being urged to "walk on water" by a young member of the Church, who would substitute for Larry Solway when he was unavailable. This man of God was dressed in his black robes and collar. He was standing by the syke, off camera, chatting with a few other participants who already had been "thrown overboard."

"When you get there? Who you're going to tell them you are?"

He had heard the director tell me to swim to the raft.

"Jesus!" I told him. "Jesus walking on water."

"Look what they did to me!" he said. "I was the first they threw off. They do not like God, or the Church."

I simulated that the studio floor was the sea, and I was swimming on it. I interrupt my narrative to explain that I have never seen this film and no one in my house ever saw it. We did not have a television. But it was a time of great fun and joy and hilarity and creative energies in this city of Toronto, now bursting its seams of restricted and conservative dullness, and burgeoning into a city of life. I have never learned how to swim. But I must have seemed professional, imitating the crawl, knowledgeable in the ways of the sea, because when I reached for the raft with my hand, and pulled myself out of the water and into the safety of the lifeboat, the first challenge to my identity was raised.

"Who are you?"

"Jesus!"

There was no skepticism, no debate, no wonder, no philosophical thought to the possibility that I might have come from a continent where all Jesuses were black ...

I was dumped overboard.

Going back to stand beside the Reverend, by the light blue syke, with the other dumped survivors, he said, "What did I tell you? This is an ungodly crew!"

Wendy Michener, the daughter of a governor general (Roland Michener), was in this game. Heather Burton, Dennis's wife; a Dr. Rich, a psychiatrist who lived near Asquith Avenue, on a small cobble-stoned street going down the hill to Rosedale Valley Road; the Reverend; two others, a man and a woman, whose names I cannot remember; and me.

The game suddenly got to be like drama. There were now three left. Heather, Wendy and Dr. Rich, who had been allying himself with another man to convince Heather Burton to throw herself into the sea. And he succeeded in ridding himself of the competitor. He is now left to convince either Heather or Wendy to commit suicide. But he had sided with Wendy against Heather in order to dump the last man. Confident that he now had Heather covered, he made approaches to Wendy. Wendy turned against him. Overboard went the good doctor.

The two women, Wendy Michener and Heather Burton were left — to reach the desert island, with provisions for two, to carry on the race!

This result was, to me, quite interesting, for the race was in jeopardy of dying out, without the possibility of reproduction. And on an island, inhabited only by two women. But no one amongst us, thrown overboard earlier in the game, mentioned this. This was my private thought, manufactured to fit the demands of fiction which the novelist indulges in as a part of being a novelist.

The good Reverend cordially invited us, Heather and me, to his home to have a few refreshments to celebrate a successful television program of this "parlour game of survivor," more than to drink, although a drink on this exhausting day was welcomed.

And he drove us in his black Volvo, as it had to be, since he was a professional man of some intellectual stature, because the Volvo in the 1960s was the symbol for that kind of sophistication.

I had not seen Heather since the night of the party at the Kilbourns when her husband Dennis burst into the crowded room to see Pierre Berton dancing with Mrs. Kilbourn; Mr. Kilbourn dancing with Mrs. Berton; Honest Ed dancing with Mrs. Mirvish; Robert Mirvish dancing with a woman I had never met; and Dr. Morty Shulman, at that time a member of Metro Council, dancing with Heather. Dennis was wearing his grey houndstooth suit, handsome in this autumnal sartorial splendour. We all envied him. And he wore the suit like an armour of morality, announcing to us who knew, that he had had a very successful year.

The Artists' Jazz Bann was playing a piece by John Coltrane, who, apart from Miles Davis,was their favourite jazz musician to imitate, not too successfully, I might add. But it was great fun.

Dennis walked up to the dancing couple.

He measured distance, calculated target and strength and velocity.

And when he landed the punch that struck the Good Doctor in his square face, it was the first time in my life, as a fan of boxing which took place on television in the basement the Ole King Cole Room of the Park Plaza Hotel, on Friday nights, it was the first time I had seen a man strike another man who fell flat on his arse from the punch. Not even Sugar Ray Robinson had done that.

Dr. Shulman fell amongst the cymbals. Gord, the drummer, held his sticks, in alarm, in his hands, wondering at the shivering sound of the dangling cymbals.

Dennis Burton took his wife to safety outside the Rosedale drawing room. The dancers and the guests were speechless. The cymbals had lost their last vibration, and were silent. The music of the Artists' Jazz Bann was struck dumb. In this silence, which had an undercoating of funniness, and wonder, and sensuality, Dr. Shulman got to his feet, rubbing his left jaw, more surprised than anyone else in the knowing room. He did not crawl, or walk, to his wife, Mrs. Shulman for succour, and assistance, and said to the room, "What did he do that for?"

What did he do that for?

It seemed that the entire room of black ties and long dress, blue jeans and thick woollen sweaters, and the corduroy suit of the artist who had met me at the bar of the Pilot Tavern that same night, lamenting the fact that he was not in the good books of Mrs. Kilbourn, and had received an invitation to this annual celebrity party, he was now drunk down the long hall of the kitchen, in this mixture of money and wealth and brain and brawn — Dennis's — and beauty and sensuality, and very good Scotch, everyone knew the answer to Dr. Shulman's unhappiness and difficulty with the answer to the question he himself had posed.

"What did he do that for?"

Heather is concerned now, about two years after the boxing match between Dennis and Morty, a match in which there was one aggressor, an unfair match in the drawing room in Rosedale, Heather is more concerned with the "impression" given, the conclusions that might be drawn from her part in the dispatching of Dr. Rich overboard, a choice that left her with another woman to fulfill the demands of "carrying on the race."

"I was worried that they would think we were lesbians."

The name had not been used before. And the idea had crossed the mind of none of the other participants. But Heather was concerned.

"Austin, have you ever wondered what happened that night, when Dennis burst into the party?"

I had not even thought of that, of the things that happened when she got dressed and left for Rosedale from Church and Yorkville; and he was home cleaning his brushes; or putting a finishing touch on the face of the beautiful lady, who had been sitting for him, on commission from her husband, in the triptych he had shown me on the easel on the second-floor apartment and studio; and had she left in her own taxi; and he, alone with the smell of paint and turpentine, his houndstooth suit with the red lining on the hanger on the nail in their bedroom, and felt the shame of not having been invited to the champagne and strawberry party of black tie and tails and long dresses?

"When he pulled me out the door, I saw the taxi waiting, and he went mad and you can imagine what happened …"

The Reverend must have been driving a Volvo, for he was that kind of a man, a middle-class, university-educated man, different from the middle-class, educated men who were white liberals and a touch artistic, who drove VWs, either the Beetle, or the station wagon; and this was almost a culture: the model of the car you drove matching your profession and, to some extent, your salary. In the mid-1950s, only ten years after the end of the Second World War, wealthy Jews in Toronto were hesitant and determined not to drive the Mercedes-Benz because of their still sharp memory of Nazi Germany, and the knowledge that the Mercedes-Benz was the symbol of Nazi industrial technology. They tended to concentrate on the Cadillac. And the irony of this relationship of the model of a car to the profession of its owner has a humorous reflection when applied to the American Negro of substance, and those who liked style and image, in Harlem and in Detroit, "the heavier cats." They too, chose the Caddy. Other American Negroes, not of the moneyed class, but who were members of the middle class in the 1950s, favoured the "Bruick," as they called the Buick 98.

Tying ends, connecting the strands of stories to complete the action and give the "conclusion" to a scene which opens as atmosphere or as context, I find myself looking at my own life, and coming to the conclusion that I have lived on the periphery of society, as society is used in its best sophistication, taking part in political decisions, commenting on those political matters which affect my life, mingling with persons, men and women of my "class," meaning men and women who have the same ethics, morality, education, talent, ambition, and desire to succeed, none of this has come into my path in the natural way in which I experienced and lived this sophisticated and civilized life, back in Barbados. I grieve that this is the lot of the immigrant. But I have never regarded myself as an immigrant to this country, because that would be to accept the Canadian meaning of "immigrant," to embrace an identity of myself as a second-class person, "visible minority status," a difference, the reservation of accepting the "foreignness" that the immigrant who is white does not have applied to his sojourn in Canada. And this is why I can see, at this stage of my life (and at that juncture in 1963, driving in the black standard-shift Volvo with the Reverend and Heather Burton), that all my life in this country has been lived on the periphery, sometimes, completely excluded from the significant decisions that are made. But the decisions are made on my behalf; and after the decisions are made, there is the assumption that I shall live with them.

At this stage in my life, in 1963, I am thinking seriously of leaving Canada, for England. America, which is just across the border, and which is living within my political consciousness like blood in the veins, touching my literary awareness, Malcolm X, Leroi Jones, Stokely Carmichael, and James Baldwin, Amiri Baraka, Richard Wright, and Ralph Ellison are all rejected, and I seek a place, a landscape, a context that is better known to me, through the condition of birth and former residence; and culture. And I chose England. I shall go there and do what I left Barbados to do: get my degree from the London School of Economics, LSE, to which I had been admitted in 1954, and after LSE, enter The Middle Temple, to which I had been admitted in 1963, to be trained to become a barrister-at-law. I was rejecting Canada and America — and Barbados — three former colonies, and confronting the Mother Country on her own soil, on her own terms.

But I knew in my bones that I had to leave Canada. It was not so much an uncertain future faced by a beginning writer, it was simpler than that. I had outgrown Canada. My patience with having to stomach the indignity extended to me, to have me live on the periphery of compromise. And what had I achieved, as a beginning writer and as a freelance CBC radio broadcaster, to make me give all this up, and make my exit from Canada? I could not go back to Barbados. Barbados does not tolerate partial success. And Barbados does not stomach writers and other artists even though they might be at the pinnacle of their success. I found myself, in my thoughts of voluntary deportation, in the position of choosing another country completely foreign to me, in the sense of having no physical knowledge of living there, only the historical connection of colonialism, and before that, slavery. And it is strange, even now, to think that I had found some solace in going to a country whose history of race relations was equally spotted by violent outbursts as that in the United States. But I was British in the sense of the colour of my passport, and Britain could not refuse me. This was my delusion before Margaret Thatcher became prime minister, and who obliterated all that Commonwealth family relationship.

I never left Canada for England. And this was before Margaret Thatcher did become prime minister and changed the immigration laws. With the foolhardiness of looking back, and wishing for greater luck, and feeling as if I would have had it, I wonder with the fool's honesty, "What would I have become had I gone to live in England? Would I have been a barrister-at-law? A schoolteacher, which I had been, for three years in Barbados, after Harrison College, before my coming to Canada? A writer? A frequent visitor to the Old Bailey, to stand before a magistrate, accused for demonstrating and protesting against racial discrimination, as many of my West Indian friends who were writers had found themselves, as I had protested its version in Canada? Locked up? Branded a criminal? Described in the newspapers as an extremist? Just as my now dead friend, Andrew Salkey, and the late Jan Carew, had been branded? Just as Michael DeFreitas, who became Michael X, who became 888, was branded and then deported back to Trinidad, and who killed an English woman, and who was made even more notorious and despicable a figure by V.S. Naipaul, in his novel, *Guerrillas*?

Whenever, in these days of 1965 and 1966, that the newspapers were writing about me, either as a broadcaster or short-story writer, they made a point of introducing me as "a friend of Malcolm X." Or, "Canada's Angriest Black Man." They never paused to see why I was angry? Or what had caused this anger, if at all I was, really, "angry"? These were after all, not too remote from the days of Senator McCarthy, and widespread paranoia in the United States; the Royal Canadian Mounted Police (RCMP), were even at that time, colluding with the CIA and the FBI.

Telephones were tapped in those days. Every black man who raised his placard and his voice in protest of racial discrimination was regarded as an "extremist." "Extremist" carried the same weight of guilt as "terrorist" today.

I wanted to be known as a writer. Even as a black writer. Or as a Negro writer. Or even as an Afro-Canadian writer. And I saw the danger, to myself, and to my career, by being associated so closely to political extremism. I wanted also to be able to separate my life as a writer from my life as a man. I did not, and still do not, consider the two to be one and the same.

And as luck would have it, I was invited, at this time in 1967, to visit Yale University, to give a reading of my short stories. How this came about is purely a stroke of luck. Luck has always followed me, in my life, in all its aspects, in all places where my life has taken me, in all conditions, and situations that include love, career, pleasure, travel, every aspect of human endeavour. It is the luck of the cat, of the black cat, no pun intended, as a reminder of the term "cat" used by the hip black musicians such as Miles and Trane and Duke and Count and Bird. I mean the nine-lives cat, falling from a fling through a window on the second floor, and landing on all fours. That kind of luck has wrapped me in its blanket of protection; and even before the demonstration of luck, I have the declaration of the Fates, the gods that Greeks and Romans consulted before any important event or act, the strong sense of instinct that is a part of being black, meaning having that ancestral connection to Africa.

It began quite simply. And unexpectedly. A professor of history at Berkeley College in Yale University, Robin W. Winks, who hailed from a small town in Iowa, was doing research into his writing a book, which eventually was published as *The Blacks in Canada, A History*, and he had come across in his research a "magazine" which I had a hand in editing, *Ebo Voice*. Could he have a couple of copies? And what would I charge him?

The "magazine" in question was nothing more than a couple of plain pages copied on a Xerox machine, perhaps they were stencilled, containing a few poems by me, a word by Howard Matthews, a poem by Charlie Roach — nothing to write home about. And I would have shouted, "Five dollars each!" had it not for the fact that my friend Jan Carew, recently emigrated from London, England, where he had lived for years, was visiting me, on Asquith Avenue; and when I told him of the request of the professor, he said, "Ask him to invite you to Yale to give a reading. You will have that in your curriculum vitae for life!"

You will have that in your curriculum vitae, for life!

Life and curriculum vitae turned out in the same mould as the luck I was talking about.

I made the trip, on the invitation of the professor, to Yale, where I gave a "tea," as a seminar at Berkeley College is called. And after the two days at Yale, I went down to New York and Harlem, where I interviewed Leroi Jones (Amiri Baraka), a second time, and Paule Marshall, and John

Henrik Clarke, the editor of *Freedomways* magazine, a black journal that specialized in black literary and political affairs; and Max Roach, who had just composed his jazz opera, *Freedom Now Suite*, in which his wife, at the time, Abbey Lincoln, screams herself hoarse in imitation of Africa's woes and joys, and protest; and I drank my Cutty Sark Scotch at the Red Rooster in Harlem; visited all the jazz joints in Greenwich Village and on Broadway, and heard Thelonious Monk on piano, wearing his beret, and dancing out of tune to the harmonic music he had just played in a solo; and eventually returned to Toronto, a man with the new tonic of prospect and a future, in academia, or in writing.

And a few months later, another flash of luck reached me. I was invited back to Yale to spend one month as a Morse Fellow at another college, Pierson College, to talk about creative writing and anything that came into my mind. Appointed with me at the same time was William Caldwell, the famous sculptor of mobiles. In the two months I spent there, I never rested my eyes on Mr. Caldwell. Perhaps, he was, like his mobiles, spinning in the wind.

But I had met the chaplain of Yale, a rebel of a man of the cloth, William Sloane Coffin, who later gained notoriety and fame and the congratulations of American college students throughout the country for his opposition to the Vietnam War, raging inconclusively in the nationalist hearts of young men; and after that, his part with the Dr. Spock burning draft cards in public in defiance of President Richard Nixon and H.R. Haldeman and John Ehrlichman and J. Edgar Hoover the FBI chief, and the thickened paranoia of the entire Nixon administration. And a scientist from Harvard who was visiting Yale, Dr. Gerry Wall, spoke to me in scientific terms that I could understand. And when Yale became too serious and intellectual, I sought refuge in Harlem and in Greenwich Village, and the Five Spot, and the Ninth Circle, because Dylan Thomas had drunk all those whiskeys at one sitting on a stool on the bar's carpet, three inches thick with the shells of parched peanuts, a record, in one night, his last night on earth, glorying in the feat of accomplishment, "not going gentle in the good night" of the Village's ambiance.

And then, my last day as a Morse Fellow, the professor of history, the author of *The Blacks in Canada*, Robin W. Winks, invited me to lunch at Calhoun College, whose master was Professor R.W.B. Lewis, an authority on Edith Wharton. Present were Robert Penn Warren, professor of English, who taught also creative writing in a system of having each student write one page each day; C. Vann Woodward, professor of history, called the Southern Historian, and Professor Sydney E. Ahlstrom, professor of American studies. The lunch was college fare, not exciting, but exciting in its context, in the Calhoun College dining hall. I do not remember what we ate. But toward the end, the question was posed by Professor Lewis, "How would you teach Afro-American literature if you were asked?"

And since I was not asked, at least I did not see the implication; and since by now I had added to by two visits to Yale to my curriculum vitae; and I could forever boast of this experience, I became expansive, and said that if I had the chance to teach Afro-American literature — certainly not at Yale, for this was beyond belief and realism — I would teach it comparative to African literature in English translation, and West Indian literature, and I reeled off dozens of names of those writers, and they looked at me, and smiled, and sipped their coffee, and I was thinking of The Five Spot and Miles Davis, and the Red Rooster in Harlem ...

CHAPTER TWENTY-FOUR

"Power Games"

The light was bad, although it was a Friday, even though Friday has always had a way of interposing itself between me in brief periods of exhilaration and moments of my despondency, providing the relief of a hiatus between the bad days and the good days of my disposition. Haze, like a curtain of voile, a blind of confusion and of indecision was covering the sun. And it covered my spirit, too, just as a curtain covers the props on the stage that give the play its meaning and its significance.

I found myself on this Friday morning, in an embarrassing posture of imprecating: applying for a visa to permit me to work in America, to work at Yale University in a one-year appointment, Visiting Lecturer in the Department of English and in the American Studies Program; and this desire following on the heels of my anti-American belligerence — after all those cold nights sitting on the sidewalk in front of the U.S. Consulate General, protesting the murder of Medgar Evers, protesting the assassination of Dr. Martin Luther King, Jr.; followed by all those warm afternoons and nights, marching up and down, with placards like Roman shields made out of paper and cardboard, with strident voice, deprecating the same America, through which front door I now enter; now, a supplicant: then, a miscreant, labelled "Canada's angriest black man," because I was a member of the culture of anti-American protest, adding my small voice to the racist treatment of black people in America, and to the bombings America carried out against the brown people of Vietnam, with extraordinary violence greater than all the violence of bombs dropped during the Second World War.

"Mr. Clarke, you are politically controversial. And I doubt whether you'll ever get a visa to live in the United States."

The American Consul General at Toronto was smiling as he told me this. It was in July 1968. He was a man of some intelligence, and sophistication; and in spite of his place and position in the diplomatic bureaucracy of the most powerful nation on earth, he had startled me with his sense of humour. I had not ever associated humour with American diplomacy. But I was aware that the powerful, at times chosen by themselves, and that are beneficial to themselves, can express bouts of humour. But this general humour, and sophistication, I have found absent, too often, from the manner of most white Americans of his position.

"You don't like us," he added. I suspected that he did not want me to like America, either, and had come to realize that anyone like me would not like America, certainly not the America of 1968, and certainly not in the same way as the amorphous "middle-American" does.

Our conversation continued in a courteous but firm manner; and the little sympathy he permitted himself to expose to me, did in no way delude me into thinking that there could ever be a change of heart. I was left to consider myself as some kind of celebrity, a kind of notorious, but dangerous, person to be watched by foreign missions, and this importance both startled me and pleased me.

"But you can always inform Yale University about your visa problems. And I'm sure Yale will get the visa to you."

He was introducing me to a structure of power, a system of academic power of which I myself was too unsophisticated to conceive. There were other powers in the most powerful nation on earth. The consul did not even have to add "In no time at all!" but he did so nevertheless. And this seemed to be the re-emphasis of what Yale University really meant, in terms of its power and capacity to solve matters of a politically ticklish nature.

I had told him, with no mincing of words, that I felt I was doing his country, America, a great honour by wanting to live within the boundaries of its cauldron of consumptive racialism. The year was, after all, 1968. And I had made it clear to him, that by going to America, I would be sacrificing whatever peace of mind I might have accumulated in the thirteen years I had been living in Canada, for one year in America; and that I had absolutely no intention of wanting to remain longer than the one year I had been contracted to teach Afro-American literature at Yale University. My appointment was in the Department of English and in the American Studies Program; jointly.

The consul could not have believed, nor appreciated the intensity of my despising his country in such a cavalier manner. In his mind, every living person, in particular poor people from poor countries (and as a West Indian I would have qualified in American eyes as a poor immigrant), still regarded America as the land of opportunity — if not the land of the free and the brave. For certainly he would have seen the long lines of Canadian applicants, European and Latin-American applicants fleeing socialism in their countries, and some few West Indian applicants, in winter and in summer, stomping the cold and the fear in their feet, as the line, long as a snake wrapped around a man's body, all waiting for the chance to go to America, to live; and "to make the Yankee dollar." And the consul would have understood how it was possible for all these people, from all corners of the world, displaced for various political and social reasons, who want to jump into the frying pan of American materialism.

The country has advantages; and he, as consul, would have to conclude, and inform his government that America was still well-liked by all these foreigners, that the motivation for this great wave of immigration was based upon something other than greed; and that because of this materialistic greed, the applicants, now transformed through their greed into supplicants, would tend not to be revolutionaries and communists and terrorists. And naturally, seeing that I was a West Indian, it was possible for him to feel that I might not want ever to return from America to Canada.

But we did not belabour the point.

He did however, inform me that my being "controversial" and "political" was the indictment decided upon, not primarily by the Canadian government (who certainly would not reverse an American indictment), nor was it the opinion of the U.S. Consulate General in Toronto. It was, rather, the conclusion of a consul general in Barbados, a conclusion based upon her memory of me, when I visited my home in 1964, soon after my first novel, *The Survivors of the Crossing*, was published, soon after I had interviewed Malcolm X in New York. This conclusion was made by a woman, by the name of Miss Eileen R. Donovan, American Consul General (as she signed her name in the *Barbados Advocate* newspaper), in a letter addressed to me.

I had been speaking in Barbados about the racial problem in America, and Miss Donovan, her country's representative to my country, felt she should explain America's position on the subject of racism. This is Miss Donovan's letter to the *Barbados Advocate*:

> I am concerned by a by-lined article which appeared on page 8 of your August 11 edition, originating in Barbados by Austin C. Clarke who is stated to be a Barbadian living in Canada, now here on assignment for the Canadian Broadcasting Corporation.
>
> Mr. Clarke, like anyone else living in a free society, enjoys the right to write what he chooses, however factually incorrect and dangerous misleading it may be.
>
> One can only wonder why the *Advocate* chooses to publish such mixed-up material advocating violence by Negroes in the United States, since the purpose of a free Press in a free society is to inform rather than incite.
>
> One must also wonder for whom Mr. Clarke speaks. If such views are merely his own personal opinions, he should say so, and so should the *Advocate*. If he speaks for some group in Canada or elsewhere which shares his views he should also say so.
>
> I can tell you and your readers, however, that there is one group for which he does not speak, and that is the American Negro citizens of my country, 99% of whom would reject and resent his views as firmly as I do. Eileen R. Donovan, American Consul General.

I cannot remember, and have no document to show what I wrote that drove Miss Donovan to express such paternalism hardly concealed beneath her more obvious patronizing superciliousness; and her attitude, when seen against the background of the civil rights movement in America, in 1964, and the cruelty of American police and sheriffs and governors and mayors, is ironic. But even more puzzling (though not to the population of Barbadians whose understanding of the racial problems in America in 1964, was, to say the least, naive), is her presumption that there is a similarity of nationalistic sentiment amongst "99 percent of the American Negro," and that she was certain that this 99 percent of black Americans agreed with her that they "regarded themselves as American." What kind of Americans? Second-class?

But Miss Donovan's position was historically consistent with American delusion regarding racism in their society: many white Americans presumed to be able "to speak for the Negro American." I found myself, as a black man living in Canada, and a Barbadian by birth, being deliberately vilified in my own country, by a foreign white woman, an American diplomat, who was justifiably diplomatic in trying to prevent the domestic racial problems in her own country, from being exposed in an area of the world where American foreign policy is to influence the thinking of this unthinking Barbadian population, and to establish good "race relations." But Miss Donovan's position was not, and could not be justified on the basis of fact. It is a trifle mundane now to say what I said then, in 1964, in reply to her letter, that America was a country of inexplicable anti-black hostility. But is it really inexplicable? The reasons for racism swirling inside America have been let out of the bag.

But it was important to me to set Miss Donovan straight. And then, I ignored her: she was not, as an intellectual thinker, important to my life.

Her decision to write the letter to the editor might have been motivated by a collective embarrassment in which her country got itself entangled, and which it had tried to make palatable through its neo-imperialist relations with some West Indian countries, in order to maintain American influence in the West Indies. But only the most gullible and messianic West Indian prime ministers would swallow this American public relations program. Miss Donovan's letter could not have been understood in all its paternalistic implication by the average

Barbadian; and it probably was not regarded by the Barbadian as either offensive or neo-imperialistic, because this class of Barbadian did not have the first-hand experience of living in America during the early 1960s at the height of the civil rights movement, and the reality of racism in which that exposure would have educated him; and he would be in the dark regarding Miss Donovan's own government's reaction to the demands of the "Negroes in America" for justice; and further-more it would have been impossible for the ordinary Barbadian to see clearly the dichotomy between the American public relations program of good race relations in the West Indies, and the application of that "good race relations" within America, as it related to the "Negroes" living in America. For these "Negroes," according to Miss Donovan, are American citizens.

But Miss Donovan had apparently not forgotten me. Nor, had she forgiven me. In fact, she had white-listed me. And she might have white-mailed me, also! But this was understandable. It was understandable from her position of power. In matters of this nature, I have, for many years, found that justice is not a significant factor in the consideration of morality. It is rather a factor of power. So, I was both impressed and startled when the American consul in Toronto introduced me to the avenues of power at Yale University. And he seemed to be suggesting that I might use these avenues of power in order to leap-frog the obstacle placed in my path by another American consul.

In this position of some irony, I felt as if I had been introduced to the "power game" itself, and had become a participant in its execution. It was a delusion that I could, and did, indulge in, at that time. Had I persisted in this delusion, the stony fact of the consequences of my puny literary and ideological entente with Miss Donovan, reminded me promptly of this home truth: I was still being haunted in Toronto, four years after the exchange between Miss Donovan and I that took place in Barbados, and thousands of miles away from Barbados, with an exchange of three letters in the *Barbados Advocate*; and the person responsible for giving this importance to my letters, was a consul general.

"I would really like to know what it is you said to our consul general in Barbados, in 1964," the consul in Toronto said to me. As he said this, there was a smile on his face. "We don't think you like us."

It was not necessary for him to have added that. He seemed to me
then, to be a man caught up in a useless intrigue of international diplomacy that was minuscule; and he was no doubt trying to bring me within
the sphere of his intrigue. He was smiling. And I had come to suspect
smiles more than growls.

To me, going to Yale University to teach Afro-American literature,
and American studies, was a diversion not so sophisticated as the parry
and thrust of intrigue. And it certainly was not diplomacy. It was, in plain
terms, a matter of bread and butter. It had put me in a serious moral
position, too: my willingness, my eagerness coupled to this, to procure
this bread and this butter while living within the lion's mouth. The terror
and the danger, if not the subconscious suicidal bent to my nature,
were also obvious to me. And though I had decided, against an inflated
moral arrogance, to make this bread in America, and even though I had
understood clearly that my intention to acquire this money in America
was, to say the least, an expression of schizophrenic behaviour, I was
still determined to permit neither the racial situation in America, nor the
pragmatism in my scheme to become bogged down in the inquisitive
tangles and smiles of another American diplomat, a consul.

Now that I am thinking of this, I do not think he was a consul. He
was definitely not the consul general. My file was too flimsy, even with its
potential incendiary phrases, to warrant the attention of a head of mission. He could have been a "tenth secretary" handling short-term visas.

Looking back now, and trying to piece together small and insignificant
details of my interview at the U.S. Consulate General at Toronto, I can
remember certain actions and attitudes that, through my instinct, I have
always managed to identify clearly, simply as a means of self-preservation
— if not the means of providing myself with a second gust of strength,
for the purpose of counterattack and retaliation.

I remember a secretary, a woman, who saw me before the tenth secretary did. She wore steel-rimmed spectacles. I remember the bland taste
of her choice of clothes; and I remember the tension in her fingers. She
spent the entire ten minutes with me, making lines on her notepad. Her
notepad was yellow and legal-sized, with blue horizontal lines, and a
red margin on the left side. But I was not supposed to be looking at her
notepad. The lines she drew on it became long, and then she thickened

them; and then, still fumbling, still doodling in her mind for a piece of diplomacy with which to make me feel comfortable while I waited for the tenth secretary, she found herself making symbols: heads of spears, or arrows. But she had attached the heads of the arrows in the wrong direction, in relation to the shaft of the spear, or the arrows. The heads of the arrows were attached in such a way that I felt she was not thinking of violence, even symbolically, so much as she was expressing a corporate decision, indulged in and decided upon before I stood before her, and in which she had shared; as a decision to turn me back.

A woman who happened, years before she told me this story, to be the receptionist and secretary in an advertising office where I presented myself to apply for a job as a writer, writing copy to sell Forsyth shirts and men's college blazers, told me that the moment I left the office, after the manager had declared his love for Barbados, and his good impression of the very high literacy rate of Barbadians, after telling me I'll hear from him, after promising me the job — "You'll be a credit to our firm, Mr. Clarke!" — he tore my curriculum vitae neatly into half, down the length of its legal size, then place the halves, evenly as if he were measuring advertising space, then reduced them to quarters, then into the small size, then held them between thumb and index finger, and, like a basketball player, dropped them into the empty wastepaper basket that sat at the feet of the receptionist-secretary. And he ended his "slam-dunk" with fingers still arranged in a delicate, dainty gesture of satisfaction. Years after this, a woman who worked as a secretary in an employment office of the civil service, told me ten years after I had been presenting myself before a supervisor to be interviewed for jobs: job as night watchman, Christmas rush postman, cleaner of the elementary school just south of College Street, one building west of police headquarters on College and University Avenue; janitor of the Baptist Church House, up from Bloor, on St. George Street; and some women who worked for the Bell Telephone Company, in its office on Asquith Avenue, these two informants told me, in strictest confidence, "'cause if it get out that it is me who tell you, I will get fired," that the officer at the desk to whom I gave my preliminary information, such as age, education and address, this man — or woman — wrote a code, a letter, a number, an exclamation mark, perhaps three black dots, the purpose of which was to "warn" the man who would interview me, that I was a Negro. "Shit! Would I lie about a thing like this?"

This secretary in the U.S. Consulate at Toronto might have been thinking of journeys and passages, of time and place; and of countries and entry and exit. And detours. Perhaps, also, her mind might have bordered on deportation. Was she conscious of her thoughts? Or, was she, as a psychiatrist would conclude, unaware of the thoughts that were crowding her head? Was she fashioning in her personal forge, in her anvil, the heads of arrows pointing in the wrong, but in my direction, subconsciously?

The heads of arrows turned into detour signs. She was telling me, through her hammering on the anvil of her yellow legal pages, that so far as my being granted an American visa was concerned, that she knew, had been instructed that I was on the wrong path. She had attached the heads of the arrows in the wrong direction, in a backward direction. I knew then, I felt it through my system, I was aware of the blow of instinct upon my reason, that even before we had discussed the matter for two minutes, what my position was. No visa was to be granted.

I cannot remember anything she said to me during this interview. It was really a preliminary interview, like the ones at the front of the employment office. But I might have been inattentive to her words. I had, by then, developed a mental mechanism that made it easy for me to switch off my hearing faculties whenever I suspected someone of telling me something that I felt the person himself did not believe in, and which I feared was detrimental to me, had I listened to it, and tried to understand it; and this ability to switch off my ears, at will, has protected me from being assaulted by hypocrisy and stupidity. And surprised. The secretary was doodling away her time in order to catch the most gentle opportune moment in which to break the gloomy news to me.

When a man has compromised his moral position (as I seemed to have done), his point of view, or his conviction; and if that compromise should force him into rationalizations in an attempt to try to justify it on grounds of pragmatism, then that man like myself stands in grave danger of being destroyed and insulted in matters of even greater personal significance. He can no longer claim that he has retained the same moral position by explaining later on (even before the catastrophe consequent upon his compromise) that "in the first place" his logic had warned him against being entangled in the matter, or in the person, or in the attitude, in the point of view and conviction, which five factors were hinged on to his moral principles.

So, when I told this American tenth secretary that I did not regard it as a favour, nor as an honour, to be permitted to live in America, anyhow, the moral poignancy of my rebuke, if at all it was still a rebuke, and had retained the significance of righteous protest, it had already been dissipated, had lost its strength and virtue, its body, and was now corrupted by an official refusal of a visa to permit my immigration to America. "In the first place," I should never have applied for the visa. I should never have accepted the one-year appointment to teach at Yale University. My moral foundation had already been shattered at the root by my acceptance of the appointment. For I had already deluded myself that I could hate America for its treatment of "Negroes" like me, and still, in the next breath, accept a situation to work within its system.

"Politically controversial," the tenth secretary had said.

My papers would have to be sent to Ottawa to be "officially processed"; and by the time they were processed, it would be six months later.

Ottawa did get the papers from the Americans.

And when I tried to sidestep the Americans in an amateurish manoeuvre and applied instead for Canadian citizenship (certainly not an expression of my desire to become a Canadian citizen!), Ottawa replied, in a form letter, couched in official jargon, and with considerably more indelicacy and less humour than the Americans, that "certain con-fidential" files pertaining to my "activities," files that could not be made public, "in the public interest," stood in my way of obtaining Canadian citizenship at that time. But I might, and could, if I still desired to be a Canadian citizen, apply again in two years. Apparently, two years is the length of time necessary to convince "politically controversial" West Indians to see the un-wisdom of their political activities. Two years was therefore the silk of time in which I could have my application for Canadian citizenship reconsidered. Miss Donovan had copied her files efficiently to the proper Canadian and American agencies. Canada, which proclaimed itself at that time, to be guided by a distinctive nation-alistic foreign policy, with no influence from the Americans, had col-laborated with the Americans in a definition of "political controversy." But the policy of the Canadian government toward black people was not different in essence and in quality from that of America. And since America had judged me as "politically controversial" for a speech I gave in Barbados, then Canada and no doubt, Britain, would have judged me as a black extremist and a black militant, which were the terms used then for any black man who talked about white racism, in terms that exploded integration as an ineffectual tactic, and inapplicable to the assurance of dignity and even of human rights.

I was becoming known outside of Toronto for something. And my sponsor at Yale, Professor Robin W. Winks the historian, had found my name cropping up here and there during his tracking down through research, information about blacks in Canada for his book *The Blacks in Canada*. The historian and the detective had tracked me down. But his intention was different from that of the diplomat, of course. And so, it was no surprise to me, some months later, when I was invited to a Danforth Foundation conference in a place named Zion, near Chicago, that Yale got in touch with me to advise me that I should not apply for the type of visa that the Tenth Secretary had suggested, but that I should apply for the visa that Yale was now suggesting. Yale advised me to apply for the type of visa that Yale wanted me to have. I was disorientated at the time.

The riots in Chicago and the tragedy of the 1968 Democratic Convention in that city were oppressing my mind. And now that I was in this place, named Zion, offered no redemption and no absolution, even of a biblical nature. My disorientation lingered. I was too near to Mayor Daley. Too near to the city of Chicago. Too near to Chicago's policemen, about whom the French playwright Jean Genet, on assignment by *Esquire* magazine, and attracted to the physical bodies of the cops, used the metaphor of the male penis in his description of the nightsticks these cops held menacingly in their tattooed, hairy, white arms.

But Yale University had demonstrated a kind of paternalistic interest in my welfare. And Yale was perhaps more powerful than either Chicago or Mayor Daley. For Yale had said in its telephone message: "Just tell the Immigration people in Toronto which plane, which hour, which day you'll be coming to Yale, and the visa will be waiting there for you, at the Toronto International Airport.

That is power. What kind of power, I don't know, but I understood it as being a simple, clean, unadulterated power. I do not know how many telephone calls Yale University had to make on my behalf; and to whom; I do not know if Yale called its senator, meaning the senator from Connecticut, a piece of intelligence given to me, right off the bat, by the tenth secretary. But I do know, from a call from my wife, that the visa was there, in Toronto, at the American immigration office, half an hour after I had received the telephone call in Zion, Illinois, from Yale University.

It had taken me four months before the U.S. Consulate General in Toronto could see me; and I had had to make that appointment myself, when I realized that the consulate might have been doodling and marking time on my application, probably in the rhythm of the death march ...

CHAPTER TWENTY-FIVE

Yale

This Friday afternoon is a day of sun and happiness and excitement. I am leaving Canada. Not for good. Not for England, the Mother Country, as I had it in my mind to do, less to register at Middle Temple and become the barrister-at-law I thought was in my stars, and more as an escape from the way my life had been balanced in the scale of unknown endings. I would walk in front of the Supreme Court, a short tack to joining demonstrations in front of the U.S. Consulate, and would take a minute to look up at Justice, a woman — sometimes I wondered if Justice was never sculpted in the body of a man? Or, a boy? — and I would wonder whether a prejudice, an opinion not necessarily dressed in law and in logic, a breath, deliberate to tip the scales, and any other aberration, what act could, like the two fingers of the shop keeper placed stealingly on the scale, to add avoirdupois and profits, in the small kerosene-lamp shop, in that weak light, back home in Barbados, and give the wrong justice. And I imagined myself in a dock in this Supreme Court, pleading for the justices' understanding that the weight of racial prejudice is more burdensome, psychologically, than in its execution, physically. For if this were not the case, then there would be no black Americans. The Middle Passage would have been their ovens and concentration camps. But we know that they lived on, through this rough crossing from one tent and grass hat, to a wooden shack of hell in America. And in the West Indies. But I am leaving Toronto, and the uncertainty that faces the writer, at almost each step of life, no less unsettling after the second book, than after the fifth, each step shaking like an unanchored flight of wooden stairs not pinned or screwed to its foundation.

This is a journey of unknown destination in the sense that although I know where I am going, I do not know where I am heading to, in the strict sense of destination. And I know it is a journey, which, whether undertaken in full, going from LaGuardia Airport in New York, to Yale University in New Haven, or aborted before its terminus, is going to change my life, forever.

So, I am in the white Connecticut limousine car, crammed and crushed against unspeaking white men and white women, professors, and students returning to various colleges and universities in the Eastern seaboard, for the September term, or entering for the first time, on the way between Darien and New Haven, early in September 1968. I tried to remember and fit together, into some perspective, things about the itinerary of my trip over this strange countryside.

Here I am, moving east and slightly north from New York City. I was more safe and comfortable in New York City, especially the part that is Harlem, for there I have interviewed, on assignment for the CBC, Malcolm X, Leroi Jones, Floyd McKissick, Roy Innis, Minister Louis Farrakhan, John Henrik Clarke, Paule Marshall, Rosa Guy, Abbey Lincoln, Max Roach, and others, as long ago as 1963 and 1964. But this journey now is over new terrain. I try to think whether some of the names of the exits from the highway that go into smaller towns and villages and residential districts, have a peculiar and specific history that I should know, in order to assist my integration.

Westchester comes into view; and from the pages of the *New York Times* newspaper social columns, I already know that a certain breed of rich and retiring, successfully retired American white man and white woman, inhabits this part of the reservation of suburban living.

I think of the number of pieces of luggage I have on the roof of this limousine, shapeless as a long, fat, green worm, painted white, that one would find on the manicured lawns of the residential area we are passing and are told the correct exits, by number and by name, that we should take, to get to the strong-drinking safe suburbs. "There ain't no niggers living up there, Jack!" Leroi Jones has told me. And I become frightened that I have moved too many of my belongings into this country of America, unsettled as a new colony. Nobody in the white limousine has anything to say to anybody else. The *New York Times*, the *New York Herald*, the *Village Voice*, *Look* magazine, *Time*, the *New York Review of Books*, *Playboy*, *Ramparts*, the *Washington Post*, *Esquire*, *The New Yorker* and *Atlantic Monthly* were all filled with commentary by America's leading intellectuals, those on the right who were not always as religious as they boasted; and those on the radical left. Not one woman in the limousine has anything to say to the person sitting beside her.

My wife, sitting beside me, mentions repeatedly her shock at the "power" that Yale demonstrated in procuring visas for her "political controversial" husband. The visa had been waiting for us earlier that morning at the Toronto International Airport. And Yale had sent her a visa, too! What other miracles of power would Yale be disposed to pulling off on the behalf of this black man and his black wife, and his two black daughters travelling in New York State now, in this white, silent, and apparently disapproving limousine heading, like an overeating suburban dweller on its way to Connecticut. Connecticut Yankee comes into my thoughts. I do not know what a Connecticut Yankee is supposed to look like; but I remember the term used in articles in the *Atlantic Monthly*. And I think someone had told me that William Styron, who had already stirred up a controversy amongst the black American intelligentsia, lived in Connecticut. Perhaps, he was a Yankee, too. But I got the impression that Connecticut Yankees were radical liberals who did not mind the integration of Negroes into their suburban communities, on gentlemen's agreements.

The black man knew that Connecticut had a history of quiet wealth and comfortable retirement, and quieter liberalism in matters of social integration with Negroes; but that in these three characteristics, nothing was ever mentioned, certainly not in the same breath, about Connecticut's Negro population, so much so, that one did not normally think of Negroes or black people when one mentioned the name Connecticut.

The black man in this white limousine going to Connecticut, sensed a certain judgment being made, silently behind the eyes and lips of these Southerned, tanned, healthy-looking young men and middle-aged men who sit like football players crowded on a bench, inhaling each other's sweat and tension, waiting for their chance to explode in the violence of the game. He knows that it is one thing to sit in the first-class section of a plane leaving New York's LaGuardia for Toronto, at eight o'clock on a Friday night, when businessmen go home for the weekend, and have some of their disquietude at his presumption and presence, wondering whether he is an African diplomat, or a jazz musician, or a star football player, or a very successful American pimp. Or a drug dealer, for he is wearing too much silk and gold chains. But he knows that it is something altogether different to sit so close to them in their limousine, which is not the same thing as a taxi, and which they know is not the normal method and manner of transportation of the lower-class members of Connecticut's residents to get from LaGuardia Airport to New Haven; and he wonders what is going through their minds as they find him, when the limousine turns unexpectedly, touching them so intimately in the loins of their weaknesses and their strengths; and on their seersucker suits. Not even during their Sunday-afternoon football games on the television, or in the flesh, do they expect this closeness of skin on skin, closeness of suspicion on suspicion, and the roaring mighty black full-back has never challenged their own conception of their strength. O.J. Simpson and Jim Brown slipped through their tackles.

The black man has to reach over two persons in order to flick his ash from his Gauloises cigarette in the ashtray. But there is no ashtray. It could have been stolen when the limousine was parked on the wrong street in New Haven. And he might want to breathe in some rehabilitative Connecticut air, although it might not be prudent to ask any of these unspeaking strangers that the window be wound down so he might catch a breath, although he can see the need to cleanse the air of the walnut-and-brown-panelled prudity inside this limousine. And he becomes a frightening person of the prejudices of choice.

He is now I. So, I think that I would hate to be forcibly integrated in the sense in which the term is being used by the NAACP and by the 1968 version of white Connecticut liberals, integrated with all these white people in this limousine; condemned through that integration to travel any considerable distance, either in space or in time or in attitude, sitting beside them with the destination being the indictment of my desire to be integrated; or else being the beneficiary of that integration. I think that of all the moral arguments that black people in America have put forward to seek an end to segregated public transportation, there have been some significant humanitarian considerations that got crushed under the heel of the political liberalism of black and white Americans who feel that to place flesh on top of flesh in this closeness during travel has anything to do with justice. At best, that kind of reasoning is symbolic.

Now, I am in the position to say categorically, that most white people feel uncomfortable when they sit beside black people. And they feel something more than discomfort when they sit beside black people in a country they know to be a racist society. They do not usually express this discomfiture in an offensive manner, although their attitude might have a racialistic origin; for white Americans have been conditioned into a public behaviour of public manners. Except of course, in the dark Southern segregationist culture of governors. So that one might hardly think that the white man or the white woman sitting beside you today, or on a bus or on a plane, is the direct descendant of, or a witness to, the cultural and spiritual genocide of millions of blacks and reds and browns and other non-white peoples, perpetrated for so many years. And then again, it is with special wonder and with some peace of mind, to see the races integrating, on the most self-respecting level, when they attend ball games. But if the violence in the genes of white Americans expresses itself through their presence beside you, it also declares a silent war of conscience within themselves. For their history is now common international knowledge. And they tend to become inordinately uncomfortable and do all sorts of small uncomfortable things, like giving you too much space, or picking up your coat or your ticket from the floor; or like standing up and walking into the aisle of a cinema to allow you to pass and sit down (when in fact you might wish to brush against their legs, to see for yourself that they are human, too; or for you to experience some small sensual titillation, for you are human, too; and white people would do all these things that are damn uncomfortable for them to do, and which they tend not to do, when the "intruder" is white like themselves). Amongst them, in white circumstances, there is more casualness; although they understand that it is normal to be annoyed at intrusion; and therefore their behaviour in these circumstances is more natural and therefore more dignified. It is like entering upon a conversation that comes back to you and to them, black people and white people, and in voices of strained friendliness. A mountain of history explains them to you, which itself explains them and which explains you; and for you to remove this legacy with them sitting beside you, and for this absolution to be suggested merely through this suspicious closeness, is to demonstrate further an inferiority which has been the presumption of their first contact with you, in a history in which you saw them as rapacious and raping ... and we are passing some names of places that have a distinct Native American cultural root. I do not know which tribe, which nation of Indians, for something in the arrangement of power has already caused me, a rather enlightened black man in spite of all, to spend less time learning and remembering things about Indians in Canada, in South America, in the West Indies, and in America, than I have spent, sitting on hard benches that have no back and no cushion, learning about King George the Sixth, and his other dead portraits of brothers and sisters, arranged along a wall of pomp and glorious history and majesty in a West Indian elementary school, in an endless chronicle of colonial conquest ... but the names are now Indian, and with no great stretch of the imagination required, I can see myself as I would have been bound to travel this route in the company of white people, against my wish, forced, and decorated with iron chains; and the stagecoach going much faster than this burdened Connecticut limousine, even relatively speaking, faster; and the silent white people thinking of the drama of travel and civilization; of the chance that they might not reach home, which was merely an attitude of brutality and conquest, to sit beside a fireside of family life procured at that great expense of death, to have dinner, to breathe into their warmth of living their strange conclusions that Indians are savages.

Travelling now, years ahead of this present year, 1968, their necks are stiff with the expectation of arrows and spears with the heads fixed on them in the correct intention to kill (not like the secretary in the U.S.

Consulate in Toronto had affixed her spear on her yellow notepad!), and as chance would have it, actually stiffened by the actual arrow and the spear, and I, or perhaps some duplicate of me, a model of me made from clay, a house nigger, a freed slave, a black cowboy, somebody like me, black, sitting in this fiery furnace and having to suffer the same judgment as the Indian, because I had entered a house of prostitution. I had had very little claim of moral rectitude, no chance of impressing the policeman who raids the brothel, precisely because I was caught inside a house of no repute. But I might have just this small chance of impressing the policeman that I had been carrying out a personal sociological study of the ways of whores, and that I was not really after certain joys of the flesh, seeking carnal knowledge. And for me to think of that excuse, is certainly more obscene than if I had swallowed my fate of circumstantial death, notwithstanding that it had been caused and brought about by the stronger force of circumstantial evidence. For I had enjoyed some mobility, vicariously, even if only it was thought, on deeper analysis, to be nothing more than motion, caused by being in the same moving white Connecticut limousine, by being a passenger in a coach: not that I was moving.

So, the Indians in the names of exits and towns rush to meet me, and I feel more comfortable because history has cleaned this passage through time and through murder and rape, decimation, pointing in a certain direction, which if I could return to this limousine and this route, three hundred years later, I might see the names of black Americans, slaves, like statues in bronze and in stone, identifying both the journey I would take then, and commemorating in ironic American thoroughness for devastation, the fact that black people had once lived in this country, and are now successfully silenced, buried by name only on signposts and exits; or in the struck faces of an American penny, or a dime, like the Indian face on certain billboards, on certain restaurants in resort areas, on certain life insurance letterhead stationery. I am living in the year 1963, which is the year of great paranoia of genocide taking grip in America, in the minds of blacks: and Leroi Jones (Amiri Baraka) has told me as early as 1964 that he suspects that America has constructed and have renovated concentration camps to house black Americans. Was Leroi being paranoid?

Many white Americans cannot face this possibility, although they had previously gone through it during the Second World War with the Japanese in California; and their humour about this denial of human rights does not permit them to look at this chapter in their history in quite the same way as I am forced to see it; for I must see it this way, even at the risk of being paranoid, if I must cling to the remaining dot of sanity within me, a sanity which juxtaposes my psychical dualism.

An Indian with feathers flaming out of his head, like a frightening diadem, or like a halo proclaiming his sovereignty over this Connecticut land, jumped out from a small precipice into the road before us: the billboards stood in our way for a few seconds, like a fort blocking our passage; and then, just as quickly, it was gone. The billboard faded, into insignificance, for we have ignored its history lesson, just as we might have ignored the waves of attacking Indians, two hundred years ago, through the superiority of our blunderbusses, since we had already made the blunder of having ignored their presence on the land, and any right that they might have had to it; and so we are accustomed to cutting them down in a pioneering determination to expand and to justify the land and all that was found in the land, for conquest of rape, in the name of various justifications based upon dogma, prejudice, concept, and many economic needs. I quote from *To Serve the Devil*, by Paul Jacobs and Saul Landau, with Eve Pell:

> The colonizers came to the New World believing that coloured people were inferior, and used that ideology to justify the enslavement of blacks, the killing of Indians and Mexicans and the importation of Oriental labour for work considered unfit for whites.

But the descendants of the colonizers driving this Friday afternoon in the Connecticut limousine with me, on this beautiful autumn afternoon, with the colours of gold and brown and red, on either side of the highway, so many years after those killings (in the markets and in the marketplaces), did not understand why certain exits and towns bore the names of Indians; Indian names; did not understand it, or if they understood it, were indifferent to it, through the passage of time and history which had now settled itself into a comfortableness and an acceptance of superiority and power which they might have thought to be inherent. They saw only the comfort and the power and the beauty in the trees along this highway, all of which made the passage so appealing to the eye and so palatable. Again, from *To Serve the Devil*:

> The identification of coloured skin, with the devil, with inferiority, infused the entire culture of the Anglo-Saxon during the first centuries of colonisation.In each case, the racialism coincided with economic need for slave labour and for land. At the same time, racist attitudes were institutionalized as laws, religion and everyday practices. Each school learned, along with the principles of republicanism and democracy, about the inferiority of the coloured peoples.

… we are travelling over Indian graves, over Indian bodies, over the bodies of slaves and Asians, over the bodies of the ancestors of the same people travelling inside the limousine with me; but nobody in the limousine is thinking about them now, or about how they got here; for America to them, is a land made precisely in the dimensions of their mental parameters and in the shape of our present comfort, because every white man has made a claim to having civilized America, and the indigenous peoples they found in America.

If this limousine with the twelve passengers that we are, were leaving the Seawell International Airport, in Barbados, where I was born, and if it contained only four white persons among its other passengers, who might have been strangers to the country, it is most likely that the Barbadian "natives" would exchange some words of pleasantry with the visitors; they would boast or otherwise disclose to the visitors their knowledge of world affairs and their sophisticated familiarity with world travel. "… England, Spain once; overnight Latin-America, and I saw Brooklyn and the Brooklyn Bridge, once. But I never went more South than Washington, D.C.!" … and the Barbadian would point out some historical landmark, and most certainly would offer to help these American strangers with their hotel accommodations, and give them the entire history of the island, in the space of time it takes to drive the nine miles from the airport to the area of the tourist hotels on the west coast.

The journey from LaGuardia to New Haven is longer than it is from Seawell Airport to Bridgetown, the capital of Barbados. Because I was brought up with this sense of hospitality, strong as a moral obligation to be polite to strangers, I can say that the silence in which a small minority of black people travelling in America in these days, and who is able to exert upon the majority of white passengers (and this does not apply only to America), is a silence that is more significant than what could have been spoken, and that is something altogether different from what is sometimes called British reservation at the meeting of strangers. Perhaps there was a better system of travel, if not a more comfortable one, for both races of people, when public transportation was completely segregated. But I won't like to press this point to any other conclusion.

I do not think that I, a black man in America, a West Indian in any other country, was like the black American, harnessed by a sense of history that was like a responsibility upon the senses, a history of the dead Indian, and that I was so obsessed by this history that I could not enjoy some aspect of the technological beauty of barrenness of the landscape over which these efficient highways had been gouged out. I could see that these highways did not only mean that I was travelling over the macadam of Indians' skulls and bones. I was aware of the comfort of good roads. No, it was not that: it was, merely, that in the silence of the white limousine, with the unspeaking white Americans, that I was forced through lack of conversation to conduct a dialogue with myself, and notice certain meanings and implications in the names of exits and on billboards rushing towards me. And these names seemed to insinuate to me that something dramatic had happened along these highways before they were highways, tragedy and drama had been staged along this journey and the fact of their history is now the names of Indians littering the landscape of these highways, which are nothing more than dried tar and congealed gravel, before these had coalesced into a new highway which was in essence merely a mixture of the Indian dead with their ashes and blown-out brains and the spreading of asphalt. It was a recognition of this history that I felt I had to face before I could assume, with ease of conscience, my appointment to teach the very first classes of Afro-American literature at Yale University; for this course, as I had conceived it, would have to take notice of, if only in passing, of the physical absence of the Indian from the literature of the country as a whole, especially from the curriculum of Yale's Department of English. And I would have to try to explain this absence in terms of the symbolical presence upon the conscience of the nation, in the form of a historical artifact: on the country's billboards, and on some American coins.

Why was the Indian's face on the printed stationery and letterheads of certain insurance companies, and on some American coins? And why was he absent from the social infrastructure of America? I would have to explain this, because the black American, like the Indian, was absent also, even although the black man's absence was rationalized as cultural invisibility. So far, no Negro head, no head of a black nationalist, no head of a "politically controversial" West Indian, no head of a Black Panther has so far, adorned an American dollar bill, or a five-cent coin. I was to discover later, that the black man in America, regarded as a psychic imposition upon the minds of white Americans, was very conspicuous on the walls of the gentlemen's washrooms at Yale. These washrooms were emblazoned with symbols and graffiti literature of the black man's sexual prowess!

But the absence of any kind of symbolic representation of the Negro's face from the face of the American dollar bill, is perhaps, a cause for present celebration. This absence can be taken to mean that the Negro (or the black man), is still alive and flourishing in the society, even although his eradication from the infrastructure of society, and from the white American's psychic concern of humanity, might still be a matter of some serious consideration. White Americans, at this time, were not quite yet dressing themselves in the fashions of Negroes, or like Black Panthers; and the costume parties of white Americans, at Halloween and at Christmas did not show them dressed as slaves on cotton plantations, or at "revolutionary" meetings, and dancing the "boogaloo." The Negro was still safe. His face had not yet been struck on the face of a coin. He is still alive. And he has not yet been featured in American "Westerns" as the unheroic suicidal impulse to white American manhood. He is invisible from certain aspects of American culture, mass-communications media, in a way that the Indian is, ironically, not invisible; and this invisibility, which is in some quarters lamented, such as the adherents of black cultural nationalism, yet it is an indication that the Negro does exist in some way, deep down in the wood work of the psyche of white Americans.

Many more Indians from the past of place names, battles, ambushes, and raids, jumped into our path; but still no one in the limousine seemed to have noticed the way in which they gave direction to our progress through time and space. We were travelling again on the skulls and bones and penises of Indians, particularly on their penises; for it was this form of the destruction of their manhood, their bravery, their culture, the clean castration of Indian "braves" in the movies of the West that had permitted American white men to see themselves as the alternative to the Indian, and to boast about the larger testicles of their own courage. I felt that my own testicles would tend to grow larger if the test of my manhood was that I had shot a "brave" coming at me in the prescribed circle of the ritual, armed with nothing but an arrow while he rode a horse. There would tend to be no contest; and no notation of the "brave's" part in the contest, simply because the author of the history of this contest, is the same man who writes with rifles.

But the smoothness of the highway and the condition of its upkeep (anyone will tell you that without looking at the signs that mark state lines, he can tell you when he has passed out of New York State and is entering into Connecticut: merely because of better roads!), a highway which has meaning today because it is the road from here to Yale University in New Haven; this highway is probably nothing more than smothered thousands of buried skulls and bones and penises appropriated into an attitude that went into the construction of the highway.

The passing Indian names on the embankments, on the billboards, are merely ghosts from a past that had got to be forgotten; because it is a state of mind that can brook no inquiry and no examination.

My own expectations were high. For even though I tried not to be overcome by the meaning of Yale, and my accomplishment there as a black man, a West Indian, a black man who had been appointed a "Hoyt Fellow," I still had to be aware of the possibility of personal failure; for it was the first time that I was to teach in a university. I had never thought of teaching in a university; and there was never any serious hidden, or half-hidden desire in the back of my mind that I might ever want to teach in a university, even though I admired a man, Professor Ashley, who walked with bended neck and bowed head, looking at the sign of autumn fallen on the path of the quadrangle in Trinity College, on the short but intricate intense arrangement of Italian ceramic squares, or the rectangles of stone quarried and shaped by masons who came over from Scotland with presbyterianism in their Bibles, mashing the yellow leaves with the brown, in the distance it takes from his professor's suite on the third floor, high with the angels and the bats and the daring squirrels in the Crows' Nest. His grey, English-cut worsted sports jacket, with one ripping-iron vent, white shirt with a tie of alternating white and blue stripes, and grey flannel trousers, brown shoes that had cracks of age and style in them, that made no noise on the obedient stones. I erased his portrait and painted in instead, my own image of what a professor looked like; this only wish, this only speculation of myself in Professor Ashley's place. No, there was never any hidden or half-hidden desire to teach in a university.

I began to think of my outspokenness against America, which in some ways represents to me, the basest condition of humanity because of America's racist practices. I also thought of what I had published about America. And then a terrifying thought hit me: I was taking part in a writers' conference sponsored by the Canada Council, and held in Vancouver, a few years earlier; and I had suggested then that Canadian writers, the serious ones, those who did nothing but write, and therefore starve because they were writing in Canada, should be offered sinecures in Canadian universities as "writers-in-residence"; that they should have no obligation to teach, or do anything at all; and that their presence on the university campus should be sufficient prestige for the university, and that the university should leave the writer alone to do their writing. Someone suggested that it was a great idea. And it was pointed out that the Americans had led the way in this regard, as they tend to do in almost every other. And then the suggestion was made that we Canadian writers ought not to look toward the border, toward America, for such sinecures. This proposal incensed me. I felt it was just another example of Canadian dependency upon America, a dependency which a former prime minister of Canada, John Diefenbaker, had said so much about, and caused him to win the biggest electoral majority when he campaigned against such dependency. Mr. Diefenbaker had, in fact, to remind Canadians, during his term in office, to be Canadian, and not be dependent on America. And I had said then, imitating Mr. Diefenbaker's Canadian nationalist political philosophy, at the height of my own arrogant clairvoyance, "I will never, under any circumstances, live in America, furthermore accept a job in that damn country as a writer-in-residence." The year of the Canada Council conference in Vancouver was 1966. Martin Luther King, Jr. was kneeling on the Southern red dust to make good the principles of non-violent protest and the premise of human equality; and Malcolm X was like brimstone and ashes, setting the fire of his oratory to describe his brand of nationalism, condemning the country he accused for its recalcitrance and refusal to acknowledge its principles of racial injustice. And in the hotel room in Vancouver, British Columbia, on the other end of Canada, far, far in the West, the other Canadian writers, all white, applauded. It was a moral and intellectual position which most of them had been forced to take, if not fully understand, through the imperatives and the embarrassment to all white people over the world, the embarrassment that the Selma marches had chiselled on their mind, and the Alabama brutalities; and in the behalf of Martin Luther King, Jr., who had forced America to kneel with him in the blood-soaked dust, in grief, as he had forced Canada and most of the world to see the full implication of American racism, and its effect on Canada.

Now, here, only a few months after that righteous stand that I had made in Western Canada, I am now heading along the Eastern seaboard, toward Yale University, my wife beside me, probably confused with her own thoughts, my two daughters in the seat in front, fascinated by the journey and the newness of things along the way, choosing perhaps which bedroom they were going to have in the university-controlled apartment that was assigned for us.

I was trying to appease and understand for myself the immorality and the obscenity that my presence in this Connecticut limousine signified. My baggage, piled on its roof, told me that there was a clear indication that I had contradicted my principles. I had in fact immigrated to America, harnessed with an impracticable principle of arrogance; and armed with an "H-1 visa" in spite of my being indicted by the very Americans, as a "politically controversial" person.

The limousine stopped at Bridgeport — or, it could have been Darien — to rearrange the passengers so that three limousines would not arrive in New Haven with one passenger in each. This preoccupation with organization, and not with comfort in travelling, was to be startlingly conspicuous during my stay at Yale and in America.

The number of pieces in my luggage was creating a stir. There was some conspiratorial discussion among the three drivers, dressed in ugly green uniforms, similar to what American GIs wear into battle. One large and quite ugly and weather-beaten, pocked-marked, and red-faced driver assaulted me by his manner, which somehow matched his face, in saying to me, without calling me by name, without addressing me, "You have to pay extra for each of these!" This was in addition to having paid the fare for each of my family. I regarded this as my first assault by white America. The driver ceased to be pocked-marked, ceased to be an ordinary man, and became instead, the ugly face of America which I had seen so many nights on the screaming shots in news and documentaries all through the summer of 1968. And I began to regard his assault upon my intelligence as a kind of microscopic exploitation, which perhaps upon face value might not have been racial, but which when taken with the meaning of my journey from LaGuardia toward New Haven, devolved into a plain case of a white limousine-driver trying to bleed an unsuspecting foreign black man. I realized there and then, by my outburst, that it is impossible to walk through a trough without carrying some of its lingering perfume in one's senses. We had both apparently watched the same drama and the same violence and the same news on the same television network, from Selma and from Alabama, and from New York City.

I do not think that he expected a confrontation from me. He had probably miscalculated my middle-class manner and appearance (clothes have a way of betraying a man's crudeness; or of representing him to be a gentleman, when he does not wish to be regarded as such!), and he might have assumed that I was going to be agreeable. But he was wrong. I knew he was trying to rob me by his claim for a tax on my luggage. And still I had some doubt that he was not deliberately trying to rob me; but we had both been cast in certain, preconceived, precise roles. Television had done that to us, many years before.

He looked like a man who drank beer for two hours immediately after his shift ended, before he captured the peace of mind to face his wife and five children; like a man who threw dice in a crap game and enjoyed doing it, like a man who might have had some recent bad luck, and the prospect of a few unsuspecting dollars from me, seemed to be the gamble in his demand. Or, he might have mistaken me for a polite middle-class American Negro ... like a friend of mine, a black professor; he and I went once to a place somewhere outside of New Haven to pick up an antique desk which his wife had picked out and which he assumed his wife had either paid for, or else had settled the price of. He went into the living room of the house of the man selling the desk and other furniture (where the furniture was kept for sale), thinking that it was the place of business, for the sign outside the house, nailed to the side, said TRADING CENTER; but it turned out to be his home. The desk in question was a very beautiful one. It had "$75"pasted onto it. Beside it was another desk, almost identical in design. I asked the man, a white man of about sixty years old, whether this one was also for sale. And when he said yes. I started to bargain with him, although he had placed the same price tag of "$75" on it, written in red ink with a felt pen.

"I'll give you sixty dollars for it."

"I couldn't take that," he said.

I really wasn't serious, for I didn't need a desk. But all of a sudden I needed this desk; and I needed to purchase it, although I really wasn't serious about bringing him down, for the price asked for, was rather reasonable. But I was testing him.

"Sixty-five," I said to him (and to myself, "... and not a fucking cent more!"), certain that he would say something like, "Mister" or, perhaps, "Boy ..."

"All right!" he said, all of a sudden.

I was laden with a desk I no longer desired. But I arranged to take it. My friend and I took his desk outside first, into the station wagon and he went back inside to pay the man. But the man was looking through the shutters at us, and he wanted to make sure that my friend understood that his wife had not already paid for the desk.

"Your wife didn't pay me, you know," he shouted. "Your wife didn't pay for the desk."

We knew what the man was thinking. But we merely laughed. When my friend returned from paying him, he was smiling.

"I saved five dollars. He took off five dollars after you got yours for ten dollars less ..."

He was excited. But he hadn't bargained. His wife obviously hadn't bargained, either. They had both taken the man's word. They were both American like he was: they are both American Negroes.

"You know, Austin, I never thought of bringing him down!"

And so, this pocked-marked man comes towards me, insisting that there is a tax ...

We were in New Haven. A hot, dusty, Southern-looking town, in late August, although it was September; a Friday; with construction going up here and going down there, old buildings being pulled down all around the town, as you enter it in a small road, like a small piece of the entrails leading to a large stomach, tagged by a blue sign that said NEW HAVEN with its reputation that leaked out inside the limousine, that the town was a "model city." No one explained whether "model city" meant that New Haven had had no recent race riots, or whether New Haven had a mayor who was a "model" of a mayor, so far as mayors go, and if he was being compared with other mayors, like Richard Daley, the Father of Chicago. No one could say whether in fact New Haven was a "model city" simply because it had begun to house its poor black population in model low-income housing projects.

But the most impressive thing about New Haven this afternoon late in August — or was it early in September — was the stifling and strangulating heat. It would be a different temperature of New Haven's climate that would come to strangle me later on. But, for the time being, I knew that where this kind of heat resides, there resides also the locust; and locusts in American summer towns are the taxi drivers. New Haven's locusts are the most unmannerly in the world. And this is taking into consideration the taxi drivers in New York City; Boston; Durham, North Carolina; Toronto; Montreal; and Austin, Texas.

A stranger to New Haven can spend up to two hours on the street, holding up his hand to hail a taxi, before some understanding resident tell him that the only way to get a taxi is to call the company's number for one. So, you just have to make that telephone call. Monopoly and bad manners, one the cause, the other the effect, leaves the stranger at the mercy of the taxi driver. But taxi drivers in New Haven complain that they do not make much money driving taxis. They never tell you, if you are black, the colour of the holdup man; and I never found out what they say to their white customers, for obvious reasons! Tipping is small; and New Haven, which is Yale University, which is mainly a student population, is not a taxi-using community.

The town is small, and its layout with an unnecessary number of one-way streets encircling the town, makes it almost entirely impossible for a successful bank robber to make his getaway from the scene of the robbery. It might also be that the one-way streets make pedestrians think twice about taking a taxi from Park Street to the Park Plaza Hotel, a distance of four blocks, but which would require the taxi to drive a distance of half of the town to reach a destination which could be walked in five minutes. But in this August heat, and with baggage, you won't want to walk this short distance; and you would therefore submit yourself to the unimportant conversation of the taxi driver with his unlit half-smoked cigar, its juice mixing with his saliva, at the corner of his mouth; and you won't mind at all if he insists that he isn't going to lift "all these bags myself," and then drives off with you in the wrong direction (after having boasted that he won't ever live in any other place but New Haven, where he has spent every one of his fifty-five years), and to test whether you are really a stranger, or a returning student, he asks you, "Do you know which corner of Edgewood Street, 228 Park, is near?"

It is his senses that you have to watch out for. He senses that you are a stranger, but he must be certain and make this dialogue with you, in order to test you, in order to lessen his conscience about deceiving you. And you say nothing, and you leave him to strangle on his guilt and suffocate in the New Haven heat. And you, if you knew then what you shall learn later on, you could have concluded then that this taxi driver is nothing but a strangler, in the same sense that the university is a strangler of the poor mainly black people in whose midst it stands like so many mounds of locusts; and this you will have learned later on.

In the summer months when nothing really happens in New Haven, because Yale is closed, and everything is dead, this death by strangulation chokes breathing as it chokes the aspirations of poor people all year round. But its dramatic pressure is felt and seen more easily at this hot time of year. And you feel, if the knowledge you are going to have were in your possession today in this taxicab, that the heat and the taxi drivers and the university itself and the dust and the university-controlled apartments, with the college rooms that have no air-conditioning, are all the same agents of some cultural and political and intellectual strangulation.

But you can't say anything of this yet. Not today, not on this first day, because you are overcome by the physical beauty of Yale University, and also by its metaphorical beauty. It is physical beauty that opens up to you on a moment's reflection, the academic and intellectual situations you can get involved in. And your mind starts to revolve on this first day, around large theories and on great themes; and you feel that the ivy on Yale's walls is really a reflection of the aristocratic nature of the university; that only the rich and the influential have a place here, can be happy here, where they come like fish swimming to spawn; that years ago one would never imagine a Jew at Yale, that a Jew could not be chairman of the Department of English, and certainly no American Negro could ever teach here, and no American Indian. You begin to feel that Yale was a place set apart for some elite of American white masculinity and brains, which of course you tell yourself, from a thumbing appreciation of the country's history, was the original intention of higher education. And you conclude, in spite of this history, that that tradition is all damn nonsense. Martin Luther King, Jr. and Malcolm X are still alive.

But you do not have this reflective disquietude about your arrival yet, because you are still affected by the bad manners of the taxi driver whose attitude is similar to that of the limousine driver; and you wonder whether this is not an occupational characteristic, or whether it is their way of greeting strangers. Something shakes this attempt to be broad-minded out of your head, and you are thrown back upon the fact of what you are: that you are black in this strange midst, no longer are you a West Indian. But whatever it is, you feel that they do not behave this way toward a white stranger. And you tell yourself that this is so, because you know you know, and you know consequently, that you are in America. And the fact that your piece of American residency is within the physical boundaries of Yale University, makes no difference whatsoever to the conclusions you might make to this confrontation ... "Do you know what they call a Negro with a PhD degree?"

This question was asked many years ago, by Malcolm X, at Harvard University. It had been put to a black professor there. And the black professor knew, although he might have, in the mixed and academic company of Harvard, refused to face, or to express the reality of his own position, still he knew the answer to Malcolm's question. And he might have kept his silence because of his ambitiousness. He therefore could be expected to have been a man of some intellectual substance (why else would he be teaching at Harvard?) but not with enough guts in his aspirations for promotion at Harvard, to resent the question being put by someone like Malcolm X. So, he refused to answer the question.

"They call a Negro with a PhD, a nigger! A nigger!" Malcolm had answered it for him...Malcolm had spent quite a lot of time in and around Dorchester in Boston, and in that time, he certainly would have passed close enough to the campus at that time, to recognize it as a campus. But the Negro with the PhD was not the first black intellectual to have had his credentials questioned; although he might have been the first such one to have had them questioned by another black man, and one who did not have a PhD. W.E.B. Du Bois, the first black man to have graduated with a doctorate from Harvard, was asked during the presentation of a philosophical paper, by his colleagues, to sing a Negro spiritual. Du Bois, fortunately, for all black PhDs following him, did not oblige his colleagues. And it is doubtful whether Du Bois knew any Negro spirituals.

Black intellectuals who teach nowadays at Ivy League colleges like Yale and Harvard, are no longer asked to sing Negro spirituals, certainly the question is not put in such precise, if unsophisticated terms; but questions about their legitimacy and about the quality of their academic qualifications are still being asked, and with not much sophistication at all. And the fact that some version of the original question, as it had been put by Malcolm X, is still being asked of black intellectuals, which does tend to prove Malcolm's point.

I had to load all of my bags into the taxi, without help from the taxi driver. Perhaps, this man knew what Yale called its black intellectuals. He refused even to touch my briefcase. And it was not a question that the briefcase might have contained explosives. He was not an intelligent man, with no erudition, not so sophisticated that he could have detected in me, the revolutionary beneath the sheep's clothing of an Ivy League suit.

"I have a bad back," he said. It was not so much an explanation, certainly not an excuse, as it was merely a statement intended to establish the bounds of our relationship. And straightaway, he seemed to be limping more pronouncedly; but it made him look as if he had a very bad leg.

I put all the bags into the trunk of one taxi, and when it was filled, I had to order another taxi. These taxis were waiting like locusts in front of the Park Plaza Hotel where the Connecticut limousine stops. It is one of the few places in New Haven where a taxi can be seen, parked. There were four of us. The first taxi driver with the bad back, had made sure there was a second taxi to accommodate us; and although the second taxi driver did not complain about a bad back, he too refused to touch our luggage.

"We are not supposed to."

It was now up to me, left with two incapacitated taxi drivers, to decide which of the two gentlemen was the more helpful in forming this bad first impression of life in New Haven, and of the New Haven Yellow Cab Company ... years ago, while on assignment in New York City for the CBC, as a freelance radio broadcaster, I had taken a Yellow Cab from the train station at Grand Central to Rockefeller Center, where the CBC studios were located. There was a black woman in the taxi with me. She was dressed in an American modification of an African costume, wearing large silver bangles and bracelets on her wrists, and a large Afro, in days when only the bravest, most secure, or most demented of black American women dared to manifest in this symbolical way, their cultural alienation from the rest of American life, a symbol which in those days was seen not only as an act of defiance, but also of some aspect of black rebelliousness and cultural separatism. My first stop was somewhere on Sixth Avenue, in the rich, tall, granite district of safety and harmony with American wealth and Rockefeller fortune in downtown New York. "Would you wait for a couple minutes?" There was no problem. The taxi driver even exchanged pleasantries with us, and offered his opinion of the chances that the New York Giants would win the World Series. We reached our destination. He stopped the cab. He let us out. And he waited until I went in and returned from the twenty-fifth floor, and he seemed quite pleased at the prospect that he might get a large tip for his courtesy. I got back into the cab. He smiled. I told him, "125th Street and Seventh Avenue." His complexion changed. He became white. 125th Street and Seventh Avenue is black. In place of the New York Giants, he was now muttering about riots and stabbings and muggings and Negroes. The black woman in the cab, knew Harlem. She lived there all her life. "I'm not going up there!" the taxi driver said. She understood what he meant. And I suddenly became very frightened because I sensed that she was waiting for me to take a militant and black stand against his obstinacy. I was going to have to show this black Africanized woman, and prove to her satisfaction, that I was one West Indian who was also a black man, equally Africanized in the rhetoric of "black cultural nationalism" that I was a West Indian who was black, possessed of big black balls, that, in other words, "I had my shit together, Jack!" The driver remained parked. The driver remained adamant. The black woman and I were inside the taxi all this time. "I am not going up there. I am not taking you to Harlem."

"I'm going to report you to the, to the … Human Rights! I'm going to report you to the N-double-A-CP! The taxicab company. What's your licence number …?"

He shrugged off his disregard of my threats, quite calmly took out his wallet and, without looking back at us, pushed the licence into our faces. He didn't seem worried about the loss of his livelihood; that his taxi licence would be taken away; that he would be chastised by his supervisor; because he was being reported for an act of racial discrimination by a foreign black man, who could pass for a diplomat. And he did not seem worried simply because he knew that he had behind him, substantiating in full argument, his callous disregard of the wound he had inflicted upon us: behind him was arrayed the entire taxi system, perhaps also the New York Police; for it is obvious that if his supervisors had had no knowledge either of the meaning of Harlem to white people, or the meaning of racialism in their country, then he could not now be reflecting their corporate response and attitude.

And then, this taxi driver did something that was very strange for the type of stubborn man he had made himself out to be. He pulled out his short sweater and then his shirt, and exposed to us a scar as ugly as raw beef, and as long as the mark left on his skin by the elastic in the waist of his underwear. The scar stretched from the left rib cage to the right rib cage. I wondered how he had survived such a slash.

"I got this in Harlem. And Jesus himself couldn't get me to go back to Harlem!"

We fell silent. The black woman born in Harlem probably understood more about the cause of this scar than I did; than the man did. For she had lived there all her life. She was the first to suggest getting out of the taxi before she was confronted with more ugly and damaging testimony of this man's experience in Harlem and of the meaning of its black ghetto life which she was to say to me, later, was more than broken ribs and broken bottles, drugs and black rage, and the black violence inflicted upon black people by black people, and the psychology that explains it, according to Franklin Frazier, who knew Harlem.

I tried to put myself in this man's place, suppose I was a taxi driver and I was in a white exclusive district and I was slashed in this way, and …

"Fucking cracker!" the black woman said.

But it was spoken more like an apology for her people, than as a rebuke.

This was the kind of powerlessness that has absolutely nothing to do with the political kind of powerlessness; for that kind may be exploited by factors which are subject to change: this kind, on the other hand, leaves the nasty taste of futility in the mouth and in the groin, and is felt more deeply for its racialism than as an act of racialism itself. The black woman and I were neutralized on the hard concrete of the sidewalk, and we could have beaten our brains out on that slab of insensibility which ironically we could still walk on, step on, trample, but which was, in its hardhearted characteristic, much like the unemotional taxi driver.

This black woman and I waited there until we saw a black man, whom she called "a Brother," behind the wheel, driving a taxi, and she waved him down. He stopped for us, and he called her "Sister," and called me "my Brother"; and then we knew we were going home. It was one hour and thirty minutes later.

But by then, with all this time wasted, and feeling comfortable in the back seat with the "Brother" driving us, I felt relaxed although there was no logical nor racialistic reason why I should more willingly entrust my safety, if not my peace of mind, to a taxi driver simply because he was black (for he was equally strange to me!), I did somehow feel I was in more understandable hand. For I was going "home to Harlem." And so, we both reclined in the back seat, and enjoyed Aretha Franklin singing "R-e-s-p-e-c-t!" Something in our bodies had permitted this trust.

The more bitter taste of the experience with the white brutalized taxi driver had by now evaporated in the Harlem air, but the strain of personal injury had already been mixed into the sensibilities of our castration. It was not a political powerlessness; and defeat was its consequence. It was deeper than that. And much more lasting and absolute. The heat in New Haven on this air-less afternoon, with two taxis at my service, but with no more assurance of service and no injury, I found to be very little different from that New York experience.

I had been told before I arrived that "New Haven niggers aren't like New York niggers"; and I can't remember who gave me this advice; but I had not been told exactly what New York niggers were like; that the city hadn't been burned down — yet; that every person who lived and worked in New Haven, which is to say, every person who worked at Yale University, held the university firmly etched in his mind, with an awesome respectability. Because of the smallness of the town, in all senses of that term, these two taxi drivers weren't expressing bravery or liberalism in taking me to 228 Park Street, for everybody knew that Park Street was safe, and opposite Pierson College, whose master was John Hersey, the novelist. I was therefore on university turf. And even the New Haven Police Department is aware of the limitations of their physical jurisdiction when it is a matter of arresting someone who is connected to Yale. In some cases, the police department does not have to be reminded, in the course of their duty and their desire, that this enthusiasm for law and order might carry them within the boundaries of Yale University's jurisdiction, which is a jurisdiction with bigger balls.

⁓

Yale University in the year 1968, is an unreal society. The people associated with it make it that; and in turn, if not before this institution has made its mark upon the constituents, the inter-relationship of its members to the university contributes to making the Yale community an unreal one. For the black person at Yale, student, faculty member, or worker who lives within the power of its employment, grasp and iron gates, it is the most adhesive college community in America. The white members of the faculty do not escape this influence; for although their position is not circumscribed by the restrictions of colour, still the fierce competitiveness and the fatalities to career that are consequent upon that, plus the politics of their respective departments into which they are thrown, against will and tactic, all these factors create the condition of a one-way allegiance that Yale expects from its employees. And in this respect, their fate is no different from that of the black faculty member. Only the most misguided or deluded black man on the faculty of Yale University, would think that either Yale College or the administration of the university could add one whit to the damage already done to his sensibilities; for he ought to have realized that the damage would have been done already, at the precise moment that he had stepped on the property of Yale University.

I sensed this from the beginning, that Yale somehow manages to regulate the lives of old and young faculty members. It exerts a loyalty that one does not usually regard as a healthy working relationship between administration and faculty member. And this has nothing to do with the loyalty of an employee. God knows, and so too does the New Haven black community that surrounds the university like so many outhouses of poverty and deprivation on a plantation; God knows and so does the cleaning staff and the janitorial staff — predominantly black people — that the university's history and attitude as employer is not a romantic one; and that it has absolutely nothing congruent with the ivy running up the walls of the twelve colleges built against time and against reason and against utility, by an equally incongruent architecture and social planning. I am talking about a kind of hidden, unspoken, but very powerful "something" that keeps the white faculty in some form of academic neurosis, a kind of official patriotism, which when it conflicts with their personal principles as men (and women), those principles tend to be conveniently subordinated in such a way as to promote their true feelings that Yale University is God, and they themselves, are mammon.

One could say, and perhaps this would be to hit the problem in the guts, that all Yale faculty members learn, very quickly, how to be diplomatic: but to be diplomatic is nothing more than to be a liar; the kind of liar whose "facts" are superimposed upon a structure of respectability and power, both of which are derived from the particular institution which he represents and which stands behind him.

One example of the diplomatic is the decision of a young Fellow of Berkeley College who tried to ensure his promotion from assistant professor to associate professor, and the chance to live in a Fellow's suite in the college, by giving a record album to the master of the college. This young man, not particularly brilliant and outstanding in his field (twentieth-century English literature), also knew a fact that everyone in his field knew, that he discovered slowly, after a few weeks sitting at luncheon with the master of the college, that the master had a passion for the poetry of Dylan Thomas. The young Fellow, quite simply putting two and two together, and by professing an institutional interest in the college, feathered the nest of the Fellow's suite he had his eyes on with the purchase of an impressive and most expensive edition of *The Collected Poems of Dylan Thomas*. He sweetened the pot of his calculation with a recorded version of the poet reading his poems. And somehow, since I was a witness at the high table at luncheon, I became a contributor at the purchase. The young Fellow's financial aspirations, probably like his academic ones, were temporarily beyond his means.

I am not saying that the Fellow bought off the master. I am saying that the Fellow's comprehension of the fierce competition for college suites, for free living accommodation, and for promotion within his department, this thoughtfulness on his part might have been the feather that tilted the decision in his favour, and against the other Fellow, perhaps more brilliant than he, but who had neglected to consider this act of calculated graciousness, which after all, is a very noticeable stone in the foundation of sophistication and culture that Yale University stands for. Whatever the reason, this young Fellow is now permanently entrenched at Berkeley College, in a free suite, and probably is a full professor.

But graciousness is not the only weapon used. Verbal and intellectual calisthenics are used more effectively. Sometimes, they border on obscurity or on contradiction. An example of this verbal and intellectual game as it is played by the university itself, comes from the highest source of power, the president of the university, himself.

The context to bring out the significance of the matter, is May 1970, the day Yale devotes to delicious frivolity: barbecues and draught beer and Frisbees and beautiful women from Connecticut College, from Smith, from Wellesley, and from Howard and Clark and Brandeis Universities — we are living still in a segregated society where blacks date blacks, and whites date whites — to be with the black students; all this suddenly became no longer important — the Black Panthers were coming. They would invade, and "occupy" Yale University; and they would close down the university. Bobby Seale was to be tried for murder in New Haven. There is anger, fear, myth, speculation, and violence in the air like the smoke coming from the kitchens of colleges, when the skies are clear. But the greatest concern is the safety of the black women students: where to hide them from the dark clouds of tear gas, and possible brutality at the hands of the New Haven police, who have a reputation as brutes toward the black New Haven residents.

So, the president, like all presidents in the country during this time, was confused; and in some cases rendered inoperative; but he did not want to capitulate to an "extremist" bunch of Black Panthers and shut down his university. What would the Board of Governors say? What would the black professors and the black students — and where are their loyalties, with the university or with the Black Panthers? — say? But of course, their opinion was not calculated to be essential to the "action" to be taken. And I am not sure if they were asked: if we were asked.

The president, Kingman Brewster, sent a directive to faculty members about the conscience and the responsibility which they must feel as human beings; and the implication that they might feel this way because they are human beings, exposes their unfeeling nature as representatives of a larger more significant society outside the iron gates of the university, although that larger society, America, might be equally unreal, and just as hypocritical as Yale.

I recognize and personally sympathize with the widespread and deeply felt concern about the prolongation of the war in Vietnam," the president said, in his directive. "I also share the general irritation with the expressed official intention to disregard campus expression such as protest and to discourage open critical discussion. In my own official capacity, however, I cannot give positive University sanction to the interruption of normal educational activities. Yale should not forfeit its educational neutrality for a political cause, no matter how widely backed.

Normally, whether to miss a class, or whether to postpone it, it is up to the student and the instructor, as long as absence or the postponement does not demonstrably impair the effectiveness of the educational process. In accord with this general policy, the University does not intend to interfere with any individual decisions about attending or postponing classes on any single occasion, including October fifteenth [Moratorium Day, 1969].

As far as employees are concerned, if there is a New Haven community exercise at midday to express concern about the war, anyone who wishes to be present should ask his supervisor if it would involve absence from working hours. I would hope that the supervisor would permit such absence at the noon hour if it would be consistent with the proper functioning of the University and if the absence could be made up by readjusting some other hours of work.

In sum, while the University does not wish to use its official authority to sponsor any moratorium of normal

activities on October fifteen, it does not want to stand in
the way of individual faculty, student and staff expression
of concern as long as the educational and other functions
of the place are not unduly hampered.

This directive from the president of the university was written on the
2nd of October. It gave those to whom it was addressed exactly thirteen
days in which to digest its equivocation. It is the kind of language more
suited to the State Department of America embroiled in moral crises
than it is bent upon translating into non-moral prerogatives for guidance.
As it happened, it put the radical factions of Yale community into greater
moral and academic conflict.

But there are graver, more deceitful implications in this directive than
that. To begin with: this directive establishes an official position for the
separation of an institution of higher learning from the realities of a
"political cause"; and in so doing, it has then decided that not only is
this university above politics — an abysmal lie as anybody who lives in
New Haven can attest to — but it also implies that this university has,
on its own, decided to choose which "political causes" are suitable for
its official sanction and involvement; and also, which of these causes can
have the prestige of being backed by the university.

And for a university to state that it cannot "give positive sanction
to the interpretation of normal educational activities," when those
"normal activities" themselves cease to be normal and relevant in face
of an "interruption" of national proportion and gravity, as is the war in
Vietnam, is further proof to emphasize how unreal a place is Yale in the
world that surrounded it, during the latter part of the sixties.

But what is even more puzzling and difficult to understand other
than the implications that may be read into this directive, is the admission that the university has abrogated to itself the position of a moral
leader in the community of New Haven, in the state of Connecticut,
and in the whole of America. It has, in taking this stand, sacrificed
whatever honour one can now associate with what has been referred to
as "institutional neutrality," with a demonstration of its politics; the politics not necessarily of the university itself as it is seen by the students,
but of what the university symbolizes and represents. This sacrifice of

honour was made at a high moral price that the students themselves were demonstrating against; and the immorality of the university's position had already been pointed out by the students, and was reflected in the very nature of the war in Vietnam.

The final paragraph of the directive really sums up the attitude of the university toward demonstrations and toward positions of conscience. And the university is, at best, schizophrenic. On the one hand, there is the intention to personalize the university (for instance the proposed presence and participation in the moratorium speeches on that very day); and on the other hand, to deny that this presence and participation is possible, while basing it on an institutional point of view, or position. For no college president in America, with the war in Vietnam threatening national unity, is able to "personally sympathize" and "deeply feel" any problem of the moral magnitude of the war in Vietnam, or a problem like black unrest and black injustice, while at the same time, seek to modify his personal and moral attitude by reminding his institution and the people associated with it, of the "institutional neutrality" which must necessarily bind the university's expression of such problems, in a directive. The entire last paragraph is meaningless, if it were to be applied, logically, to a college in Vietnam.

The real importance of this directive as it affected the overall consciousness of the university is this: no president, no member of any standing in the administration, could have afforded to write this kind of diplomatic jargon, unless he had behind him the assurance or the complicity of the entire faculty; and by faculty in this case, I am referring to the heads of departments and other members of the ruling junta of Yale, such as the masters of the colleges. The real significance of this directive is the ridiculousness of it. It made the students laugh. But even in their merriment and ridicule, in their victory of being told by their institution that their institution itself was not serious on moral matters, lay the very powerlessness that that merriment occasioned. Yale University is big enough, powerful enough to jive, and be laughed at, without one stem of its ivy being tarnished or ripped from its walls. And it is not the ridiculousness of Yale that would postpone this destruction, but rather the students of Yale themselves, over whom the university had an ungodly power.

The tendency on the part of the administration to make Yale more personable is illustrated in the attitudes of those who find themselves associated with the place. Yale becomes Mother Yale. The most ironic and perhaps obsequious expression of this kind of matriarchy is to be seen in the way black students relate to Yale. The personalization of Yale as their mother, as a place providing such comfort to them, conflicts with the nationalistic and racialistic responsibility which they boast of possessing. It is a personal conflict and one that further challenges the larger self-proclaimed responsibility they talk about: their racial accountability. The black student who comes to Yale from the projects and places like Harlem, and places that stand for Harlem in terms of deprivation (even if this particular student does not have this Harlem experience in the real sense, he certainly has a symbolical experience of deprivation in America), will admit that there are some very good things about being at Yale.

The place is quiet, usually when he needs it to be quiet, when he needs his personal breathing space in an otherwise hectic environment, the student can find peace, perhaps during which he might be caught up, if only temporarily, in pondering his suicide; or pondering the suicidal amount of work that the Yale instructor has assigned him.

Work is synonymous with Yale, for faculty and for students. Work is also reality for faculty. "Publish or perish." At Yale University, this is not merely a euphemism for intellectual diligence; and it certainly is not a cliché.

Because of tradition, and because of the romanticism that overcasts the place, Yale can and does attract some very important lecturers and visiting professors. They come from the ultra-conservative rank of America, to the blackest Black Panther Party member. But mainly the presence of these visiting lecturers and professors generally has no relevancy to the interests of the black students. The black student would, in spite of his confessed bewilderment over the university's choice of visitor and the subject of his talk, still regard such a selection of guest as having some substantive bearing upon his own presence in the university, and as a contribution to his education in the Black Studies Program (later to become a department), which was a demand he had made upon the university.

For instance, Herbert Marcuse might have been a brilliant modern philosopher; but what he says during a guest lectureship at Yale has very little to do with the lives of the black students there, or with the lives of black people elsewhere. Mayor John Lindsay might have been a good mayor, something of an evangelist, and, in addition to being a radical politician, something of a "hip" mayor who dared to walk through the Black and Puerto Rican ghettos of New York City during the threat of "riot and racial apocalypse," as every politician was saying — and some, hoping — and in spite of Mayor Lindsay's "radicalism" that Harlem and the barrio and other "mean streets" still existed during his administration; and they exist today, 2005, almost untouched by his liberal-radicalism. So, in spite of every act and promise by his jurisdiction and administration, what contribution could he make, and did in fact make toward the existence of the black student at Yale? Canadian literary critic Northrop Frye may be the best scholar of William Blake, but what insight and solution does he — like those other world-renowned thinkers applied to help solve the problem and the culture of the American ghetto — offer to improve the black student's existence on the campus of Yale? Or the welfare of the black student on any campus in America?

I doubt whether the social and cultural position of the black student at Yale is ever considered in lectures by these men, although I am told that a black student here, did manage to get a very good recommendation from Mayor Lindsay when he applied for admission. Did the mayor know the black student?

The university does not take the black student into consideration, does not take the black student seriously when guest lectureships are being planned. World-renowned visitors to Yale University do not come from the world of the black student, or from any other world that he is culturally acquainted with.

It is only when Imamu Amear Baraka (Leroi Jones) comes to Yale that Yale becomes important and "relevant" to the "existence" of the black student. Otherwise, the latter's cultural alienation is complete. And even although the black student might not understand what Baraka is trying to tell him about his presence at such an institution as Yale, still there is a great amount of knowledge that might be gathered and conveyed from the podium in the Yale Law School, which is a symbol of excellence.

This kind of knowledge, vicarious though it might be, this kind of black presence on a white landscape, the black student himself readily calls "relevance." When a man like Mayor Carl Stokes of Cleveland spends an afternoon with John Hersey, the master of Pierson College, both the college and the university take on an aura of "relevance" so far as the witnessing black students are concerned. But it may be a superficial "relevance." But that act might very well be construed to show that the university is contemporary and is politically non-neutral, in spite of what the directive of the president said, would say, or feel.

There is a feeling of uncertainty which comes over the black student from the very head of his adopted institution, and which grips him and binds him into a confusing relationship to his "alma mater," a term used consciously and constantly by these black students who can boast, and in some cases can wish that they all had been born in a ghetto background. They therefore castigate themselves and their striving parents who fought for middle-class standards for their own lives and the lives of their children, so as to escape the very meaning and experience of "ghetto background" which their educated black sons and daughters, black students at Yale, now think of as the badge of legitimacy. But it is only a black student at a place like Yale University, or at any other Ivy League college, who would willfully yearn to have come from the guts of a ghetto. The black student at the University of Texas at Austin does not indulge in such fantasies. His presence on the Campus at Austin is too close, and is measured too deeply in the spilling of blood and the bludgeoning of balls and testicles, for him to yearn for, and indulge in, such images of social desolation, and consider it "cool." So, this kind of "wishing for ghetto origin" on the part of the Yale black student, is the first stage of a conditioning, a state of mind that permits him to look at his life through a romantic prism of equally romantic "legitimacy" and wanting that legitimacy to connote something that he himself is fleeing from.

If the black student who yearns for the legitimacy of "ghetto background" were really to be thrown back upon that dump heap, he would readily repudiate any kind of allegiance to an institution such as Yale. And whether his repudiation is spoken "silently or loud," as Amiri Baraka says in a poem, and spoken openly, or within the close and tribal gatherings of black students in college dormitories, the voice would be the same. He would reject the black ghetto background as he has, from the pit of his guts, already have rejected Yale. "Yale is a motherfucking racist institution," they say all the time. And they use "institution" to connote incarceration in a federal prison. This is what the black student thinks of the school he is attending; Yale. But he is there, at Yale. And he is there as one of the most ardent constituents of Yale. Yale "is a racist institution," to use his words; everybody knows that; but what everybody does not know, is that the black student, after having made this pronouncement, continues to see and to crave that his mental development shall be measured in the strict terms of success, or of failure, using the slide rule of Yale University's standard. And he makes a desperate effort within the framework of his militancy not to step beyond the bounds of radicalism, which Yale and the faculty expects him to, at least, stutter.

This expectation of radicalism from the black student, this expectation of black militancy even, is natural at Yale, as it is the expectation of loss which a businessman makes provision for in the setting of price of his items, and which he understands to be an aspect of his success in carrying on his business. But the pertinence in the statement, "Yale is a motherfucking racist institution" lies not in the fact that it comes from the mouth of a black student, but rather that it lies in the presumption that any black student at Yale could be so bold as to disregard the implication in the concessions being made (and understood by both parties), to bring him here to study.

So you find that these black students, in their desire to be associated with a first-rate university, and at the same time not wanting to be seen as "Uncle Toms" or "bourgeois Negroes" by the "heavy relevant brothers in the ghettos" or by the "brothers in less heavy" Ivy League colleges, are caught up in the same two-faced posture of hating and loving the institution in the same breath, as they are in their schizophrenic relationship to the larger American society. They are forever locked into a position of duality of existence, and perception. Theoretically, no black student should ever go to Yale University. He or she may not attend this kind of an institution, and still claim, or remain, black. Or, perhaps, Yale should have been permitted to remain purely, pearly white, so that at that cataclysmic moment when pertinence and the spirit of equality and equal opportunity visited the university to make it contemporary and relevant (even to white youths), then Yale and its tradition could more easily be buried under the unreality that emanates from the entire administration and faculty, in particular the Department of English, which sees fit to repudiate all that is modern from its curriculum of study, associating "modern" with the untried and the unproven, and the uncriticize-able, and which for years to come, perhaps, will continue to study the "classics" of the dead language of dead English writers in English, and forget the existence of modern "black literature," which will always be relegated to "Black Literature" or "Post-colonial Literature," or "African American Literature." Never simply Literature!

And when the necessity or the demand to be modern, does come, when the twentieth century has to be considered, this Department of English considers a book like *Rosencrantz and Gildenstern Are Dead*, or *The Horse's Mouth* as its two selections of good modern fiction. No professor with political power or with academic brilliance in the Department of English faculty, when the list of modern and twentieth-century fiction was being discussed, thought to include *The Systems of Dante's Hell*, or *Invisible Man*, or *The Man Who Cried I Am*. James Baldwin, Richard Wright, Arna Bontemps, and Langston Hughes were not even thought of. But the latter named three books, written by Amiri Baraka, Ralph Ellison, and John A. Williams, were enthusiastically relegated to the Black Literature list.

There is something safe in studying only the works of dead writers: there is enough critical material already written about them. And the authorities of this kind of criticism are already — like cement blocks — entrenched in the Department of English. Conservatism is as important a critical point as is critical judgment in Departments of English. But critical material of this kind is stale, and it does not reflect the sensibilities of people who are living today and are studying this dead literature in contemporary times. There is something destructive to the mind, morally and socially, if one could only emphasize with Dante and the Romantic Latin Poets in Translation, to the exclusion of important contemporary works like *Herzog*, or *The Chosen Place, The Timeless People*. The latter novel is written by a black woman, Paule Marshall; and her work would have to obtain literary legitimacy, not from the work itself, but from the Department of English at Yale, before it could be placed on the curriculum of study for English Literature.

The predisposition toward dead things, toward dead writers and dead ideas, becomes a great concern to the black student at this university; for to a large extent, his background in literature and his experience, the essence of it, is in clear contradistinction to the underlying philosophy that might be culled from the study of such works. The whole cultural background against which these works have been produced is anathema to him. He can no more relate fully to Dante than he can relate to the chamber music concerts in some of the colleges in the university. There is never any intention to feed him with the poetry of Amiri Baraka, for Amiri Baraka himself as a man and also as a poet, is the contradiction of Yale. He will get Amiri Baraka only in strict relation to "Black Studies." Black Studies and Black Literature, so far as Yale University is concerned, has not yet achieved "academic legitimacy" as a discipline. Perhaps this attitude is based upon the quality and the credentials of the black professors on the faculty; perhaps it is based upon the feeling, and this would seem to be the more honest reason, that "Black Literature" has not yet become a sufficiently intellectual discipline that scholars, both black and white, can study and criticize without being embarrassed into feeling that they are either radical, or stupid. For serious professors to specialize in "Black Studies" at this time is to bring down upon their heads the criticism which scholars like Melville J. Herskovits of Northwestern University suffered, when, early in the last century in which 1969 occurs, through study and scholarship, he found out that the Negro was worthy of serious study, and that the Negro was not a "myth." The academic prejudice against "Black Studies" is prevalent today, 1969, in the same proportionate intensity as there is prejudice against the black American in his own society.

But to look back at the black student at Yale: someone who finds himself boasting that he is from the ghetto, in a physical sense, from any ghetto in America, although if you checked his records, you would be informed that not many like him do in fact come from such harsh beginnings. But the concept in their minds of "machismo," of being black, requires them to invent this metaphor of the ghetto, which has come to have significant meaning, and which, when exhibited against their present position in an Ivy League university like Yale (which only began to admit black students in any reasonable number), this insistence upon a romantic "black ghetto" background, even when it is false, even when it is pointed out to you that there is not even a significant fraction of them who have ever even visited a ghetto, let alone lived in one; and this exhibitionism is just part of the total deception that they are forced, through their presence at Yale and their duality of feeling for Yale, to indulge in, I am told that quite a large number of the black students are wealthy children of wealthy parents, doctors, lawyers, businessmen ...

Although Yale has its share of wealthy and influential students, students who sometimes flaunt this wealth and this influence and this privilege most indiscreetly, to be black and to be wealthy at Yale, does not mean very much to his status vis-à-vis the university; because it is the blackness, the peculiarity of that blackness which becomes phobogenic, and which in turn defines the student and follows him throughout his university career. He is plagued by his colour, whether he is an avowed black cultural adherent or a black nationalist, or just "a nice Negro boy." And it is this blackness that strikes the campus policeman first. And their reaction to this blackness upon the landscape of Yale, which to them is clearly a white college, suggests that not only is the campus policeman's attitude a reflection of the university's, but also is its way of seeing black students. It is merely a slice of the perspective from the same fruit of presumption, that the larger society, America, assumes to be the correct and precise one with which to regard a black student or a black man.

One gets the impression sometimes, judging from incidents of blatant racism caused by the campus policemen and the bad manners of some university officials, in college dining halls, and from the elevator operators in the library, most of the white employees at Yale feel themselves to be inherently superior to the black student, and to the black faculty. One can therefore imagine how they feel toward the black employees.

The black student has been assaulted, harassed, and persecuted by the campus policemen; and in spite of proof (which the black victim is always called upon to demonstrate as his proof of racism), the president of this university would still insist that he does not have the power to correct and to put an end to this treatment of black students attending his university. If one were to seek some reason, or some rationalization for this kind of persecution, one might have to conclude that Yale University forgot to inform and to brief its campus police, and some of its college staff, including college masters and college deans, that the university had officially accepted so many blacks as students, and that their sudden presence in the college quadrangle and dining hall and at the college mixer, was not the anticipated and feared eruption of New Haven "delinquent blacks" on its campus. These officials were probably not told that the sudden number of blacks were not "from the community" (meaning that they were "outside blacks"), in spite of the fact of cosmetic similarity of colour.

It was an assumption on the part of the university, that the campus policemen and other university staff would accept the sudden dramatic appearance of so many blacks on the campus in 1968 and 1969. And it was an assumption of equal importance that the university authorities would understand that the black student was there, by right, and that he had the same rights as the white student.

I have always felt that policemen and guns have no place on a university campus. Their presence is an anachronism: even in spite of the concept of law and order, rampant in America. Law and order in 1968 was beginning to be rampant even among some professors as a modus vivendi. To see these stout, ugly, overfed white men in their dark suits, their hips bulging over their leather belts, because of too much food, hamburgers and pork chops and steaks with the blood still in them, and milkshakes that look like white, sweet glue; and from too much sitting at their desks, or in their parked cruisers; and to see their buxom hips, and to know that part of that bulge around the waist is not the result of their higher standard of living, but rather is the reflection of their higher worth or status, in the society, that they were wearing guns, making all this become very frightening.

The campus policemen at Yale do not draw guns on white students. The campus policemen at Yale do not beat up white students. The campus policemen at Yale do not question a white student entering a college gate to attend a college mixer, or some other function at which there are women, white women from neighbouring women's colleges. And everybody at Yale knows that many of the white youth who attend the social functions of the university are not Yale students, that some of them are under the legal age for drinking liquor, and that most of them are not even invited as guests of college residents. It is conceivable that a campus policeman who has to stop someone from entering a private party on the campus would tend to stop a "New Haven–type black person," since to him, with the predominant white enrollment, he is going to be more accurate in his un-random sample of intruders if he forbids only black persons from entering. But his accuracy is based upon his own racial prejudice. Nothing more, nothing less. So, the white official at the wrought-iron gates of the college, does nothing about the white "students," for they all look alike to him; and they are all white to him.

This practice of unfair judging reached a climax one night at Calhoun College, of which I was a Fellow. A very popular black rock group was playing there at a college mixer. (A college mixer at Yale is an affair at which girls from the neighbouring all-women's schools are brought to Yale in a bus, transported sometimes at the expense of the college hosting the mixer; and they are then escorted into the dining hall of the college, where beer is served free, where the men mix with the women, just as freely, and get to know the women in ways that a man gets to know a woman. After the dancing and after the mixing, should the girls so desire, they can return to their own college, or else remain in a man's room. This overnight stay in the man's room, though not officially permitted, is not too seriously prohibited. This kind of mature way of treating men and women is one of the good things about Yale University.) This black group was so popular, the music so good, that every black person in New Haven having heard of the dance, decided to attend the mixer. At this mixer, most unusually, an admission fee was charged, thereby making it public, and moreover, legal for anybody, student or visitor, to enter the college gate and attend the dance.

The usual thing happened. White teenaged girls, younger than the state's drinking age, were admitted by the campus policemen guarding the entrance to the college; and of course, it is fair to say that it is not really the sole responsibility of a policeman to question every young woman about her age. Some of the regular dates of the black students, both those resident in the college and those from other colleges, were refused entry. Or, else were asked to show their identification. Only blacks were questioned. Perhaps, the policemen were more versed in the history of Calhoun College than it was generally thought: that the college had had over the years, a very large percentage of white students from the Southern states in America, that the Rebel flag and the Rebel battle hymns were sung regularly in residence.

But at one point during the mixer, the college dining hall where the dance was being held, was so crowded, and there were so many black faces on the dance floor of this college named after John C. Calhoun, who by no means was disposed to this kind of mixing of the races, that fear ran through the Calhoun College white students, and through the white college administrators of the mixer, when they saw so many of their women dancing with black men. Had Senator John C. Calhoun been present at this mixer, his entire endowment to Yale University would have sweated away at the sight of this miscegenation.

Rumours spread. Like incidents of police brutality, like charred black-ened pieces of paper in the wind. Somebody said there was going to be a race riot. Panic gripped the student organizers of the mixer. They called in the police. The feared campus police. The whole affair deteriorated into a distasteful reminder to the black students of the racism on the Yale campus. And it was distasteful to those black students who lived at Calhoun College, reputed amongst the university's black students, to be the most undesirable place to live.

The night this incident took place, I was having dinner with the master of this college at the Master's House of another master, a novelist. We had been drinking in the manner in which Yale faculty drinks: as much as possible, just before complete insensibility takes over; in enormous quantities in enormous drinking glasses that could hold almost two beers poured, or one-fifth of a bottle of Wild Turkey Bourbon, as if we had made a vow with ourselves to break records, to erase, to drown out from our senses all meaning of our life at Yale. I had been thinking of going to the mixer after dinner, because I too had heard of the good quality of the music. But something had happened to postpone my arrival there. Perhaps I too had been insensibly drunk. So, I did not go to the Calhoun College until the next day, when I heard the story from the black students (white students at Yale never mentioned any distastefulness about racism and police brutality to me, or to any other black faculty member), about the previous night's happenings.

I felt it was in my position, as some kind of a figure in the eyes of the black students, to at least try to inquire what had really happened; and also to find out the truth in what I had been told by the black students; and to see what the master of the college intended to do about the situation. I felt this responsibility also because I was a Fellow of the college. The black students who lived in the college expected this involvement from me. So, I stopped by the college that Monday during the "tea-and-cookies" afternoon of fellowship, when the master's wife serves; and there and then, I brought the concern of the black students to the attention of the master. Not only had he heard not a word of their side of the story, he had not even heard the whole story. And naturally, he had done nothing about it. Doing nothing about matters of this nature and gravity was, I learned, the characteristic response of the University, to things that smelled of racism.

"What do you think I should do?" he asked me, as he would have asked a student of his who had got into some intellectual difficulty over American Literature.

I could see in his eyes the earnestness that you sometimes see in the eyes of a plaintive. The man was approaching this problem as if it were an academic matter. I was not sure whether he felt that as a black man, as a faculty member closer to the black students than a white professor normally is, I was therefore in a position to offer a solution, or to give some advice. But I resented his question. "What do you think I should do?" It had absolutely nothing to do with me. It was an administrative problem; and he, as master, was the chief administrator of the college.

"I think I should do something," he went on to say, "But ..."

"I think you should do something," I told him. "I do not know what you should do. But whatever you do, you should do it quickly. And it should be something to make those black students, who attended the mixer in their own college, feel that you are serious. But what is more important, you should make the black students in your college feel as if they belong in your college."

I then watched him, and his manner did not change from the academic. He seemed far off, away in some textual intricacy of an "American Adam." I watched that face made purple by bourbon, a face that I had seen often, close up, during many nights of drinking in his living room, with the huge

untitled painting above a large couch, and I would see how this painting was transformed, and in its place there appeared another "portrait,"
the stained-glass window in the lounge of the college, just as you enter
by climbing the two cement steps of the dining hall door opposite the
Porter's Lodge, that stained-glass window that shows a planter from a
Southern plantation, planting his foot (it seemed then, that the foot was
planted for an eternity, and not symbolically), on the head of a Negro, a
slave, a black man, even a black student, as he would come to be known ...

Something in the irony and the metaphor of that stained-glass
window told me that it stands, not so much, for an aberration in history,
the history of America, the history of the relationship between the
black students and himself, but that it was the printed, stained reminder
of the black students in Calhoun College and in the university, that
neither their presence nor their academic achievement should ever be
measured against the rod of their collective knowledge of origin in
segregation, on plantations. The foot was no longer planted, in a real
sense, on the neck of the black student at Yale; certainly not during the
time of this college master. But in a symbolic sense it was still there.
The foot has always been there; and it seemed that it would be there
for some time to come. And the master must have been thinking about
this, because he said, "You know, Austin, Calhoun is not the most racist
college on campus. Why Branford College could not make Professor
Houston Baker, a black faculty member, the college dean, because the
white students protested, and were against it."

He had travelled full circle: from the point, the intellectual, at which I
first met him, to that point which black Americans refer to as "bullshitter."

This was the same man, who during those days of grief, following
the murder of Dr. Martin Luther King, Jr., had watched the funeral
along with me; and had insisted upon sending up to the guest suite in his
college, during the time I was a Hoyt Fellow, a bottle of Scotch, one day
of that long period of national mourning and embarrassment, and fear in
New Haven and in the rest of America, gifts to act as his own assurance
(so it seemed now), that the passion and the sorrow and the hate of the
nation's black population would not catch like a match nursing a fire and
spread to New Haven and Yale, and to Calhoun College, and tear down
the ivy from the brick, and the brick itself, fistful by clenched fistful.

And even then, my tendency to come to some conclusion about the meaning of his patronage, his kindness, the possibility that he was buying me off, a complete stranger then in his country, that he thought I was so important in the struggle for racial justice and thereby angered by its absence, to be bought off, just as it might have been in those days in the era of plantations when the master gave the slaves an inordinate amount of rum and liquor to drink on holidays before the slaves were obsessed by murder and revolutionary rape, and their black bodies would be imbued and deadened by the spirits in the liquor which would bring about a prostration in that metaphor of drunkenness which in later years came to be regarded and to be held by white masters, on plantations and in colleges, as the image of the Negro.

The master had told me one afternoon, during that precarious time that required love and black allegiance, a need emphasized and magnified during this period of fear, "I am glad that you are living upstairs in the guest suite. I'm sure the blacks won't think of burning down Calhoun."

And when, on this Monday afternoon, following the confusion with the mixer, that "Calhoun is not the most racist college on campus," I went back to that time of mourning, America's mourning for its loss of racial innocence; and I had to wonder, in what other ways and in what number of times, he might have used my presence as a visitor in the college to assure himself of protection from the wrath of his own black countrymen. I wondered also whether my life would not have been worth it, had New Haven's blacks stormed the ivied battlements of Yale University, and razed it to the ground as the Black Panther Party had threatened to do with words of black cultural nationalism. Would I lie, consumed in "the fire next time," useless in the ruins of his sincerity?

"Calhoun is not the most racist college." In this confession lay all the extenuation against any act, against any attitude, before, and even up until then, might have been deliberately racialistic. An act that he himself might have admitted to, as racialistic. But I feel certain that in spite of the great American conspiracy, an immorality of silence, the master's own silence must have rebelled vociferously inside his heart. And if I were to analyze his statement, spoken with all sincerity and pride that is characteristic of a Southern gentleman who confesses that he is a segregationist, and who would maintain that his state, let us say, Louisiana, "is not the most racist in the country," and that it is in fact less racial than either North Carolina, or South Africa during its apartheid regime, and would attempt to use this statement in a logical way against his enemies who may be black and white liberals, the statement that "Calhoun College is not the most racist college" can be taken as a reflection of the attitude of the university itself, a confession that seeks to bring about some extenuation of its heinousness. It is the kind of statement that I have heard used many times at Yale, when the university was challenged about the quality of its Black Studies Program. I can hear the president saying, "Yale is not the most backward college on these matters, gentlemen." And in this context, "not the most racist" means the same thing as "not the most backward."

The Calhoun College Committee carried this report of the mixer which had caused the problem, a copy of which was given to me by the master. Here is the relevant portion of that report:

> A greater than usual crowd of High School and younger students attempted to get into the mixer. This was due to a mistake of advertising the dance over WYBC-FM [the Yale radio station], to all of New Haven, while we expected it to be broadcast only to Yale students. WYBC was asked to retract their invitation, but they did not do so. By 9.30 the crowd of young people outside the gate was so large and rowdy that the gates were closed by the police. Almost all ID's were checked through the gates. In the living room, the people who had gotten past the gates now had to get past Jack Shaw. They did not want to pay the $2.00, nor have their ID's checked again by him, and by 11.00 he was being pushed bodily through the doors. Finally, in the dining room, certain inebriated Sophomores were heard discussing the possibilities of starting a fight. The crowd conditions would have made a fight and the resulting flight from the dining hall disastrous. The Social Committee and the University would be liable for any injuries incurred as a result.

Jack Shaw then stated that he decided to check all ID's of all people when he noticed a lot of too young looking people trying to get in and when he heard people had been coming in through windows in the Grotto, the Fellows Lounge and the Master's Garage. Furthermore, he noticed ID passing and people faking the stamp on their hands.

Stan Royal added that he saw an atmosphere of fear from the beginning that something might happen, and attributed this to the Soc. Comm. and the police being frightened by the mass of Blacks inside and out.

Clay did not deny this. A partial [underlined in the report] purpose of this mixer, of paying the extra money to have "Au Natural" play was to attract Blacks. The "fear" came from the name calling outside the gate, and rumours that Sophomores looking for fights, and the number of High School and younger students who seem to have gotten into the dance by various methods, for whom we are liable. The responsibility of the Social Committee is to Calhoun students alone; if outsiders cause disruption we do not want them here. By agreement with the police, the mixer was closed down at 11.00 to prevent trouble.

The above clarification led to a discussion of the possibilities of prevention of re-occurrence. Tony Salzman began by proposing that the checker be moved from the main door to the living room. It is impossible to do that because there is no way to keep the people from coming up through the basement and keep the ladies room open at the same time. Next he proposed that we strictly impose ID checking. It was explained that we have been doing this, but perhaps with not enough scrupulosity. Then the problem of whom to let in was discussed. The people to be let in for free are Calhoun men and their dates and females showing college ID's. Those who should pay are other Yale men and their male guests. No others should be let in to the college during a mixer.

Stan Royal then asked if the problems at last week's mixer meant that "Au Natural" and similar groups would not be asked to play again. Bennett replied that was definitely NOT TRUE. More precautions should be taken beforehand, and the mixers should not be advertised. The Committee ordinarily cannot afford to pay $250 for their band, however. The price of the band in this case was offset by the intake at the door of $130, of which Jack Shaw was paid $20.

It was at this time, and through this incident, that I first began to regard myself less as a West Indian, and more as a black man living in America, a black man who previously would boast openly and proudly of the fact that I was West Indian in origin and in attitude. And I would brag that this West Indian background gave me a special perspective of the racial problems in America. The West Indian perspective also relieved me of much of the automatic distrust with which I noticed most, if not all of the black students regarded both the university and the white people associated with the University. "When the Master talk, and I hear that Southern accent," a black student of Berkeley College told me, at lunch one day, "it just reminds me of the South." And in their distrust of white, the black student included other blacks, those few local New Haven blacks who had recently been hired by the university in positions with very high-sounding titles, with the minimum of power and influence, to change the ingrained condition of black neglect.

I would tell myself before this incident with the mixer, as I stood chatting with a white professor, or to his wife, a now faded Manhattan beauty dressed in wools, or as I stood in the kitchen of the Master's House in any of the colleges, exchanging jokes for jokes, parrying with vague academic ideas with his wife, that I was Austin Clarke, and that by that identification, being Austin Clarke, I was therefore, my own man: capable of entering a relationship with the university and with the faculty on terms which if I did not myself establish, at least were terms I could break, that I was "man enough to handle," should the implications and innuendos in those terms attempt to slice away from what my black students constantly called "my manhood." I could stand up at any cocktail party, sit at any dinner table in the university, in the president's huge mansion on Hillhouse Avenue, in the dining room of John Hersey, novelist and master of Pierson College, which was across the street from my apartment, accepting his invitations to dinner, at which I was introduced to the stellar company of his friends, such as Dave Brubeck, a Knopf publisher, or the son of a publisher, without once feeling out of place, or that I was "a token Negro," that "my manhood" was being compromised. I could swap anything they were swapping, and still be able to tell myself that I was Austin Clarke, and unattached from what Roy Bryce-Laporte, the head of Black Studies called, "the racialistic obligation of being a black man at Yale," from the collective image of having to be black, and bad, a sentiment I suspected all black students to have, and which I had refused to accept as the barometer of my social intercourse with the Yale community. I was pretending instead, that I was whole and free. But I was self-indulgently delusionary. It was a tenuous, self-destructive posture of individuality. And individuality on the part of a black man who teaches at Yale, or is a student there, is an impossible philosophy of life and of behaviour, to maintain with any semblance of consistency. For you are not looked upon as an individual.

In those days of beautiful weather, in the early days of the first semester in 1968, I was the only black man, not a little popular with the men and the women, students, professors and wives, and I was teaching anything related to a Black Studies Program that Yale was trying to conceive as an established and serious academic curriculum related to the life of black students and black people.

I am certain now that the program that I helped to initiate at Yale will never be anything more than a scant concession to the presence and the pressure put upon the program by black students; and to the psychological pressure of the students themselves, to the larger black community both around Yale and throughout America. When a comparison with the programs at other universities is made, Yale bluntly insists that its program is the best. This is probably the case. It is certainly not the worst. For Yale is Yale. And the best Black Studies Program must therefore be instituted first at Yale. This was the intention. But has the ambition to be the first amongst the Ivy League colleges been achieved?

I had suspected that the black students had fabricated an image in which they meant to put me; one that was acceptable to them. They could see me only as a black man. Perhaps, also, as a foreign black man. Any cultural distinctiveness that I might have would be viewed by them against the pervasive black cultural nationalism which their own chauvinism would readily tell them that they were superior, if not contemporary to my West Indian background. And in my present predicament, I might even have conceded the point. But they had never thought it worthwhile to advise me of the precise image in which they wanted me to operate. And since I resent categorization of any kind, and from any source, I tended to reject both the image imposed upon me, and the black students' own attitude about images. I am a writer. And I regard myself as a writer; and if I am not, then I am nothing. But I also know that even if only for the sake of being practical, when I am in America, I am black. Black. Phobogenically black. "Unforgiveably black," as they said of the great black heavyweight boxer, Jack Johnson. I also have no delusion that for some, I am first and foremost, a black man, a Negro, a nigger.

It is irrelevant that Yale University, in a moment of panic in June 1968, and due also to the shortage of "qualified professionals" to teach in the recently formed Black Studies Program, presumed that I was academic and qualified enough, capable to be on its faculty to teach its students. All that is irrelevant. And because it is, I deliberately ignored the pain and the confusion and the loneliness of the black faces I could see around me, waiting across the plaza of the Bieneke Rare Book Library, after the sun had fallen behind the ugly brick, so strong and everlasting and terrifying in its unwillingness to rot and crumble, and the other durable buildings of the Old Campus, and after this sinking sun had eaten off the topmost pillars of Woolsey Hall, I would see these black students rushing to dinner there, dressed in the walk and posture of the pimp of Harlem (whom they were then imitating as a symbolic gesture of their own rebelliousness), a walk, which if anybody knows anything about black people, is a manifestation of black rebellion and alienation — at the same time — against the temporary surroundings in which black people find themselves, encircled so to speak, as if they were in fact, part of the cold, heavy, formidable architecture surrounding them. For they hope, these young black students at Yale, to emerge untouched by all this architecture, by all this "bullshit" which is what they call the architecture, and which they claim is; and they expect too, that their sojourn here, three to four years, will not hold them suspect in the eyes of the more healthy, more "un-colonized brothers" who remain in the

American ghetto, because they cannot leave it; and who die of hunger and frustration, but with their "shit together," which is to say too, that these untouched, unspoiled "brothers" have lived a life that did not have a university in it, to add to their confusion, that no university had muddled their heads with useless philosophy and theorems, out of joint, with the rhythm of their lives as men, as black men; and useless in the practical sense that the rewards to them from such an education are circumscribed by the condition of racism in the country.

I refused to accept the image I could see reflected in the smiles of some of my colleagues. I did not regard many on the Yale faculty as colleagues: not in that professional sense. There were however, a few exceptional exceptions. And these were men with whom I would drink and discuss matters of life, my life and theirs, as that "life" could not be touched by such a commonplace and topographical phenomenon as race in this country. These were men brave enough to want to talk about things that had nothing to do with the racial situation in America, at the time.

And although the question of race ("Now, as a black professor, what do you think of the social life at Yale?"), was never brought up, there still lingered some preoccupation with it that I could discern, in many ways, on the face, in the handshake, in the invitation — or lack of invitation — in the little hasty chats along corridors in the Hall of Graduate Studies ... "Tell me, who is the gentleman sitting next to me?" a senior professor in the Department of English once asked his neighbour at a department meeting. "Oh yes, of course, Professor Austin Clarke. I've heard a lot about him!" That was the time when I was the only black man attending these meetings. A singular experience. The preoccupation had been allowed to slip out as a mild shock; and soon all such preoccupation with IT could be "externalized" and seen as liberalism. But IT was there then. IT was there with the ivy, with the now-defunct "Rebel Nights" at Calhoun College, when white students from the South used to sing songs that contained messages and insults, as if they had not heard of the outcome of the American Civil War, and therefore could not accept a northerner's version of the history that the war was indeed over.

When the rumour, "There's a lot of stealing nowadays," began to circulate, and Pierson College, which almost faces the escape route to the New Haven black community locked its gates after six o'clock in the afternoon, and nearby Branford College followed suit, some felt that the stealing was being done by black youth, and that the gates were closed against their rambling through quadrangles and into students' rooms. IT was there. And IT is there in the whole question of enrollment of black students; and in the inordinate number of black women serving in the kitchens of the dining halls of the twelve colleges, with the cleaners of rooms, this extraordinary number of black hands doing manual labour; black hands and black help in the positions which have traditionally been reserved for the descendants of that black man cut into the stained-glass window in blazing colours when the sun hits it, in the lounge of the dining hall of Calhoun College.

I saw IT and I refused to believe that it could ever apply to me. Everyone knew or should have known that I was already an established writer before I came to Yale. Everyone knew I was a West Indian, and they should have known too, that there was no point in trying to keep me close to them, as assurance and protection from the racial apocalypse which so many people, Norman Mailer, Malcolm X, James Baldwin, and Stokely Carmichael, thought was in the next rainfall, and which was on the minds of so many persons, as it had been in the mind of the master of Calhoun College, following the murder of Dr. Martin Luther King, Jr.

The master of Calhoun College had said he was glad I was living in his college; my black presence might prove to be the bulwark against the possibility of black violence which some of his own black students might have been induced into inflicting against their alma mater; and I, the West Indian, was going to be the protector of the master against the Black American!

Looking back now, with considerably more objective judgment, on a time characterized by a national lack of objectivity, I do not see the insult in the master's statement, as vividly as I saw it then.

A distraught black female undergraduate told me one day, "Yale niggers is supposed to be the brightest niggers in the country!" She said something else which challenged both the truths contained in her statement. But the more significant part of her statement, spoken in rage and disillusionment, was that although she herself was at Yale, she was still regarded as a "nigger." She probably regarded herself as a "nigger." How could this be? She was, after all, married to Yale, although she confessed that she tended to forget that she could never be regarded as a "Yalie" in the same way as one would regard George Pilling, the author of the Calhoun College Social Committee report, to be. For Mr. Pilling did manifest a close identification with his institution, in almost natural ties of kinship. And this young black woman can never see Yale in that same sense. She sees other black students as "niggers," and her view of them in this context, has nothing to do with the brotherly, loving use of this term. Her rage disqualified her use of the term "nigger" from being an affectionate one, or a compassionate one.

The young black woman's remarks caused me to wonder if I myself was seen as the Calhoun College "show nigger" in the same way that I would say that the tall, handsome, and intellectually brilliant man from Trinidad is the Branford College "nigger." I know that Ken would have repudiated this description. And he would argue that there was nothing about his relationship to his college, or to Yale, that should make me conclude this. But in the final analysis, it has nothing to do with him, and it has nothing to do with his own definition as a "radical," and this is beyond anything that he might think of himself. For it is the definition that the university attaches to his association with it, and with Branford College, that counts.

And the fact that at Branford, the master makes a more serious attempt to dispense his broadmindedness, and use his New England brand of liberalism against the more recalcitrant other masters and faculty members to demonstrate that there are "legitimate" black intellectuals at Yale, still it can be said that my friend, Ken, in spite of all this, is a "grander show nigger." I think that Ken understands this. For he is, like me, a West Indian; and like me, has lived in Canada, and in England, for many years. America cannot therefore put much over on him. And although he shuns us, his black colleagues, because we are not radical, and probably also because in his estimation we are not bright like him, yet we, students and faculty alike, know that, as the black American hipster puts it, he's "got his shit together." Because if he hasn't, time will tell him that his only allies at Yale are the black occupants of his similar incarceration.

It was therefore with a tinge of envy, though with understanding, that I — we — saw Ken towering in every way over the audience and the students, in more senses than the obvious one, in the Ingalls skating rink that night of symbolic crisis (Yale itself is in some ways, synonymous with symbolic crises), when the university, gripped in its rivalry with Harvard over the question of radicalism, tried to do something equally radical (as Harvard), about the presence of the ROTC on its campus. The Harvard students had already played out their dramatization of radicalism, on the Cambridge campus and in the newspapers of the entire country, on the question of the Harvard ROTC. So, Yale therefore had to manufacture a similar concern for the ROTC, and for the war in Vietnam, and for related moral protests. And when that happened, you should have seen this man, not unlike Frederick Douglass in stature of dignity and of brilliance, but in some ways also more like Dr. Martin Luther King, Jr., guiding the multitude of Yale's white students, instructing them in the fieldwork of the principles of revolution and confrontation tactics to be used against Yale, his employer, in the same way as he might have opened their minds in his college seminars, showing them as he eventually succeeded in doing, with a modicum of success, how to fight the university on the issue of its moral responsibility, because it was a sponsor of the ROTC on its campus.

Some of my black students told me that they regretted Ken's refusal to associate with them, that he did not want to be their "adviser," and that they looked upon his decision to spend all his time with the white students and the organization, Students for a Democratic Society (SDS), as one result of Yale's power "to change a brother." They also looked with criticism at his exclusive association with other whites; but yet they knew, so they assured me, that Ken's image was assured, for with his brilliance and brains, they were willing to admit that "the brother is heavy."

And suddenly, events overtook his best planned and cultivated image. The Black Panthers were coming. To Yale. To occupy it. And take over its administration, perhaps only symbolically, recruit all the black students and some of the black faculty to their theology of Black Power, to disrupt the university, and to provide a sympathetic environment for the trial of Bobby Seale for murder, in a New Haven court. The SDS was the Panthers' vanguard. Jerry Rubin preceded them with a rousing speech in the park. Rumours of impending riots, the disruption to regular classes, the head of Black Studies in a quandary, uncertain, uninformed on university policy and strategy by the president of the university, unable therefore to advise his black faculty members. And underlying all this confusion, the safety of the black women students was on everybody's minds, just in case things got out of hand, as they were getting out of hand in many American cities, and especially in the black communities. And the directive authored by Kingman Brewster, meaningless in a meaningless confusion, with nobody knowing what was the best thing to do, to save Yale. For it was felt that Yale was about to be burned down. Certainly disrupted to the degree that its normal operation and administration were seriously threatened. The presence of the SDS and the threatened presence of the Black Panthers on the Yale campus in this week of May 6, 1970, had us all reeling, like fish thrown to the surface of a lake, to catch breath.

Everybody was talking about liberation. But liberation from what? The war in Vietnam? President Richard Nixon's oppressive administration, during which civil rights were trampled, and wire-tapping strangled free expression of political views? The spreading of racism and the increase of police violence against black people in the inner cities of America?

There arose in the midst of this chaos mixed with national uncertainty about the means of controlling it, incapable of solving it, for no one seemed to have a solution, they sprung up, all over the Yale campus, and on other Ivy League campuses in America, semi-formal "institutions" called "the teach-ins" — impromptu lectures given by the more radical black professors. At Yale, they were also known as "Liberation Schools." I have a copy of a broadsheet that came off the presses at this time, like the spreading of contagious diseases, like mosquitoes and flies in the summer cottage time, at the lake. It is dated Wednesday, May 8th. The year is 1970, the year Yale, in a fit of fear and guilt, was convinced that the Black Panther Party was going to "occupy" the university, close it down to ordinary classes, and turn it into indocrination camps teaching black cultural nationalism.

This is what was advertised for the afternoon and evening of May 6th, in one of the Liberation Schools set up by the black student body and the black faculty:

Liberation School
Wednesday May 6
Black Literature and the Process of Liberation
Houston Baker and Austin Clarke
2PM Branford

Liberation and What We Can Do
Ken Mills, Roy Bryce-Laporte
2PM, Morse

Yale and the Community
to organize and coordinate action workshops
Ken Mills
Margaret Leslie, from United Newhallville
Branford Dining Hall
8PM, Wednesday 6th

The enthusiasm and the excitement that surrounded these Liberation Schools stated very clearly the underlying concern that swept through the entire campus; and this concern was the physical safety of the black women students, and what to do with them, how to protect them in case "armageddon" fell like bullets from police guns, or fell like slashes of billy clubs in the hands of the police. It was the first time that the meaning of the term "armed camp" had a nervous connotation, as I walked from my apartment on Park Street, through the quadrangle of Pierson College, out on to York Street, through Branford, and out to the Old Campus. In the park nearby, the SDS had already set up their soapboxes like pulpits to deliver the lesson to Yale. The night before this morning that broke clear and hot, Jerry Rubin had laid down the political platform of the SDS. But the whole country already knew what that political theology was: we had heard it many times before, from Columbia, to Harvard, and to Princeton. The Black Panthers were no way in sight. But their presence was heavy and real and scary as an omen. The New Haven Police and the Connecticut National Guard were already lined up along the streets, tense, unsmiling, muscle-bound, and with their hands wrapped round their brown billy clubs held in front of their bodies as if they were protecting their testicles. I felt that this armed guard expected, and perhaps relished, the possibility of having to use them in a few hours, when things got out of hand. I felt that they wanted things to get out of hand.

It was still early on this May morning, and I was walking through the park and the quadrangle of the Old Campus, like a soldier counting bodies and arms of the dead, although the dead in the Battle for Yale had not yet been started; but start it would; and in the haze, perhaps imagined in the new lexicon of warfare and battle, or perhaps more correctly, the humidity which someone told me can rise like a thin white cloud, in this unclear morning, I imagined the sound of guns and the smell of tear gas. And with this anticipation, I placed my white handkerchief to my nostrils, and imagined I was being attacked by the soldiers holding their sticks in the same tough way a man holds his prick standing like a conqueror over a white porcelain urinal. But nothing was happening. Just the accumulation of police and troopers, waiting for an order, or waiting to act out of fear, in case the order came too late for their impatience. No black students were in sight. No black woman students. They had been hidden from view, taken into safety. I walked back the same route almost, and came not immediately, but taking my time, in this inspection of event and result not yet happened, and when I got close to Calhoun College, I started to smell the smell of tear gas. Something had happened. My white handkerchief was no longer white. It was black. Not from the tear gas, but from the haze of humidity and New Haven dust. The streets were quiet now. Only the brute-force image of New Haven Police and State Troopers. And they were lined along Park Street, across from Pierson College, guarding the empty streets, in case the invisible Black Panthers should fall out of the sky. I walked beside them, for the road was narrow, close; and I could smell their perspiration, and their hate; and saw the way the police gripped their guns, their tools, caressing them in the way described by the French playwright, Jean Genet, who knew something about thighs and limbs.

No one had commissioned me to make a tally of things, to report like a scout in war, jot down and take notes of mortalities and injuries. It was the boredom of the morning, the boredom of the event, the boredom of the May Day weekend, now without the gaiety of unprofessionally stilled beer, and red hot cinders of steaks large as a brick; and hot dogs like boys' penises; and hamburgers burnt to sweet blackness; and for those whose constitutions could afford its sting and strength, bourbon and whiskey, and the playing of Aretha Franklin, Sam and Dave, James Brown, Otis Redding, and some Miles Davis and John Coltrane sneaking through amongst the heavy beat of rhythm and blues. And not a note, not a whisper, not a chord of calypso. I am in America.

This was a time of craziness: and the proclaiming of crazy ideologies and romanticism. This craziness was caused by one fact: the barbarians were at the gate.

John Hersey, the master of Pierson, had recently written a book, *Algiers Motel*, and he wanted to set up a foundation to receive the royalties from the book after the second year. The royalties from sales in the first year were to go to the Detroit families. But the barbarians were at the gate. He wanted then to give the royalties to the Black Panthers. But there was a condition. The royalties were not to go to the Panthers' political program. I did not see how he could exclude one from the other.

Houston Baker, now head of Black Studies at Duke University, startled us with, "The Black Panthers are the new Denmark Vesey," because, to him, they see visions and had white support.

Doug Miranda, who was a member of the Black Panther Party, regarded white radicals as "the crazies." He was certain that the Panthers could not have got the New Haven black community or the Black Students at Yale (BSAY) to bring about the confrontation with the university, as some had been enticing them to do, so, according to Doug Miranda, he allowed the "crazies" to do it for them. "Maximize chaos" was the tactic. At any rate, he felt that the Panthers are not hung up on the white radicals, "the crazies."

A large number of white faculty, old and young, were beginning to chastise President Brewster, because they felt that they had been abandoned by him. They were not supporting him in the statement he made about the trial of black revolutionaries. Part of this statement was the institution of a "voluntary" or an "involuntary" tax on the university faculty: one percent of basic salary, or one percent of salary over $12,000. This money would be taken annually to create a foundation. This money will be given as Yale's contribution to the black community.

And talking about salaries, which in my time at Yale was smaller than at most universities, came one of the most intriguing incidents that seemed to have been the colour and the character of the Black Studies Programs in America. The shortage of qualified black professors. We were like surgeons, constantly on call. And during most weekends none of us were in Yale, but travelling out into the provinces, so to speak, to other universities and colleges who wanted to hear our views on everything that was black. "Black Aesthetics" became a watchword, to cloud or to bury intelligent argument, and point of view. You had to know something about this "black aesthetics" key, otherwise you could not unlock the vault of "heavy bread." You didn't really have your shit together. The times were good. Money was being made. Money the middle name of Americans. And the places where this money was most easily found, and mined and offered to any black professor at Yale, the leaders in the Black Studies Programs, where "black aesthetics" was best taught, was the State University of New York system of universities, SUNY.

You drove from Yale on Friday mornings, to Williams College, to Clark University, to Connecticut College, to Wellesley, to the various SUNYs, to Duke, to Princeton, all over America — wherever a plane alighted; and if there was no airport, you were picked up and driven to your lecture. And you came back with your pockets full and heavy.

I was in a classroom at Brandeis University in Waltham, Massachusetts, teaching Afro-American Literature, Richard Wright's *Native Son*; and it was four o'clock in the afternoon and I had to get up to Boston on the train from Waltham, and hire a car, and be driven by one of my students to Williams College to give a lecture on Malcolm X and the Black Muslims in America, and have a discussion with Betty Friedan, who confessed that the women's liberation movement gathered its technique and political tactic from the blacks in the civil rights movement. This had never been expressed publicly before. And the irony is that the women's liberation movement did not lift a sincere finger to assist black women who were suffering, and still do suffer, a more heinous persecution of inequality, inequalities in all aspects of their lives.

There was something about that lecture at Williams that reminded me of Canada. The name of the auditorium was the name of a Canadian beer, or rather the name of the owner of Molson Beer. I remember another humorous thing about that lecture, which was pointed out to me by my friend, Jonathan Aaron, who was an assistant professor, like me, at Yale in 1968. Jonathan said that he held his breath, in fear that my opening sentence was so long that I had forgotten the subject, and therefore could not find the finite verb to close the thought I was making about Malcolm X's importance in the civil rights movement, and in the liberation of black people in America. Long sentences, not only written but spoken, seems to be my calling card, seems to have started at that lectern that night in Williamstown. And this does not mean that I do marvel at the length of opening sentences in my fiction, and sometimes, at the omission of the finite verb.

But this story is about my friend, Ken. Ken's reputation mounted after the Liberation Schools he organized during that historic May Day Weekend at Yale. People began to notice. He was being invited all over the Eastern seaboard to dispense his radical wisdom in philosophy. One of the SUNYs snapped him up. This was not unusual amongst black professors. At conferences, he gave paper after paper, like another West Indian who had come over from England where he taught in a second-rate university, for an interview at Yale; and who was instructed, as a visitor, to take the Connecticut Limousine from LaGuardia Airport to Berkeley College, at the corner of Elm and High Streets; and who arrived a little late, in a yellow taxi, a trip that cost more than one hundred dollars; and that was not apologized for as an extravagance, but as a cultural misunderstanding. "A limousine in England is the same as a taxicab. Or a hansom."

In Ken's case, there was not this misunderstanding. But those of us who were spying on him, discovered that he owned a very rare, and expensive English car, which he never drove on campus, but which had been hidden away in a garage some distance from the cluster of the twelve Yale colleges. One man who knew of this car was Doug Miranda, who borrowed it almost every weekend, who kept Ken's secret, who had to be given the courtesy, since he and Ken were radicals, and the bond of being "brothers" could not be broken.

Ken would sneak out from Branford College and drive down to his SUNY to attend conferences, and give guest lectures, and hobnob with the New York "brothers," all of whom made almost twice the salary that Yale paid Ken. Ken was not tenured. No black professor in Yale's Black Studies Program was tenured, and this was another contention during the lectures in the Liberation Schools.

A position at the SUNY was offered. And Ken accepted. The money was too good not to. He must have heard about the West Indian who mistook a taxicab for an airport limousine, and who held three full-time teaching jobs at the same time, who lived on planes, who changed his clothes in the washrooms of planes, who drew three hearty salaries, and drove a white Cadillac and smoked Cuban cigars, to settle his nerves and soothe his anxiety, to help him to remember which city or town, which campus and university he was in, at that moment of restless insomnia.

The money was too good. Ken was appointed associate professor, with tenure. And things went well. He drove back up in his roaring English foreign roofless roadster, his long Afro blowing in the breeze, to take his seminars in Branford College. And then, one Friday, at a conference on some aspect of Marxist sociology, or the sociology of Marxism — was it the Marxism of sociology? — at which the chairman of sociology at Yale was a speaker, looking at his program, he saw the name, the title, the position of one of his own faculty members in Yale Department of Sociology …

This dialogue between the SUNY chairman of sociology, and the Yale chairman of sociology, has been repeated many times by many black professors:

"Is this Ken Mills?"

"Do you know him?"

"Yes."

"We think very highly of him!"

"So do we. He's on our faculty!"

"Ken Mills?"

"The same Ken Mills!"

"The same Ken Mills?"

We do not know anything of the conversation between the chairman of Yale sociology, and Ken. We do not know what passed between the SUNY chairman and Ken. We do know however, what words were exchanged back at Yale, between the chairman and Ken.

"You have to make a choice."

"I choose Yale."

Ken had been shortlisted for a prestigious fellowship. Ken was short-sighted about the philosophical aspect of loyalty to Yale. Ken sacrificed a very large salary, plus tenure at his SUNY, for the prestige of Yale.

He was awarded the prestigious fellowship. For one year.

He was fired when he returned to Yale.

He died, unfortunately, too young, soon after this declaration.

CHAPTER TWENTY-SIX

Aquarius

Norman Mailer comes roaring into the Calhoun College lounge, to be made a Fellow of the College, fresh and burly from his success in a thoughtful article written for thousands of dollars and for thousands of Americans to read, including the rebellious young black students at Yale, and published in *Look* magazine, on his favourite subject, civil rights in America, and the black problem. No other matter on the minds of Americans was as worthy of such intellectual attention as "the black problem."

And in this hour of strained relations between black and white Americans, in particular between black students and white intellectuals like writers of Mailer's stature, the relationship was strained tight as a bow about to be snapped. The black students came from many of the colleges to hear Mailer, who was one of the biggest draws in this field of civil rights and freedom and protest against the war in Vietnam. His book on the subject, *The Armies of the Night*, had created a great positive literary stir; and had placed him in the forefront of American intellectuals who were against the war. He was numbered amongst luminaries like Dr. Benjamin Spock; Yale Chaplain William Coffin; and the Nobel Laureate, Dr. Gerry Wall of Harvard. But the black students in the Calhoun master's lounge that night were a rebellious lot, intent upon taking Mailer to task for his "appropriation" of a black voice that they thought ought to have laid down this Law of Black. John Henrik Clarke, the editor of

Freedomways magazine that came out of Harlem; Harold Cruse, the author of the controversial book of "black ideas"; and even James Baldwin: this triumvirate they thought ought to have been lecturing them on this evening of sociable entertainment, but of most unsociable discussion.

The evening for me, was one of curiosity: observing the successful American writer in an academic atmosphere, surrounded by Americans, some of whom were black, in this time of racial stress and torment, and comparing the man now known as Aquarius, christening himself thus, as a brush of objectivity, as a means of controlling his material and escaping the criticism that his views were too personal, this new Aquarius was appealing to me, in the comparison with Canadian and West Indian writers, who did not, and possibly could not, command this "rock star" attention.

I had not met Aquarius before this. My interest in him was caused at the time by his reputation that centred on the incident of stabbing his wife, and being arrested. I thought this was the stuff that made a man a writer, this brushing, this facing, this tempting the prison bars, fate, destiny, daring — or madness. And I had hoped to find the wife-stabber in his personality. When I met him, all that gossip and history became myth, a picture now faded out of all relevance, rendered now in the heat of debate, as a misrepresentation of a past that bore no relation to civil rights and Vietnam and Richard Nixon and the burning of draft cards. We were all legionnaires in the armies of the night. And the night was black. I observed Aquarius in the same way as I had observed George Lamming the Barbadian, who wrote *In the Castle of my Skin*: watching him like a hawk, not to see anything about his character and personality, but how he held his cigarette, how he exhaled the smoke, how he held the glass with the whiskey and soda, how he used the English accent in his poet's voice, something like Dylan Thomas, these things of great value to me, a writer who had not yet written a short story, furthermore, a novel. But what was I observing Aquarius to find? Was I searching his body, his hands, his fingers, looking to see if the machismo in his words in fiction was reflected in his personality, in the way he looked, in the way he positioned his body on the receptive couch? Was I trying to imagine how his body would have lurched to deliver the stab that was dramatic and life-threatening?

At a dinner party given in Aquarius's honour, in the master's dining room, my wife was seated beside him. She had read *Armies of the Night*, and the things written about his past with knives and wives.

"He's not like that, at all!" she said. And she related the stories he told, and was impressed by his sense of humour. "Those things are all lies!" she added, contradicting the popular gossip about his temperament.

Let me not continue as diarist, pretending to be Samuel Pepys or James Boswell, and let Aquarius use his own voice to describe that night at Calhoun College. He gives his own narrative in *Of a Fire on the Moon*, published in 1970. He is describing two things: a dinner party in the Houston home of a mutual friend, a millionaire who dealt in oil and oils and sculptures from Africa, and his meeting the students at Calhoun College.

> There was also a Negro in his [Aquarius's] host's living room, a man perhaps thirty-five, a big and handsome Black man with an Afro haircut of short length, the moderation of the cut there to hint that he still lived in a White man's clearing, even if it was on the very edge of the clearing. He was not undistinguished, this Negro, he was a professor at an Ivy League college; Aquarius had met him one night the previous year after visiting the campus. The Negro had been much admired in the college. He had an impressive voice and the deliberate manner of a leader. How could the admiration of faculty wives be restrained? But this Black professor was also a focus of definition for Black students in the college — they took some of the measure of their militancy from his advice. It was a responsible position. The students were in the college on one of those specific programs which had begun in many a university that year — students from slum backgrounds, students without full qualification were being accepted on the reasonable if much embattled assumption that boys from slum were easily bright enough to be salvaged for academic life if special pains were taken. Aquarius had met enough of such students to think the program was modest. The education of the streets gave

substantial polish in Black ghettos — some of the boys had knowledge at seventeen that Aquarius would not be certain of acquiring by seventy. They had the toughness of fibre of the twenty-times tested. This night on the campus, having a simple discussion back and forth, needling back and forth, even to even — so Aquarius thought — a Black student suddenly said to him, "You're an old man. Your hair is gray. An old man like you wants to keep talking like that, you may have to go outside with me." The student gave an evil smile. "You're too old to keep up with me. I'll whomp your ass."

"It had been a glum moment for Aquarius. It was late at night, he was tired, he had been drinking with students for hours. As usual he was overweight. The boy was smaller than him, but not at all overweight, fast. Over the years Aquarius had lost more standards than he cared to remember. But he still held on to the medieval stricture that one should never back out of a direct invitation to fight. So he said with no happiness, "Well, there are so many waiting in line, it might as well be you," and he stood up.

The Black boy had been playing with him. The Black boy grinned. He assured Aquarius there was no need to go outside. They could talk now. And did. But what actors were the Blacks! What a sense of honor! What a sense of the gulch! Seeing the Black professor in this living room in Houston brought back the memory of the student who had decided to run a simulation through the character of Aquarius' nerve. It was in the handshake of both men as they looked at each other now, Aquarius still feeling the rash of the encounter, the other still amused at the memory. God knows how the student had imitated his voice from the chair. There had been a sly curl on the Black man's voice whenever they came across each other at a New York party.

It was in this New York townhouse, at a party where I first met Norman Mailer. My agent, a tall, handsome Princeton-educated black American, Ronald Hobbs, had, through a friend of his who was private secretary to the owner of the townhouse, and the owner of the Magritte in the Houston mansion, had introduced me to the millionaire, Jean de Menil, and his wife. Mrs. de Menil is an art historian. She was the artistic force responsible for the production and publication of *The Image of the Black in Western Art*, by Harvard University Press. At this time, Ronald Hobbs was the agent of Larry Neal, Leroi Jones, H. Rap Brown, and other rising black talent.

I would spend weekends in the New York townhouse, even when Mr. and Mrs. de Menil were away, either at the Houston mansion, or in Paris. Jean would call me at Yale and arrange for me to be looked after by the staff. "Are you coming alone? How many staff do you want?" It was exposure to a style of life unimaginable. But I learned to spend comfortable weekends, alone in the three- or four-storey townhouse, filled with more priceless things than the mansion in Houston.

The first night I was introduced by Ronald Hobbs was at the birthday party for Mr. de Menil's private secretary. Mailer was there. We ate lobster and drank champagne; and danced to music played by a small orchestra. I observed that Mailer, whether through the amount he had drunk, or through lack of balance, did not handle the slow pieces with much confidence. Lots of New York and international celebrities were at that birthday party. I remember each guest had two bottles of wine, one white, placed at his table, just before the butlers served the lobster. At the end of the party, I stood at the door, thanking my host, and chatting with Ronald Hobbs about the time the last train from Grand Central left for New Haven. Mr. de Menil heard our concern, for it was very late; and he instructed a driver to take me. Believing that I was to be dropped off at Grand Central, I repeated my thanks, said good night, and got into the limousine that was called. It might have been lurking round the corner. A liveried chauffeur opened the door. And when I thought I had recognized the avenue leading to the train station, I told the driver, "Turn here."

"No, sir," he said. Through my mind flashed the encounter with the taxi driver refusing to drive me from Rockefeller Centre to Harlem, some years before. I did not know what to do, or think. And then the chauffeur explained.

"Mr. de Menil said I am to drive you to Yale."

One weekend, alone in the townhouse, I called a cousin through marriage, George Carter, a schoolteacher and a painter, who lived in Harlem.

"Come and visit me, cuz." It was a Friday night, about six o'clock, still in time for dinner.

"Where're you?" he wanted to know. "When did you get into the city?"

"I am on Park Avenue, in a townhouse ..."

He did not let me finish.

"Get-outta town, nigger! Shee-it! This nigger ain't coming downtown, brother. Park Avenue did you say? This nigger's safer in Harlem, cuz."

"There are some things I want to show you. As an artist, you'll appreciate them. This place has four stories, and each floor is decorated in different period, furniture, and paintings in such good taste, and ..."

George would come, for a minute, since we were cousins, to take a peep at the paintings. I told the cook, the only member of the staff I thought I needed for the weekend, to prepare dinner for two. "Would you like appetizer, soup and main course, sir? What should I serve?"

Medium-rare lamb chops, asparagus, spinach, spring tomatoes, split-pea soup, Boston lettuce, small tomatoes, garlic, olive oil. "And would you mind choosing the wines for us?"

The doorbell went. George. I opened the door, and before he took the next step inside the darkened front hall, he said, "Shee-it! Did you break in here, brother?"

We went up and down in the lift, one of those with the concertina door, that you close behind you, and then press a soft bell, and try to hear the noise of the pulleys, but cannot, because everything in this townhouse is soft and civilized and noiseless. On each floor, George showed his amazement and joy at the treasures in this magnificent house.

"Jesus Christ!"

We were on the second floor, going up. The furniture and the sculptures and the paintings he recognized.

"Originals! Masterpieces, brother!"

On the third floor, we entered a small sitting room, and sat round a table of polished mahogany with inlaid pearls, on which were two antique ashtrays, for people smoked in houses in those days. George took a cigarette. It was French. Gauloises Filters. His eyes took in the room.

"God-damn!"

He was holding an art book in his hand, turning the leaves in an almost absent-minded way, nodding as he recognized the pieces of ancient sculptures. And then he was pointing to an object. He touched the object, all the while pointing at the illustration of a piece of sculpture in the glossy-paged book.

"Ain't this a mother …?"

The piece he was touching was the illustration he had been looking at in the art book.

I could not believe my eyes. He could not believe his eyes.

"This thing was made, or discovered in something-B.C.!"

And we went down in the voiceless lift to the dining room, on the first floor, with a view of the sculpture garden, blessed in the soft shower of electric lights, bringing out breasts and limbs and torso, and the green leaves of plants surrounding them.

I had indulged in a taste of Victorian manners and mannerism, and had asked the maid to place George at one end of the oblong mahogany dining table, and I at the other. I wanted him, as much as myself, to experience the distance in dining that men of wealth, or of cold demeanour, lived with at breakfast, luncheon, and dinner. George would know this. George would have experienced this: he came from good West Indian stock.

We carried on the kind of conversation that Victorian gentlemen, and ladies, at dinner would engage in; and when it was over, when we had our salad and a glass of champagne "to cleanse the palate." The maid asked, "Where would you like coffee to be served, sir?"

"The library, please."

When I said, "please" I was unsure about the protocol to be used to household servants. Should I have said, "The library?" Or, "The library, thank you?"

George knew as well as I did, that in this kind of refined atmosphere and environment, one takes one's coffee in the library.

I had never seen the library. I did not mind George knowing this. But I could not afford to have the maid know that I had never entered the library; did not know if there was a library; but was sure that in a house of this kind, with these art treasures, there was bound to be a library. The lift was still silent. There was some anxiety. I wanted to find the library and sit in the proper state of expectancy, before the maid entered it. The lift was made to stop at the floor above the dining room. I made a quick inspection of the room, and there was no library. On the next floor, in the murmurless lift, my spirits fell: I had one more floor left to investigate, and find a library. It was not on the second floor. Nor on the third. And the lift did not go higher. We were approaching the private apartments of the de Menils.

We went back down to the second floor. And there it was. We had hardly sat in reading chairs and lifted a book, any book, to give the impression that we were cool, when the maid as silent as the lift, entered the library. On her tray were espresso coffee in demi-tasse cups, and two large crystal snifters. I could smell the rich, seductive strength of the Armagnac Monluc, VSOP...

I was teaching in the summer of 1969, at the School of Letters, Indiana University, when the call came from Jean de Menil, in Paris, inviting me to Houston, Texas, because "Norman's going to be there, writing a piece on the launching on the moon, for *Life* magazine, and it would be good to see the launching ourselves ..."

I was working on a short story in the Wilmington humidity, restless because of it, worried to be told by one of my black students doing graduate work in black aesthetics, that "the motherfucking Klan was born in Bloomington-Indiana, Jack, this ain't no shit, Brother!" Wondering if they would take it upon themselves to march from the "nine miles from here" and occupy the Bloomington campus of Indiana University. Or if the Indiana State Police and National Guard would do it for them. On the campus this summer, there were six blacks: two women, and four men, and me, and we formed a little society to protect ourselves from the humid Bloomington humidity and from boredom. The short story was not going well, and it was in the midst of this torment of trying to make sense of the words that the telephone call came from Paris, from

Jean, to visit him in Houston. I tried to shuffle out of the obligation by informing him that travel by plane from Bloomington to Chicago, then to Atlanta, then to Houston was not only precarious because of the small planes necessary to hook up to the larger planes, planes that "rattle and shake" like flimsy kites in the Barbados wind, but that I was busy with my work and with my graduate seminars. He would not have no for an answer, and with Parisian skill and diplomacy, he sent a special delivery note to my uncomfortable apartment on the brink of the campus, a section that seemed to be in the middle of a forest. And as I got to know my surroundings and environment, it turned out that I was indeed living in the middle of a forest. The Klan, nine miles away, had the necessary camouflage to attack me any moment of the deepened black nights so peculiar to the South. I thought of Macbeth and Duncan and the three weird sisters, and the prediction of invincibility and duplicity in language.

"Be bloody, bold, and resolute," the Second Apparition assures Macbeth, "laugh to scorn/The power of man, for none of woman born/Shall harm Macbeth." Macbeth ignored the caution and wisdom of believing an "apparition" who went on to give stronger, more curried assurances: "Macbeth shall never vanquish'd be until/Great Birnam Wood to high Dunsinane Hill/Shall come against him."

Who, murderous king, struggling writer, superstitious leader of men going into battle would worry his head over the possibility that the "Apparition's" reassurance, that his safety and invincibility lay in the unnaturalness of walking forests? Still, with the Klan just nine miles down the street, I could not be certain that they would not turn themselves into trees and tree trunks with the green camouflage, and come after me ...

But these were unreasonable thoughts. I really did not want to take the long flight from Bloomington-Indiana to Houston-Texas, Texas being the most reprehensible state I had heard about, from the point of view and the mouths of runaway slaves, and those who did not have to run away but had lived through that plantation horror.

Jean's letter said, "Don't worry about the complicated flights, my jet shall come to get you at Bloomington, like a breeze!" The exclamation mark was most functional. And conspicuous. I fell for that punctuation mark. I told my students, who spread the news throughout the summer school classes, that "their professor" was going to Texas on a private jet.

The day of departure arrived. I was at the small Bloomington Airport, a two-roomed shed, dressed in American summer wear of grey-and-white-striped seersucker suit, blue shirt, college tie of Calhoun College, and brown suede desert boots; and having packed short pants, bathing trunks, and sandals to contend with the Texas heat and humidity. And a hunger for a swimming pool and "coloured television" in which to drown myself for the two weeks of my invitation.

The private jet, a Lear jet, came into the Bloomington Airport like a breeze. I was sitting in the lounge, no larger, no more impressive than a room in a downtown bowling alley, than a room with a pool table; and then all of a sudden my name was called out; and I went to a telephone in the airport manager's office, and Jean's voice was on the intercom, and the voice of his wife, and he told me he could see the tiny airport, and that I should come on the runway and see the jet, coming in to land "like a breeze"; and before it did land, I was taken to the VIP waiting room, and everyone at the airport looked at me differently, and I pushed out my chest, and went on to the runway to meet the jet, and walk aboard up the steps, and I thought I heard applause. I had paid the taxicab the nominal rate, about five dollars from my apartment in the middle of the forest, and when I returned from Houston, witnessing the landing on the moon, the fare was doubled. I was a celebrity. I had travelled on a private jet. The taxicab man had to get his share in my new celebrity. And I paid him his inflated fare without a murmur of protest or emotion.

Houston, Texas! The land of bigness. Big houses, big Cadillacs, big steaks, big swimming pools, big portals in the Southern imitating Roman architecture, big lawns mowed to an evenness that matches artificial grass, and greener; big wages, big passions and tempers, big violence, big bigness. I saw myself driving from the airport in his white Cadillac. Perhaps, as a Frenchman, he had a Citroën. Or a Mercedes-Benz. And his mansion would have the white stately columns so characteristic of the antebellum South, lined with magnolia trees. And the swimming pool, though not shaped in the passion and romance of a heart, or some shape of the human body, would be large, as big as a football field, in which I would float on an inflated bed, with a gin and tonic floating beside me on another floating object. And at dinner, I would be dressed in my grey-and-white-striped seersucker suit; and at night after dinner and espresso and Armagnac, watch television on a screen as large as one in a movie house.

The plane landed at Houston. And it taxied to a shed. Beside the door to the shed were two Hertz rented station wagons, in the most ugly baby blue colour. Jean got out and entered. Where was the Cadillac? Where was the Citroën? The Mercedes-Benz? The Lincoln Continental, then? Jean was a phony. To come all this distance, and park a Lear jet, and enter a rented car? I knew then that I had made a mistake in accepting his invitation to watch the landing on the moon.

But we drove in silence, through the neighbourhood of wealth and silence, and I discovered then, in this winding drive where there was absolutely no noise, even though there were Mexicans, or Indian-looking men, short in stature, but tough in the limbs, especially in the waist, with pangas in their hands, bending over, almost in the shape of hairpins, attacking the luscious grass with an expertise that no powered lawn mower could match, in this visible exertion of energy and power, but no noise rising from the grass sprayed like confetti that is green ... and in this silence, the rented awful baby-blue Hertz station wagon, with Jean and his wife and I and his private secretary inside, all silent, all wondering, all thinking that we were lost — except his wife who would have made this trip as many times as Jean — waiting for the proof of our deception that Jean was not what he said he was.

And then we enter River Oaks, and there is this silence again, nothing moving, nothing shaking, nothing blowing, for there is no breeze, and the station wagon turns into a driveway, and my heart sinks. There is no house immediately visible. Then after a few yards, the roof of a house emerges in the first sign of dusk, and the station wagon continues, and my disappointment increases with every yard it travels, and then we stop. There is no house. Only a roof is visible. The roof of a bungalow. Sunk into the ground. But we are moving to the front door, and then, as if in a miracle, the house emerges from the ground and is taking up all the space before us. When the front door is opened, there is a welcome that takes the breath away. I shall let Norman Mailer describe it, in the same book, *Of a Fire on the Moon*:

The mansion was modern, it had been one of the first modern homes in Houston and was designed by one of the more ascetic modern architects. With the best will, how could Aquarius like it? But the severity of the design was concealed by the variety of furniture, the intensity of the art, the presence of the sculpture and the happy design in fact of a portion of the house: the living room shared a wall with a glassed-in atrium of exotics in bloom. So the surgical intent of the architect was partially overcome by the wealth of the art and by the tropical pressure of the garden whose plants and interior trees, illumined with spotlights, possessed something of the same silence that comes over audience and cast when there is a moment of theater and everything ceases, everything depends on — one cannot say — it is just that no one thinks to cough.

There had been another such moment when he entered the house. In the foyer was a painting by Magritte, a startling image of a room, with an immense rock situated in the centre of the floor. The instant of time suggested by the canvas was comparable to the mood of a landscape in the instant just before something awful is about to happen, or just after, one could not tell. The silences of the canvas spoke of Apollo 11 still circling the moon: the painting could have been photographed for the front page — it hung from the wall like a severed head. As Aquarius met the other guests, gave greetings, took a drink, his thoughts were not free of the painting. He did not know when it had been done — he assumed it was finished many years ago — he was certain without even thinking about it that there has been no intention by the artist to talk of the moon or projects in space, no, Aquarius would assume the painter had awakened with a vision of the canvas and that vision he had delineated. Something in the acrid breath of the city he inhabited, some avidity emitted by a passing machine, some tar in the residue of a nightmare, some ash from the memory of a cremation had gone into the painting of that gray stone — it was as if Magritte had listened to the ending of one world with its comfortable chairs in the parlor, and heard the intrusion of a new world, silent as the windowless stone which grew in the room, and knowing not quite what he had painted, had painted his warning nevertheless. Now the world of the future was dead rock, and the rock was in the room.

At the dinner party to which Aquarius was invited, and Jean de Menil had asked me as his houseguest whether I approved of the invitation list, and of course, who was I to have scruples about the guests, who included Alberto Moravia, the famous Italian novelist; Dacia Moraini, Aquarius; another Italian journalist; and myself; with Mr. and Mrs. de Menil, our hosts. I realized how restricted my education was: I was the only person who could speak only one language. At dinner the conversation moved from English, to Italian, to French, with all the other guests taking part without a slip of syntax. Except Mailer and I. And it was so natural for them to speak in three languages, as the conversation moved to their seat at the table, without effort, making it more embarrassing for me, who knew only one language.

When the moon launching was about to begin, Mailer had by now gone back to the launching pad, I was surprised to find that there was no television in the main house, and that we had to go into the servants' quarters to watch the takeoff. And we did that.

The next morning I wanted to take some photographs of my surroundings, of Houston, and I asked for directions to the nearest film shop; but Jean thought he should call ahead and tell the shop owner that I was coming. It was a polite and understated way of telling him that I was black, and that I was visiting the de Menils of Houston. I picked this up from the courteous manner of his dealing with me. I bought a Polaroid camera, which Jean paid for, and I set out to take pictures of my environment, of the house, of the Magritte, of Norman Mailer, of Alberto Moravia, of everyone, including the maids in whose rooms we had watched the launching of the moon the previous night.

It was time to leave. To return to Bloomington's humidity and to the nearness of the Klan, only nine miles away from the apartment in the middle of the forest; and when I got to my graduate seminar and was asked what happened in Houston, I said, "There was a dinner party, and this Italian writer, Alberto Moravia, and Norman Mailer, and Dacia

Maraini — whom I learned later was the lover of Moravia, who had recommended her for one of Italy's most prestigious prizes — were there." They voiced their astonishment that I did not know that "Moravia is only Italy's best novelist!" And they gave me as a going-away present three paperback copies of his work. It was on my return to Bloomington that the taxicab driver, the same man who had taken me to the airport two weeks earlier, charged me twice as much as he had charged on the way out, in the private Lear jet. I paid for my celebrity.

The next time I saw Mailer, who was no longer Aquarius, but was simply Mailer, was in Chapel Hill, at the University of North Carolina, and the next day, at Duke, to give a lecture and tell the same joke, which drew no laughter from the Chapel Hill students, but which was uproariously greeted on the Duke campus. I wondered why there was this difference in appreciation of dirty jokes, which was what Mailer had told, about his former wife, and her inefficiency in bed, in the sexual game. Not "game": more like a battle. She turned the tables back on him when he speculated about her sexual dexterity, blaming him for any lack of appreciation and effectiveness on that score. It was during this visit that I made him my famous omelette of sardines and eggs, in the home of the chairman of Religious Studies, at Duke, Professor Clarke. No relation of course. This omelette is described in my book about cooking, *Pig Tails 'n' Breadfruit*, later reissued under the title *Love and Sweet Food*. It was on this occasion that I knew that Norman Mailer and I were friends.

I would see Mailer some years later, in Toronto, when he came to give a lecture at the university, after the publication of his blockbuster novel *Arabian Nights*, at a late dinner party at my house on McGill Street, at which were Cynthia Good; Barry Callaghan, who picked a fight with Mailer; and Susan Walker, who did not pick a fight with Mailer.

CHAPTER TWENTY-SEVEN

The Old Boy

Into my life came a man of intrigue, of danger, of drama, of fear, of experience with guns, a man who handled great sums of money, who had consorted with kings and dukes and lords, a man who knew about arms, and about overturning governments, a man not unknown to countries with low political esteem and lower financial dependability, governments tottering from corruptions of all kinds, a man not of the people, but a man to be reckoned with. He christened me, "Old Boy." And I called him "Old Boy" in return. A man of dramatic intrigue, a man who wanted to be a duke in the British system of the peerage; and who was confident that he could convince someone, slightly less royal than the Queen, that it was his right, by birth, that as a Barbadian he had the right pedigree to be so anointed. And he promised me a dukedom, too. He decided that I would be called Lord Austin of Flagstaff. And he laughed, a full-bodied laugh that took all the surrealism out of the joke, and made it serious; and within reach; and it no longer seemed absurd and idealistic. Lord Austin of Flagstaff.

He had just emigrated from London, where he had spent many years, and returned to Barbados where his friend was now Prime Minister. He commanded an important presence with the Cabinet, spent money in large cash amounts like a sailor, but understood better than his beneficiaries that it was an investment in his future and equally an investment in their personal destruction; as the story went — the story goes — for he had created myths around his persona, was larger than life in Barbados, called Little England, for its imitation of English culture and country life, was a Lord in the eyes of the avaricious politicians whom he fed cash to, and with the granting of the only government licence to open and operate a bank, he created another myth that he had buried gold bars in the country district of the Parish of St. John, in which he was born, and had wired them with electricity and dynamite and gun powder against predators, and politicians who were predators.

He booked himself into the Barbados Hilton, at the time the most prestigious hotel residence in the West Indies; and spun a web of carefully scripted behaviour that caused an accounts clerk to draw to the attention of the manager that the Old Boy had racked up a long-distance telephone bill of two thousand Barbados dollars within one week. The alarm went up, and out. And the manager, intimidated by the myth that surrounded the Old Boy, walked soft along the thick carpets of the special suites and tapped like a mouse on the door of the Old Boy's room. And mentioned in equal timidity the small question of the telephone bill. It was, at that time, the largest telephone bill ever racked up in the Barbados Hilton records.

"Of course, Old Boy," the Old Boy said, without batting an eyelid. And he went to his briefcase, strategically open so that the hotel manager could see the contents, and he counted off the required amount of money, in Barbados dollars, and paid the received manager.

"We are sorry to bother you, sir," the manager said, with sincere regret that he had indeed bothered the Old Boy. And downstairs again, in the office, he scolded the worker for almost embarrassing him.

The Old Boy racked up hundreds of dollars in telephone calls to Britain and to his far-flung "empire"-making deals with armaments and weapons, and keeping millions of dollars and pounds in guarded protection, in trust, in the buried vault of his mercantile bank, safe from the clutches of succeeding dictators of the Middle East. Barbados was the safe haven of these gold bars that increased in number as the myth swelled like the bladder of a butchered hog.

When the Old Boy left Barbados, he left a long list of casualties who had accepted money in cheques with his name on them. He went back to a suburb in New York, where he lived with his "daughter." And bided his time, calculating risks and more adventure; and then he called me, from the Toronto airport one cold day in November.

"Old Boy?" He wanted help in finding a place for his two dogs. They were with him, at the moment, in a motel near the airport, and were being fed and petted by the maids. I did not know that dogs were welcomed in motels and hotels in Toronto. "When you are a conservative, the system opens up to you! If you are a radical, the system closes down around you." It was a lesson in politics that I have kept in mind since that cold November morning, when I went to collect him, in my Mercedes-Benz. He was at home in the Benz. In London, they said that he went about in a Rolls-Royce, and dressed in morning suit, complete with silk top hat. But no insignia with the Royal Seal, attesting to the fact that he now wanted to be made an earl of the realm. Some lord, indeed! He was without his "daughter," whom he consistently addressed as "his daughter" and behaved toward her, in public, as if she was in fact, "his daughter" until once, twice, three times in one month of what my mother called "a slip of the tongue," he forgot to mention that she was his daughter! The look in his eye, the glint of the previous night's satisfaction, in bed or in the exchange of a thought, his passion for progeny had been struck.

We all who knew him, knew and hoped and loved the young woman. But numbered amongst "all of we," were the women in our lives, sisters, aunts, and wives. These three groups of women, and as women they were wiser than all of us men put together; all these women saw the "rudeness" in his calling "his woman his daughter."

"We smelled-that-out, long time ago, boy!"

But his magic and the truth in his word were founded in the "presence" of his clothes, suits cut to an English gentleman's taste, and shined shoes, always bright and oiled like a dog's stones. His loyalty to friends, men and women, was expressed not only in the size of "the little something" he gave to politicians, but as a mark of their confidence in his generosity, they took these "little somethings" in the form of cheques; and, with their names on these documents, the other paragraphs in their personal histories were thrown open for the Island-nation to hear and laugh at; but this is the world of West Indian politics and power, and the heavy humidity of sexual boredom, which propelled these desires into gatherings at the home of a foreigner, who saw the opportunity to brag about his political connections and raise his value in the eyes of other foreigners, his friends in Trinidad, who liked these sexual extravagances; so he wired his flat for film and audio, and then captured libelous sexual enjoyments of the Island's aristocracy, and the destruction of their political careers; and sent the evidence captured on raw film and audiotape, by certified letter, to America, to *Playboy* magazine. *Playboy* spotted in this film, the faces of politicians and barristers-at-law, judges and businessmen; and understood the scandal that would erupt in the small Island-nation, and sought corroboration, and asked the Old Boy, safe up in England, to say who is who, and who was who, on the exposing film. The effect was instantaneous. And irrevocable. And men vanished. One in a large fishing boat, out to sea, at Gravesend Beach, tied they say at his ankles with bangles not of silver, as in the days of first slavery and transportation from Africa over the bilious waves of the Atlantic Ocean, but shackled by the material of concrete blocks custom-made to suit his delicate ankles and dropped deep into the concealing sea. "Never to be seen again." And indeed, the promise made by those whose reputation was blemished by the images on the film, was kept, just as members of a secret society keep promises. Not even the three daily newspapers wasted an item of news to commemorate the historical event.

The negatives of the film were seen by the Old Boy, and the price of silence asked for them was paid in cash — not cheques this time! — in hard, cold English pounds, translated into Yankee dollars. The negatives were handed over to the Old Boy. I am told he made a barbecue of the evidence and dropped them one bright morning into the water below a bridge that spanned from Manhattan over to Brooklyn, just as he would have dropped the ash from a Trumpeter cigarette, back years before, into the silky, thick, high-smelling water of the Barbados Careenage.

Suddenly the news left Barbados and came to the United States, in the vacationing warmth of Florida, where men and women retiring from careers and from scandal always appear. And it was no different for The Dipper (Errol Barrow, as he is known), who all of a sudden exchanged the discussions in a Cabinet room for the argument of practical politics in a graduate students seminar. They say he was brilliant. The heavy showers back in the Island which could spoil an early morning of shooting small birds and then skinning them and then eating them in one or two mouthfuls of sweet crunching bones and skeletons and little flesh, washed down with rum punch made from Mount Gay Premium twenty-five-year-old rum, freshened by fresh limes, squeezed also over the baked birds, to clean the mind and erase the blemish of the past of stress and anxiety over West Indian "Governaunce," to use the English word used by the Old Boy, still wanting to be an English earl. Earl Old Boy of Sin-Joseph — the Parish in the Island where he was born.

I was a professor on a one-year contract, in the Black Studies Program at the University of Texas, at Austin. The telephone call had come from a man named Bernth Lindfors, one last-minute night, because "George Lamming, who was appointed, cannot come, and we wonder if, with this late notice, hope you don't mind if you could come and take up the appointment?"; and when I asked him where he calling from, and he said, "The University of Texas, at Austin ..."

"Austin? Is there a town named Austin?"

"Austin-Texas."

"Well, if they can name a town after my name, then I'll come ..."

You could bathe in the swimming pool of the apartment building built round the rectangle of the pool; and you could walk a quarter-mile up a slope and enter the "all-night" grocery store, and come back home to the townhouse-apartment, connected to all the other townhouse apartments of two and a half bedrooms each, on two floors, with furniture left there by the builders, "rented furnished, sir," the real estate agent said, "so you, as a professor won't have to waste your time looking for furniture, for we've thought of everything to make your life in Austin, comfortable, Austin. I hear your name is Austin. This will be a good, happy place for you for the year!" And you could walk through the aisles in the grocery, and feel you were walking through rows of flower gardens in a luscious tropical garden back in the Island. And I changed my habit of shopping and shopped only at night now, in the thick Texas humidity, and in my basket were the same items time after time: lamb chops; North Carolina sweet potatoes; fresh peanuts in the shell, also from North Carolina; fresh pecans; small, round beets; large beefsteak tomatoes; Brussels sprouts; virgin olive oil; long grain basmati rice; a Virginia ham, pepper-coated, made in Smithfield; pork rind and salted pork parts with which to season the rice; canned peaches cut into halves; sour cream to serve on the peaches; champagne and red and white wines for the cooking. One night I bought a lobster; and, after that, changed my shopping, substituting the lamb chops for racks of lamb. Going up the slope, from the lake from the river that flowed behind the furnished townhouse, and not looking back to see the vista and how beautiful my Texan surroundings were, my full concentration seemed to be, at this time, for this long year, on food. This was before the introduction of cooking shows on television. I cannot remember whether I had a television. I had a Mercedes-Benz, bottle-green in colour, automatic gearshift, a 250S, which I had bought the year before in Chapel Hill, North Carolina, when I taught at Duke University. This Mercedes-Benz I used for the visits to my mother, who lived in Brooklyn at the time; filled with 8-track cassettes, filled with the music of Aretha Franklin, James Brown, Sam and Dave, Johnny Mathis, Billie Holiday, Dinah Washington, Nina Simone, Sarah Vaughan, Miles Davis, John Coltrane, Barry White, Otis Redding, Jimmy Witherspoon, Louis Armstrong, Duke Ellington, Count Basie, Errol Garner, Billy Eckstein, Rufus Harley (a man who played jazz on Scottish bagpipes), B.B. King, Sam Cooke, Sonny Rawlins, J.J. Johnson, Elvin Jones, Art Blakey and the Jazz Messengers, Ahmad Jamal, George Shearing, Dizzy Gillespie, Charles Lloyd, Keith Jarrett. And one track of a song, "She Loves You, Yeah, Yeah, Yeah," by a British group, named the Beatles, which I never listened to, and which was given to me on my birthday one hot July in Texas, by a young beautiful white woman, the best student in my seminar on creative writing. Driving to Brooklyn from Austin, Texas, was an exciting journey, passing through all those Southern towns, and one-pump gas stations, things that appeared almost daily with different disastrous associations in the newspaper and on television, charting the progress of the slow pace of racial integration in the entire country of

America, not only as northerners, — including Canadians — thought was the case; but the excitement ended the moment I reached New York, and parked the Mercedes-Benz. And to reach New York, and hear some of the jazz musicians recorded on 8-tracks in the boxes that held the tapes, either in person in Greenwich Village, or through the German speakers in the Benz, life was beautiful. And this excitement turned to fear, and the fear of loss, the minute the Benz was parked and locked up in the laneway beside my mother's house on Avenue A in Brooklyn, or even inside the locked chain-linked gate behind the house, beside the dog, under the watchful window with the light that came on to frighten the thief, when any motion was close enough to turn the security light on. The dog was still sleeping when I walked through the back door. And to hate to open the eyes the next morning, to see that the glass on the driver's side was broken, or the entire glass taken out, in the darkness the security light did not pierce.

This cold November morning is the third time they have broken into the Benz. All of the 8-tracks have been stolen. The thief is careful; tidy. He has left the mark of his carefulness behind. It is expressed in the three boxes that he has left behind. Closed. On this third break-in of the Benz, parked always "close to the house so the thieves would think we watching them," all the other 8-tracks were taken out. The Beatles tape is left back. It is as if the thief was scornful of the juxtaposition of jazz and rhythm and blues so close to rock and roll. And the handwriting on the piece of paper, torn out from my own notebook that lay on the front seat, to hold notes of direction from the Deep South to the North of Brooklyn and integration, and in scratchy handwriting, set down in the haste of burglary, with the one word.

Mutthurfucker!

"You think the thief was telling you something?"

It is only a mother who could think of this, and ask a question to make you think of her question.

"You think you should keep more of the Beatles in your car, when you are travelling up from the South, again?"

The reputation of the Prime Minister Errol Barrow was known outside of Barbados. I had no trouble discussing his invitation to give a guest lecture and the conditions of the visit to the campus of the University of Texas at Austin, including the red carpet that was to be stretched from the plane in the small airport to the door of the terminal entering the VIP Lounge. And the fee, five times the usual "honorarium" pittance that universities get away with, "with murder," my mother explains their "damn cheapness, inviting big people and paying them peanuts," the fee that the prime minister was offered, without negotiation, caused him to accept the invitation as an honour, and as a "good thing to get away from Miami for a while."

It was not a departmental lecture, but a university lecture in the sense that students and faculty from all departments were invited; and, as it turned out, did in fact attend. The lecture was to be one hour; and if the prime minister wished, he could take questions. The topic, of his own choosing, was not announced before the lecture, and when he was approaching forty minutes, and was entering into the sixtieth minute, I went back in memory to his campaign speeches when he was in an election, when we would stand for three hours, and follow his words, remembering that he was a brilliant defence lawyer, when he was the Leader of the Opposition, when it was in his interest to talk longer than anybody else in the House of Assembly. Here now, he was on a campaign swing; and his audience was students listening to every word that fell from his lips, in a convocation hall, since no lecture room was large enough — in anticipation — in this university in the Deep South, in 1975, still close enough to the civil rights movement, for memory of bloodshed and brutality and injustice to be fresh enough in the mind.

When it was over, when the questions from the audience were answered, it was ten-thirty, still too early for a prime minister to be going to bed. He was known as "a night hawk"; but it was the first time I was a host of a prime minister, and a university campus is not the most sophisticated atmosphere in which to provide suitable entertainment for a head of government. So, I tried the easy way out of my obligations.

"If it wasn't so late, Prime Minister," I said, "I would take you to my apartment, with a few graduate students, and have a drink, and if it wasn't so late, perhaps prepare a snack ..."

"You know that I don't go to bed early!"

"I have some lamb chops, but they're frozen ..."

There were four graduate students, members of my creative writing seminar; and they were eager to continue the question and answer part of the lecture; and they needed a drink; and as students, always hungry, and already acquainted with my cooking — I'd had them over to the apartment many times, they were urging me, suggesting that there were three cars available to take us to the apartment beside the river ...

"It's a lake, sir."

"It's a river!"

"Lake!"

"River!"

We stopped at the all-night grocery, and got some more lamb chops, and champagne, and when we got to the apartment, with the water in the swimming pool placid as a sheet of smooth ice, it was as if we were back in the Island, preparing for a party with tourists.

"You don't have to thaw out meat before you cook it. Lamb chops and steak can be put into the oven, frozen. It improves the taste, and you can control it better, if you want rare, or medium rare ..."

Years later, when he had appointed me the general manager of the Caribbean Broadcasting Corporation (CBC), in Barbados, there were many occasions at which I was at his table, formal and informal; at the official residence, and at the private retreat down in the country, where we ate small birds, no bigger than a small fist which you put into your mouth, and crunched the delicious taste of bones and head, and tender meat; and there were occasions when the roasted pork with the crackling like a sheet of gold on the white meat of the pig reared and grown by him, Saturday nights of the local delicacy of black pudding and souse, washed down with the strong glasses of Tanqueray gin and Kola Tonic.

But before Barbados and CBC, there was the appointment as cultural attaché at the Barbados Embassy in Washington, D.C. It was
during the administration of Richard Nixon, president of America,
during the Watergate scandal, during a time when diplomats, at the
ambassadorial level were being snatched from their offices, from their
chauffeur-driven cars, from their guarded residences and chancelleries,
in an epidemic of diplomatic kidnappings. The prime minister said
to me, "Tom, I want you to go up to Washington, perhaps two days
a week, or on weekends, and become my cultural attaché. And about
salary, you don't need any more money. You're working here at the
university. Perhaps, an honorarium. What about a hundred dollars a
day?" I took the appointment out of respect and love for the prime
minister, out of a sense of nationalism, out of stupidity, and for the
year I was in the employment of the embassy, my salary was less
than that of the chauffeur, Forde, a retired policeman from the Royal
Barbados Police Constabulary.

The Barbados diplomatic corps, consisting of ambassador; counsellor; first and second secretary; and myself, cultural attaché. Those who
had diplomatic immunity developed the contention that there was no difference in the "prestige" and "status" of Barbados, a tiny, poor country
and that of Canada; and with this argument, a "private and confidential
— eyes only" was sent by diplomatic pouch to The Right Honourable
Prime Minister, Privy Counsellor, at government headquarters. The note
respectfully inquired of the prime minister the procedure to be followed,
in case His Excellency the Ambassador was kidnapped in the brewing
spate of diplomatic kidnappings now boiling up in Washington, D.C.

Ambassadors from large, powerful nations had been kidnapped,
and enormous sums of money in cash were demanded; and some were
indeed paid. One can imagine the jocularity of the Right Honourable
Gentleman as he opened the "eyes-only" note, perhaps during a full
day of prime ministerial appointments; or perhaps, down in the country on a Sunday morning, crunching the brittle delicious bones of a
baked bird; even, perhaps, drinking a refreshing glass of Tanqueray gin
and Kola Tonic, the Gentleman's jocularity can only be imagined, in
the bemused company of Cabinet members. Certainly, one is justified
in this speculation.

The prime minister, with a Barbadian apprehension of Barbadian arrogance and the prejudice bound by class and to a lesser extent, also by education — throwing intelligence and common sense to the wind, replied as was his duty, and diplomatic responsibility to do.

"Let us hope and pray," the letter, sent in the diplomatic pouch, under the confidential seal, and with EYES ONLY stamped on the red, white, and blue airmail envelope, "that they do not ask for more than twenty dollars, Barbadian — (BDS) $20.00 — otherwise, he gone through the eddoes!"

The matter of kidnapping and the anxiety manufactured in the heat of the epidemic spreading through Washington D.C., was never brought up again. But before this decision was made, to the disappointment of some, as I listened to them at luncheon in a nearby Indian restaurant, eating Saag Gosht and basmati rice, and drinking Heineken beer, arguing and speculating and hoping that the amount of money for their ransom to be paid by the Barbados government, for their release, would reflect their importance, and be comparable to the hundreds of thousands of dollars in American currency that was being paid, almost every week, for diplomats from the "developed" countries. But after the receipt of the prime minister's note, advising caution and respecting modesty, the arguments of personal worth, and national embarrassment by the kidnapping, all this evaporated in the humidity of egotism.

Back home! Barbados. I am now at the radio and television station. It is in the Pine. It is 1975. I grew up about one mile from where I am now. It is a Friday morning. I am at work. The members of my staff are shocked that I would come to work on the first day of my appointment as general manager of the Caribbean Broadcasting Corporation. The chief announcer, a woman, expresses her shock. "But, Mr. Clarke, you're the general manager! We didn't expect you to come to work on the first day ..."

But there are things to do. Behaviour to be corrected. Behaviour, sanctified by years and years of incompetence and disregard of the station's customers, to be changed, and improved upon. I feel I have been appointed to this job to "Barbadianize the station" — putting the emphasis on news, current affairs features, sports, and especially education, in a Barbadian context, so that the image of Barbados, in music and in social behaviour, would be the focus of broadcasting. And the first item on my schedule is to cut down on the time senior staff takes for lunch — three hours, instead of the regulated time of one hour. This behaviour is typical in a colony: senior staff take the liberty and assume the privilege of taking three-hour lunches because they feel that senior staff can behave in this way, a way that expressed their superiority to the other staff, in particular the non-skilled staff, and their self-importance.

On the first day, I am leaving my office to be driven into Town, by my chauffeur — I cannot drive because I do not know the way— to have a business lunch. I come out of my office, near the entrance, and I see a white Barbadian sitting on a chair, waiting to see someone in the advertisement department; and I recognize him; we were at Harrison College together, years ago. I greet him and he greets me, "Oh Christ, Tom! Welcome back home!" I am having lunch at Brown Sugar restaurant, a favourite place for the upper middle-class Barbadian to eat. But more compelling than this status is that the food is excellent. It is "Bajan food." Souse; split pea soup, complete with pig tails and flour dumplings; cou-cou and steamed flying fish; roast pork; dried peas and rice; yellow split peas and rice; and cassava pone — and many other Bajan delicacies.

I am having lunch with Harold Hoyte, the managing editor of the Barbados *Nation* newspaper, an enterprising daily started by him, a middle-class Barbadian, and run almost entirely by black Barbadians, to compete with the conservative, older daily the *Barbados Advocate*. When I was at the embassy in Washington, D.C., in 1972, the board of the *Nation* newspaper, seeking investors, approached me for that financial support, but I was in no position to invest. Another ironical bit of history common to me and Harold Hoyte is that when he was in Toronto studying journalism at Ryerson, he was the first important editor of *Contrast*, a black weekly that specialized in reminding the Canadian black community of the existence of racism, especially the "racial profiling" rampant throughout the country, and in Toronto in particular; and when Harold had to return to Barbados, at the conclusion of his studies, I was asked to act as editor until the newspaper could find a permanent replacement.

So, Harold and I had a lot to talk about in this historic reunion. Also present was Eddie Rochester, who went through Combermere School for Boys with me; and then I met him, a second secretary, at the embassy in Washington, D.C., when I was the cultural attaché. Eddie was on holiday. As it would turn out, Harold Hoyte, whom I considered to be a friend, turned out to be my most effective detractor, writing articles which compromised me, encouraging his staff to write columns that assaulted my character, all in the name of "the freedom of the press."

With my installation in a house near to the Cave Hill campus of the University of the West Indies, and helped in my orientation by woman chosen for me for her political loyalty to the Democratic Labour Party, the party now in power, Harold would come often to lunch, cou-cou and Bajan stew made by my maid, in such lip-smacking deliciousness, unsurpassed by any other maid in the entire country.

It was a leisurely lunch. Two and a half hours. When my chauffeur parked the small car in the space reserved for the general manager, when the dust in the parking lot had risen and blinded our vision of the entrance, and when it cleared, the same businessman was sitting in the same chair, waiting to be taken into the studio, to record his advertisement, which had been discussed and which was supposed to be aired that same evening, during the seven o'clock television news.

"Are you still here?"

"Still here."

"Who are you waiting for?"

He called the name of the staff member.

"How long you been waiting?"

"Three hours, Tom."

I knew I was back home.

I took him into my office.

The worst was to come. The staff, from the heads of the radio and the television departments down to reporters and directors of news, all resented my management. The union steward set in motion a campaign designed to undermine me; and the stupidity of it was such that I ignored his machinations. It was the first of many mistakes I made. Another mistake I made, this one more disastrous, was based upon my ignorance of social custom and the effect social custom has on class, and colour, and status. I decided I had to meet every member of staff from the janitor up to the assistant manager, in a social atmosphere, the two of us, to assure every one of my employees of the fairness of my treatment, and the protection of their rights. I decided to take some of them to lunch at a restaurant, and some to my home. I thought it was a wonderful experiment. But as I said, I had forgotten the ingrained class and colour prejudice that lurked in all aspects of social behaviour, after all these years still, in Barbados, from the 1930s right up to the 1970s. My mistake was applying a Canadian mould to the unsettled, shifting volcanic mentality of the Barbadian.

The first demonstration of annoyance came from the leading announcer, a woman. She resented the fact that the general manager would invite a junior staff member in the radio department to his home, to lunch, before he had first invited someone of her status. And the volcano erupted in whispers of disbelief that were not heard outside the clique of the aggrieved announcer. Things became worse: the union began thinking of a strike; and thinking of strikes, the animus turned to the contemplation of assault, the atmosphere at the station became tense, and there developed a tinge of animosity between myself and the staff, particularly those who were in the camp of the woman who resented the luncheon arrangement initiated by me.

Things grew worse than I had imagined possible. The prime minister heard about this, and what he heard, in more detail than my own spies were able to uncover.

"There are threats on your life," the prime minister said.

"You gotta be kidding!" I wanted to tell the prime minister. But you can't speak to a prime minister in this manner of disrespect.

So, my disbelief remained silent.

"Go the police inspector and get a gun."

"A gun?"

"Get a .38."

My speechlessness was barely able to contain my astonishment. The last time I had held a real gun was at the disastrous Cadet Corps Camp at Walkers, in 1950, at this time, about twenty-five years before; and the gun I had used; lying on the damp sand, behind a wall of bags filled with heavy, wet sand, lying on my stomach, holding the machine gun, following the instructions of the regimental sergeant-major, a gravelled-voice Englishman with a Cockney accent: "Squeeze the bloody trigger, boy! Squeeze the bloody trigger!"; in a euphoria of self-importance, becoming a real soldier, which was my ambition to become at that time; following in the cut-down brown polished boots, now made to look like shoes, of Second Lieutenant Frederick "Sleepy" Smith, who taught me Latin, who taught me to like Latin and Virgil, and made me "sing of a man and a hero, who first sailed from the shoes of Troy ..."; and before that two weeks of pretending to be real soldiers and seeing my ambition crystallize like the breaking of morning so close to the sea, in tents on the soggy sand the colour of coral, the guns I used in training, in drill, in parades for the King's Birthday, for Victoria Day, for the new Queen's coronation and following birthdays, were the rifles chiselled and sawed by the school carpenter, made of board; and then the relics of the Boer War, .303s that had their firing pins pulled out like rotten teeth. We could not, with this precaution, shoot out our small, still unriped testacles, by accident.

"Yes, Tom," the police inspector said. I was in his office, at Central Police Station, in the Main Guard. Years before, corresponding with my days at Combermere School for Boys, I would be in this same Main Guard, delivering my stepfather's "food." He was a private then. And he rose in the ranks, to become a lance corporal, which was his final rank when he left years later, on the brink of retirement. The inspector knew who I was: not only general manager, but "Lance Corporal 434 Luke's little boy"; and "Jesus Christ, Tom, welcome back home. Now, the gun the prime minister want you to have ..."

The inspector called me by the nickname I am known by in Barbados. The way he used it made me comfortable; and took the seriousness out of the meeting and the cause of the meeting. "Tom, Tom the piper's son, stole a pudding and away he ran..."

"You ever fire one o' these, before?"

"No, Inspector."

"You want me to show you? Incidentally, wha' kind o' gun you want?"

"I don't know."

"You sure you know how to use one o' these?"

"I was in the Cadets."

"This isn't no board-gun, Tom. This is a .38."

I held the .38 and was shocked by its weight, and its ugliness, and its danger, and the sudden thrust of blood in my veins and in my head, and the violence which the spasm made me think of; and I was a New York cop, with a gun holstered under his armpits so that its ugly bulk would not be seen under the ill-fitting jacket, and I wondered who I would shoot first ...

I put the .38 into the waist of my trousers. I did not have a holster.

"Oh shite, Tom! You want to lick-out your two balls, in case there's an accident? Wear it some place else ... in a safer place."

I was ready to go, and I wished the inspector well; and he wished me well; and good aiming; and my chauffeur was bringing the car around under the trees which bore yellow berries and dropped them on your head, and you then pressed them, to a small report, under your shoes; and as I held my hand on the rear door, the inspector came out, smiling, enjoying himself, at my expense.

"You forget these, Tom!"

In his hand was a small box.

"You going need the bullets, man."

My unpopularity spread to the point where I became the subject of a song by a famous calypso singer, Sir Don. The song, titled "Tom Say," became a national hit. I reproduce the lyrics below.

> If I only acting and you are shivering in your shoes
> Dotting your i's, crossing your t's, and minding your p's
> and q's.
> When they really appoint me, you can imagine how it will be.
> I have come to change the system, just you wait and see.

Chorus: A Barbadian-language station (Tom say), every man, Jack (under)
My administration have to get in at eight o'clock
The weatherman from television must wear a shirtjack
I know you don't like me and you discuss me behind my back

My name all is in the paper and you're trying with all your might
To run me back to Canada, but I don't care whether he have the right
Regardless how you bad-talk me, I am putting it to you
I was born and bred in this country and I will do what I've come to do

Chorus

You can ask anyone who know me, anyone who know where I'm from
They will tell you that you've got to show me the ball that shoot down Nelson
When I make a final decision, only heaven could change my mind
But you're butting against a rock stone when you butt up to me this time

Chorus

You must be seeing my chauffeur driving, how I sit down in the back
How impressive I just be looking, do you envy me just for that?
Now let me tell you I am a hard seed, loaded with sex appeal
And all the women have agreed I can do whatever I feel

Chorus

The controversy continued to rage over my suitability as general manager and my daring to instill discipline and improve the technical efficiency of the presentation of news, the dress, and the image of the presenters on the television news, all part of my intention to "Barbadianize" the radio and television station. I was getting fed up. I was realizing that I should have taken the advice of my friend, William Ashleigh McMurtry, who had advised me not to accept the appointment. It was in the roof bar of the Park Plaza Hotel, when the bar took up almost all of the space on the roof, and was, as such, filled on Friday afternoons with successful writers, meaning writers of advertising copy, and advertising executives, when for sinking a ball in the putting competitions rewarded you with a bottle of champagne, which social activities were staged, until too many young women, forlorn through broken love, took the shorter route to happiness and jumped off the roof. But that Friday afternoon, Bill said that I had left Barbados too long, more than twenty years now, and to return after such a long absence would be a big mistake. "It will never work out," he said. "You can't go back home again!"

With the ugly revolver in my waistband, ignoring the caution of the Inspector, I would walk through the television studios, with the handle of my .38 visible, each time I thought I needed to remind the staff who was boss, pulling back the tunic of my shirt jack suit to let them see that I was armed, that I "carried a piece" … all my friends who were Cabinet ministers, and especially my friends in the Loyal Opposition, either carried their "pieces" hidden under the tunics of their shirtjack suits, or in their glove compartments. One carried his revolver, "an American piece," in his briefcase bought in America.

On this Friday afternoon, I am home in the master bedroom, whose window opens on to the backyard turned by me on weekends, into a kitchen garden, with a few beds of roses. Rose bushes begin from the porch under which the car is parked; on that whole side, right round to the back, under the bedroom window. I am in a deep trough of slumber caused by exhaustion and by the humidity, and I go off into a sweet pleasant dream, and Miles Davis's trumpet is carrying me on a peaceful wave of "Someday My Prince Will Come," and all of a sudden I am outside my bedroom in the dream that is in Toronto, and the humidity turns to a chill, and I am not on green, thick grass, I am in a snow bank and the snow is thick; and I am barefooted. My legs begin to get cold. My body is cold. I am shivering. I am dressed in blue pajamas, blue with white stripes; and I am once again in the large queen-sized bed, pulling the sheets up to keep me warm; and I see the muzzle of a gun, and when I look carefully, when my eyes filled with rheum, clear, it is not a muzzle of a gun. It is the cock of the pipe of the garden hose. And water, in full cold force, is coming at me like bullets from a machine gun. The water clears my head, and brings me back from the snow and cold of the dream, to the bed now soaked, and just as cold.

My gun!

I jump out of bed, and rush outside, without the gun.

I rush back inside for the gun. In drawers, under the bed, under the pillow, in the desk … I found the gun.

I rush back outside, tearing skin from my face in my collision with the rose bushes, and I am shouting. "Who's there? Halt! Who goes there? I'm going to shout you! Who's there?"

I have to go back inside the house. I have forgotten the bullets. I have never loaded the gun. I have never walked with bullets in the gun. I have never walked with bullets in my pockets. And I cannot remember where I put them.

So, I stand on the wet grass, and I imagine that I hear footsteps running down the hill behind the house; and I imagine that I hear a car starting up, down the white gravelled road; and I wait for the car to drive past my house; and I wait with the unloaded gun in my hand, for the car to pass. There is no other way for the car to go. And the car comes slowly toward me, and no dust and no pebbles in the road, rise from the tires and from the slow speed.

"Hello, Tom, what are you doing with that in your hand?"

It is my neighbour, the barrister-at-law. "I going to the supermarket."

And he drops me at the supermarket. And he bought a bottle of Mount Gay Rum and I bought a bottle of Bombay gin and two steaks. And I forgot about the intruders. Or was there only one intruder?

~

It is another Friday, and things have got even worse. The Cabinet met on Thursday. Cabinet meetings are confidential, the most confidential occurrences in the country. But word leaks out that the general manager of the broadcasting corporation, Tom Clarke, the name I am known by back home, will be fired. I scorn the leaked information. I went to school with every member of the Cabinet; and the school tie in Barbados is thicker than blood.

The prime minister's car drives up in the yard of the broadcasting station. Word spreads. Whenever the prime minister drives up in the yard, in his maroon beaten-up Mercedes-Benz, woe is in the clouds over the yard and the buildings, and word spreads faster than a fire in a cane field. Somebody is going to be fired. Someone is going to be sacked from the Cabinet. Somebody is going to be scolded. Something tragic is going to happen. Even, sometimes, a prime minister of another West Indian country is going to be called "a bandit"; or the United States is going to be called an "imperialistic, bandit country."

You are cautious to call a prime minister your friend, even though the relationship you had with him started out friendly; the prime minister visiting your house in Toronto whenever he was in Canada bargaining and exchanging memories with Pierre Trudeau, the prime minister of Canada at the time, the two of them (along with Fidel Castro, and Forbes Burnham, first president of the Republic of Guyana) having attended the London School of Economics at the same time; you are cautious even though the prime minister comes into your study, selects books he would like to have, would like to borrow, "I taking these, Tom. You could always get another copy, around the corner, tomorrow morning!"; even though he would eat with us, and sometimes, he and the minister of foreign affairs, Sir Cameron Tudor, would join talents, and cook in a suite in the Park Plaza Hotel, for years and years the hotel frequented by Barbadian officials; even though the prime minister and the minister of foreign affairs were driven by me, in the old Mercedes-Benz, down Spadina Avenue, south of College Street, to Kensington Market, and I watched the two men put their hands in the brine barrel, and twirled it round, to select the right pieces of pig tails to cook with their peas and rice, the minister of foreign affairs taking advice from the prime minister; even though he and I visited the President Lyndon Johnson Library the morning after his lecture at the University of Texas at Austin, telling me in all seriousness, "Johnson was the best president the States has ever had. History will prove me correct"; even though I did not take him seriously; even though these anecdotes were the ribs in the structure of our relationship which began when he had first returned to Barbados from England and the Royal Air Force and the London School of Economics, and Lincoln's Inn, and was the junior barrister-at-law at the bar, and, as such, had to take a murder case with no possibility of victory in his defence of the man condemned to hang by his neck, even before he stepped into the dock to hear his history, and was saved by the inexhaustible summing up ... the other junior barrister-at-law, Julian Marryshaw, saw the guilt in the brief of another man brought up for murder, and saw the futility of wasting too many words, and addressed the jury in his summing up, for one hour, fifty-nine and a half minutes, and in due diligence associating time spent with the evaporation of innocence, found the man guilty, and he was taken from "that place, to a place and hanged by his neck until he was dead, dead, dead. Fifty-nine and a pivvy of minutes it took Julian Marryshaw, LLB, Barrister-at-Law, Gray's Inn. But "The Skipper," "Dipper-Barr," talked for three days, wore the attentiveness of the twelve men, the peers of the condemned man, in the grip of his longevity and legal mastery of English law.

So, even though this was our history, the Friday afternoon when he entered my office, without knocking, just pushing the door open. The door was already open; ajar.

He addressed me as Mr. Clarke. Tom I was to him, on occasions when things between the two of us were good. Austin, when things between us were not so good. But Mr. Clarke was reserved for reprimand, criticism of my broadcasting policy, to remind me who was who, and who was prime minister.

I knew then that something had happened to my support from friends in the Cabinet. Erosion had taken place. Perhaps, they had been helped along in their change of heart and, my constituency dissolved by the same usage of longevity and mastery of law that he had used years before to get the murderer off.

"Mr. Clarke, can I have a gin and Kola Tonic?"

I knew the gin he liked. I knew the Kola Tonic he liked. I knew the proportion of gin to Kola Tonic he liked. I knew the amount of ice cubes he liked in his drink.

He was holding his leather briefcase on his lap. He was running his right hand over its rich, cured leather. The noise of the ice cubes in the crystal half-pint tumbler was the only sign of life in the stifling office. My stupidity and my amateur comprehension of diplomacy made me speak first. And the moment after I opened my mouth, I knew the battle was lost.

"I understand, sir, that you are not satisfied with my work here."

He took a sip of the gin and Kola Tonic, the colour of burnished gold in the glass.

"I feel that if you did not like my work, since you came to my house in Toronto, and told me I could contribute, since I had made enough money in Canada and you came to my apartment in Austin-Texas, to ask me to take this job, you would tell me, you would be the first to tell me that something was going wrong …"

He took a sip of the gin and Kola Tonic.

"I am not your advisor," he said.

"But you came to my house in Austin-Texas, and in Toronto, and asked me to come home to be in charge of the broadcasting …"

He took a sip of the rattling ice cubes in the glass with the gin and Kola Tonic.

"I am not your minister. Peter Morgan is your minister."

"But I would have thought, sir, that you could have advised me …"

He did not take another sip of the drink.

I had lost all sense of judgment, of proportion, or respect, of propriety, and of self-preservation.

I go back to Toronto, to the Kensington Market, to the Royal Suite at the Park Plaza Hotel, to the Johnson Library in Austin-Texas; to the meetings we had in Washington in his hotel, about a vicious article written in the *New York Times*, to which he wanted me to reply to lessen the sting of scandal hinted in the newspaper article, to the early Sunday morning meetings down in the country, in St. Lucy, when we crunched the skeleton of small birds, heads and spinal cords, Lilliputian in size but gargantuan in taste and delicacy; and ran our teeth along the symmetrical alignment of bones in the skeletons of barbaras, jacks, and flying fish; and washed them all down with rum, and jokes about other West Indian prime ministers, and slamming dominoes and dealing cards: impromptu games of five-card stud. And now, he is talking and the crystal glass with the melting gin and Kola Tonic is silent. The ice has become cold water, like the veins left in his body for I am killing him.

"And Mr. Clarke, I would like to buy the bookshelves you put in the house, when you leave. Not that I am saying when you are to leave, I am not saying that, but when you do leave I wonder if you can leave the bookshelves. I will buy them. Janine wants to move into the house, and she likes reading ..."

Before it has come to this state of betrayal and cold realization that you cannot invest time and sincerity in a friendship with a prime minister, before I was able to see the multiple personalities in the character of this man, before I saw with equal chilliness how I had allowed myself to be a victim in the friendship, I had arranged for him to teach at Yale University as a visiting lecturer; and he was going to be made a Fellow, with full privileges, to eat in dining halls, to do research in all the libraries on campus, and to receive one thousand American dollars a month, for the three months in a term. He was excited and chest-puffingly proud of this; and became arrogant in mentioning it to members of his own Cabinet. Yale! Yale was better than the place he had been teaching at in Miami. My friend at Yale, now Master of Berkeley College, Professor Robin Winks, was enthusiastic to make these arrangements for the prime minister. Professor Winks was invited by me as my guest, at my expense, to spend two weeks in Barbados. He was going to look at the Centre for Race and Multicultural Studies on the Cave Hill Barbados campus of the University of the West Indies; graduate students in his history classes were going to come to Barbados, and write papers on the collection of books bought from Richard B. Moore, a Barbadian who owned a bookstore in Harlem and lived in Brooklyn, and cooked cou-cou and steamed flying fish every Friday night; and these papers would be left in Barbados; and an exchange of Barbadian graduate students and faculty would go up to Yale. It was a coup for Barbados.

All I wanted from the minister of tourism, who was the minister in charge also of broadcasting, "my minister," was a free ticket for Professor Winks, in gratitude. The Professor was bringing his son, and had paid for his son's ticket. The house I was providing. And I had asked my maid to be the Professor's maid during his visit. I had asked Freddie Clarke, a solicitor to rent me the house on Paradise Heights that had the swimming pool. It was more than a fair exchange. It was robbery by the Barbados government. One airplane ticket from LaGuardia in New York, to Bridgetown. The minister refused. And the prime minister, through him, told me I was "too cavalier" in the arrangements I made for the exchange of scholars.

I called Professor Winks, even before I left Barbados for home, and told him that I could no longer be the negotiator between Yale and the Barbados government. He advised me to call the whole thing off. "Authors and prime ministers!" he said. And nothing else.

I informed the prime minister — now Mr. Barrow to me — that the "deal" was off. He made no comment. It was like a nod of the head, in a conversation.

I am back home. In Toronto. It is 1977. The prime minister is no longer prime minister. He is Mr. Barrow. Leader of Her Majesty's Loyal Opposition. I am a Progressive-Conservative candidate for the Ontario riding of York South, in the provincial elections; and if I should win, and I am confident that this will be the judgment, I am sure I shall be a member of William Davis's Cabinet. But I do not win. Donald Macdonald, then leader of the New Democratic Party, takes the seat with remarkable ease, and plurality. I come second. With the questionable distinction of having got the most votes any Progressive-Conservative candidate has ever got, in the history of elections. And the highest, up until the last elections in 2004!

Things back in Barbados are bleak. One day, to be prime minister: the next day, to be Leader of the Opposition, is best described in Bible terms: "thriving today, tomorrow to be dead." The prime minister was dead. A dead fish in the sea floating amongst swimming sharks and attacking barracudas. And he was lonely.

My book, *The Prime Minister*, is published in 1976. The prime minister of Barbados now is Mr. G.M. "Tom" Adams. He mistakes that *The Prime Minister* refers to him. Political events and fortune have overturned the context. The novel, set during the reign of one "monarch," is published when that monarch is no longer ruling, and his successor — the same kind of monarch: "six o' one, half-dozen o' the next" — assumes not only the crown and sceptre, but also the personality and persona of the other. The temperament of ruling is the same.

The Prime Minister is, I must admit, a vindictive book. But it is not unfair. It is taken out of context. And it is banned. And the author, though not officially banned also, is encouraged not to visit Barbados, and this is said in a language that is filled with the nuance of deceit and nuance that characterizes Barbadian language, that is spoken with foreboding. But I do not mind. The book is selling well, in spite of scorching, negative reviews. The book is smuggled into Barbados and sold at great profit; and everybody reads it, not through interest in its literary value, but to try to "detect" the real person in the society from the "fiction" of their character in the novel. But whether the author has written a note that "any similarity of the characters of this book, with persons in real life, is purely accidental, and is not intended," the public disregard this, and pick out their neighbours from amongst the "fictional characters."

But my mind is on politics; and becoming a minister of government. Perhaps, minister of education. Or, minister of multiculturalism. Or, minister of the black diaspora. Or, the black minister.

I lose weight, canvassing. Climbing stairs, going up to the penthouse in apartment buildings and working down to the ground floor, stuffing pamphlets into mailboxes, and finding some of my campaign material placed in less conspicuous places, in the garbage chutes, or on the floor, or in the lobby; and in turn retaliating; for this is a kind of war; and losing house through the enormity of debt; and losing face, when the West Indians are insulted that I would run for the "conservatives"; and losing patience. But mainly, losing weight, and having to take my suits and trousers to a tailor who specializes in reducing the sizes of waists and shoulders and thighs, and paying him almost the same amount of money for this reduction as for a brand-new suit; and then there is the voice from the past on the phone. The voice of the former "Priminister."

"This is Dipper Barrow."

"Oh, Prime Minister!"

"I didn't know you were a conservative?"

"I am a conservative when I am in Canada, and when I am in Barbados I am a member of the Democratic Labour Party."

"Good luck in the elections."

"Thank you, Prime Minister."

For me, once a prime minister, always a prime minister.

Pleasantries were exchanged. He wanted to know how I was. He went back to the election campaign. He wished me luck, again. And then he came to the point.

"That visit to Yale that you were arranging ... you think you can still arrange it?"

"I can arrange it, Prime Minister. But I can't promise you'll get the same money, because ..."

"Money is no problem. I'll go for nothing. I just want to get out of Barbados ..."

Weeks later, and I am defeated at the polls, and I am relieved of the pressure of canvassing and campaigning, and keeping the hours of craziness, and having always to be on guard about what I say, when I hear from my friend Professor Robin Winks, that the visit to Yale has been approved: "He will get a little something as fee, there will be his suite, and full library privileges. We will do this for Mr. Barrow. And how do you feel after your campaign? Incidentally, Austin, we will need a letter of recommendation from you, for Mr. Barrow, before Mr. Barrow can take up his Visiting Fellowship ... as soon as possible."

The publication of *The Prime Minister*, and the notoriety it gathered round it, like a piece of iron in the sea, when the salt in the water corrodes and rusts it and its shape is crippled like the limbs of an old man, this novel declared a "roman à clef" brought to the surface, a lot of men and women who now aligned themselves with the conservative party of Barbados, the Barbados Labour Party. The irony in Barbados politics is that both main political parties have the word "labour" in them, although everyone knows that the BLP is a conservative party, whose members were, years ago, white planters and businessmen, and a few black barristers-at-law, principle amongst whom was Grantley Adams, the father of Tom Adams.

One of the most important men now arraigned against the fallen government of the Democratic Labour Party is the Old Boy. He is now in Toronto. Without access to his mercantile bank, out of reach of the dynamite-wired princely wealth buried in a certain place in St. John. Sometimes, perhaps he has forgotten where he buried it, probably in the dark of the darkest night, it is in St. Thomas. At other times, as if to confound persons and thieves and former ministers he says, openly, that the loot is buried in St. John. St. John is the location of Codrington College, named after a slave owner, Codrington College, affiliated to Durham University in England, where you go to become a priest in the Anglican church or to read for a degree in the classics, St. John is the seat the former prime minister still holds. Perhaps it was in this St. John constituency that the treasure was buried. The Old Boy is now installed in a mansion in Toronto's upper-class residential neighbourhood. Behaving like the earl he wants to be, reading the rules and regulations of heraldry and the peerage; and offering titles to me, today a dukedom, the day after; and picking out members of the Cabinet in the new government — he is a member of Dipper Barrow's party, the DLP — men he had given money to, men he has given assistance to, men he has given secrets to, to boost their confidence. He behaves like the leader of a government-in-exile; and indeed, there is a document written by someone, a disgruntled former official in the Barrow government, entitled "Private & Confidential: Eyes Only — The Establishing of a Government-in-Exile." People living inside and outside of Barbados want to overthrow the legitimate government of the day. There are also rumblings of political discontent and political terrorism and political treachery in Trinidad, where Black Power raised its head and almost secured a foothold; and there is Grenada, where the government of Sir Eric Gairy was overthrown by Maurice Bishop, a London-trained barrister-at-law. I saw his list of persons in Barbados, and a few names of politicians in Trinidad, Jamaica and in Guyana, who were "traitors" to black people. The

Old Boy was a staunch supporter of Black People, and black people throughout the world.

That Sunday when he asked me to help him find a place for his two purebred dogs, beloved by him in greater affection than he would love his "daughter," I took him, in the company of a real-estate broker I knew, through some streets where there were basement apartments for rent, for he wanted a "place to keep a dog." But he had something else in mind. He wanted a house suitable for a peer of the realm. We visited Forest Hill, we drove through the cold Sunday afternoon, and visited homes in Cabbagetown and, on a whim, I suggested Rosedale. The real-estate broker knew of three houses for sale in this distinctive area. And then we found the house on Crescent Road, recently vacated by the owners, who moved within the same neighbourhood, leaving behind, like an abandoned chair, a room full of books to be taken by the real-estate agent, by the new owners, by men who rambled into the house to sleep on the floor; by homeless men. A mansion for his dogs. The Old Boy was adamant that this was the place he was looking for. He did not even go through each room. It was the way the mansion looked, and the size of the building. He must have lived in one of these mansions in London.

"It's the address, old boy!" he told me, as we went to the office of the real-estate agent, on the penthouse floor of a building that housed a branch of the Salvation Army, near the popular restaurant at the time, Fenton's.

The real-estate agent serves chilled white wine and cheese and white seedless grapes; and I partake of this in quantity not recommended in books of etiquette; and I glance over by the window where the Old Boy and his "daughter" are standing in over a large leather, old fashioned box-like valise, with noisy double locks. I have just taken a glass of white wine to his "daughter" and some grapes. The Old Boy does not drink. "Can't do what I do and drink alcohol, too. A touch of cognac at nights, before bed, well …" I had seen the label of the bottle he bought from the Vintages Store, and was impressed by his taste. He asks me to wait a moment. He has just unlocked the vault of a valise. Exposed are plateaux and hills of money. English pounds. American dollars. Barbadian dollars. "Help me count the money for the down payment, old boy."

To buy a house in Toronto, you ask for the selling price, and if you agree to it, you deposit at least, 10 percent of that price. You have your lawyers search the property, checking against liens, outstanding taxes, whether the house is a house, and things like that. And after one month, or two, or even three…depending upon the agreed time for the closing, you will then pay the required amount, taking the mortgage into consideration. The house the Old Boy decided on, was very expensive. In the value of the house in the current market of that time, was about five hundred thousand. The Old Boy suggested a deposit of thirty thousand. He paid in American dollars. In hard, cold cash. And he did not ask to be paid the difference in the exchange between American dollars and Canadian dollars. The real estate agent pocketed the exchange. She had never had such a deal. But the Old Boy, whether deliberate or through ignorance, had confused a "down payment" for a "deposit."

To make a long story short, as the saying goes, the Old Boy lived in the Rosedale mansion for about two years. He moved out of my life, and went to another residence, a townhouse near the Lake. And he would have languished there, for it was not a place like the Rosedale mansion with its sophisticated environment, where he could have mixed with his neighbours and visited their boardrooms, with tales of adventure and daring, and the making of millions of dollars, where he could have regaled them about trans-oceanic journeys on sailing boats which were stopped by the coast guard of islands, who accused him of "invading" their peaceful sleepy kingdoms who put him in jail for months, until his contacts overseas, in Canada and in England sent a private jet to take him "home" to London … where it was the barking of the pup, now a loving fully-grown dog, that woke him up, on his release back in London, so that he might take his prescriptions of medicine; and stay alive …

"This dog saved my life," he used to say, "that's why I love him"; that's why he bought steaks from the Rosedale grocery store and rice from Loblaws and cooked the two of them together, and fed them to the two dogs, the brother and the sister, the one who had barked opportunely, and saved his life. The dogs were eating better than many Rosedale families. "This dog saved my life. She barked in my ear until she woke me up, so I could take my tablets ..." He rubs his right hand, palm down roughly over the shining golden pelt of the she-dog, then roughens up the dog's ears, then, like a quiet vacuum cleaner he passes the same hand, palm down still, over the cocked spine of the dog, as if he intend to soothe it to sleep. And then he slaps it on its backside. The dog turns her head, acknowledges the act of love, and slurps its long pink tongue over her master's face, over his mouth and eyes.

CHAPTER TWENTY-EIGHT

Home

I have left home two times. The first time on the September 25, 1955. I arrived in Toronto with six dollars — in three denominations — in my pocket. Two American dollars, one Canadian dollar, and three Barbadian dollars. On my second time leaving home, I arrived with six dollars. All six were Canadian dollars. I have read of immigrants who boast about their hard work and their success measured against the small amount of money they came with, and the vast amount of wealth they accumulated in five or ten years, to show not only their conquering the odds of such quick success, but to illustrate their love of hard work. I have always felt that such boasting is out of place. And there is no one correct way of measuring success in a new country of immigration. I mention the six dollars in my pocket in 1955, and the six dollars in 1976 that I arrived with, at the same airport. It does not measure anything but coincidence, for I did not come at the first time as an immigrant, but as a student; and the second coming was as a returning citizen. What then is the significance of the six dollars? Even though in the first case the currency was from three different countries; and at the second departure from home, twenty-one years later, the six dollars were the currency of Canada, my new home.

So, it must be the idea of home, and the meaning of home that is the significance of the six dollars. I am not boasting of typical immigrant conquering of the odds, for I did not picture myself as a disadvantaged foreigner seeking either employment or refuge. So, it really does not matter what the size of my wallet was in 1955 and in 1976, for it was not the size of the wallet at entry, and the size of the bank account five or twenty years later, that would verify and describe my success. My success was more simple: the escape from the country where I was born, to the pleasure, the relaxation, the sight of the lights of houses and streets and the headlights of cars, so similar to the cold, blood-freezing glow of Christmas trees and their lights, that warms the heart. And when the plane was losing altitude deliberately to land, and I was almost level with the Christmas-tree lights, although it was in August, I remember the words of my friend, Bill McMurtry, on the roof of the Park Plaza Hotel, ten months before: "You can't go back home again."

It was therefore this confirmation, through disappointment and failure in the country where I was born, that settled the ambivalence that Barbados was home and Canada was home, that caused me to enter politics and seek a seat in the Ontario Legislature, and by so doing, declare in terms more realistic than metaphorical, that I had become, not Canadian, but a Canadian.

It was years before 1976, in the bar of the Four Seasons Hotel — across the street from the CBC building when it was on Jarvis Street, No. 354, exactly where the new building to house the National Ballet of Canada is now up — that I was having drinks, ironically with Bill McMurtry and some other friends, among whom was Larry Zolf, in those days suggesting through columns in the *Telegram* and the *Star* newspapers, that he ought to be made a senator — a plea, and an ambition not yet realized, through the lack of intelligence and class of the governments in power, at those times of desire and self-promotion; but it was Bill McMurtry who first raised the question: "Why don't you stop rabble-rousing and run for mayor?" It was a dare. Not to keep me silent, to seal my lips, to stuff my radical pronouncements with balled-up pages of the newspaper, or with a ball of cloth stuffed into my mouth to keep me silent. It was his suggestion that I should, perhaps through popularity or notoriety, jump into the mayoralty race now raging; and be a "role model" to the voiceless black population, both the native black community, and the immigrant West Indian community.

I took up the dare. And a remarkable development happened right then and there, in our presence. I called the *Toronto Star* newspaper, and told them, "I am Austin Clarke, and I am entering the mayoralty race."

Before I had left the Four Seasons Hotel, my entry into the race for mayor of Toronto was broadcast on the six o'clock television news. I had no idea the *Star* would take me seriously. But it said something more serious than this dare, than this entering municipal politics. It said that something historical was happening, even although I was not mindful of this at the time. But it showed, upon reflection, and in the few weeks I remained in the race, that others thought it was a "good thing" for a black man to enter municipal politics in Toronto, in Ontario, in Canada. And it made me into some kind of "model," into some kind of madman, into some kind of "uppity" West Indian, into some kind of a symbol.

When I got home that evening, the woman I was married to was angry, was puzzled, was nonplussed, was stunned that something happening, something that embraced and included her, against her knowledge and her will, against her history — for she was born in Canada, of Jamaican parents, father a railroad porter, mother a former domestic servant who had come to Toronto to study the Bible and become a missionary in Africa, something dramatic and at the same time, something humorous was being played out in her quiet, private, and very conservative home. This was one more case of "craziness" from a man she had married, perhaps against her better judgment, the first stroke of madness being his decision to be a writer; and now this, running in a mayoralty election when never before in the history of Toronto, of Ontario, of Canada, and in the history of Negro-Canadians, no one had shown such craziness as to think that white Canadians would vote for a Negro man, would want a Negro to be his mayor.

"All the damn newspapers and television stations. Calling here, knocking down my door. Wanting interviews. And you didn't even call to warn me. You're running for mayor. And you don't tell me you are running for mayor! When you decide to run for mayor?"

It was a question I could not answer. I did not decide to run for mayor. A dare decided that for me.

I had just started to teach at Yale University, and I was kind of commuting, coming home about two or three times a month; and I would have to be a commuting mayoralty candidate. My heart was not in it. I regretted that I had been so romantic to take up the dare. I regretted entering the race, now that I knew that Professor Stephen Clarkson was a serious candidate, and that my presence in the campaign might divide his support.

The good thing about my "running for mayor" in 1969 is that it convinced, soon afterwards, many black Canadians to enter politics: working in various capacities, in campaigns, being candidates and canvassers; and not only for municipal office, but for provincial legislatures and the federal House of Commons. The Honourable Lincoln Alexander, a former minister in the federal government, formerly lieutenant governor of Ontario, and the Honourable Leonard Braithwaite, the first member of the Ontario Legislature for the Liberals, are the two important leaders in this trend for black citizens to take their place, rightfully, in Canadian politics. We must not however, forget Rosemary Brown and the Honourable Howard McCurdy, both of whom were members of the New Democratic Party.

Today, without taking credit for this impressive increase in political activity, and their successes in it, of black candidates, I am happy that my first assault upon the previously all-white reservation of elective politics, though short-lived, provided the impetus for this new political interest, and renders it now almost as a natural consequence in the life of every black man living in Canada.

We can learn a lesson from the South Asians, who put themselves up as candidates for office.

Epilogue

"The seas were calm as only Caribbean seas can be calm, and the sun was pouring down on us, and we wished the sails could shade the sun from our eyes, and from our backs; and especially the stupid Canadian boy who I'd hired to sail the blasted boat, this fellow spends all his time smoking; smoking grass, but it was the sun more than the smoke from the blasted pot he was smoking, trying to be in the shade on a boat in the Caribbean Sea, and we were far out to sea you know, Old Boy, far-far out, bypassing Barbados, for why were we troubling ourselves by sailing into Barbados waters; but it was the sun pouring down, and the deck of this boat we were sailing on, cutting through the water like a cutlass mashing up a green water coconut, how it does hit the skin clean, making the wound almost hard to see, the blade is so damn sharp; and how it goes through the soft coconut no more than a half-inch thick, clean-clean was this sun pouring down on our backs in the Caribbean Sea; and all of a sudden I am watching this blasted Canadian boy, who playing he is a captain with knowledge and know-how of ships and compasses, but the blasted boy not watching the quadrant or what you call it, he not watching for the horizon, or watching out for other boats in the Caribbean sea, in the area where we sailing — not to Barbados, as I tell you, but mainly because we didn't have any business with Barbados, we were not doing business with Barbados. We were bound for Dominica, that little poor-arse country that Eugenia rules over, whiching

I can's understand how anybody in his right mind would see any profit in our sailing the blasted boat in the direction of Dominica, which a country that can't buy a blasted sweetbread, father-less the kind o' 'things' we were carrying on board, 'things' that I don't need to tell you, in clearer terms, what they consisted of, and don't listen to the press in these parts, the West Indian press, a pack o' fools and inventors of news, don't know what the hell they print or get their news from, America feeding them propaganda, Britain feeding them outdated intelligence. If they want to know real intelligence, they have to go and work in the Middle East, in Iran and Iraq. And even the Gulf States, the Saw-dees, and them-so; but the Caribbean as a source of news and intelligence? And don't mention the *Nation* newspaper, one of the worst rags of journalism in the world, if you really want to know.

"I have to go back to the sun pouring down on us, sailing in the clearest waters imaginable, and the sun burning my back, although I had on a broad-brimmed straw hat to shield my back from the sun, and in addition to the sun you have to contend with the salt in the waves, 'cause even although the seas were calm for the most part, a wave once in a while, would lash the blasted deck of the sailboat, and splatter-you-up like hell, so you had to be careful, while the blasted Canadian boy, laying-down flat on his back, looking up to God or the heavens, or the clouds, and the whitest clouds you ever saw, you saw right there in waters off Grenada, which as I said, was never our destination. I don't know where the hell they got their news from, and if it wasn't for the blasted Canadian boy falling asleep after smoking so much dope, we would have accomplished our mission, got the money, deposited it in a certain bank, gone back to Britain in a private jet, and forgotten about the West Indies!

"But you hear what you hear. And you read what you read. And you make your own theory, and draw your own conclusions, and spoil my reputation. And I was born in the West Indies. I tell you the blasted Canadian boy was smoking grass. And he fell asleep at the tiller. And the blasted boat drifted off course. And all of a sudden. Coming down from the clouds and the mists that started to gather, coming down like the sun, although it was night now, and the sun was not shining.

"Coming through the clouds was a Coast Guard. A coast guard boat. With guns. With megaphones and loudspeakers. Announcing my name.

"How they know my name? How they know that a man with my name was aboard? How they knew my latitude? And my longitude? And arrested me. For planning to invade Dominica. There are worse bastards in power down in the West Indies. I know all of them. I deal with all of them. I talk with all of them. I do business with all of them. I lend money to all of them.

"When I got those negatives showing all those Cabinet ministers and high-ranking judges and famous barristers-at-law, in their sex parties, and the editors of the magazine in question called me from New York, I knew what I had to do. I had to protect the government. I could let that Trinidadian bastard bring down a legitimate government. And embarrass a prime minister. It cost me money. But what is money if it can't be put to use? To good use? And to bad use? Money made in those circumstances, and off those countries, is money you have to invest in the protection of certain governments.

"I am a man of peace. I am a right-winger. But still a man of peace. I know how the world powers look at right-wingers like me. They welcome me. They protect me. They protect me because they know I will not conspire to bring down their democratically elected government. I know these governments. And I know these leaders."

"I have travelled through the jungles of Brazil, near the Guyana border, providing safe conduct to a man who wasted all the blasted Latin and Greek he learned at Harrison College. No country in the Caribbean wanted to give him refuge and a place to live. And the money he left with soon ran out, and what could the blasted fool do? I gave this man safe conduct through the bush and jungles bordering Guyana until we could hide him and then put him on a private jet for Brooklyn. As you know, he went into the Church, not the Anglican Church, but some Pentecostal mission hall, giving sermons partly in Barbadian dialect, and partly in Latin. In Pig-Latin, if you ask me. Snakes, agoutis, which we ate for food, crocodiles, which we avoided, mosquitoes as big as house flies, the smell and stench of dead animals, bloated bellies, eyes eaten out, flies buzzing like confetti tossed on wedding guests, but black, and the humidity of the British Guyana nights. I know them all. I saved them all. And I can topple them all. But I am a nationalist. I am a loyal Barbadian. I will never invade my own country.

"But going back to the negatives which I had to buy and pay for, in American currency, in hard cold cash, in American 'smackeroons,' cash on the line; in hard cold cash. And when I got those negatives, what you think I did with them? Toss them out through a porthole while crossing the Bermuda Triangle? No! They are buried in the same place as the gold bars, and wired for security in case some blasted politician or newspaper editor feels brave enough to meddle with my treasure.

"But I have to conclude my story about the blasted Canadian boy who fell asleep on the job, smoking marijuana when he should be looking after the tiller, and charting the journey in the sailing boat, a really wonderful boat that one of my arms-dealer friends loaned us, to carry our assignment, and to be stopped by a blasted Coast Guard boat and charged with bearing arms, bearing weapons, charged for treachery, charged for being a revolutionary with intent to overthrow a Caribbean nation, with a planned invasion of Barbados, my own native land. Would I do such a stupid blasted thing? For who would I shoot, who would I put in my sights while I am carrying out this revolution, and who would I kill first, to seize power as a consequence, do they think I am so stupid, a man like trained in England and in the best brigades and intelligence armies, to be now arrested like a common thief? A fowl-cock thief?"

"They placed me in solitary confinement. But my people heard. And before the first month was over, they sent a private Lear jet and took me to an undisclosed destination, you will understand, Old Boy, that I cannot tell you the name of the country in which the destination lay, nor the man who flew the jet, nor the safe house where I was taken to, to recover from the torture those West Indian bastards put me through. But I am tough. In this business of weapons and transferring cash and gold bars from one country to the next, you have to be tough.

"And this is why I love this dog as if she is my daughter ..."

Today is a Friday that I am telling you these things as I 'member them.

Afterword

'Membering. It is also a Friday. Late at night. I am convinced of his affection and loyalty to dogs. I do not have a dog. I do not like dogs. I do not have a dog. I do not like dogs, but I appreciate in this final chapter of remembering the loyalty he extends to his pets. At this end, very late at night, in his Rosedale mansion, I listen to his explanation of his life. He has been convincing us of his beliefs in being a right-winger and although he demonstrated his love for his country of birth, proudly reminding me of his loyalty to his country of birth. I see in the irony in his embracing these views of loyalty as a black man living in England at the time of racial convulsing, this kind of nationality in an England transfixed by racial discrimination.

Credits

Care has been taken to trace the ownership of copyrighted material used in this book. The author and the publisher welcome any information enabling them to rectify any references or credits in subsequent editions. The following are listed in alphabetical order:

"I Come from the Nigger Yard," Martin Carter, *University of Hunger: Collected Poems & Selected Prose*, ed. Gemma Robinson (Hexham, UK: Bloodaxe Books, 2006). www. bloodaxebooks.com.

Geoffrey Chaucer, *The Canterbury Tales* (New York: Bantam Classics, 1982).

"We Are the Hollow Men," T.S. Eliot, *Poems 1909–1925* (New York: Harcourt, Brace, 1932).

Paul Jacobs, Saul Landau, with Eve Pell, *To Serve the Devil* (New York: Vintage, 1971), xxi.

Excerpt from OF A FIRE ON THE MOON by Norman Mailer. Copyright © 1969, 1970 by Norman Mailer, used by permission of The Wylie Agency LLC.

Ian McEwan, *Amsterdam* (New York: Anchor Books, 1998).

Richard Outram, "Ophelia Illumined," used with permission of the Literary Estate of Richard Outram.

Caryl Phillips, *Crossing the River* (New York: Vintage, 1995).

Dylan Thomas, "A Child's Christmas in Wales," used with permission of Orion Children's Books.

By Dylan Thomas, from A CHILD'S CHRISTMAS IN WALES, copyright ©1954 by New Directions Publishing Corp. Reprinted by permission of New Directions Publishing Corp.

Selected Fiction
by Austin Clarke

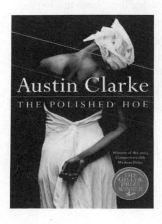

The Polished Hoe

Winner of the 2002 Scotiabank Giller Prize and of the 2003 Commonwealth Writers' Prize: Best Book (Canada and the Caribbean)

When an elderly Bimshire village woman calls the police to confess to a murder, the result is a shattering all-night vigil that brings together elements of the African diaspora in one epic sweep. Set on the post-colonial West Indian island of Bimshire in 1952, *The Polished Hoe* unravels over the course of twenty-four hours, but spans the lifetime of one woman and the collective experience of a society informed by slavery. As the novel opens, Mary Mathilda is giving confession to Sargeant, a police officer she has known all her life. The man she claims to have murdered is Mr. Belfeels, the village plantation owner for whom she has worked for more than thirty years. Mary has also been Mr. Belfeels' mistress for most of that time and is the mother of his only son, Wilberforce, a successful doctor. What transpires through Mary's words and recollections is a deep meditation about the power of memory and the indomitable strength of the human spirit. Infused with Joycean overtones, this is a literary masterpiece that evokes the sensuality of the tropics and the tragic richness of Island culture.

More

Winner of the 2009 Toronto Book Award

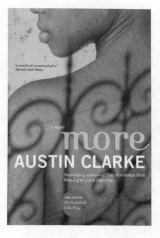

At the news of her son's involvement in gang crime, Idora Morrison collapses in her rented basement apartment. For four days and nights, she retreats into a vortex of memory, pain, and disappointment that unravels a riveting dissection of her life as a black immigrant to Toronto. Idora has lived in Canada for twenty-five years. She has struggled to make ends meet and her deadbeat husband Bertram has abandoned her for a better life in America. Left alone to raise her son BJ, Idora does her best to survive against very difficult odds. Now that BJ has disappeared into a life of crime and gang warfare, she recoils from this loss and tries to understand how her life has spiraled into this tragic place. In spite of her circumstances, Idora finds her way back into the light with a courage that is both remarkable and unforgettable. *More* is a powerful indictment of the iniquities of racial discrimination and the crime of poverty.

Available at your favourite bookseller

VISIT US AT

Dundurn.com
@dundurnpress
Facebook.com/dundurnpress
Pinterest.com/dundurnpress